Trans and Gender Diverse Voices in Libraries

This book is number thirteen in the Series on Gender and Sexuality in Information Studies, Emily Drabinski, series editor.

Trans and Gender Diverse Voices in Libraries

Kalani Keahi Adolpho, Stephen G. Krueger, and Krista McCracken, Editors

LIBRARY JUICE PRESS
SACRAMENTO, CA

Published in 2023 by Library Juice Press

Library Juice Press
PO Box 188784
Sacramento, CA 95822

http://libraryjuicepress.com/

This book is printed on acid-free paper.

Library of Congress Cataloging-in-Publication Data

Names: Adolpho, Kalani Keahi, editor. | Krueger, Stephen G., editor. | McCracken, Krista, editor.
Title: Trans and gender diverse voices in libraries / Kalani Keahi Adolpho, Stephen G. Krueger, and Krista McCracken, editors.
Description: Sacramento, CA : Library Juice Press, 2023. | Series: Series on gender and sexuality in information studies; no. 13 | Includes bibliographical references and index. | Summary: "Centers the lived experiences of trans and gender diverse people in LIS work and education. All authors and editors will be self-identified trans and gender diverse people"-- Provided by publisher.
Identifiers: LCCN 2023002394 | ISBN 9781634001205 (paperback)
Subjects: LCSH: Transgender people in library science. | Gender-nonconforming people in library science.
Classification: LCC Z682.4.T73 T73 2023 | DDC 020.86/7--dc23/eng/20230522
LC record available at https://lccn.loc.gov/2023002394

Table of Contents

Section 2: LIS Education

Section 3: Public Libraries

Section 4: Academic Libraries

Section 5: Archives and Special Collections

Section 6: Professional Reflections

Introduction

Kalani Keahi Adolpho, Stephen G. Krueger, and Krista McCracken

Who We Are

Krista McCracken (they/them) is a queer, non-binary, settler archivist and public historian. They are a Researcher/Curator at the Shingwauk Residential Schools Centre located at Algoma University in Sault Ste. Marie, Ontario, Canada. Krista is passionate about trans and gender diverse inclusion in the Canadian library and archives context. They regularly speak, write, and stitch about gender identity.

Kalani Keahi Adolpho (they/them or he/him) is a mixed Kanaka Maoli (Native Hawaiian), queer, and trans person living in Richmond, VA. They are a Processing Archivist at Virginia Commonwealth University, and a former diversity resident librarian at University of Wisconsin. They hold a B.A. in History and an MLIS from the University of Wisconsin-Milwaukee. Kalani writes and presents on diversity residencies, ethical description, and trans and gender diverse inclusion.

Stephen G. Krueger (ey/em or he/him) is a queer, white, trans person living in New Hampshire. In addition to being the Scholarly Publishing Librarian at Dartmouth College, he writes and presents on trans inclusion in libraries. Stephen holds a B.A. in English from Warren Wilson College and an MSLS from the University of North Carolina at Chapel Hill. His publications and opinions can be found at www.stephengkrueger.com.

What is This Book?

In the genre of professional literature for the library and information field, this book may seem a little unusual. We'll get into what it isn't shortly, but first we'll start with what it is. In essence, that's basically what it says on the tin: *Trans and Gender Diverse Voices in Libraries*. In the call for proposals, we had two requirements for potential authors. First, they needed to be involved in library and information science (LIS) work or study, or have previously been so. Second, all authors needed to be trans and/or gender diverse.

This seems like a good place to discuss our word choice, and whom it covers. "Cisgender" means a person whose gender matches the one legally assigned to them at birth; "trans" is often used as an umbrella term for everyone else. However, these definitions create a flawed binary, just as "male" and "female" do. Gender is far too complex and fluid for such concrete lines to accurately cover everyone's experience of it. There are many genders and individuals all over the world who do not fall under any of these binaries–male or female, trans or cis. We use "trans and gender diverse" in an attempt to cover the glorious range of gender diversity that exists without squashing anyone under terms that do not fit them. These few sentences are, of course, a vast oversimplification of an enormously complex and fascinating topic, and we encourage you to learn more about gender diversity on your own. But this is a book introduction, not a gender education workshop, and we must move on.

So in practice, all of the authors in this volume are people who self-identify as trans and/or gender diverse people in library work or LIS education. Beyond that, we had no set requirements. The purpose of this book is to be a space for sharing whatever the authors wanted to share about gender identity in this field of work. The book is not a scholarly collection, though some of the chapters lean in that direction; it includes personal reflections, anecdotes, and even some poetry. The authors are LIS students, library workers of all types, and a couple of people who have left the profession entirely. The variety of perspectives and contents is not a mistake; it is the point.

Having briefly covered *what* the book is, we will now spend a little time on *why* the book is. One pragmatic answer is that as part of his 2019 book *Supporting Trans People in Libraries*, Stephen collected a few short pieces of writing from trans and gender diverse library workers, which he thought ended up being the most interesting element; this book is that concept expanded and given the attention it deserves. (An earlier book in the Series on Gender and Sexuality in Information Studies, *Out Behind the Desk: Workplace Issues for LGBTQ+ Librarians*, deserves credit for demonstrating the viability of this type of volume and serving as an inspiration for our own, gender-specific version.) A broader answer is that the book's intention is to begin to fill an enormous gap in the literature and, perhaps more importantly, in the awareness and understanding in the library field as a whole.

We do not know how many trans and gender diverse people are part of the library profession. The 2017 ALA Demographic Study includes only male and female in its gender options, which leaves out any number of people and gives no information at all on how many of the respondents are trans or gender diverse.[1] This book cannot begin to answer that question, and it does not try to. The point is that trans and gender diverse people exist, and we are not counted. But we are here. This book has fifty-three chapters and fifty-seven authors (plus three editors), and we are only a small representation of the uncounted numbers of us throughout the profession.

First and foremost, this book is for us: for all the trans and gender diverse library workers who are the only one they know of in a department, or a whole institution; for the LIS students who do not know if there is anyone like them in the profession they hope to join; for those who have been lucky enough to be welcomed, those who are surviving as best they can, and those who have been forced out of a field that

1. Kathy Rosa and Kelsey Henke, "2017 ALA Demographic Study" (Chicago, IL: ALA Office of Research and Statistics, 2017), https://www.ala.org/tools/research/initiatives/membershipsurveys, 1.

they loved (or at least that they were led to believe had a place for them). We aren't only invisible in the data—in a world and a profession that assumes that we don't exist and often punishes us for doing so, we are invisible to each other.

Secondarily, this book is for the rest of you. Perhaps you consider yourself an ally (which does not mean that the people you want to support feel the same); perhaps it has never occurred to you that trans and gender diverse people are your colleagues, your classmates, your employees, your supervisors, your students, your teachers. Perhaps you think that the profession is already as welcoming and supportive as it needs to be (it is not). This book is to show you a small part of the reality. You cannot read these chapters and claim that Safe Zone stickers and "libraries are for everyone" signs have done the job. You cannot assume that everything is fine in your workplace because nobody has spoken out. You can no longer pretend that we don't exist.

About the Editing Process

As editors, we centered values of inclusion and anti-oppression. We wanted to provide authors with space to express themselves, even—or especially—when the experiences and opinions did not reflect our own, with the exception of content that perpetuated the oppression of others.

We approached editing this book with a desire to include as many trans and gender diverse voices as possible. We wanted to break down some of the barriers that exist in publishing and offer space for people to speak their truths, and we wanted to demonstrate the extensive variety of experiences that trans and gender diverse people have in library work and LIS education.

Now that we've covered *what* this book is and *why* this book is, let's discuss what this book isn't. This book isn't peer reviewed. This was an intentional choice. We didn't want someone judging the experiences of trans and gender diverse people against an arbitrary academic standard. Likewise, we didn't want authors to feel as though they needed to justify their lived experiences by citing scholarly sources (especially when academic materials that accurately reflect these lives do not, for the most part, actually exist). The experiences, feelings, and thoughts included in this book are hugely varied in form and content and represent individual lived realities. These realities are valid without peer review.

This is a book grounded in sharing personal experiences, in all of their messiness and glory. We didn't edit out personal feelings or personal anecdotes as they relate to trans and gender diverse identities and libraries. We also didn't edit the tone of the chapters. We let people say "fuck." Many of the chapters express anger and push back against the professional norm (and myth) of neutrality. We did ask authors to edit out identifiable references to people other than themselves: names of bystanders, coworkers, and others have been changed. Some authors also chose to anonymize themselves and their workplaces or schools to keep themselves safe.

As editors we worked to support authors through an editing process that included a lot of opportunities for engagement. Throughout this process, we held a number of information sessions with the authors, which led to the creation of a Discord group for those who were interested in sharing community and communication with one another. One of the best parts of editing this book was engaging with the authors and creating space for trans and gender diverse people in libraries to connect with each other. We hope that these types of connections can continue and grow following the book's publication.

Author Safety

One of the main concerns throughout this process, both of the editors and the individual authors of this volume, has been personal and professional safety. As you'll discover while reading this book, some of our authors are out at work and in their personal lives, while others are selectively out in specific contexts. While many authors in this volume have published under their names, others have published anonymously or under pseudonyms. We gave each author the choice of whether to include a bio statement with their chapter—some did and some did not, and some of the former opted not to include identifiable information in their bios. The decision to publish under one's own name in a project such as this can be quite complex. On the one hand, it could be beneficial professionally to include authorship for a chapter in a book published by Library Juice Press on your curriculum vitae. On the other hand, authoring a chapter under your own name for a volume called *Trans and Gender Diverse Voices in Libraries* may make it difficult to go stealth in the field, or to pick and choose the contexts in which you're out (since simply being named as part of this volume publicly outs one as being trans or gender diverse). Even without naming names or workplaces, there are some experiences that cannot be fully anonymized if described accurately. Because of this reality, several prospective authors withdrew during the editing process. Some of them referenced concerns about professionally outing themselves while they are pre-tenure, or about how contributing to this volume may limit future career opportunities.

These concerns are not unfounded. According to a 2015 report from the National Center for Transgender Equality, 77% of trans or gender diverse survey respondents reported that, in the past year, they had to hide or delay their transition or quit their job in order to avoid workplace mistreatment. Nearly one quarter (23%) of survey respondents reported workplace mistreatment, such as being told they needed to present as the wrong gender in order to keep their job, or being outed at work. Overall, 67% of survey respondents reported that, in the past year, they were fired, denied a promotion, forced to resign, or not hired for a job they applied for due to their being trans or gender diverse. These statistics are higher for trans and gender diverse people who experience transmisogyny, and for people who are multiply marginalized along the lines of race and disability.[2] This book includes accounts of people who have been harassed and even forced out of the library profession after coming out at work. Concerns around safety not only limit who is able to contribute to this type of book, anonymously or otherwise, but also

2. Sandy E. James, et al., "The Report of the 2015 U.S. Transgender Survey" (Washington, DC: National Center for Transgender Equality, 2016), 148-150, https://www.ustranssurvey.org/reports.

how transparent someone can be about their experiences and the types of content they might include in their chapter.

Many chapters in this volume express frustration, burnout, despair, and anger. The possible consequences for contributing to this volume, and being honest about one's negative experiences in the field, are greater for trans and gender diverse authors who are marginalized in multiple ways. In a white supremacist culture, anger from BIPOC (especially Black people) is perceived as an overreaction or as a threat. In addition, the skewed racial demographics of library workers (according to the 2017 ALA Demographic Survey, 86.7% of respondents were white) mean that it is far more difficult for BIPOC authors to be anonymous, whether they publish under their own names or not.[3]

Prioritizing author safety means that this book is by nature incomplete. The fact that these safety considerations were necessary shows just how far the library profession has to go.

Patterns and Themes

One goal of this book is to show a wide variety of experiences and perspectives, and demonstrate that trans and gender diverse people can and do have lives as varied as anyone else's. That said, we observed a number of patterns as we read through the chapters—not necessarily universal, but recurring elements that we wanted to draw attention to. This section is not intended to claim that all trans and gender diverse people share these experiences or feelings; even within the book, this is demonstrably untrue, and perpetuating the myth of a monolithic trans and gender diverse community or universal trans or gender diverse experience is exactly what we want to avoid. Instead, consider the themes below as patterns that seem to be part of the library profession—ones that point to where the work of dismantling the oppression of trans and gender diverse people could start.

3. Rosa and Henke, "2017 ALA Demographic Study," 2.

The first of the recurring themes is anger. This is, in large part, not a happy book. It is full of rage, isolation, pain, frustration, fear, and exhaustion. Every one of these feelings is justified, and it is entirely appropriate to express them. These feelings are not inherently part of being a trans or gender diverse person, however; that is not the lesson. Often, these feelings come from being oppressed or helpless in a situation—whether in a classroom, conversation, workplace, meeting, or institution—where one's identity is ignored or disrespected, or where there is active harm because of bigotry or ignorance around that identity. More accurately, the theme is the frequency with which these situations occur in the library field; the anger and pain and fear are one result. It is not our responsibility to hide those feelings; it is the responsibility of those with the power to eliminate the oppression, discrimination, and harassment that causes the feelings to do that work.

Another common theme is the ways in which library and LIS program diversity, equity, and inclusion initiatives often focus on the appearance of inclusion, without making any lasting structural or systemic changes. This can be observed in the ways that, while pronouns in email signatures or on name tags have become more normalized, actually using trans and gender diverse people's names and pronouns remains an issue. This book is full of stories about library administrators, LIS faculty, and others treating the oppression of trans and gender diverse library workers and LIS students as a patron-only issue or something for HR to deal with. Meanwhile, there are corresponding accounts of trans and gender diverse people being forced to defend their restroom use, fighting to be called by their name and pronouns, and ultimately leaving workplaces or the entire profession. It is clear that our profession needs to take gender diverse oppression and exclusion more seriously. It needs to invest in structural changes which acknowledge that trans and gender diverse people aren't just our patrons; they're also our employees, coworkers, students, teachers, and volunteers.

There are plenty of other themes we could discuss, but we'll conclude with this one: regarding how trans and gender diverse people are treated in many workplaces and classrooms, the bar is appallingly low.

Many authors were relieved when they found a place where they could be out without fearing for their job; many others do not have even that. A classroom in which the professor respects students' names and pronouns is notable because of all the ones where this does not happen. Often, the hope is not for acceptance and true support but for survival. These expectations are not out of line with how library work and LIS education operates; on the contrary, this book demonstrates that for many people, this is the reality. From physical spaces to policies to interpersonal ignorance and bigotry, the experiences recounted in this book demonstrate that the library profession continues to fail its trans and gender diverse members over and over again.

What's Missing?

Despite the broad nature of our call for proposals, there are many voices and perspectives that are missing from this book. As noted above, there are issues around safety and the difficulty (perhaps the inability) to be truly anonymous and transparent about our experiences as trans and gender diverse people in libraries.

Some of the perspectives that are missing are related to the demographics of the field such as race, gender, and disability. While the profession does track the racial demographics of library workers, there is less detailed data around disability and none at all about transgender and gender diverse library workers. The racial demographics of our authors reflect the demographics of our field, with far more contributions from white trans and gender diverse people than from BIPOC. The experiences represented in this book are also all from majority white, English-speaking, settler-colonial countries, predominantly from the United States and Canada, with one author from Australia. It is difficult to say whether the gender demographics of the contributing authors of this book are representative of the field, given the lack of data available for us to compare. The majority of our authors are nonbinary, trans masc, and trans men, with fewer contributions from trans women, trans femmes, and Two-Spirit people (we have no contributions from authors who, in their chapters, explicitly self-identify outside of the colonial gender system beyond this).

Other gaps relate to who has the capacity to publish; plenty of potential authors with valuable experiences to share do not have time for such a project (the large number of chapters from academic librarians may be related to this, as such positions more often provide support for professional writing than non-librarian roles or other types of library work), and others may not have seen the call for proposals at all. We have a few chapters from people who have left the profession, but we assume there are many more such people whose voices are missing from this volume. The majority of our contributing authors are academic or public library workers or are LIS students. This book lacks the experiences of LIS faculty, library volunteers, and retired library workers, as well as employees from school libraries and many types of special libraries.

This book is not intended to be the definitive guide to trans and gender diverse experiences in libraries, but instead to start the conversation. It is our hope that this book will help trans and gender diverse people in libraries realize that they are not alone, and that their experiences are worth sharing.

How to Read This Book

We are delighted that this book has so many chapters and authors, and thus so many different perspectives on what it is to be trans or gender diverse in library work and education. The number of chapters may, however, make it tricky to navigate for readers. With that in mind, we have a few suggestions for how to approach this book.

1. **Everything.** Read it all, cover to cover. If you have time, or can make the time, please do this. Each chapter is important. Each one covers something different from the others. Do this especially if you are new to the idea that trans and gender diverse people are members of the library profession, since it will begin to demonstrate the range of identities, roles, and experiences. Reading each chapter will help break the

assumption that all trans and gender diverse people have similar backgrounds and opinions.

2. **Sections.** Read the section(s) most relevant to you. We have organized the chapters broadly by topic. That said, there is a great deal of overlap; the chapters all include personal experiences to some degree, and many touch on LIS education as well as professional work. The Personal Experiences section includes chapters in which the authors center their own thoughts and backgrounds rather than a specific type of library work or education. Professional Reflections contains chapters with a focus on theory or discussion of topics that are not limited to a particular aspect of the field.

3. **Index or keywords.** This book has an index, which can be used to identify particular chapters of interest. In addition, we asked each author to choose up to five keywords for their chapter. These are not standardized terms; they reflect what each person wanted to highlight for readers, as one goal of this book is to create space for authors to express themselves in their own words. Some authors used the keywords for identity terms (e.g., *BIPOC* or *trans woman*); others used them for work type or broad concepts. Skim the table of contents to identify the chapters you find most interesting.

Note: It is important to note that keywords are meant to describe chapter content, rather than the authors themselves. Keywords for identity terms around race, disability, gender, etc. have been used when these identities are a major theme of the chapter. This is one reason why there are more keywords for marginalized identities than privileged ones, because these chapters include content around being multiply marginalized. Authors should not be assumed to be white, neurotypical, or able-bodied because there is not a keyword indicating otherwise. That being said, we do encourage readers to reflect on what it means that some identities are normalized through not naming them explicitly.

After all, chapters may not be explicitly about privileged identities, but privilege impacts the kinds of experiences we do or do not have, in and outside of libraries.

What to Do Next

This book is not intended to be read and then forgotten. Our hope is that many readers will take what they learn and incorporate gender inclusion practices into their work in libraries and LIS programs moving forward. As stated previously, we also hope that this book can help foster community amongst trans and gender diverse people in LIS. With all that in mind, here are some tools to help begin or continue that work.

- **Trans Inclusion for Libraries** (www.zotero.org/groups/2412905/trans_inclusion_for_libraries/): An ever-growing list of resources on all aspects of the topic. It is an open Zotero group that anyone can access and add items to. Unlike this book, most of the resources in the collection are centered on research and recommended practices, so it's a good place to start learning more.

- **Trans Inclusion in LIS Presenter List** (bit.ly/trans-lis-presenters): A list of people who offer presentations, workshops, and consultations on gender inclusion in LIS. Different people offer different areas of expertise. Hire them for workplace trainings or class sessions.

- **The Trans and Gender Diverse LIS Network** (https://www.stephengkrueger.com/trans-lis-network): A closed support group for trans and gender diverse library workers and students. We appreciate the allyship of cis folks, but this one is not for you. Do tell your trans and gender diverse coworkers and students about it, though.

So read, and reflect, and then go forth and do the work. It is not optional.

Bibliography

James, Sandy E., Jody L. Herman, Susan Rankin, Mara Keisling, Lisa Mottet, and Ma'ayan Anafi. "The Report of the 2015 U.S. Transgender Survey." Washington, DC: National Center for Transgender Equality, 2016. https://www.ustranssurvey.org/reports.

Rosa, Kathy, and Kelsey Henke. "2017 ALA Demographic Study." Chicago, IL: ALA Office of Research and Statistics, 2017. https://www.ala.org/tools/research/initiatives/membership-surveys.

Section 1:

Personal Experiences

Reflections of a Non-Binary Asian American in LIS

Alvina Lai (they/them)

Keywords: Asian American, Chinese American, non-binary, early career librarian, tokenization

Note: In the attempt to make the writing as accessible as possible, the author strived to only reference sources that were open access (OA), or accessible at public libraries. In addition, in the interest of uplifting underrepresented scholars, the author strived to only cite Black, Indigenous and People of Color (BIPOC) and/or gender diverse voices.

Intro

This text is for the non-binary Asian Americans in LIS. I'm writing for you so you can compare notes, add to your inventory, and take what you need during your journey through the profession.

This is how I ended up in LIS. I was raised in Brooklyn by immigrant, Cantonese-speaking relatives. Helicopter grandparents bubble-wrapped their grand "daughter" by sheltering me from the dangers of cable TV, playdates, and the general outside world. Instead, I did homework, read books, and helped with the laundry. Then came high school. In a wild act of teen rebellion, I secretly applied to an art college in Manhattan. I enrolled without permission (got into *so* much trouble) and plunged head-first into the wild, unaware that I was about to enter a different society an hour's train ride away.

Bewildered by change (as one often is), I fumbled through undergrad with stunted social skills and complete naivety of white American pop culture. The world outside of the Chinese enclave of Brooklyn travelled on a different orbit. In the eyes of (mostly white, middle-class) college peers, I was moneyless, Asian, and awkward. I was a hermit crab changing its shell, and every so often the shell was crushed under someone's heel.

At the same time, art school in NYC in the 2010s was also a time of exploration. *Non-binary* and *demisexual* were added to my vocabulary and I practiced describing myself with those words. I bookmarked them for later—I was too busy with classes and trying to make enough money for the next monthly tuition payment. After completing undergrad, I worked in a university fundraising office, where I encountered database management for the first time. I wanted a promotion, so I went right back to school to build my technical (and social) skills. While in library school, I joined LIS associations, met people, and volunteered. I bounced between academic, non-profit, and corporate positions. I veered from database management to digital archiving to digital asset management (DAM). In 2021, almost a year after graduating and during an international pandemic, I started in a corporate DAM librarian position. On my first day, I added "they/them" to my email signature.

My name is Alvina and I'm a non-binary Chinese American. This is the mapping of my experience in LIS, and these are the practical lessons I learned along the way. I hope my journey can be useful to you as you go forward on your own path in the field.

Tokens and Monoliths

If you are open about your gender identity in the workplace, you might be conscripted into being "the expert." Chinese-American clinical psychologist Sand Chang sarcastically says, "As a nonbinary person, I am expected to be a spokesperson for *all the transgender and gender nonconforming people across the land!!!*" That's not your burden. As Chang describes,

"This is a responsibility that I do not want, and it's a position of power that I should not be given."[1]

You may also be unwillingly conscripted into conversations as The Asian. Peers may pop their head over your cubicle half-wall and say, "Do Asians really x?", "How do you pronounce this Asian name?", "How do you say x in your Asian language?" The Asian American experience is not a monolith. Resist the urge to try to summarize whole cultures into one sentence. Resist the instinct to people-please. Resist the tokenization. Resist.

Co-Existing

In 2017, I received an email from my mother with some career advice:

> You are too young to know what future will be when you see yourself as part minor group, but I am observing this everyday. I have coworker who is 'he' told me in tears that she couldn't find job for a long time because she dress up like man. Maybe some law will protest [protect] them, but in realty, business and majority are refused to accept them. People like them may find job in west village, but it is hard for them find job at up east side or west side. If you want to achieve your career dream in these areas, think about it seriously…
>
> Dear alvina, it is painful to see that you are going to chose a way that would hurt you deeply and we as Chinese parents couldn't help you to avoid from what is happening. Please listen to us, people in New York are living in different life, some easy, some difficult, who want to chose difficult one? Not smart people.

We no longer talk.

People try to tell us who we are and who we are not. To survive, we learn to navigate and negotiate our identities. We compromise. We learn to engage with the egos of our office-mates, teammates, professors,

1. Sand C. Chang, "TOKEN: TO·KEN /TŌKIŊN/," In *Nonbinary: Memoirs of Gender and Identity* (New York: Columbia University Press, 2019), 49.

managers, directors, committee members, co-authors, colleagues, clients, patrons, everyone. We learn to co-exist.

Communities

When I entered LIS, I was advised to find my library family. After all, "Members of marginalized groups, especially people of color and those who identify as LGBTQ+ [lesbian, gay, bisexual, transgender, queer, plus], experience hidden workloads, microaggressions, early burnout and lower retention."[2] There are librarians of color who had those experiences—they've written about it, created communities because of it.[3] There are trans and gender variant librarians who have also created communities, like Trans and Gender Diverse LIS Network, as well as resources like Que(e)ry, which brings "attention and support to hidden queer collections, and to provide a fun social space for queer librarians (and all who love them)."[4] These communities do the essential work of sustaining their LIS constituents.

So where do we fit among these different library communities? As non-binary Asian Americans, we exist at an intersection that requires

---

2. Camille Thomas, Elia Trucks, and H.B. Kouns. "Preparing Early Career Librarians for Leadership and Management: A Feminist Critique," *In the Library with the Lead Pipe*, April 17, 2019, https://www.inthelibrarywiththeleadpipe.org/2019/early-career-leadership-and-management/

3. Joanna Chen Cham, "You Are Not Alone," in *In Our Own Voices, Redux: The Faces of Librarianship Today* (United States: Rowman & Littlefield Publishers, 2018), 59–64; Sofia Leung, "Letter to New People of Color in LIS," in *In Our Own Voices, Redux: The Faces of Librarianship Today* (United States: Rowman & Littlefield Publishers, 2018), 257-263; Michelle Lee, "We Need Diverse Librarians: The Asian/Pacific American Libraries Association's Past, Present, and Future," in *Asian American Librarians and Library Services: Activism, Collaborations, and Strategies* (United States: Rowman & Littlefield Publishers, 2017) 23-40; Sai Deng, "From Birth to Maturity: The Chinese American Librarians Association," in *Asian American Librarians and Library Services: Activism, Collaborations, and Strategies* (United States: Rowman & Littlefield Publishers, 2017), 41-50; We Here, accessed June 16, 2021, https://www.wehere.space.

4. Stephen G. Krueger, "Trans and Gender Diverse LIS Network," accessed June 16, 2021, https://www.stephengkrueger.com/gender-variant-lis-network.; Que(e)ry, accessed June 16, 2021, https://www.queeryparty.org.

nuance. Jayden Thai, a psychologist and queer, trans man of color, explains,

> Trans API [Asian Pacific Islander] individuals may have to negotiate between their trans identity (influenced by U.S. individualistic cultural values) and their API identities (influenced by API collectivistic cultural values). In addition to balancing cultural values and spaces, trans API individuals also encounter double discrimination from their communities such as racism from their predominantly White trans and queer communities and transphobia from their API families and communities.[5]

When society sees identities as separate buckets, we have to navigate the empty spaces between them. Here's an example. In 2020, a (Chinese-American) relative connected me with a university staff member for an informational interview. The calendar read: "Ms. Alvina Lai." If I asked the university staff member for a correction, my relative might find out. And that would cause drama. So, I didn't. When the personal and the professional collide, when different social expectations clash, there is identity negotiation.

Thai's research states: "They noted not feeling like they belonged in either the trans community as an API person or their API culture of origin due to being a trans person."[6] Here's an example of this phenomenon at work. At one organization, I was encouraged to join some company groups. There was a LGBTQ+ community group. Will I be the only person of color (POC)? The company also had an Asian heritage community group. Will I be the only non-binary individual? These concerns are part of identity negotiation. We reflect, weigh, negotiate.

Is there a way to understand this experience? Vani Natarajan, a queer South Asian American librarian, explores this.[7] They talk about the queer

---

5. Jayden Thai, "Transgender and Racial Identities Negotiation Processes of Transgender Asians, Asian Americans, and Pacific Islanders: A Transcendental Phenomenological Examination," *Electronic Theses and Dissertations*, August 1, 2018. https://doi.org/10.18297/etd/3048.

6. Thai. "Transgender and Racial Identities Negotiation Processes of Transgender Asians, Asian Americans, and Pacific Islanders: A Transcendental Phenomenological Examination."

7. Vani Natarajan, "Counterstoried Spaces and Unknowns: A Queer

and transgender people of color (QTPOC) identity. They explain that QTPOC LIS workers develop forms of capital, or abundances, to sustain themselves in library spaces. Two forms of abundances are familial abundance and resistant abundance. We generate familial abundance by creating communities to support one another. We generate resistant abundance when we develop reactions to inequality.

Inequality varies for different people. Our experiences as QTPOC are different from white people (including LGBTQ+ white people). Our experiences as QTPOC are different from POC who are not queer or trans. Even among QTPOC, there is a range of experiences, such as those which are specific to Asian Americans. When we are in communities created for one identity, our other identity may be ignored or shunned. From what Natarajan's saying, it sounds like QTPOC need to, and do, create their own.

Creating a community is a long process, one that requires bravery, energy, and persistence. Even with a library family, there is still the day-to-day grind in the office. What does it mean to be a non-binary Asian American when serving patrons, when sitting in meetings, when writing literature? The way one dresses and is seen, speaks and is heard, writes and is read—these are all part of co-existing.

Dress Code

When people and popular media think of librarians and dress codes, they think of the cardigan. Cardigans and items of dress are often gendered, based on the gender binary system. That can make it difficult for LIS workers whose gender expressions don't fit into that system.

My dress is androgynous. Androgyny is ambiguous and deliciously indifferent. Unfortunately, some people (stores and websites too) still think of fashion as "men's" or "women's" wear. Just as white supremacy

---

South Asian Librarian Dreaming," in *Knowledge Justice: Disrupting Library and Information Studies through Critical Race Theory* (Massachusetts: Massachusetts Institute of Technology, 2021) 141-157, https://doi.org/10.7551/mitpress/11969.003.0011.

normalizes whiteness to create a harmful othering of POC folx, masculinity is normalized as the default gender expression and creates harmful othering of non-masculine gender expressions. This distracts from the charm of androgyny, and puts androgyny on this gender expression scale of more or less masculine.

For non-binary folx, androgyny may almost seem like a mandatory uniform. As Chang describes it, when they dress in femme clothes,

> I won't be seen as 'trans enough' — my clothes will give people permission to treat me as a woman or feel entitled to use the wrong pronouns. Even people who claim to be accepting of non-binary gender still expect that our expression must deviate from the norms associated with our sex assigned at birth.[8]

It's one thing to be in androgynous dress because it is what I want, and another thing to dress that way because it is expected. I remind myself that I don't need outward affirmation of my gender and choices of gender expression. I can adopt any kind of dress and still be a non-binary person regardless of what people think I am.

There's one more thing about androgynous dress: it's different when you're Asian. No matter how I dress, I'm navigating stereotypes (and racist histories) victimizing Asian American bodies. For example, when Chinese laborers came to the U.S. in the 1800s to build the nation's Transcontinental Railroad, it made white men insecure—as a result, white workers directed violent, racist, and emasculating attacks at Chinese men, which we still see today. Meanwhile, Asian women in American history were "hyper-sexualized yet demure and submissive… This stereotype in turn fostered the over-prevalence of Asian women in pornography, the mail-order bride phenomenon, the Asian fetish syndrome, and worst of all, sexual violence against Asian women."[9] The violence is still vis-

8. Chang, "TOKEN," 51.

9. Sunny Woan, "White Sexual Imperialism: A Theory of Asian Feminist Jurisprudence," *Washington and Lee Journal of Civil Rights and Social Justice* 14, no. 2 (March 1, 2008): 29, https://scholarlycommons.law.wlu.edu/crsj/vol14/iss2/5.

ible and present. In 2021, eight people, including six Asian women, were killed in anti-Asian hate crime shootings. Tie sexualization and sub-missiveness with any service industry (like a service desk?), and the situation reveals how vulnerable we can be.

What does that have to do with dress codes in LIS? Well, in the above, stereotypes of Asian men and women assume a binary. That itself is a problem. In a digital asset management system, a photo of me might get tagged as "Asian" and "woman," in which image tagging is another whole can of worms. More importantly, I don't want to displace the conversations about stereotypes of Asian men and women. How do I dress in an androgynous way without perpetuating the harmful stereotypes of the effeminate Asian man? How do I dress in a way that does not get misinterpreted as dismissing the struggles of Asian women? Can I be myself without silencing others?

Can I wear cardigans?

Ultimately, dress codes are problematic; everyday gendered language around dress is problematic. It's uncomfortable. Discomfort is both physical and emotional. Instead, I consider dress as a form of communication and a factor of comfort. I can never control how others interpret my communication. All I can control is how I express myself to the best of my physical, emotional, and financial ability.

Spoken Voice

In 2018, I went in-person to volunteer at an archive. Volunteers were invited to provide their pronouns during introductions. The majority used he/him or she/her. By the time it was my turn, near the end, folx were zoned out. Through the gray silence, I said, "My name is Alvina. My pronouns are they/them." Heads swerved. Faces. I paused. Silence.

My voice has a higher pitch, thus perceived as feminine and young. On calls with interviewers or new colleagues, I'm often "Miss." I've attempted to lower my voice down to a vocal fry, but that was unsustainable. I realized I was trying to be "trans enough" so I stopped. I realized I don't have to perform for anyone.

In conversations, people sometimes do a mid-sentence edit. "Her-their", "She-their", "hers-theirs." "It's thems-theirs." "Excuse me." "Sorry." Once, I was held back at the end of a meeting—I thought I was in trouble, but the speaker actually wanted to apologize for misgendering me. I responded, "Thank you, I appreciate it." It was a little awkward, since I was the reason for someone going out of their way, but it was also my right to be recognized for who I am. Plus, it's charming in that one could see the speaker's mind rewiring, internalizing new speaking patterns into normalcy. It's unfortunate that it isn't already normal, but it will be.

If a speaker redirects mid-conversation to (over) apologize and self-berate about misgendering you, be careful. It may suck energy from you. You might feel pressured to have to forgive them, and actually console them, even though *you* are the victim. Resist. There is already a lot of emotional labor in LIS—don't bear this additional burden. Be workplace appropriate, but don't be afraid to redirect them. "I appreciate it. Thank you. Let's return to our tasks." Don't get pulled into their ego whirlpool.

When I refer to myself in the third person, I sometimes mistakenly use "she." I don't intend for it to happen. It's a habit. I'm also rewiring. I forgive people and myself, and move on.

The best moments are when pronouns are used right. "This is Alvina, they're my classmate." "This is Alvina, they're our new librarian." They're! Simple, easy, satisfying.

What about silence? Silence occurs when misgendering goes uncorrected. "She'll be working on the project." Tumbleweeds. These moments are awkward, but can be resolved. If you have an ally in the office, they can follow up with, "They'll be a good addition to the project." I've witnessed self-championing colleagues interject mid-conversation, "Excuse me, my pronouns are they/them."

When I am being misgendered, I may not volunteer a correction. I find it easier to correct the misgendering of someone else, but not myself. Trans and gender diverse folx get accused of being attention-seeking, of being trans "trenders". It is not that the squeaky wheel will get its grease; rather, it is that a nail that sticks out will get hit. I'm not a wheel but a nail. I felt looming self-doubt, anxiety, and insecurity. By speaking out, am I seeking attention? Am I being problematic? I am. I'm in a downward spiral. I forget that it was someone else who made the mistake. No, I'm making the mistake, for causing problems. Why did I say something?

It's uncomfortable to be misgendered. But the discomfort of gender dysphoria didn't temper or cure the anxiety of imposter syndrome. Instead, they co-existed, contradictory and present.

To be clear, every non-binary individual has their own history and reaction to misgendering. Some non-binary folx express anger, irritation, frustration, and exhaustion. I tend to feel discomfort which dissipates, or resignation. The body is temporary. However, I occasionally feel shame for not speaking up, not because of the misgendering to me specifically, but because misgendering could be inflicted upon another person, and I didn't do anything to stop it.

During a symposium, a lovely poster titled, "Addressing the Transgender and Non-Binary User Experience in an Academic Library" was presented. The presenters described updates to their identification fields, changing bathroom signs, etc. Heads bobbed in agreement. Then it was the time for Q&A. A participant came forward. She (she clearly declared) wouldn't want to be called an "it." Gasps. Silence. Glances. The presenters, their faces expressing the same shock I felt, began to explain the pronouns. In discomfort, I left. Maybe I should have stayed, to witness and understand how these situations are (or aren't) resolved.

Like prefixes and gender-related words, names can be verbalized incorrectly. After the 2021 Atlanta shootings, a wave of media coverage by non-Asian news anchors, journalists, and public figures attempted to pronounce the victims' names. Due to the cultural ignorance of American media, some sources misspelled or shortened the names into something unrecognizable. Name butchering is not new for the Asian American community. Names get butchered during conferences, panel introductions, graduations, in-office meetings, virtual calls. It's disrespectful and tiring.

Fortunately, there is a fix. It shouldn't be your responsibility, but you can encourage folx to ask for name pronunciations, and then give it to them. Here's an example from an email from the Visual Resources Association: "Please take a moment to respond to this email with a phonetic pronunciation of your name so we can say it as you do."

Words can confuse people. Confusion can make people defensive and hostile. Their fear and insecurity are not your fault and not for you to manage. It is not your responsibility, or your power, to control how other people feel. They don't get to control how you feel, either.

There are practical actions you can take in the office. For example, build prefixes, pronunciation fields, and inclusive options into templates, forms, and surveys. Update policies, documentation, standards, and procedures. Add it as a bullet point for the next one-on-one check-in with your manager. Take a look at any database fields. In 2020, I worked with a database where the standards stated, clearly, that Mx. was *not* a replacement or placeholder.

What else? Add international holidays and monthly celebrations to the office calendar. Seek out those who contemplate and celebrate with you—find your support and ask them for help. An organization's inclusiveness can be reflected in its processes, but its processes can indicate, and change, workplace culture. It sounds aggressive, but in the bigger picture, this is just institutional growth, and you're fostering positive change as a diligent and insightful LIS worker.

If you come up against complicated bureaucracy, I find purposeful, persistent, and positive communication to be key. Changes can take months, at the director's quarterly or bi-annual meeting. Record all your efforts. If you hear a "no," you have two choices: you can keep trying until you burn out (maybe you'll make a dent of a difference and that would be worth your while), or you can take it as permission to start your job search. At your exit interview, cite "lacking diversity" as an issue, and tell them you tried. Your tone is professional, but you have your receipts. You deserve a place where you and your work can be appreciated.

Digital Identity

The first word on my resume is Mx. In whole, the first line says Mx. Alvina Lai. To use a self-determined prefix/salutation is a simple yet effective moment of empowerment. Hiring managers will make gendered and ethnic assumptions based on names anyway, so this will clarify preconceptions from the start. Though once at an interview, I was asked what my legal name was (the interviewer thought "Mx. Alvina" was my artistic name). Amused, I explained it was my gender identity and they said, "Oh, thank you!"

My email signature includes "they/them." At one company, the employer provided a signature template that linked to mypronouns.org. Despite my signature, I'm often referred to as "she" or "her" in emails and chats. Nonetheless, I continue this practice because it may empower someone else who sees it.

The biography statement; a lot of unexpected edits can happen here. The first occurrence was early in my career, when I submitted a bio for an organization's social media caption. The editor changed "they" to "she," which I saw when the post went live.

Uncomfortable with the change, I started to avoid pronouns in my bios. "Alvina Lai, Title. Responsible for X, Y, and Z. Attended Institutions." At one office, the proofreader recommended I start sentences with "She." I said no.

Avoidance only works for a while, because it eventually makes things awkward. This is true in life, and also in writing bios. As I increased my professional development engagements, the bios became longer. I returned to the third person. "Alvina Lai is the Librarian at New Company. They previously worked at Old Companies." However, with more text, there is more potential for unexpected edits. In 2019, I submitted my bio to a library association only to have it returned with red strikes. "They" have once again become "she." I was puzzled; my heart sank. I turned to Library Twitter, expressing bafflement.

Remember what I said about communities, how they're supportive? Here's an example. Minutes after my post, LIS colleagues came to my support, aid, and defense. Many folx were surprised; some folx were angry on my behalf, others sympathetic. The allyship and solidarity disbursed the gloomy cloud over my head. With clarity, I crafted a response email. I simply explained my pronouns, and the editor wrote an email back with an apology. The bio was retained and my relationship with the editor, to this day, is positive.

The most impactful piece of digital identity is the thoughtful (oftentimes scholarly) text. For most of American history, the only "important" texts were those written by white cisgender men (usually about white cisgender men). Articles, journals, books, etc. were often inaccessible. Now, it's a little bit easier. There are texts about the history of Asian Americans in literature and LIS.[10] There are texts about being queer and Asian American.[11] More text is becoming accessible online. These texts become impactful because they can be read, and also because they can be cited. Scholar Sara Ahmed states, "Citation is how we acknowledge our debt to those who came before; those who helped us find our way when the way was obscured because we deviated from the paths we were told to follow."[12] The process of writing and citing from writers of our own communities is empowering. For example, now you know about all the folx cited in this piece of writing. You can see the history of this work, and it gives you somewhere to go next.

Future

There are two things you need to bring with you into LIS. First, bring yourself. That's the easiest and hardest thing to do. You always have it with you, but sometimes you can forget you're there. Your environment can trick you into thinking you need permission from peers, managers,

10. Janet Hyunju Clarke, "An Overview of Asian American Literary History," in *Asian American Librarians and Library Services: Activism, Collaborations, and Strategies* (United States: Rowman & Littlefield Publishers, 2017) 3–15.

11. Alvin Eng, *Q & A Queer And Asian: Queer & Asian In America* (United States: Temple University Press, 1998).

12. Sara Ahmed, "Living a Feminist Life," in *Living a Feminist Life* (Durham, NC: Duke University Press, 2017) 15–16.

or institutions to affirm you and your work. Don't be deceived. In college, I wasted so much time, money, and energy (all of which I had humble quantities of) trying to get external validation for an internal insecurity. It was financially and emotionally draining. LIS will ask of you the same. I learned to see and take care of myself, and was glad I did, because I needed to see and take care of myself a lot in the field.

The second thing you need is your support, or a plan to get support. While you are always empowered to love yourself, it is easier when you have folx to help when things get hard. I found friends in my cohort, on Library Twitter, and in various LIS associations. These are the people who will support you during difficult times. They will talk about issues you may feel afraid or insecure to have alone. They helped me find energy to launch into new endeavors. Look for the people who can relate to your fears, uncertainties, and frustrations, and see you beneath it all. Self-validation is energy, and support is momentum and direction. You'll need both in LIS.

There are tasks ahead. We are the present and future of QTPOC in LIS. Let's sustain communities, create resources, foster growth and self-love. I look forward to seeing you.

Bibliography

Ahmed, Sara. "Living a Feminist Life." In *Living a Feminist Life*, 15–16. Durham, NC: Duke University Press, 2017.

Chang, Sand C. "TOKEN: TO·KEN /TŌKƏN/." In *Nonbinary: Memoirs of Gender and Identity*, 10. New York, NY: Columbia University Press, 2019.

Chen Cham, Joanna. "You Are Not Alone." In *In Our Own Voices, Redux: The Faces of Librarianship Today*, 257–63. United States: Rowman & Littlefield Publishers, 2018.

Clarke, Janet Hyunju. "An Overview of Asian American Literary History." In *Asian American Librarians and Library Services: Activism, Collaborations, and Strategies*, 3–15. United States: Rowman & Littlefield Publishers, 2017.

Deng, Sai. "From Birth to Maturity: The Chinese American Librarians Association." In *Asian American Librarians and Library Services: Activism, Collaborations, and Strategies*, 41-50. United States: Rowman & Littlefield Publishers, 2017.

Eng, Alvin. *Q & A Queer and Asian: Queer & Asian in America.* United States: Temple University Press, 1998.

Krueger, Stephen G. "Gender Variant LIS Network." Stephen G. Krueger. Accessed June 16, 2021. https://www.stephengkrueger.com/gender-variant-lis-network

Lee, Michelle. "We Need Diverse Librarians: The Asian/Pacific American Libraries Association's Past, Present, and Future." In *Asian American Librarians and Library Services: Activism, Collaborations, and Strategies*, 23–40. United States: Rowman & Littlefield Publishers, 2017.

Natarajan, Vani. "Counterstoried Spaces and Unknowns: A Queer South Asian Librarian Dreaming." In *Knowledge Justice: Disrupting Library and Information Studies through Critical Race Theory*, 141–57. Massachusetts: Massachusetts Institute of Technology, 2021. https://doi.org/10.7551/mitpress/11969.003.0011

Que(e)ry. "Que(e)ry." Accessed June 16, 2021. https://www.queeryparty.org/.

Thai, Jayden. "Transgender and Racial Identities Negotiation Processes of Transgender Asians, Asian Americans, and Pacific Islanders: A Transcendental Phenomenological Examination." *Electronic Theses and Dissertations*, August 1, 2018. https://doi.org/10.18297/etd/3048

Thomas, Camille, Elia Trucks, and H.B. Kouns. "Preparing Early Career Librarians for Leadership and Management: A Feminist Critique." *In the Library with the Lead Pipe*, April 17, 2019. https://www.inthelibrarywiththeleadpipe.org/2019/early-career-leadership-and-management/

We Here. "We Here." Accessed June 16, 2021. https://www.wehere.space/

Woan, Sunny. "White Sexual Imperialism: A Theory of Asian Feminist Jurisprudence." *Washington and Lee Journal of Civil Rights and Social Justice* 14, no. 2 (March 1, 2008): 29. https://scholarlycommons.law.wlu.edu/crsj/vol14/iss2/5.

About the Author

Alvina Lai (they/them) is a Digital Asset Management Librarian. Their academic interests include DEI in LIS, as well as LIS representation in pop culture. They served in APALA (2019-2022 Mentoring Committee), CALA (2020-22 Northeast Chapter Officer), and VRA (2021-22 Equitable Action Committee). Their writing is on Play the Past, Brooklyn Botanic Garden's "Plants & Gardens Blog," and New York Times' "Metropolitan Diary."

Alvina holds a MS in Library and Information Science from Pratt Institute, a BA in Creative Writing from The New School, and a BFA in Photography from Parsons the New School for Design. In their free time, they enjoy webcomics, video games, and drinking tea from their home in Brooklyn, NY.

"And What Would We Have Been If We Were in the Stacks?"

A. Gamble (they/them/theirs)

Keywords: cataloging, Internet culture, poetry, school libraries

They didn't know what to do with me, so they put me in the library.

In the quiet spaces filled with bright displays and dusty corners is where
I found the rainbow.
Not in books—there were few books about us in the library—
and if there, they were coded—women "friends" —
or about serial killers who wore dresses.

Not books, but the Internet, on the computer dedicated to the Oregon
Trail and Simulators:
with strangers on message boards,
bisexual erotica, atheists and agnostics,
LARPers and poets crashing the digital Westboro Baptist Church.

Fourteen, making a website of my writing, structured to Edward Gorey's
Gashlycrumb Tinies:
Gorey and his beard; Gorey and his coat.
Gorey and his queer
"Something." I was in love with a girl and dating a boy.

The Something lived in me, too—"That is not a straight child," as Eddy told me in the hospital

Thirty years later after the first library, when I collapsed
From the weight of hiding, the abuse of invisibility
The lack of words to describe who I was.

It took two decades for the words to come to my library

Through the voice of a student:
"I go by ____, my pronouns are they/them,"
And a copy of S. Bear Bergman's book about chosen relations, glitter families.

If the words had come earlier,

if I had known how to say the Something,
how to write the Something,
what would have happened?

They didn't know what to do with me, so they put me in the library. But it wasn't on the shelves that I found the words for myself.

About the Author

A. Gamble is a non-binary bisexual librarian and LIS doctoral candidate. They originally meant to write a research piece for this collection, but some things can only be captured in poetry.

Multiple Identities in a Trench Coat: Navigating Library Systems While Black and Trans

Bran Eveland Cron (they/them)

Keywords: coming out, first-generation students, anti-Blackness, non-binary, microaggressions

The university system is a pyramid scheme. There are a few people at the top with multiple degrees, and considerable amounts of money and influence. The promise of upward mobility, or rising in societal ranks, are whispered to members of each of the lower tiers. The top is advertised as the ultimate goal, but is inaccessible to most. The economic, emotional, and physical costs of education for people at the bottom of the pyramid are devastating, particularly for those of us who have had to navigate these academic systems on our own.

I have put a lot of work into my education over the years, but my education is only a fraction of who I am. This is the main reason I hold some resentment for the academic system; I do not feel my full self represented. I have learned incredible life lessons off-campus that changed me for the better, but lived experience is not valued in society as a reliable measure of one's intelligence. Lived experience doesn't often pay the bills, either.

I am a high school dropout with a master's degree. I had a lot of shame about being a dropout until I got my bachelor's degree in 2016. A few people in my life completed school years before I did, and I projected a sense of failure onto myself because of it. When I did attend university, I was lucky to have support throughout the experience, for which I am endlessly grateful.

Unfortunately, I felt pressured to enter academia for several years. The people who pressured me never got detailed about why academia was important, other than the insistence that earning a degree was necessary to find life-sustaining work.

Since I was a child, people have told me that I am well-spoken. Their natural conclusion was that I should be in school. Hearing this upset me and made me want to scream. I didn't have the language when I was younger to explain why I had such a painful reaction. Just what was I supposed to do with this information?

I initially reacted by nodding or saying thanks awkwardly in order to get through the interaction as quickly as possible. I learned that not every Black kid around me got the same attention, which made me angrier. I did not understand why strangers were finding me in grocery stores and other public places, and approaching me with this as if it were a cookie.

I believe I understand now. The way that I spoke did not match expectations, and people found that worth celebrating. I wish I could step in front of the child version of myself and tell each of these people to piss off, because I was not interested in being celebrated for that. No one was listening to my actual words, which made each interaction feel superficial and forced. While the adoptive parent I was with would beam at these encounters, I couldn't help but wonder what parts of me had to die so that this well-spoken Bran could live.

Policing behavior—including speech—is one way that people encourage racialised children to tone down certain aspects of themselves that make them so uniquely brilliant. This policing started in my own home. Despite growing up on Tongva land (Los Angeles), which is blessed with such incredible linguistic diversity, I was encouraged to speak what my parent called "proper English". This required adhering to some rigid personal language rules of hers, such as not ending statements with a preposition. I obeyed the rules at home, and disobeyed them at school.

I was good at disobeying all sorts of rules in grade school and would frequently get into trouble. I was receiving excellent marks, but annoyed my teachers by asking too many questions. I needed more to do on my own. The rules, both at home and at school, seemed concerned with being proper to the point of exhaustion. They did not make sense to me.

I found reading to be a lovely world with fewer confusing rules. I could ask myself questions about the book's contents, and never had to worry about being reprimanded. Reading was partially a form of escapism, but mainly a form of nourishment, especially when it came to fantasy and science fiction. Novels, comic books, and other forms of media allowed me to feed on complex stories led by equally complex characters in spectacular worlds.

Television shows also became especially powerful for me as a kid. *Sailor Moon*, for example, was unlike anything else I had seen. It put grade school girls with extraordinary powers at the centre of the story. Erik-Soussi observes that the series was "raw and honest, putting focus on the huge, mostly female cast's struggles with morality, friendship, jealousy, sexuality, vulnerability, and the desire to protect loved ones."[1] I deeply appreciated these smart, capable, beautiful young women who fought for love, and for a better world. The North American version of *Sailor Moon* attempted to hide its queer themes from the audience, but they still seemed loud to me. In fact, the themes spoke directly to me as I was coming to have a better understanding of myself. The show was foundational for me coming to terms with my own queerness, and my unconventional approaches to gender.

My gender wasn't a big deal for me, but other people loved to make it their business. I was frequently reminded at home that ladies didn't sit the way I did, or run around the way I did when I played. "Maybe I'm not a lady, then," I'd retort, having no idea how soon I'd come to know it.

I found out about National Coming Out Day in 1999, not long after I had turned fifteen years old. I saw this day as a unique opportunity to be more honest with myself, and with the world around me, during

1. Magda Erik-Soussi, "The Western Sailor Moon Generation: North American Women and Feminine-Friendly Global Manga," in *Global Manga: "Japanese" Comics without Japan?* ed. C. Brienza (Routledge, 2015), 23-44, DOI: https://doi.org/10.4324/9781315584898.

a time when I felt unappreciated and invisible. I happily came out as bisexual to the people I considered myself closest to in high school. I already knew some people on campus who were out as bisexual or gay, so I felt safe sharing with them. When I got home, my choice to share made me feel unsafe. "I went through that stage too," my adoptive parent murmured unhappily.

This is a very unfortunate way to respond to a person who has decided to be honest and vulnerable. I never thought I was straight. Sharing that felt like a formality. I never backed down from acknowledging my queer identity to anyone, but I did learn to make myself small at home, as it became clear that queerness was not welcome. I made myself small at school, and did the same with my gender, for fear that I would be invalidated again.

I used the word "genderless" to describe myself for the first time in 2007. As I typed the word into my LiveJournal, a certain chill ran down my back. I had already gotten the sense that being out and trans was not very safe, based on my interactions with my parent about being bisexual. I had heard horrible stories about how trans people were treated. I would not begin to get loud about my gender until a few years later, after I moved away from California. I didn't really have much of a trans community until I moved to the Pacific Northwest in 2009.

It was easy for me to feel safe among other trans people. I volunteered for the Gender Justice League (GJL), a Seattle-based organisation that advocates for trans rights in Washington State. The members made me feel at home, which was a new and exciting feeling for me. I also learned to do the same, shedding some of my strange Californian assumptions in the process. "Dude", for example, is not gender-neutral. I still thank the first woman who yelled at me about this, because it forced me to interrogate my own assumptions about the word and its meaning in broader contexts.

Volunteering for GJL was a true joy. I learned a great deal. Trans people are not a monolith by any stretch, and our experiences can vary greatly, but not having to explain myself in certain ways on a regular basis was freeing. People respected my name and pronouns. This feels very small in the grand scheme of what trans people need to survive, but sometimes the little things matter too. I enjoyed helping to set things up for Trans Pride, which GJL runs in Seattle each year. It was fantastic being in community with other volunteers and attendees during the marches on Capitol Hill. It was like breathing and existing as my true self for the first time.

Being trans is a gift. Realising I was trans helped me to like myself better, and also helped me to understand myself better. It gave me the power to look at myself in the mirror and, occasionally, not be repulsed by what I saw. I have used a handful of words to describe my experience: genderless, genderfucked, genderqueer, agender, non-binary. Each of those are ways of describing that the person I am now is a truer me than the girl I was pretending to be.

I have come out a few times, as there were a few closets I had to escape from. I have been out as gay since 2018, and it feels equally liberating. The more time that passes, the more love I discover for myself and the unique ways in which I move throughout the world.

Feeling stronger in my queer and trans identities was necessary before I could complete university, but that wasn't all I had to wrestle with. I am a first-generation student in every possible sense. I am the first in my family to earn a bachelor's degree, and the first in my family to earn a master's degree. Those achievements come with their own set of unique challenges. Most of my peers seemed to be prepared for university in ways that I could not be. Perhaps their parents paid for their education in full, or were able to give their children tips on how to be successful in higher education, based on their own experiences. I had occasional help with finances, but no roadmap to guide me through surviving university. I wasn't even aware of these things that put me at a disadvantage until I was already in school.

Despite said disadvantages, I flourished at university. My professors welcomed my flurry of questions. I tried my best to reserve the more complicated ones for office hours, so as not to disturb the flow of lecture sessions. I went to university in Canada, and despite the challenges of living outside of my home country, I did my best to get as much out of my education as possible. I majored in linguistics because I wanted to learn more about how and why people communicate in the particular ways that they do. I participated in my school's Linguistics Student Union and took on plenty of other activities outside my major. I completed my bachelor's degree in my thirties, treating it as though it was my last chance at undergrad, after previous attempts and failures. My passion for studying languages made me take a deeper look at further interests, and librarianship resurfaced almost immediately.

Libraries are a sanctuary to me, but they are not only important in terms of content such as materials and programming. Libraries are also important in terms of space, and how patrons are able to navigate these spaces. Wandering the Los Angeles Central Library as a child made me feel like a whole person. I felt free to explore on my own there. I had the power to ask for what I wanted from a library worker or a kiosk without fear of judgment. I spent a lot of time in public libraries as a teenager as well. My undergrad institution became my first choice because of a visit to the school's library during a campus tour. I easily visualised myself there. I imagined printing assignments, using study spaces, and recharging after lectures by sitting in a chair and looking out the window at the beautiful landscape around me.

In my second year of university, I began to talk about my desire to pursue librarianship to my trusted professors. As a first-generation student, I didn't have the foggiest idea about how to make sure I was a competitive candidate for grad school; I was struggling enough through undergraduate work. Two of the professors I confided in alerted me to an undergraduate scholarship from the Association of Research Libraries (ARL) that was geared toward racialised students such as myself. I applied and won my first scholarship ever. The scholarship was one of eleven that ARL granted to undergrads that year. The scholarship allowed me to work in the Special Collections department of my school's library, where I met people who seemed dedicated to doing really meaningful work for their community members. ARL also coordinated sessions that helped us understand what to expect in library and archives work, factoring in nuance for racialised library workers. The scholarship and work experience only strengthened my resolve to apply to library school. The application process added stress to an already stressful academic load, but I leaned on that support from my trusted professors and librarians. Their expertise was invaluable. It is largely because of them that I went on to be accepted to one of the best Library and Information Science graduate programs in North America.

Prestige looks lovely on paper, but it isn't everything. It doesn't tell you about those pesky rules that you have to follow in a class setting, which I struggled with as a youngster. I learned that I swore too much for the Canadians in my undergrad, and that I also swore too much for the Americans in my grad school. Back home in California, swearing felt like a natural way of expressing oneself. In an academic setting, I learned that it is considered rude.

I have been seen as rude, sassy, angry, uppity, and a number of other adjectives which are coded to describe Black people in terrible ways. Within the walls of academia, it feels especially personal. There have been days where I have had to hold my reactions to microaggressions inside myself. I vented about things at home, when I had the energy. Calling out a racist comment may have made things worse for me at work, and I feared sabotaging my opportunities. Multiple people have addressed me incorrectly in grad school classrooms. Most of the time, I have said nothing in response. Doing so in that moment would have brought a group discussion to a grinding halt. To someone who does not regularly experience these microaggressions (small acts of discrimination), the above events may not seem like much. They do, however, have ways of adding up, and doing long-term damage to a person.

I have often been the only Black person or the only trans person in an academic setting, which feels very disappointing. Being the only one sometimes means having a fair share of encounters where it is unsafe to stand up for oneself. This is especially the case in environments where the appearance of positivity is valued above all other feelings. Through the lens of librarianship, it has a specific name: vocational awe. Fobazi Ettarh describes this as "the set of ideas, values, and assumptions librarians have about themselves and the profession that result in beliefs that libraries as institutions are inherently good and sacred, and therefore beyond critique."[2] Viewing librarianship as an unalloyed good is a very popular belief. It only contributes to the increase of workspaces that enforce "positive vibes only" culture. This sort of culture may help preserve the semblance of good morale in a library work or class setting, but it can have an exponentially negative emotional and physical cost. It also does nothing to establish a safe space for racialised and other marginalised peoples.

As a recent graduate, I feel it is my responsibility to be transparent about my academic experiences, for the sake of those who come into librarianship after me. This includes the stuff I had to overcome. In order to improve upon the things we love, we have to face the harsh truths about them and do the healing work together. I adore what I have accomplished so far in the field, and I am fiercely proud of my profession. We still have to be better. The library field is frequently seen as LGBTQ-friendly, but it is rare that I see interrogation of which of those letters get accepted. I believe we have miles to go in terms of what it means to honour trans identities and racialised identities in library spaces.

Library spaces are overwhelmingly white-dominated, which can make the pyramid scheme of university systems seem all the more impossible if you're not a member of that team. This sometimes means that I have to be less of myself when I am in libraries, or figure out how to express myself in a way that is more palatable to whiteness. I can't be too forward about any problem that I am facing, which is frustrating. Workers are encouraged to share the positives of librarianship with anyone who will listen, but are discouraged from sharing negative experiences, which tends to make the negative experiences worse as a result.

On the bad days, a lot of who I am appears incompatible with library work. It doesn't take long before I remind myself that Black librarians are not new or odd and that I have plenty to contribute that is worthwhile.

---

2. Fobazi Ettarh, "Vocational Awe and Librarianship: The Lies We Tell Ourselves," *In the Library with the Lead Pipe* (2018), https://www.inthelibrarywiththeleadpipe.org/2018/vocational-awe/.

Change is excruciatingly slow within a large system, often making it seem as though it's not happening at all. However, I am well-equipped to handle challenging systems. I can even find ways to flourish within them. It's not my goal to succeed alone, though. I am determined to do whatever I can to make space for anyone who needs it, especially those who have difficulty seeing themselves in librarianship.

Bibliography

Erik-Soussi, Magda. "The Western Sailor Moon Generation: North American Women and Feminine-Friendly Global Manga," in *Global Manga: "Japanese" Comics without Japan?* edited by C. Brienza, 23-44. Routledge, 2015. DOI: https://doi.org/10.4324/9781315584898.

Ettarh, Fobazi. "Vocational Awe and Librarianship: The Lies We Tell Ourselves." *In the Library with the Lead Pipe* (2018). https://www.inthelibrarywiththeleadpipe.org/2018/vocational-awe/.

About the Author

Bran Eveland Cron is a Black agender person born and raised on traditional Tongva land (Los Angeles). They have the privilege of living with their wife Mikah on the ancestral, unsurrendered territories of the Squamish, Musqueam, and Tsleil-Waututh peoples (Vancouver). Bran is an archivist and a librarian. They believe academic research should not come at the cost of the livelihood of its participants, nor should it only be for the benefit of the institutions that fund them. They have a hard time turning their brain off when they are supposed to be sleeping.

On Fear, Professionalism, and Being That Trans Guy Library Technician

Caleb Nault

Keywords: health science libraries, library technician, student, fear, visibility

"One of the most damaging outcomes of institutionalized homophobia and heterosexism is fear. The fear of what *might* happen can be [debilitating]."[1]

In my daily life, being transgender is not at the forefront of my thoughts. I remember a time when that was not the case, and I feel grateful to be in a relatively stable space where my mind is typically untroubled by anxieties that come from navigating the world as a trans person. Here in my late thirties, my trans body is a palimpsest of tattoos, scars from multiple surgeries, motorcycle accidents, and the remains of teenage piercings, removed. Over fifteen years of testosterone has broadened my shoulders, deepened my voice, and nurtured a glorious ginger beard while robbing my noggin of hair. All of this, in concert with whiteness, has coalesced into cisgender passing privilege. In most cases, I get to

1. Donna Braquet and Roger Weaver, "Out All Over: Giving Voice to LGBTs on Campus," in *Out Behind the Desk: Workplace Issues for LGBTQ Librarians*, ed. Tracy Marie Nectoux (Duluth, MN: Library Juice Press, 2011), 69-82. The original quote used the word "crippling" in place of debilitating. Fear of transphobia and/or transphobic violence exacerbates clinical depression and anxiety, and can in fact lead to debilitating physical and mental outcomes. I am writing from within disability rather than using it as a writing device, however the word crippling is descriptive of a particular type of physical disability, and the original author was likely using it metaphorically, which I wanted to avoid.

decide whether people know that I am trans, and that has had a profound and positive impact on my mental health.

Being trans is a part of who I am, and while it may not occupy my daily thoughts nor claim top-spot as my main identity, it is always there. In my personal life, transness shows up during conversations when I momentarily stop listening to determine if I'm ready—or if it's worth it—to out myself so I can pass on a helpful personal tip about healing from a hysterectomy. My transness is there when I suss out if it is safe to mention that I used to play girls' softball, or that I used to be a dyke, or when mail shows up addressed to my birth name, even though I legally changed everything eons ago. In my working life as a library technician at a medical library in Toronto, Canada, being trans has led to hilarious and awkward conversations with colleagues, moments of genuine connection, and exciting professional development. I've also felt the impact and toll when transgender issues enter workplace discussions. My experience of being a trans library technician has been positive overall, but there is always fear.

It wasn't until my early thirties that I recognized the library as a place to work, as a professional destination. A friend pointed me towards a job posting for a position as a library technician and I quickly ascertained that specialized training would speed up the process of being hired. So, I did what millennials do best—I signed up for more student debt and went back to school. I started an accelerated library and information technician college diploma in May, 2017, a whirlwind of two years' worth of content—including two 3-week internships and an unfortunately timed teachers' strike—packed into one year. Within days of starting the program, I and the other queer or queer-adjacent students found each other and formed a group of formidably sassy weirdos. We were immediately open with each other and found safety in being able to be who we were without (too much) judgement.

I didn't immediately come out as trans to my fellow library technicians-in-training, despite the out and proud nature of our group. I enjoyed the first several months of the program just existing as a queer man among them, uncomplicated by transness. Cisgender passing privilege afforded me the ability to be seen as who I was at the time: a queer guy in a non-monogamous relationship with a queer cisgender woman. I connected with one friend about the pains of feeling erased as a queer and/or bisexual person in a perceived-as-straight relationship, while forming a flirtatious bond with another as the only two gay guys in our group.

I routinely forced everyone outside for our lunch hours to enjoy the fleeting sunshine and heat that summers in Toronto afford, and on a particularly scorching noon hour, we gathered around a picnic bench with lunch boxes and takeout containers and talked about one of our favourite topics—sex. The women in our group were very interested in what gay dating and sex apps were like and demanded stories of scandal and adventure from myself and the other gay guy in our motley crew. In response, I hauled out my phone to scroll through the grid of local suitors to potentially illustrate my storytelling, and as the phone left my hand, I had a flash of panic as I realized that my profile on this app specified that I was trans.[2] After several long moments of holding my breath and trying to play it cool as they inspected the app and pointed out the gentlemen they personally found attractive, I prodded with "So, I'm guessing you all saw what my profile says about being trans...."

They had.

And it was a non-issue, mostly unremarkable, just another piece of me that they had learned about that day. It didn't detract from how they experienced me, it wasn't accompanied by claims that I had misled or deceived them, and it opened up parts of myself that I hadn't realized I'd wished were open. Still, the fear is always there regardless of how many times the outcome is positive.

As the summer relented and autumn arrived, I began the first of my two student placements in the technical services department of a college library affiliated with the University of Toronto. My supervisor, the Head of Technical Services, was also a martial arts instructor who

2. In hindsight, I am horrified at this breach of the app users' confidentiality and do not recommend anyone do this.

offered lunch time classes on campus several days a week. After learning that I had spent six years in martial arts as a kid, he encouraged me to attend his next class. I agreed, and the next day we made small talk on the walk to his makeshift dojo while I tried to calm my rising nervousness about the fact that I needed to change into appropriate clothing and had forgotten to put on underwear that morning, and I had no idea what the change room situation looked like.[3] This would be the first time I had trained in martial arts as a man with other adult men, and frankly, I was terrified that they might overpower and hurt me on the mat, or worse, notice my trans body in the change room and physically or sexually assault me.

I was also several months on the other side of a cervical spine surgery for a chronic pain condition. While I felt able to tell my supervisor about my fears of triggering pain through practice, I definitely didn't feel like I could say, "Hey, so when I said that I did martial arts for six years, I forgot to mention that I was a young girl and because of my age and sexism everyone took it easy on me so the prospect of training with a bunch of giant men is kind of freaking me out." And it's too bad that I didn't feel comfortable disclosing being trans, because when we got to the change room and he tossed me his spare gi, he might've offered me another place to change. Instead, everyone started undressing in the closet-sized change room, elbow-to-elbow. I panicked and ducked into the hallway, sputtering "Sorry, uh, I'm…shy?" and then proceeded to feel like an idiot as I hopped around on one foot, trying to get the bottoms on before anyone could see my naked trans body.

This is likely an experience that resonates with shy cisgender men as well, but their bashfulness isn't rooted in potentially being outed as trans and the threat of anti-trans violence that may follow, be that humiliating questions, verbal invalidation of identity and humanity, or physical and/or sexual violence. Again, whiteness and cisgender passing privilege have currency, but the thing about cis passing privilege is

3. Add this to the list of "things my colleagues now know about me that they probably shouldn't."

that it is temporary and easily revoked. It's there until it's not. As someone who has trauma from being on the receiving end of men's physical and emotional violence, I do not operate on the presumption of safety. While my experiences so far have been positive and while I would like to believe that men who are employed within the library and information services profession are progressive, being wrong could have potentially deadly consequences.

My second library placement happened in the early spring and came fresh on the heels of an exciting and heartwarming experience of volunteering at and attending my first Ontario Library Association Super Conference (OLASC). I'd had the pleasure of affixing a ribbon with my pronouns to my conference badge and encountered billboards outside of the bathrooms that proclaimed the restrooms to be all-gender spaces that everyone could safely use. I came away from that conference feeling like the library profession was the perfect place for a nerd like me, and after attending a session specifically about making libraries trans-positive spaces, it also felt like a pretty great career for trans people, too. Coincidentally, a member of the volunteer coordination team for OLASC was also my supervisor for my second placement, so I had the opportunity to introduce myself and start establishing a dynamic several weeks before officially beginning at the hospital health sciences library. I didn't immediately disclose being trans to this supervisor but (correctly) assumed that he had put the pieces together himself since 1) my résumé reads like a who's who of getting paid to be trans (i.e., my previous career in community-based research was exclusively projects on transgender health), 2) the first thing I did upon starting at the health science library was propose constructing a resource guide for hospital staff about trans issues in health care, and 3) he identifies as gay and could interpret these signals. Being queer and trans within the professional library setting involves frequently negotiating boundaries between personal and professional life and attempting to be cognizant of the balance between what is appropriate versus what is not. How much of ourselves are we allowed to bring to work? In my experience, working with people who identify as queer or LGBT and/or who are open about their care for and commitment to queer and trans issues (i.e., "allies"), brings a sense of ease to navigating these professional boundaries and encourages genuine conversation and connection.

But the fear is always there. Even as I write this chapter, I worry about what—and how much—I can say without feeling I'm potentially sacrificing or damaging my career because I'm easily identifiable. The health library world is an even smaller subset of the already small special library field, and this can increase pressure around (per)forming and maintaining a professional reputation. As far as I know, I am the only trans library technician working in a hospital library in the Greater Toronto Area, across Ontario, or in Canada (but if I'm wrong, feel free to reach out and say hi!). I'm effectively "that trans guy library technician." Visibility is complicated. The consequences can be simultaneously beneficial (professional development opportunities relating to being trans within the LIS field, like this publication) and disadvantageous (for me, becoming the token trans person and becoming overcommitted and burnt out; for others, the consequences can be far worse). But in my case, visibility is necessary for personal and professional reasons. I need to be able to be my full self at work, in all of my bald, bearded, queer, tattooed, chronically-in-pain, clinically depressed, sarcastically funny, trans glory. The library profession needs the experiences and knowledge of people like me. Fear be damned.

Bibliography

Braquet, Donna, and Roger Weaver. "Out All Over: Giving Voice to LGBTs on Campus." In *Out Behind the Desk: Workplace Issues for LGBTQ Librarians*, edited by Tracy Marie Nectoux, 69-82. Duluth, MN: Library Juice Press, 2011.

About the Author

Caleb Nault (he/him) is a white, queer trans guy who currently works as a library technician in a health sciences library in Toronto, Ontario,

Canada, while concurrently completing his MLIS online from the University of Alberta. In his barely existent moments of free time, Caleb likes to ride his motorcycle, go to concerts, pet cats, camp using other people's gear, read way past his bedtime, and stroke his beard while gazing off into the distance.

A Different Breed of Cat: Finding My Queer Self

Karl G. Siewert (pronouns: any[1])

Keywords: genderqueer, non-binary, coming out, exploration, self-definition

There is a standard narrative of the trans experience that has come together in recent decades. A trans person grows up knowing that they are in the wrong body, either a girl in a boy's body or vice versa. At some point they are exposed to the idea of being trans. They recognize this in themselves and begin the process of transition, which involves puberty blocking drugs (if they are young enough), hormones, and surgical procedures. They emerge from this process having flipped a switch from F to M or M to F and proceed through the rest of their life in a body that resembles the gender they were born to be.

This is highly simplistic; it in no way represents the variety of experiences of all binary trans people (let alone non-binary ones), and it ignores the enormous burdens that often lie behind the story. Financial hardships, mental/emotional stress, and family trauma are just a few of them. However, to the extent that modern American society has accepted the existence of trans lives, this is the story that it condones.

It is not my story.

I grew up in a small city in the Great Plains and had a conventional upbringing. I was, to all appearances, a straight White male in a

1. 'I rarely feel misgendered when I'm called by any pronouns. I do experience euphoria when called "she" at a time when I'm dressed in a traditionally femme manner. The only thing that truly bothers me is being called "Sir."

German-descended Lutheran family. We went to church and Sunday school every Sunday and to choir practice every Thursday night. My parents came from Minnesota and North Dakota. My mother was an elementary school librarian who was politically liberal, while my dad worked for a big corporation and was more conservative. We were solidly middle class; I went to parochial school through eighth grade and then to public high school. I never wanted for anything, especially books, and had opportunities to play sports and take art and music lessons.

I attended a state college on an academic scholarship. I met a girl (also a straight White Anglo-Saxon Protestant) while working a summer job, and we dated for five years and then got married. We have three kids. I went to graduate school for Library Science and when I took my first library job, it was back in the Plains. I still live within four hours of where I grew up, and within three hours of my parents, who are still married.

Below the conventional facade, though, other things were going on. I've often said about my childhood that I was never very good at being a boy. I had no interest in horseplay or sports. I would much rather play with the girls or, as I got older and they rejected me, sit by myself and read. I wanted in on all the girly trends, like friendship pins and sticker collecting. Most of all, I was emotionally fragile. It was easy to hurt my feelings or make me cry, and I was a target for bullying from an early age. This rarely took physical form but was instead a kind of constant emotional torture, with even the kids who called themselves my friends teasing and making fun of me whenever I felt a little bit good about myself.

I have come to believe, in hindsight, that this was a form of gender policing. My peers saw the ways in which I wasn't conforming and tried, consciously or unconsciously, to make me change. They wanted me to be literally scared straight—and it wasn't just the kids. Over the years, many adults tried to help me address the bullying, but their solutions were just another way of policing my gender expression. I should "toughen up" or "be less sensitive." If there was behavior that caused me to be targeted, I should stop behaving like that. Extreme suggestions were that I should fight back. I should *be a man*.

Back then, in the late '70s and early '80s, I had no way of understanding what I was. I knew that there were gay people, but I definitely wasn't gay, because I was strongly attracted to girls. I knew that trans people existed, but only as the kind of binary female-to-male or male-to-female I described earlier, and they were presented as people on the fringes of society on shows like Phil Donahue and Jerry Springer. As MTV came to prominence, I began to see models of alternative gender expression like Boy George, Twisted Sister, Prince, Eurythmics, and others, but I had no concept of gender as a separate thing from sexuality or of the possibility of being something other than male or female.

At the same time, I was completely fascinated by what I would now define broadly as "queerness." In high school, and especially college, I sought out gay and lesbian memoirs and coming out stories. I befriended queer-seeming people. I played with gender expression in the guise of hippie and goth styles. I grew my hair out, and this became a significant part of my identity to the point where I experienced a kind of existential crisis when I had to cut it off for a role in a campus play. At the same time, I was coming of age politically, recognizing injustice against people marginalized due to bigotry around race, gender, and other identities. I joined environmental groups, protested the Gulf War, and was a founding member of a gay/straight alliance at college.

Much of this was related to people I got to know in person, but even more, it was fueled by my early adoption of the Internet. At college in the early '90s, I was introduced to Usenet and in the *alt.* hierarchy of newsgroups I found subcultures, countercultures, and proto-social-networks in which queerness was something not remarked upon. It was merely one of many possible ways of being, all of which were accepted and even celebrated by people who had been lifelong misfits and were now finding community. Around the same time, I was invited to the Iowa State Computing Association Bulletin Board System (ISCA BBS) and in that group and similar bulletin boards, I established some of the closest friendships of my life. Some of those friends were trans.

After college and three uncomfortable years teaching English in rural high schools, I moved to Minnesota for library school. My political awakening continued there, as I was living in a large city for the first time and exposed to a more diverse population. I made my first close friend who was gay and out. He was a co-worker of mine, and he introduced me to queer cinema and took me to my first gay bar. In my mind, I was still a curious observer rather than a fellow queer person, but I felt a kinship with him and the friends to whom he introduced me. I recall a specific conversation that seems pivotal in retrospect:

> Karl: What would you call someone like me who is straight, but fascinated with the lives of gay and lesbian people?
> Friend: Before I met you, I would have said "closet case," but that's not you. I really don't know. I don't think there's a word for that.

After library school I moved to Oklahoma for my first full-time position as a librarian. Returning to the Bible Belt involved a lot of culture shock. I had truly become a different person in Minnesota. Becoming a librarian was the fulfillment of a lifelong dream. I was that rare child who, when asked, "What do you want to be when you grow up?" would answer, "A librarian!" But it also had another consequence. I had always been a voracious reader, but except for a brief few months working at Waldenbooks, I'd never been surrounded by books all the time. I found that my reading habits began to shift as I discovered new things in the stacks during paging and shelf-reading. It was during this time that I encountered three books that truly changed my life.

My first introduction to the notion that gender expression was a thing apart from gender or sexuality came from reading *Sissyphobia: Gay Men and Effeminate Behavior*.[2] The author reflects on his personal experiences in gay male communities and the disdain and disgust that he's seen directed at expressions of effeminacy. He then draws connections outward to general anti-feminine sentiments in society and misogynistic ideas about weakness, powerlessness, and vulnerability. Reading

2. Tim Bergling, *Sissyphobia: Gay Men and Effeminate Behavior* (New York: Harrington Park Press, 2001).

Sissyphobia started me on a path toward reframing my childhood experiences as gender policing and expressions of patriarchal dominance.

Stone Butch Blues: A Novel is, first of all, one of the most powerful and moving works of fiction I've ever read. It's a semi-autobiographical novel in which Jess Goldberg, a butch lesbian, is exploring various forms of gender expression (including passing as a man) in search of a way of being in the world that satisfies hir personal identity, hir desires to love and be loved, and hir need to survive.[3] This had a profound emotional effect on me, and it taught me about the concepts of gender fluidity and the intersection of multiple marginalized identities. Jess is a butch lesbian, but also Jewish, working class, and a Communist. All of these identities are inseparable and inform every experience zie has. As I sought out more information about the author, Leslie Feinberg, I also learned that zie used non-binary neopronouns, and I read hir other books: the follow-up novel *Drag King Dreams* and the nonfiction *Transgender Warriors: Making History from Joan of Arc to Dennis Rodman.*[4] All of these works broadened my understanding of what gender could be. No other single individual has been more significant in my gender journey.

Tragically, Feinberg died in 2014 at the age of sixty-five. According to a life history published by hir spouse:

> Diagnosed with Lyme and multiple tick-borne co-infections in 2008, Feinberg was infected first in the early 1970s when little was known about the diseases. Zie/she had received treatment for these only within the last six years. Zie/she said, "My experience in ILADS care offers great hope to desperately-ill people who are in earlier stages of tick-borne diseases." She/zie attributed hir catastrophic health crisis to "bigotry, prejudice and lack of science"—active prejudice toward hir transgender identity that made access to health care exceedingly difficult, and lack of science

3. Leslie Feinberg, *Stone Butch Blues: A Novel* (Boston: Alyson Press, 2003).

4. Leslie Feinberg, *Drag King Dreams* (New York: Carroll & Graf Publishers, 2006); Leslie Feinberg, *Transgender Warriors: Making History from Joan of Arc to Dennis Rodman* (Boston: Beacon Press, 1996).

> due to limits placed by mainstream medical authorities on information, treatment, and research about Lyme and its co-infections.[5]

When I found Kate Bornstein and her book *Gender Outlaw: On Men, Women, and the Rest of Us,* I was delighted by her funny, frank voice.[6] The book is compellingly readable, well-researched, and at times painful. It is part memoir, part essay collection, and part manifesto, with the full script of a two-act play thrown in. Some of her information seems dated from the perspective of 2022, but though Bornstein identified as a woman at the time, she spent a lot of time questioning the gender binary (as the subtitle implies). *Gender Outlaw* was the first place I saw someone clearly spell out the differences between sex, gender identity, gender roles, gender expression, and sexuality.

All of this reading was leading me in the direction of answering that big question: "What am I?" And really, the question behind the question: "What do I call myself?" In many of the memoirs and coming out stories I'd read in the past, a queer character would look in the dictionary under "gay" or "homosexual" or some other term and have a powerful moment of recognition. Names, labels, and categories are important for humans. They are the ways in which we determine who we are like and unlike, who we belong with and who we shun. A metaphor I have used in the past is that any cat will tell you there's a big difference between being put into a box and putting *yourself* into one. For me, the final step in crystallizing my gender identity was hearing a single word: "genderqueer." I wish I could remember where I first heard it, but I know that it must have been sometime in the mid-2000s, and I know that it felt perfectly right to me. Genderqueer was my box. It combined so many ways of thinking that felt right to me:

5. Leslie Feinberg and Minnie Bruce Platt, "self – LESLIE FEINBERG," Internet Archive, March 27, 2014, https://web.archive.org/web/20210726214430/http://www.lesliefeinberg.net/self/.

6. Kate Bornstein, *Gender Outlaw: On Men, Women, and the Rest of Us* (New York: Vintage Books, 1995).

1. It reclaimed a slur and turned it into a point of pride.
2. In a throwback to earlier meanings of the word "queer," it represented bending rules, shifting categories, making things strange and uncomfortable. It's a word of activism and unrest.
3. In academic circles, "queer theory" takes a text that may not have been intended to evoke LGBTQIA+ themes and puts a reading of those themes onto it, like reading Gilgamesh and Enkidu or Beowulf and Hrothgar as if they were lovers rather than friends. In a very real way, this is what I was doing with the story of my own life as I came to understand my gender. I was "queering" my self.

At this point, I was approaching forty years old. I had spent all that time with an incomplete understanding of my identity, and it took me a while to experiment with this new frame of reference. I had never experienced any kind of gender dysphoria, which is a primary reason that I didn't identify easily as trans, but once I started thinking of myself as non-binary or of presenting as more feminine, I experienced enormous gender *euphoria*. This was the way it was meant for me to be in the world. Once I reached a certain level of comfort and self-acceptance, I began to think about coming out. How would I tell the important people in my life this essential truth about myself?

As one might expect of someone for whom online communities and social media were so significant, I decided that I would post on Facebook. I used the "Notes" feature and made a public proclamation in March of 2011 which read, in part,

> I tend to value aesthetics above practicality, feelings above analysis, love above power, creativity above acquisition, relationships above status, and emotional expression above stoicism. On small group nights there is invariably a moment when I look up and realize that we've split up, with men on one side and women on another. When that happens, I'm with the women every time.[7]

7. Karl Siewert, "Guy :-)," Facebook, March 12, 2011, https://www.facebook.com/notes/10164321179275290/

Other milestones followed. In the fall of 2012, I began using a personal "logo" on Facebook, Twitter, and other websites which combined a rainbow flag, a genderqueer flag, and the library symbol.[8] I had pierced my left ear back in high school, when it was fashionable for guys to wear a single earring, but in January of 2017 I had my right ear pierced as well, and I began intentionally wearing pairs of earrings in dangly feminine styles. I experimented with nail polish and makeup, including at work, and later that year I participated in a public event called Ignite Tulsa, where I spoke for five minutes about my own experience of non-binary gender.[9]

Then, in June of 2020, I came out at work. I spoke first to my supervisor and then to my colleagues in a staff meeting about my gender and told them that I was going to begin wearing skirts and dresses on occasion. I invited questions, and the general response was positive. This was in keeping with the pattern I had seen thus far. Most of the people who responded to things I put on social media or to my appearance in public and private were complimentary, but at this point something changed. As I started wearing more feminine clothing at work, I started to take selfies and post them on Instagram, Facebook, and Twitter.

To me, "dressing out" seemed to be a natural next step, an outgrowth of the things I'd already been doing. I thought that, by sharing the things I had on social media, I had prepared those closest to me for this, but that was not the case. Some members of my family felt blindsided. They hadn't seen this coming, and they didn't react positively at all. This is something that I am still trying to work on, but some relationships have become strained to the breaking point.

Despite this, I remain committed to being my authentic self, both internally and externally. I consider dressing femme to be a privilege, but also in some way a responsibility. Because I am able to wear a dress and still keep my job, it's important for me to be visible—to stand out

---

8. Karl Siewert, *GQlibraryweb_400x400.jpg*, Twitter image, 2012, https://pbs.twimg.com/profile_images/1410547301/GQlibraryweb_400x400.jpg.

9. TulsaLibrary, *Karl Siewert: Queering My Self: How Not to Be a Good Boy, Ignite Tulsa 2017*, 2017, https://www.youtube.com/watch?v=es3u3NWmgtY.

and stand up for those who can't. This is even more essential in a place like Oklahoma, where bigotry is displayed as proudly as any rainbow flag or drag outfit.

This is far from the end of my story. I will turn fifty-one in a few months, but in a way, my queer self is not even an adolescent. Every day, it seems, I learn something new about myself, and I am fortunate to be able to explore it safely. Many do not have that luxury. I hope to continue to be an advocate and activist in the library community and beyond, and I encourage you, my colleagues, to do the same.

Bibliography

Bergling, Tim. *Sissyphobia: Gay Men and Effeminate Behavior.* New York: Harrington Park Press, 2001.

Bornstein, Kate. *Gender Outlaw: On Men, Women, and the Rest of Us.* New York: Vintage Books, 1995.

Feinberg, Leslie. *Stone Butch Blues: A Novel.* Boston: Alyson Press, 2003.

Feinberg, Leslie. *Drag King Dreams.* New York: Carroll & Graf Publishers, 2006.

Feinberg, Leslie. *Transgender Warriors: Making History from Joan of Arc to Dennis Rodman.* Boston: Beacon Press, 1996.

Feinberg, Leslie, and Minnie Bruce Platt. "self – LESLIE FEINBERG." Internet Archive, March 27, 2014. https://web.archive.org/web/20210726214430/http://www.lesliefeinberg.net/self/.

Siewert, Karl (@yoyology). *GQlibraryweb_400x400.jpg.* Twitter. 2012. https://pbs.twimg.com/profile_images/1410547301/GQlibraryweb_400x400.jpg.

Siewert, Karl. "Guy :-)." Facebook, Notes, March 12, 2011. https://www.facebook.com/notes/10164321179275290/.

Siewert, Karl. "Karl Siewert: Queering My Self: How Not to Be a Good Boy, Ignite Tulsa 2017". TulsaLibrary. Video, 5:12. July 3, 2017. https://www.youtube.com/watch?v=es3u3NWmgtY.

About the Author

Karl has been an academic librarian in Oklahoma since 2013. Prior to that they spent eleven years as a reference and teen services librarian in a public library, and before that they taught English, poorly, in rural high schools. They are a maker of many things, from fiber arts to musical instruments, and they love their kids like nobody's business.

Section 2:

LIS Education

I Don't Want to Write This, or, Against Explanation

Jess Epsten (they/them/theirs)

Keywords: MLIS student, academia, genderqueer librarian, invisible labor, burnout

I don't want to write about my experiences in my Library and Information Science (LIS) program. As a genderqueer student, I struggled and watched fellow transgender and gender diverse colleagues struggle with the visible and invisible labor within academia and the LIS field. In an attempt to cope, I started a list of all the little and big things I had to do to get through the day, or did in an attempt to leave things a bit better for other trans and gender diverse folks. Making a list and reflecting on what I went through gave me some comfort and a place to put my rage and frustrations, to put pen to paper, to have a record. The list included work like sending a multitude of emails to various departments on campus to see if I could have my name on my ID card, my library account, my diploma (etc., etc., etc.); attending meetings with the dean and administration of the LIS program about getting a gender-neutral restroom in the building, which I left feeling tokenized and defeated; and giving presentations to the university's library staff about gender and my uncomfortable experiences navigating their library systems. All the while I also dealt with energy sucks that left me feeling extremely despondent: correcting people when they misgendered me or others, not correcting them (which takes its own emotional toll), fielding apologies from those doing the misgendering, checking out a book at the library when I knew the person on the other side of the desk was seeing my deadname, and hardly ever being able to make it to the nearest gender-neutral restroom on breaks because it was in another building. In the classroom and in my academic assignments, I was also constantly engaged in topics related to my identities because it often felt like no one else was going to bring up trans topics or question binaries. All of this together kept me steeped in an awareness of issues around my identities and trans inclusion in general; by the end of my program, I was emotionally burnt out, sad, and angry.

Originally, I planned to write this chapter about the extra labor related to gender inclusion I did during my LIS program as a genderqueer person. I was going to detail the visible and invisible work, the intentional and unintentional work, the painful and valuable work, the physical and emotional work; I was going to explain how the work overlapped, melded together, and dragged me down. But when I sat down to write this chapter, to write about these experiences in some succinct manner, to describe the added stress and emotional distress it all caused, I couldn't do it. My body and mind kept screaming, "NO!" I think I hesitate because writing about all this labor feels like a continuation of the work, and deep down I do not want to reproduce the labor even in the telling of the issues that I faced. They are all still too fresh. So I will not be recounting these exhausting, painful, and sometimes empowering experiences. Instead, I'm going to reflect on my discomfort and resistance, and ask questions.

When I started my program, I made a conscious choice to stand strong in my identity as a genderqueer individual. I knew it wouldn't be easy within academia and that I was going to be frustrated, but I didn't count on how much it would chip away at my energy and my mental wellbeing. The additional work I took on, consciously and unconsciously, willingly and unwillingly, as well as the subsequent silencing I faced, were definitely the most difficult things about graduate school. So much of the extra work I did was just to get through school with some semblance of dignity, to support other trans students, and to make sure trans issues weren't ignored in the classroom. So much of the extra work I did was reminding/asking/imploring people to treat trans and gender diverse people with respect—to take us seriously. My stories about graduate school are difficult and vulnerable, and to describe them feels like I am putting my choices, my identity, and myself under a microscope. I feel uncomfortable sharing these experiences, and I don't think I should have to do so in order to make the point that transgender and gender diverse people are not safe or protected in academia, that we struggle and are burdened with extra emotional and physical labor in LIS programs. I am refusing to put myself and my experiences under that microscope. Instead, I am asking: do my stories and my vulnerability need to be displayed for people to see transgender and gender diverse experiences as legitimate? Do my experiences need to be dissected for people to see transgender and gender diverse individuals as legitimate?

Now that I've graduated and have the degree, I cannot say that I've come away feeling excited, hopeful, or safe in this field. I mostly feel exhausted and cynical. I know that academia and work in the United States (read: capitalism) are extractive. They demand that you instrumentalize yourself and your identities for the bare minimum in return, while you simultaneously receive messages to prioritize self-care and maintain a strong and healthy work-life balance. But how is it possible to "leave work at work" or "not bring work home," especially when that work (or extra work) is so directly tied in with your identity? Because work is never just what is in your job description. It is also all the extra work you do behind the scenes or the work of fielding all the inappropriate questions and comments flung at you. And I am faced with an overwhelming dread of an unending future of extra work and the agonizing decision: to take on the work of advocating for trans and gender diverse people or to know that it won't get done.

I cannot answer these questions, and it should not be left to me and other trans and gender diverse people to answer them alone.

Instead, I am asking cis people in libraries:

What are you going to do take burdens off of transgender and gender diverse students and coworkers?

How are you going to transform systems to make them more equitable and inclusive for transgender and gender diverse people?

How are you going to break the rules?

About the Author

Jess Epsten (they/them) is a white, queer, genderqueer, chronically-ill southerner who recently earned their MSLS. Their interests include digital literacy and skillbuilding, community data, accessibility, and STEAM (Science, Technology, Engineering, Art, Math) services. Jess is currently working on a free, online curriculum for LIS folks on gender identity and supporting trans and gender diverse people. Prior to starting graduate school, they ran a farm with their partner, as well as a business supporting queer-owned small businesses and social justice nonprofits with website creation and coaching. Jess also loves plants, baseball, astrology, zines, comics, and the Fast and the Furious Saga.

Being Seen

Blanca Hernandez (he/him/his)

Keywords: student, BIPOC, microaggressions, LIS classroom experiences

I have always had a deep love, appreciation, and connection to school and public libraries. I experienced first-hand how they can transform a desert of a community into an ever-blooming information garden. The profound James Baldwin once wrote, "You cannot love if you cannot be loved, you cannot see if you cannot be seen."[1] Growing up as a queer Brown kid of immigrant parents in the cracked asphalt streets of Southside Chicago, it is nearly impossible to see yourself reach past the daily task of surviving. Chicago Public Schools in Black and Brown neighborhoods tend to be severely underfunded, and there are few teachers and mentors who expect these youth to grow beyond the impoverished and gang-ridden neighborhoods they are born into. It is an unspoken fact that the encouragement of "you can be whatever you want to be when you grow up" does not apply to kids like us. There is one place though that transported me to fantastical worlds like Jeanne DuPrau's *City of Ember*, gave me a peek into the terrifying world of R.L. Stine, and made me feel seen when opening the pages of Sandra Cisneros and Pam Muñoz Ryan's novels; that space was my local Chicago Public Library. It also connected me to the world outside of my own little neighborhood through the internet, which I could only truly access at the library. Libraries can be powerful spaces for LGBTQ+ youth; in my

1. James Baldwin, *Just Above My Head* (London: Penguin Books, 2007), 84.

case, I was able to discover and explore my gender identity in ways that my community and culture did not allow me to through internet access and library programming. Libraries can be one of the few places in communities that offer support groups, programming, and internet access for LGBTQ+ youth to have the opportunity to connect with others in their community. Aside from those experiences, the library also saved my mother's life. As an undocumented person, she did not have health insurance, but through our local public library we were able to find a hospital and a doctor able to give her a lifesaving surgery at no cost.

School libraries are equally transformative spaces for underrepresented youth. I experienced these positive effects first-hand, as it was my high school librarians who connected me to a college prep program that helped me get into university. Despite this, I rarely saw myself reflected in either the school or local public library staff, which robbed me of the idea that I could be behind the reference counter or facilitating library programs one day. Even now not much has shifted; according to the AFL-CIO's Department for Professional Employees, in 2020 over 83% of librarians identified as white. This is an alarming contrast to the 9.9% of librarians who identified as Black or African American, the 9.9% who identified as Hispanic or Latino, and the 3.5% who identified as Asian-American or Pacific Islander. There are currently no clear demographics for transgender and gender non-conforming librarians in the field, and this lack of information speaks for itself.[2] So, I ventured on another path to pursue an Arts Administration degree for my undergrad. That path unfortunately turned into a short-lived career as that space also has an ironically clear "glass ceiling" for Black and Brown professionals. I took an opportunity to live in Osaka, Japan for a year to teach English and figure out what to do next. One hot summer day I was feeling nostalgic about losing track of time perusing through library stacks, so I walked down to the Osaka Prefectural Central Library. Even if I could

---

2. Katie Barrows, "Library Professionals: Facts, Figures, and Union Membership - Department for Professional Employees." AFL-CIO, Department for Professional Employees, June 10, 2021, https://www.dpeaflcio.org/factsheets/library-professionals-facts-and-figures.

not read any of the Japanese writing in the books, I just wanted to feel that old book smell hit my nose again. Standing in that Japanese library, I realized that I needed to give back to my community for all the years of support and joy it had brought me as a young lost kid; I wanted, or more so needed, to be the guiding light for other at-risk youth just as other librarians had been for me. Now the task of starting the journey to become a librarian began.

I do not want this chapter to be a bleak representation of Masters of Library and Information Science (MLIS) graduate programs and I promise I have heartening stories to fill these pages, but it is more important to shed light on unfortunate microaggressions and barriers for trans and non-binary individuals, for if we do not call out injustices, then we cannot fight to break them down. Returning to my hometown, I did end up finding a great program at a university located in the Chicagoland area at the beginning of 2018. Around the same time, I began my social and medical transition as a transgender man. Of course, I still had trepidations regarding entering librarianship as a Latinx person, but more than anything I was terrified of being a queer and trans person in this space that I registered as only for clean-cut professionals. I felt too different. Would they reject me when they saw a person with facial hair pick up the name tag with the name "Blanca" at the informational session? Would they not respect my pronouns and misgender me? Would I be the only one who looked like me? Who sounded like me? All of these fears of the unknown kept me from showing up to three informationals that I had signed up for. I felt defeated. It took another year to gather up the courage to finally speak to a recruiter and show up to an open house during the spring of 2019, and that fall, I applied and was accepted into the MLIS program at my university.

Sometimes I wonder if there are other trans and non-binary individuals who are going through the same hurdles, discrimination, and lack of representation now. For that reason, I spoke up one day in my Advanced Reference class when the topic of lack of diversity in librarianship came up. The question from my professor was, "What is one action you will take to diversify the library field?" and even if I did not want to answer the question as one of two people of color in the classroom, all heads turned in my direction. Despite my nervousness to disclose my gender identity, I remembered the feelings of fear and regret I had for almost two years and imagined there were many others out there with the same hesitations that desperately need the support of the university. I began to explain that the university does not have any diversity recruiting efforts, and that unless there are clear signs that transgender, gender non-conforming, and BIPOC prospective students are welcome and wanted, then my experience would be a painful cycle for my community at this university. Let us say that the response did not go over well. The mentioned professor received her MLIS from the same university, has tenure, and has a lot of pride in the school. These should be great qualities in an instructor, but they have led her to ignore harmful truths, not just about the school but about the profession as a whole. The instructor responded by stating that the school does more than enough to promote diversity within the program. The justification for this statement was that she believes the university has a diverse Information Studies faculty and that should attract students from diverse backgrounds by itself. Despite my personal feelings about this response or this professor, the response was a direct connection to all the statistics touching on the lack of diversity I had read to this point. The reality is that MLIS programs fail to even see that there is a problem with lack of representation of trans, non-binary, and BIPOC individuals. If the problem cannot be seen, then it cannot be addressed. I have moved on from this moment in an effort to not let it sour my graduate school life, but it does make me worry for the future of librarianship and how we are not at all fostering a space for potential librarians who are transgender or non-binary.

Since I am hoping to soon be a public librarian, the course I had been looking forward to the most was the Public Libraries course, with a revered professor who has been teaching for the school for several decades now. I will admit, I am that student who reads the entire syllabus, so I sat one morning reading through the document sent before classes started. I was dumbfounded when I reached a section about pronouns. There was an entire section dedicated to the use of "they/them/theirs" pronouns and how although it is better to use gendered pronouns, the professor would allow the use of gender-neutral pronouns. The syllabus went on to state that students would have to be clear we were referring to a person or we would have grammar points deducted from assignments. I felt deflated. Yes, he was allowing us to use gender-neutral pronouns, but he still had to make it clear that he had an obvious distaste for them. For a while I thought I was being sensitive about the subject until I learned the origin of that section in the syllabus. A few years before my time at the school, another transgender student took his class. To my dismay, I learned that the student had to fight tooth and nail to be seen and recognized as a trans individual by the instructor and was purposefully misgendered in front of peers. The issue was escalated and taken to administration; they, in efforts to deal with the situation, facilitated a meeting between the student and professor. The result of that meeting manifested in the paragraph that I read in the syllabus at the beginning of class. For all that I learned in that course, I could not shake the fact that there had been clear discrimination in the classroom towards another trans student and there were still microaggressions occurring during my time in the professor's class.

Our profession is not as black and white as we might imagine, and both of these statements are true: librarianship and library services can be problematic and need serious restructuring, and at the same time they are spaces of refuge for underserved populations that can also hold amazing opportunities for underrepresented groups within the profession. I do, though, have hope for the future of our profession. Two semesters ago, I applied for an Instruction Librarian Intern position at my university library. I felt like all odds were against me. I am queer, trans, Brown, have no prior library experience, and I was two weeks post-op from having top surgery at the time of applying. I was ecstatic when I was given the news that I was one of two students chosen for the position. I was able to teach information literacy sessions in English undergraduate classes, create and run my own one-shot workshops, work on instructional videos and materials, and complete so many other wonderful projects for the library. It was my internship supervisor who drew my attention to this book proposal and encouraged me to submit to it. At the end of the two-semester internship, I gave a presentation to the school faculty, including the Dean and Provost, where I displayed statistics that demonstrated the clear lack of diversity in the MLIS program and called on faculty to support and fight for students like myself because we are worth it. The presentation was well received and for the first time I felt as if my gender identity and race were not a hinderance to me in higher education, but a tool to fight for those who have little to no presence in spaces that unfortunately are mostly white and cisgender.

To recap, libraries have been and will continue to be life-affirming and even lifesaving spaces for underserved populations. That said, librarianship cannot stop there, as there are still clear issues within the profession. Transgender, non-binary, and BIPOC individuals must see themselves reflected in their information institutions, whether that means public libraries, school libraries, or something else. University MLIS programs must create recruiting efforts for the mentioned groups, or poor diversity statistics will continue to be our reality. Universities must listen to the needs and issues of trans and non-binary students so that an issue like the one that occurred in my Public Libraries course does not repeat itself. I know that I will face other obstacles once I graduate and enter the library world outside of my school walls, but recalling Baldwin's words, if other trans and non-binary people can see me and see that they belong in library spaces, even if it is just one person, then that is a step in the right direction.

Bibliography

Baldwin, James. *Just Above My Head.* London: Penguin Books, 2007.

Barrows, Katie. "Library Professionals: Facts, Figures, and Union Membership - Department for Professional Employees, AFL-CIO." Department for Professional Employees, AFL-CIO, June 10, 2021. https://www.dpeaflcio.org/factsheets/library-professionals-facts-and-figures.

"Freaky Gender Fluidity": Navigating Distance Education as Non-Binary LIS Students in a Default Cisgender Environment

Anonymous (they/them)

Keywords: LIS students, online learning, nonbinary, transphobia in the classroom, experiences with LIS faculty

It was the middle of the semester, in a class about analyzing literature for teenage patrons. On this particular evening, my classmates and I were presenting in groups on the works of an award-winning author of our choosing, with my group presenting on Ursula Le Guin. With our PowerPoint at the ready, the group collectively took a breath and followed the script we had spent the last several weeks meticulously hammering out together.

That was, until, the words of one of my group members brought the presentation to an abrupt and screeching halt. "I personally didn't like this book," she proposed, thinly-veiled malice slipping off of her tongue in a move that we had certainly not rehearsed as a group. "The aliens in this book have some kind of freaky gender fluidity, and I just personally think transgenderism isn't something we should be promoting to kids."

My groupmate continued on with her rant for a while as a somewhat stunned atmosphere draped itself over our class. I found myself dumbstruck, grateful for the class rule of only one camera being allowed on at a time. I was trying to process not only what I had just heard, but the way my professor had simply let the remarks slide with an uncomfortable encouragement to move to the next slide. This was a professor I had worked a great deal with, both inside the classroom and beyond—someone who knew that I was nonbinary—and there was no comment, no opportunity for a learning moment to be found. It was simply a small fluster that had been abruptly swept under the rug, never to be addressed.

I had not yet realized it at the time, but this was not a one-off experience. I had only pulled back the curtain. After this interaction, I began to see the discomfort my department had with trans students almost everywhere I turned: A professor getting flustered when a fellow nonbinary student corrected him on their pronouns; another professor stumbling over himself when he remembered my own pronouns halfway through an example but never correcting himself; my advisor continually misgendering me in email correspondence despite my pronouns being attached to my signature.

When other students saw the passivity of our faculty when it came to making safe spaces for transgender people, the atmosphere took a turn for the worse. In the same course in which our group member went rogue, casual transphobia bled into multiple classes. Emboldened by the example before and, arguably, by virtue of the class being virtual, other students joined in. We had discussions on whether librarians should have to promote, or worse, "tolerate" what several peers called "transgenders." I was a lone voice in the class, desperately trying to defend myself and others who might also exist outside of the gender binary but weren't comfortable enough to speak up, and I was ruthlessly cut down again and again. There were only awkward attempts to change the subject and nothing more.

This behavior exhibited by the faculty of our department challenged me. In all of my classes, I only had the pleasure of studying under one professor in the department who used all students' correct pronouns and actively worked to make her classroom a safe space for gender diverse students. Despite only one professor actively holding space for trans students, I had issues pinning down the why of the situation. Why were my faculty tripping over themselves to pretend horrible, transphobic encounters weren't happening? Why did they struggle so much with using trans students' pronouns? Was it a lack of care, or was it something else entirely?

I took a look at the facts in front of me: I had a department that applauded itself for its commitment to diversity and inclusion, with multiple members who openly declared themselves members or allies of the LGBTQ+ community, but I also had a faculty that was hesitant to do the work required to make their classes safe. I knew I needed to backtrack—to see what our department considered inclusivity to be. What did they really mean when they continually spoke about creating a culture of care?

Like many other schools and departments existing in 2021, ours has a web page declaring their commitment to equity, diversity, and inclusion in the field of library and information science. In reading this document, there do seem to be good first steps in ensuring equity within the department. The department outlines expectations for their faculty, though they are vague in that they say faculty will receive "*supplemental material that will focus on other equity issues such as gender, disability, and sexual preference.*"[1] In their outline for students, their only currently proposed plan is to have an anonymous feedback form, where they will "*uncover and attempt to address student concern*s".

This last point in particular is what troubles me. Beyond the vagueness that the plan shows to LGBTQ+ students at large, it feels peculiar to me that the onus is on marginalized students to report issues that the department will allegedly "attempt to address." Think back to the scenarios I have listed throughout this chapter, if you will. The department has shown time and time again that, despite their well-wishes and aspirations for inclusivity, they fail to rise to the occasion of protecting transgender students. A simple policy such as "we do not tolerate language that is othering to students of any background" might have helped make the environment one where casual transphobia was not left

1. School of Education, "Equity, Diversity, and Inclusion at LIS," UNC Greensboro, accessed September 10, 2021. https://soe.uncg.edu/academics/departments/lis/lis-equity-diversity-and-inclusion/.

unchecked. It would've saved me evenings of muting my computer and disrupting my studies so that I didn't have to endure a stream of transphobic consciousness from a particularly dominant group of my peers. I wouldn't have cried into a pillow, wondering if this was the lesson our future librarians were going to spread wherever their lives took them.

Why would I feel that any report I submitted to my department would be taken seriously? I have endured several instances of blatant transphobia at the hands of my peers, and there was never once a situation in which the faculty stepped in to effectively help. Each event felt like the faculty didn't know, or care to learn, how to navigate it. Why would I feel confident that these same people would do anything to protect me and my transgender peers? Asking transgender students to seek help from the same people who have continually turned them away isn't as supportive as faculty seem to think it is.

I don't believe my department is acting with malice. These are my mentors, my future colleagues, some close enough to be considered friends. They do not have actively bad intentions, and I do feel that at their core they want to make their department as inclusive as they can. But good intentions don't add up to much without the constant work that is required to take those intentions and turn them into actions. Our faculty doesn't know what to do. They haven't received guidance—they most likely think that their current approach of simply saying they are a safe space for transgender students is enough. And when they face situations in which their perceived inclusivity is challenged, they flounder. In floundering, they allow their online classrooms to become hostile environments for trans students.

I propose the following adjustments to make the University of North Carolina Greensboro Library and Information Science Department more inclusive for transgender students. First, the responsibility of reporting discrimination should not be placed solely on students. The faculty and staff of this department should be regularly evaluating themselves, and the department should require their participation in programming about creating safer environments for trans students. Second, the department should develop a policy on how to conduct these evaluations, what metrics they are holding themselves to, and specifically outline their commitments to upholding their commitment to equity, diversity, and inclusion. This policy should include multiple components. One should be clear guidance on what to do in the event of transphobic rhetoric being spread in class and how to handle it safely. In addition, there needs to be guidance for all staff regarding pronoun use; some ideas include information about how to use different pronouns they may encounter, how to incorporate language that does not encourage gender and pronoun assumptions, and how to normalize optional pronoun sharing in the classroom. Third, steps need to be written out to outline an active plan to ensure the safety of gender diverse students. Finally, this document should be made publicly available to students so that they can continue to hold their faculty accountable.

By the time this chapter has been published, my time with the department will already be at an end. I will, unfortunately, not be able to see what changes, if any, are to come from my writing this. I admit, the prospect does cause me some trepidation, but the time for silence has long gone.

Step up to the plate, UNC Greensboro. Be the inclusive, equitable space that I know you want to be, that you can be.

Your trans students need you.

Bibliography

School of Education. "Equity, Diversity, and Inclusion at LIS." Accessed September 10, 2021. https://soe.uncg.edu/academics/departments/lis/lis-equity-diversity-and-inclusion/

About the Author

Anonymous is a recently graduated nonbinary student living in eastern North Carolina. In their spare time they fancy themself a bit of a home chef, loving cat & plant parent, and ceramics enthusiast.

Genderqueerness in Bloom

Monica Hunasikatti

Keywords: Desi, South Asian, genderqueer, Indian, non-verbal communication, fashion

Gender identity, for me, initially felt like a performance. My clothes determined my act, made it authentic. The truth was, I had complicated feelings about my body, my chest, and my small frame. Fashion helped form my ability to understand my gender, as well as the bubble of safety I cultivated through my outfits, my hair, my wigs, and my tattoos as tools for navigating the often-intangible landscape of gender identity. The connection I had with my culture—specifically, weddings and other celebrations—allowed me to take a deeper look into how clothes ruled the South Asian community's economic and social hierarchy. South Asian Indian (Desi) culture and experimenting with my clothing choices within the safety of my graduate school's library helped shape my understanding of my personal identity of gender queerness.

The library gave me sanctuary, not just to challenge the rigid rules of academia, but also to understand what gender means to me and how it impacts the kind of librarian I aim to be. My own complex journey with gender impacted how I interacted with other students in my program, how I approached labor relations with my union colleagues, and how I assisted patrons of my library with a focus on providing safe and accessible spaces to discover, find, and retrieve information. Solace and wisdom were found from fellow queer and trans MLIS students, and safety from one professor in the department whose classroom allowed me to express myself openly and to be as loud with my wardrobe as I was with my voice. My hope is that with the ever-turning tide of the socio-political landscape we're in, more people (both those in LIS and those who love the nurturing environment of their hometown library) can find community in those stacks.

Where I found more power and joy was in working at my library. As a library assistant, I was free to curate displays, plan interactive events, and create programming to document our collective knowledge about marginalized communities, providing information to all passersby. The pillar by the door was perfect to broadcast news. It was a sweet spot: right at the entrance/exit of the small library. This pillar represented opportunity. With eye-catching and colorful displays, my colleagues and I were essentially free to broadcast whatever news we wanted. Our displays drew people to what we had to say and made people pause. In many ways, dressing that pillar was much like how I choose to dress myself. There was always something to say.

I guess my library wasn't anything particularly special. It was housed in a concrete monstrosity in the cheesiest state of the Midwest. Its furniture was bright and stylish but did not exactly ooze comfort. The stacks were lined with books, zines, dissertations, and dust. Gaggles of undergraduates filled the tables, and students filtered in and out almost every hour from one of the three classrooms connected to the library. But this was home. Or at least, some version of it. I guess one could argue I had some kind of academic Stockholm Syndrome. It's probably not that healthy to have been so attached to an academic library, but there I was, one of the only visibly brown graduate students in my cohort, working to become a librarian.

In addition to being a safe harbor, the library was also my stage. I could dance about, flit in and out at almost all hours of the day. I wore my wigs, my suspenders, my thigh highs, my nerd jewelry, my bowties, and my flouncy dresses, and felt unencumbered doing so. I felt free to explore my gender identity within that tiny library for librarians. To be brown and visibly genderqueer was liberating on a scale I had not experienced before.

Class and Status as Communicated Through Clothing

From the motherlands to the place of emigration, class follows. Extravagance does not even come close to describing the level of spectacle that Desi weddings contain. Matrimonial events are given top consideration—they have been culturally important for thousands of years. It was from these events that I first really began to understand the importance of clothing and fashion. To Indians, what you wore was a symbol, not just of beauty, but of wealth as well. Its function as a class indicator is nothing new. For South Asians, specifically Indians, what you wore became not just an individual identifier, but one that declared your family's class status. Your jewelry, your handbag, your shoes, and of course, your saree/salwar/lehenga all spoke volumes about your socio-economic standing. This public display of devotion to one's family provides social currency needed to survive intra-community politics. While this display of over-the-top wealth might be off-putting to many, to those celebrating, it is a source of immense pride. It represents the ultimate form of love and affection, not just to those getting married, but to the family members who have come from far and wide to celebrate with them. It is the collective, not just the couple, who is meant to be celebrated. These celebrations are expensive. Thousands of dollars are spent on flowers, food, alcohol, new outfits, gifts to relatives and close friends, decorations, venue(s)...the list goes on. These ceremonies are extremely auspicious and vital, especially to the older generations. Based on ancient marriage customs and laws, many of these events are seen as mandatory. From an early age, these weddings taught me the visual and cultural power of clothing, and how it connects to gender roles, class, and social hierarchy.

British colonialism violently upended Indian cultural norms, especially in regard to sexual orientation and gender identities. Hindu mythology and Indian society have a 4,000-year-old history of gender and sexual fluidity, but with British invasion came criminalization and pathologizing of the hijra community along with a damning eye towards anyone existing outside of heterosexuality. Despite the fact that the very gods we worship do not adhere to the gender binary (I mean, it's not even subtle how badly our gods give the finger to the classification of gender), British colonial attitudes about gender and sexual diversity resulted in South Asian bigotry towards queer and trans people. It's these aspects of my experience—from the extravagant world of Desi weddings, to sites of free learning in libraries, to navigating American views on gendered garments—that have shown me how clothing has become an indicator of how a person is treated.

Throughout history, the Desi diaspora have often bargained with the dominant culture, whether it be the British and other European colonizers or upper caste/upper class aristocrats, for how they will be perceived. Will they be seen as exotic? Or as a threat? This psychological bargaining demands that only socially acceptable clothing be worn by the marginalized. This bargaining has caveats, of course. When it suits the dominant power, our clothes are seen as shiny objects to ogle at and to covet, and at many times, to appropriate.

Do Clothes Make My Gender?

When I felt like I looked good, I was confident and even bolder than usual. My clothes were often a prelude to what my mouth was about to say. I was loud in my classes, I asked questions, and I challenged professors. I did not allow the hierarchy of academia to intimidate me.

I also felt as though I was a fake, a facade. I felt like my reliance on clothes to describe my gender identity made my experiences strictly superficial. I had no issue with being considered a woman, but why did it still make me pause when someone referred to me as that? I enjoyed feeling androgynous. I felt safer and more comfortable when I explored my masculine wardrobe. Rejecting expected characteristics of subservient womanhood made me happy. Strong femmes in pop culture, on Instagram, and in anime were awe-inspiring. However, admiring Utena from *Revolutionary Girl: Utena* and Haruka from *Sailor Moon* didn't quell my anxiety about trivializing what it means to be genderqueer. What is gender anyway? That was a question that existed in some form or another the entire time I was obtaining my Master's degree. It still exists now, even as I am typing this essay. It wasn't just my climb in academia that made me feel like a fraud. It was also because of how tumultuous my understanding of my personal identity was. The confusion I felt towards my body resulted in pushing those mixed-up emotions away.

> I think that it... happens differently with everybody. So with fashion, I was always very expressive. As soon as I had the means to make it happen, like I did.... There are other places in my life where I am not as confident, like speaking or writing.... I am not able to express myself as much as I can if I'm wearing a wig. And like that was a lot easier for me to come to, than learning how to write or like learning how to communicate myself with language.—Sandeep Gill[1]

Clothes are my microphone. They are akin to shining a spotlight on myself and allowing me to be heard without saying a word. Not that I needed to showcase more differences between myself and others around me during graduate school; I was neck deep in a sea of white midwestern conformity. There were times I felt alienated from my peers, especially when it came to talking about diversity and equity within the information world. Librarianship is still largely populated by white women, and my experiences involved reserved, quiet, and modest students. While I cherish so many of my classmates and am grateful for the conversations I had during and beyond the classroom, white complacency and silence in the information sciences was, and continues to be, thunderous.

Conclusion

Clothes are a way for me to express myself. Clothes are tools that allow me to communicate in a non-verbal and powerful language. From the

1. Sandeep Gill, interview with Sameer Desai, South Asian Stories, podcast audio, 12/28/2019, https://southasianstoriespodcast.com/2019/12/28/sandeep-gill-celebrity-stylist-and-image-consultant-and-her-mission-to-help-people-look-and-fee#l-their-best/

earrings dangling from my lobes to my sweet kicks, I want my clothes to say something. They indicate joy, sadness, vulnerability, sensuality, protectiveness, and a myriad of other emotions. My clothes become my weapons or my shield. They defend me and keep me safe. Clothes can render me invisible. They can also shine a spotlight on me. What I find affirming in all these facts is that I feel as though a protective power has been given to me. Being brown and visible was my reality, and I did not want to hide my skin. Due to the queer-friendliness of my graduate school cohort, I felt safe to explore my gender expression. Since I was so far from home, it was important for me to cultivate meaningful bonds around me. What I did not expect was to find kindred spirits in the happy queers around me. It was blissful to see happy gay people living ordinary (and not so ordinary) lives. I experienced this first in my library. It made me question: What does it mean for us to create a safe place within our libraries that looks like what I experienced? I think for me, it started with how organic it was simply to exist as a person in a particular space that nourishes the queer folks that walk through it. This nourishment of experimenting and challenging and reexamining cultural norms in a safe environment is key to revolutionizing our information spaces.

Bibliography

Gill, Sandeep. Interview with Sameer Desai. *South Asian Stories.* Podcast audio. December 28, 2019. https://southasianstoriespodcast.com/2019/12/28/sandeep-gill-celebrity-stylist-and-image-consultant-and-her-mission-to-help-people-look-and-fee#l-their-best/.

About the Author

I am a South Asian librarian who enjoys their genderqueerness. I received my undergraduate degree in African American Studies and Gender, Sexuality and Women's Studies from Virginia Commonwealth University. I received my Master's degree in Library and Information Studies from the University of Wisconsin at Madison. My librarianship focuses on reaching out to a variety of diverse communities through educational programs, community gatherings, and public displays of a wide variety of books that uplift marginalized people. I am a connoisseur of anime and nerd media. I love exploring the intersections of race, gender, and sexual orientation in pop culture.

Genderqueering the MLIS

Anonymous

Keywords: student, genderqueer, nonbinary, misgendering, being out in academia

In this chapter, I will discuss my personal experiences navigating the Masters in Library and Information Sciences (MLIS) as a queer and genderqueer online graduate student in the United States. The MLIS program that I attend, which I have chosen to anonymize, has taken multiple measures to help transgender and gender diverse students express their gender identities. These policies and norms have made it easier for me to express my shifting gender identity, but some recent institutional changes and experiences have caused me a great deal of frustration as well. I am writing through my own specific lens, and while many of these issues are commonplace for transgender and gender diverse students in higher education, I can only speak about how these situations have impacted me as an individual. The transgender experience is by no means a monolith, and my experience is only one of many, as I am sure you will discover by reading the many perspectives contained in this book.

When I began drafting this chapter, I had included the name of my program and my initials. I'd been prepared to praise and critique my program as a current MLIS student, despite some anxieties about the possibility of readers, and potential employers, discovering my identity. That was before my university decided to migrate their student and staff information and course registration system—the previous iteration of which I had planned on praising for its flexibility for transgender and gender diverse students. These changes made me lose some faith in my supposedly welcoming program, and made me question whether there could be repercussions for my career if future employers figured out my identity. I will also be discussing specific incidents that occurred in my program, and I don't want to burn any professional bridges. As a result, I will be omitting some details about the program, as well as personal details, while knowing that students or staff in my program will likely be able to ascertain exactly which school I am talking about.

When I was initially applying to MLIS programs, the program I currently attend stood out to me because of their policy on diversity, which explicitly recognizes diverse gender identities. Part of the application process for my program involved writing a diversity statement. In mine, I discussed the intersections of my identity and my personal commitment to justice as a person and as a future librarian. Given the historical and contemporary trends of libraries, archives, and museums in upholding hegemonic traits and values, I was glad to see that this program requires applicants to think about how they are situated within a historically white, middle class, (cis) woman-dominated field. To make it clear, I am a white, queer, genderqueer individual, and I recognize that there are issues with requiring diversity statements in applications. By listening to the experiences of BIPOC (Black, Indigenous, People of Color) library workers and students, I learned that requiring diversity statements in applications can also be a frustrating and draining experience for the very people they are intended to support, and that these statements are an imperfect Band-Aid for greater structural inequities.

After I was accepted into the program, I was delighted to find that the school's online portal allowed students to enter their names and pronouns in free-form text fields. Students who used names other than their legal names could easily update them in the system without jumping through any bureaucratic hoops. The same applied to pronouns: students could write in their pronouns, as many as they wanted. Names and pronouns could be updated indefinitely and immediately. As my comfort with certain pronouns changed during the course of my program, I found it an incredible relief to be able to update my pronouns without having to contact administrators or get permission. I felt empowered to explore my gender freely, and it was validating to be able to do that in an academic space when I wasn't out in other spaces.

Unfortunately, the online portal was later changed to a new system that severely limited options. Users now needed to use a drop-down menu of pre-selected pronouns, and the number of pronouns that users could select was initially limited. There was also a required and non-editable "Gender" field with the only options being "Male" or "Female"—which is inaccurate, as male and female are sexes, not genders, and the choices perpetuate a binary that excludes many intersex people and forces trans and gender diverse students to identify with an assigned or legal sex that may not correspond with their gender. There was now a Legal Name field, in addition to a Preferred Name field, which could be triggering for individuals who have not legally changed their names given at birth, but use a different name now. Finally, there was also an editable "Gender Identity" field. Having both a non-editable "Gender" field and an editable "Gender Identity" field implied that gender "identity" is less real and less legitimate than assigned or legal sex. That being said, institutions should move away from requiring the recording of legal sex in the first place, to be truly trans inclusive.

Since the launch of this new online portal, several transgender students brought these issues to the attention of the staff in charge of integrating the system, which resulted in some changes and compromises being made to accommodate these concerns within the limitations of the chosen technology, legal requirements, and staff unfamiliarity with best practices for trans and gender diverse inclusion. The "Gender" field was changed to "Biological Sex," and the options in the drop-down menu now include "Male," "Female," and "Not declared." Additionally, more pronoun options were added, and explanations were included to describe the legal context for some of the required fields. While it is frustrating that students had to advocate for these changes to be made, the responsiveness and willingness of staff to accommodate these concerns is important to recognize. Many students in higher education do not even have the "luxury" of attending an institution that actively works to make it easier for transgender and gender diverse students to accurately and safely self-identify.

That being said, the changes were compromises at best. Students still have to select from a limited drop-down menu of available pronouns, requiring them to request additional pronouns be added if theirs aren't available. The "Biological Sex" and "Legal Name" fields, required by state law, are needlessly invasive, and it is unclear if that information is made visible to staff. The "Biological Sex" field may also create a headache for transgender students who have transitioned—are they expected to select their birth sex even if they have medically transitioned and changed their legal documentation to reflect their gender? And what about those who haven't yet, can't, or don't want to transition? Why should it even matter? Students in higher education have much more important things to worry about than arbitrary and invasive questions about their bodies.

Faculty and student behavior, which help create and sustain cultural norms, play a significant role in how welcoming and validating the environment in my MLIS program is for transgender and gender diverse students. Many professors who teach in my program include their pronouns in their email signatures. It's a detail that might be easily overlooked by someone who has never questioned their gender or been misgendered—but it's a detail that I appreciate. It makes me feel seen to know that LIS faculty members actively participate in creating a culture where gender and pronouns are not assumed. This practice also makes it easier for transgender and gender diverse students to display and introduce their own pronouns, which can be extremely anxiety-inducing when it isn't the norm.

One specific instance that made me feel validated was when one of my professors created a webpage that included photos, names, and pronouns of each student in class. It is important to acknowledge that some closeted transgender and gender diverse students might find this practice invasive and even dangerous. Some individuals might feel comfortable listing their pronouns in their student profiles, but may be reluctant to share them with classmates and faculty, or they might list incorrect pronouns in their profiles to remain closeted. Personally, I found this practice helpful, because it can be difficult to get to know fellow students beyond their replies to discussion board posts. If, at the time of taking this class, I had wanted to change my name or pronouns, I would have experienced some embarrassment and discomfort at having to contact my professor to update the webpage. While this approach is imperfect, I appreciated the effort my professor took to attempt to ensure that students had an easy way to correctly refer to one another.

The second instance that made me feel validated was when another instructor held a live video meeting at the start of the semester so the class could do introductions and ask questions about the syllabus. He instructed us to introduce ourselves with our names, our pronouns, and a number of other facts. I was struck by how easily my professor demonstrated this in his own introduction, sliding through his pronouns without fuss. I was both nervous and excited when it came time to introduce myself, especially after I learned that there were several other students in my class who, like myself, used they/them pronouns.

The third time I felt affirmed was something of a mixed bag. It was, once again, a video meeting to start off the semester, but this was my first class where live video meetings would be required every week. This meant that there would be more opportunities for people to misgender me. My professor hadn't set a precedent for introducing pronouns and I wanted to make sure that I wouldn't be misgendered, so I included my pronouns next to my displayed name. At first, I was the only one with pronouns displayed. But as the meeting went on, I noticed that more and more classmates, and then my professor, displayed their pronouns as well. Before it got to my turn to introduce myself to the class, several classmates had verbally introduced their pronouns as well. It was such a simple, validating thing to see my classmates respond supportively and ensure I wasn't alone in proclaiming something that is so important, and yet so often taken for granted.

Being in an academic environment where some professors make an active effort to validate transgender and gender diverse students has helped me recognize the need for flexibility when asking students to self-identity in a community space. During video introductions for the class where students were asked to introduce their pronouns, several students skipped their pronouns. I was hurt that some of my classmates might not have seen the importance of normalizing a practice that can make life so much easier for everyone. At the time, I was making several problematic assumptions about these classmates: I assumed that they were cisgender, I assumed that they perhaps scorned the idea of introducing their pronouns, and I assumed that these students didn't know that pronouns and genders should never be assumed. After all, if I hadn't introduced my pronouns, my classmates would have taken in my appearance and incorrectly assumed my gender and pronouns.

However, I now recognize that it is important to leave room for people, regardless of gender identity, to keep their pronouns to themselves. I myself have grappled with this issue on social media, at work, with loved ones, and in my program. There are some spaces where I feel safe to ask people to refer to me as "they/them" and others where I'd rather let people assume that I use a particular set of pronouns, because it feels safer. It would be hypocritical of me to assume the worst when a classmate skips their pronouns in an introduction.

There have been slip-ups, of course, and moments when people could have made more of an effort to be inclusive. During a group project for an online class, my group members and I introduced ourselves via email. I made sure to list my pronouns in my email signature, as did another group member who used they/them pronouns. The other two group members were cisgender women. Despite the effort that the two of us they/them users made to ensure that the correct pronouns were used for us, there was an instance in a video call where my group member who used they/them pronouns was misgendered while not present in the meeting. It was a non-malicious slip of the tongue, but I found myself unable to correct the group member who had made the error. In retrospect, I wish I had, and I also wish the burden hadn't been on me to do so.

I've also been misgendered during class video calls, multiple times, by classmates and a professor despite my pronouns being right next to my name. It's incredibly embarrassing to experience that over a video call, when my face and pronouns are so visible, and I'm supposed to be focusing on class discussions. One time, after being rapidly misgendered, first by a classmate and then by my professor, I wanted to slam my laptop shut and storm outside, stand in my backyard, and scream. Instead, I typed "they/them please ☺" into the chat box, bit my tongue, and sat with my feelings.

Nobody acknowledged my correction, which was almost worse than being misgendered in the first place. I know that my classmates and professor could see the message, because the chat box was frequently used during class. It was humiliating to have to stick up for myself and then to feel ignored by my class's complete lack of response. In a class where we often discussed readings on implementing social justice, activism, and equity in the library, not one person, not even my professor, felt the need to acknowledge the fact that my identity had been denied by two people in rapid succession. This is so much the norm for transgender people. I only experienced this a handful of times, and I almost feel grateful for that. The bar is laughably low.

It can be difficult to know how a cisgender person will respond to being corrected or called out for misgendering a transgender person, especially if you aren't familiar with how educated they are on transgender issues. When you are transgender yourself, the burden of correcting these missteps weighs that much heavier, because it's your own identity at stake, regardless of whether you're out or closeted. How someone responds to being corrected can determine whether it's safe to be authentically yourself around them. And sometimes, I'd just rather not know than face that pain. There are people in my life who I know I cannot risk coming out to because of the things I've heard them say. There are people in my life who I am out to, but who still express frustration or get defensive when I correct them. There are also those who panic and over-apologize, which then requires labor on my part to tell them it's not a big deal (but, truly, bless them for actually caring). I find it frustrating to try to hand-hold people through the process of putting in the basic effort required to correctly refer to myself and others.

It's exhausting to always be fighting people's traditional, learned assumptions about gender and pronouns, especially when learning or working in an institution that doesn't affirm you. I'm not out at my public library job because I don't feel ready to navigate being misgendered by people who should know better. I don't want to do the labor of educating coworkers about my identity or correcting them when they inevitably slip up. At least when people don't know they're making a mistake, I can't fault them for not trying. When a library patron or coworker refers to me with gendered language, despite the stab of annoyance it inevitably brings, I know that person is making an effort to show me respect, or even friendliness.

If I had a pronoun pin on my lanyard at work, how many people would look at me, and then intentionally misgender me to my face? How many would forget, or simply ignore it? How many would ask me what those words mean, out of supposedly harmless curiosity or scornful suspicion? How many times a day would I have to justify my right to take up space in the fullness of who I am, when my right to be should be a given? These are questions I'm still wrangling with, and I'm not sure when I'll be ready for the answers.

For now, despite the slip-ups and headaches, I've found that it's been good to live my truth in an academic space. My program still has a lot of work to do, as their recent step backward shows, and I hope that in the future, faculty will keep transgender and gender diverse students in mind when implementing new policies, procedures, and technology. I hope that more faculty members take it upon themselves to learn how to be good allies in the classroom so that transgender students don't feel silenced, ignored, or othered. All that aside, I feel safe to be out at my program because they, however imperfectly, make it a point in their policies, in their culture, and in their infrastructure to make it *easier*, if not easy, to be transgender. I hope that I will one day feel safe enough to be out at my workplace, too.

Operationalizing Bias

Calvin Cantina

Keywords: LIS PhD programs, transphobia in education, medical issues, librarians against information science

The following text is excerpted from journal entries that I wrote for a course project in 2013, during my first year as a Ph.D. student in a Library and Information Science (LIS) program.

As a trans person who was forcibly assigned female at birth, my gender is not my own. Despite gender being viewed as a social construct, a mere declaration of maleness has never been enough for me to earn its assorted privileges. I require an intramuscular shot of testosterone every other Tuesday to keep my body phenotypically male enough for others to call me "he" and "Mr. Cantina." I'm relatively fortunate that my hormonally-induced bald spot and patchy facial hair allow my appearance to be classified as male most of the time, although the times that my disguise doesn't work are incredibly painful.

Before the spring term begins, my body decides to rebel against me; my reproductive system emerges from a four-year hibernation to make its presence visible again. I lived as male for several years before I was deemed mentally healthy enough to start hormone therapy under a doctor's supervision. That process was an incessantly painful vicious circle: my mental health was suffering because I couldn't access hormone treatment, but I couldn't access hormone treatment because my mental health was suffering. I'm amazed by how one medically unexpected event is powerful enough for my emotions to snap right back into that old space. After my anxiety attack finally subsides, I calm down long enough to call my doctor at the student health clinic.

I am very fond of my doctor. As far as I can tell, she is the only doctor at the health center who has attended the campus LGBTQ ally training; she's certainly the only person I ever see there who is wearing a button that proclaims her to be an ally. Upon checking me in, the nurse practitioner follows the typical routine: she asks me how I am, checks my blood pressure, and asks me the date of my last period. I look surprised and half-jokingly ask what I'm supposed to say. "I don't know why that question is on the form," she says, "but it's here, so I asked it. Sorry about that." We both laugh uncomfortably as she leaves the room and I wait for my doctor to arrive.

My doctor promptly arrives, and I tell her about my psychological woes and reproductive ailments. She has two pieces of bad news for me: 1) she is referring me to the university's mental health clinic for psychiatric treatment, and 2) she will have to refer me to the university's women's health clinic for a thorough examination that may include a biopsy. The first news item is frustrating, though unsurprising, but the second is devastating. As a general health practitioner, she does not feel that she has the expertise to do a biopsy, even if university regulations allow her to do so.

While acknowledging her valid point, the very idea of entering a women-only space for a painful medical procedure fills me with horror. I teach an on-campus course and am used to seeing former and current students around campus—I can't go to the main library without running into at least one, it seems, and I occasionally see some on my bus to and from class—but most of my students don't know that I'm trans. My decision not to reveal this can easily be construed as a textbook example of using my privilege to keep myself safe, which is exactly what it is. (There are more salient parts of my identity that I can never conceal—my sexual orientation and working-class origins, for example, are near-public knowledge in my department; I am occasionally reminded that my sexual orientation apparently is not a secret to anyone in town, judging by the occasional epithet that obnoxious strangers feel comfortable tossing in my direction.) My doctor is kind enough to validate my anxiety, promises that she will see what can be done to make this biopsy as easy on my psyche as possible, and assures me that she will be in touch. I am clearly a classification problem, and one that appears to have never been an issue before on this campus with over 40,000 students.

Before the appointment ends, I ask her if she has any idea why the nurse practitioner asked me when my last period was. She looks me up in the patient management system, and discovers that my gender is listed as female. "But I thought I changed that!" I exclaim; I graduated from the university years ago under my old name and gender, and spent much of my first semester asking the health center's medical records department to correct my information in their patient database and the pharmacy's database. It turns out that there is yet another database containing my health information. The Internet truly is forever. My doctor tells me that she will contact the director of the medical records department to explain my situation and will let me know if I have to do anything; she now has to speak with at least two of her colleagues about my health care issues. I consider nominating her for sainthood.

While my doctor is busy conducting a guerrilla Trans 101 workshop on my behalf, I start my preparation for the spring semester ahead. I will be taking a mandatory course in research methods, which will turn out to be surprisingly painful. As it is mandatory for second-semester doctoral students, everyone in my Ph.D. cohort has enrolled; this is the second course that we have all taken as a group. Each week, we meet at an oval table. Each week, we sit in the same seats that we've assigned ourselves, the gap between the L and the I in LIS—a concept often mentioned by the instructor of our first mandatory group course—made manifest. The four of us who are particularly interested in critical theory and library work sit together on one side. As the semester goes on, it becomes readily apparent that we four are all too literally surrounded by colleagues who question the validity of our research. Unfortunately, this frequently includes the instructor.

The usual instructor of record for this course is on sabbatical for the school year and as a result, another tenured professor is teaching in their stead. The major assignment for the class will be a fairly lengthy research proposal, the idea being that we can use such a document as the basis for a dissertation proposal when the time comes. The instructor informs us that he has a lot of experience reviewing funding requests for the National Science Foundation (NSF) and can give us insider information on how that entire process works. I briefly find myself wondering what will happen when I share my decidedly non-scientific research interests, but I tell myself to be optimistic for a change. Maybe this class will offer information from a wide variety of perspectives. We watch *The Mystery of Picasso* on the first day of class, which I take as a good sign.

As the weeks go by, the good signs start to disappear. At first, it's difficult to say how much of this is based on the instructor's own inclinations and how much is due to student participation; after a while, the distinction ceases to exist or to really matter. We spend a lot of time discussing what factors make research worthwhile: it needs to have a high impact factor, identify something that is previously unknown, and be replicable. The only way to prove impact is with statistics. Everything has to be logical and empirical. For three hours a week, we enter a world where Big Data and text mining are the prized gold standards, and all worthwhile data must be machine-extracted. I joke to a friend that I am going to start typing it as "BIG DATA" to emphasize its utmost importance; he jokes back that he will start using "lis" (as opposed to LIS) to make the new priorities in our field as visible as possible.

As time goes on, this joke gets a little less funny, especially when we begin working on our research proposals, which we are expected to review and revise throughout the term. The format for this assignment is roughly modeled on an NSF grant application; our proposals follow a similar template, but stop short of actual requests for funding. In a surprisingly literal interpretation of peer review, we will be discussing each other's proposals during class; each student will leave the room while their work is being critiqued. Each student is assigned three different proposals to officially review, leading and summarizing the discussion for one of them. We are asked to leave our names off of our written reviews (which seems an odd request, given that a matrix of assigned reviewers has been posted), and to make copies for all of our classmates to read.

For this first round, our instructor informs us that we only need to submit an informal rough draft; one or two pages will do. I take the research statement that I used when applying to this program and clean it up to some extent. My research agenda concerns subject classification for materials about marginalized populations; my basic argument is that if the labels we use to describe information about people don't match the labels that they would use, we have a problem. This is basically an analysis of library subject headings from a poststructuralist perspective, an effort to interrogate the power balances that are created and constantly validated when we classify oppressed groups. I choose to focus on queer and trans people because I think that my research will be most effective if it hits me where I live. In an attempt to give my classmate reviewers something measurable, I propose that I will create a subject thesaurus for trans and queer identities. I know that my classmates don't have much experience with classification research, but I hope that I can manage to get my point across nonetheless.

Even though I only have to review three, I decide to read all of my classmates' research proposals—partly out of genuine interest, and partly to see how my proposal-writing ability matches up with theirs. Most of them have gone well over the two-page limit, submitting fairly formal proposals with statistics and citations. I immediately panic: does the phrase "rough draft" mean something different to doctoral students? Is this a test? Have I failed? After I calm down about the formatting, I finally do a close reading of the proposals' content. A substantial number of the proposals deal with BIG DATA and text mining in some way or another, which is unsurprising. My fellow critical theory admirers have submitted ideas that also handle marginalized populations; of course, I find these other three proposals the most interesting.

Reviewing these proposals proves to be a difficult task on several levels. Are we to decide if our classmates' research is worth conducting at all, or should we analyze how well they present their research ideas? I decide that everyone's research is worth conducting, and I try to offer criticisms on how to strengthen the actual proposals. *Go into further detail about your methodology*, I write. *Can you contextualize this within the field of LIS?* It never occurs to me to question if someone's research is valuable in the first place; I'm a colleague and a classmate, not the course instructor, and I'm not interested in power trips.

Once we actually discuss these proposals in class, it turns out that we all have wildly divergent ideas of what the review process should entail. We spend twenty to thirty minutes dissecting each other's work in relentless detail, whether we know anything about their research area or not. After three BIG DATA-intensive proposals in a row are discussed, I decide to stop prolonging the inevitable and leave the room for my turn. I have to wait for the discussion to be summarized in writing before I know what anyone has said, but I can hazard a guess, especially after hearing the critiques of a proposal to study institutionalized racism in academic libraries: *This proposal needs to operationalize racism; what happens if it turns out that institutionalized racism isn't embedded in librarianship at all?* This is the point in the class when it finally hits me: those of us working with oppressed groups of people are repeatedly being asked to justify our interests, and the instructor has no plans to change the conversation. I have a sudden urge to leave and never come back.

After class, I ask a couple of my classmates to tell me what the discussion about my proposal entailed. They inform me that the professor suggested that I incorporate straight, non-trans people as a control group, an idea that leaves me utterly bewildered. I also learn that a classmate who is also queer became so frustrated with the discussion about my work that they had to leave the room. It sounds like my initial assessment was sadly accurate. The actual written feedback follows the trajectory that I've come to expect: *Is there a way to demonstrate that this is a problem? Are only LGBTQ users having problems searching for information on queer or gender non-conforming topics? Could this study contribute to FRBR?* I entertain the idea of answering their questions with more questions: How do we document the act of inaction? If users cannot find materials about their own identities, isn't that indicative of a problem? How does a conceptual model for bibliographic description relate to inaccurate language in subject headings? I realize that while just a few of my classmates use the critical theory that I want to apply, even fewer of them seem to have much experience working with controlled vocabularies. I start to wonder what I'm supposed to be getting out of this work.

I seem to have a lot of trouble seeing what I'm supposed to get out of anything I'm doing these days. During my first visit with my new psychiatrist, he expresses alarm at the cocktail of medications that I've been on for several years. The medication that I take for my ADHD has some particularly nasty neurological interactions with another medication of mine. He suggests that I stop the ADHD medication and try something new—something that the university's pharmacy doesn't cover and will require me to pay out of pocket. He says the drug manufacturer offers a coupon for a free 30-day prescription so I should try it and see how I feel. The local pharmacy takes five days to fill this prescription because it is a special order. When I go to pick it up, I idly ask the pharmacist how much this scrip would cost if I were paying for it. The figure is the same as my monthly rent, yet another hilariously absurd example of the need for universal health care. I take it for a few days and notice no effect besides a massive headache, so I stop. Life as a grad student with uncontrolled ADHD is not as exciting as it might sound. All I do is worry obsessively about the work that I need to do and sleep at odd hours to get away from the worrying. By the middle of the semester, I am hopelessly behind in everything, finding that it takes me hours and hours to write anything, even a 500-word essay on a topic that is very familiar to me. I start setting alarms so I can get up early and work on my course assignments; every Monday morning, I shrug and fall back asleep.

In the research methods class, we are taking a break from discussing our research agendas to discuss those of faculty members in our department. We each interview a professor about their intellectual history and methodologies, and report back to the class. I watch a classmate laugh as they recount how the professor they spoke with had once accidentally attended a conference program about human-computer interaction from a feminist perspective—gasp! —and found himself grudgingly admitting that these feminist researchers were making the same types of arguments he was; his sexism is presented as a lovable foible. The instructor smiles indulgently.

Meanwhile, I've heard back from my general doctor. After speaking with a colleague, they have worked out a way that I can check in at the regular clinic desk and then be sent to the women's health clinic with no one the wiser. Additionally, she and her colleague have discussed my situation and chosen to spare me the horrible pain of an endometrial biopsy; instead, I will have a marginally less uncomfortable transvaginal ultrasound. She knows that this is the equivalent of offering me a firing squad with four rifles instead of six, but it's the best she can do. Everything is ready to go as soon as my schedule allows it.

Armed with this knowledge, I let six weeks pass before I call the clinic back to schedule the appointment. I tell myself that this is because I just keep forgetting to call, which is partly true; of course, my mental health issues play a larger role than I'm willing to admit, but the largest unnamed culprit is my own custom blend of self-hatred. The archetypical trans narrative classifies physical transition as successful when a person is frequently assumed to be cisgender. Due to a combination of luck, various forms of privilege, and some disposable income several years ago, I have had chest surgery and am on hormone therapy, so my body looks pretty phenotypically male—unless (or until) someone sees me naked. While that qualifier is a pretty substantial one, the vast majority of my daily interactions with other people require all of us to be clothed, so it is generally within my power to disclose my gender identity at will. This type of medical care can easily remove that agency, which makes me worry that I will be treated poorly by health care professionals; this worry comes from my lived experiences, and is more of an expectation than anything else. My inability to distinguish between my fears and my expectations is where my own transphobia resides.

The day of the ultrasound arrives. I bring a friend for support. Everything happens exactly as my doctor said it would: I check in with the same receptionist as I always do, and a nurse surreptitiously leads me up the stairs to a side entrance for the "women's" health clinic. Everyone is perfectly respectful and nonchalant about the process, which is indeed incredibly painful, but is otherwise a complete non-event. As usual, I was worried about the wrong thing.

In the research methods class, it's time for us to submit the second drafts of our research proposals, which are supposed to incorporate the feedback we received from the first round. Having received very little useful feedback, I decide to just make every section longer. In addition to thesaurus construction, I add a new goal of interviewing metadata workers about their classification practices. I add a couple of stories from frustrated library workers about searching for "queer" in their catalogs and finding nothing relevant. I mention an IFLA report in an attempt to demonstrate that improving subject access is important and has high impact. I have no idea if this is what I am supposed to do, but I have to do *something*.

This round of discussions is not particularly different from the first, except that I receive even less feedback from my classmates. Here is the entirety of the written feedback: I should state the core issues more explicitly. Additionally, I should expand my work's impact beyond the IFLA report I cited and operationalize FRBR. That's all. This second comment leads me to conclude that most of my classmates do not know what FRBR is, let alone its relationship to subject classification, though they do seem to know what "operationalizing" is, so they're one up on me in that regard. A few of my friends in the class confirm what I suspected about the class discussion: the students assigned to review my work seemed unprepared and did not appear to fully grasp the idea of transphobic subject headings. It isn't until weeks later that I learn that the professor used the incorrect pronouns for me during this discussion; it isn't until later yet that I learn that he has *repeatedly* used the incorrect pronouns despite being corrected by others. I'm not sure why this act feels like such a betrayal—the course has been racist, heteronormative, and cissexist, so what's a little overt transphobia?—but it genuinely does. Due to the privileges that I describe above, many of the students in my department do not know that I am trans, and being called "she" against my will and consent is not a way that I want them to find out.

The BIG DATA/critical theory divide in the class grows even more pronounced once we start to discuss any type of qualitative method. The information scientists choose to express their discomfort with qualitative methods by repeatedly mentioning their distrust of anything that isn't replicable or measurable. *How are you supposed to do research based on talking to a group of people one time? Humanities research has a low impact factor.* During one class, I find myself trying to explain that there is no true objectivity in any kind of research because human beings can't be truly objective; we all bring our own perspectives with us. My outburst is mostly ignored, and I curse myself for not being articulate enough to start any sort of discussion, nor witty enough to offer Irigaray-inspired mimetic rejoinders to their dismissiveness.

My medical issues continue unabated. The ultrasound did not reveal any abnormalities, meaning that my reproductive issues are idiopathic; I grimly amuse myself by facetiously conceptualizing my body as a space of resistance that denatures the category of "trans male." I keep meaning to call my psychiatrist to discuss my medication options, but I only remember to do so when the clinic is closed and I can't actually call them. I continue to sleep and worry, rousing long enough to work on my annual student review. The meeting goes well, even though I confess to the two members of my committee that I am woefully behind in my coursework due to writer's block. They are sympathetic and offer useful suggestions that I promptly forget to try. My progress towards the degree is found to be satisfactory, and I wait for the Doctoral Studies Committee to examine my annual review documentation and make their own decision.

Consumed with mounting guilt and anxiety over my incomplete assignments, I email my research methods professor to inform him that I am aware that this is an issue and that I am working to resolve it. He asks me to meet with him at a local coffee shop to discuss this further, and we schedule an informal meeting for the end of the week. I mention this to my advisor, who asks me if I would like them to come to the meeting. I decide to go alone, and we arrange to have a debriefing afterwards.

Our meeting is under an hour, and my instructor is friendly and avuncular; we spend part of the time chatting about the title of the book I've just checked out: *"Raw Data" Is an Oxymoron*, an anthology edited by Lisa Gitelman. He can't understand why I'm having such trouble doing the work when I've been published before, so I confess my undermedication saga. He then tells me that my writing and course participation show an unwillingness to step out of my comfort zone and that he wants me to put myself "out there," because that is what getting a Ph.D. is all about. He then tells me that my comments on the difference between postmodernism and anti-foundationalism (namely, that I have no idea if there is a difference) make me sound as if I don't know what I'm talking about and am choosing to namedrop instead.

I nod and agree with him, because I'm afraid to speak truth to power. I can't bring myself to tell him that, these days, just showing up to class feels like putting myself out there. That making any comment in class that isn't a joke or a request for clarification makes me feel no less vulnerable than having a transvaginal ultrasound does. That the antagonistic class discussions create a toxic environment and his inaction feels like an endorsement. That I feel defeated. I don't tell him that some of the information science students in the course have taken to telling my partners in critical theory that their work isn't situated in LIS and they shouldn't be here. The fact that my white male privilege has kept me from being critiqued in the same way is painfully salient, but I see no purpose in mentioning this to a full professor who is even more steeped in white male privilege than I am. I apologize for falling behind, promise that I will get my work done, and quickly retreat to my advisor's office to debrief.

When I get there, they inform me that my instructor sent a letter to them and to the chair of the Doctoral Studies Committee stating his grave concerns about my success in the program because I haven't participated enough in class and am far behind in my assignments. He wants this information to appear in my annual review; however, he didn't send the letter until after the submission deadline for annual reviews had already passed. My advisor assures me that this does not mean that I will be kicked out of the program. We discuss steps that I can take to get some work done. I cry in their office out of pure embarrassment. They assure me that I am not the only student in this course who is struggling, and I am not the only one who is behind in the assignments. I don't know if I am the only student who has been flagged in this fashion, though I can hazard a guess.

My advisor suggests that my instructor seems to be unfairly targeting me, an idea that genuinely hadn't crossed my mind. I have been chalking up his exclusionary views of gender and sexuality to benign, if obviously frustrating, cluelessness. If he is singling me out, it's because I'm behind in my work, so I must deserve it. I begin to realize how much of the class discourse, both spoken and not, I have internalized. Due to my own experiences, it is easiest for me to minimize the poisonous classroom environment, to classify it as a product of my own actions or inactions. Taking the easiest path, however, is exactly the type of behavior that I want to threaten with my research, and with my approach to classification in general: if we continue to follow inaccurate and painful systems without question, we reinforce our own oppression. We will never be able to use the act of description for social change if we do not disrupt the traditional descriptive process.

Epilogue

With my advisor's assistance, I reported my professor's behavior as bias-based harassment to the university's office of inclusion. In late 2013, that office moderated a meeting between the professor and me; the most memorable part of the meeting was when he said, "I knew you were transgender, but I didn't know which way!" (If it weren't for the journal entries included above, this is the only thing that I would ever remember his saying to me.) The office mandated that he attend the university's LGBTQ and trans ally training sessions—since I never spoke to him again, I have no idea if he actually did.

I got a B-minus in his course. I later wrote my dissertation on the topic I presented in class; it was defended successfully with no revisions.

The LIS program that I attended now includes out trans students in both the Master's and Ph.D. levels. I hope that their experiences do not mirror mine.

Two Sides of a Coin: Individual and Institutional Support for Non-Cisgender LIS Professionals in Academic Institutions

Kai Fay (they/he)

Keywords: academic libraries, graduate school, online learning, transitioning, transphobia in the classroom

My library and information science (LIS) career began ten years ago when a change of major and a minor existential crisis led me to take a student job in the library. Coincidentally, that was only a few months before I also began questioning my own gender identity. The juxtaposition of these two timelines means that, for me, the bureaucracy of transitioning and gender-related policies is inextricably linked with my development as an LIS professional.

During my first few years working in the library, I was transitioning in my personal life, but not in my professional life. It was not until I started graduate school that I felt ready to begin transitioning in my professional life as well. By that time, I had changed my name and pronouns, but none of my legal documentation had been updated to match, and my school did not have a system for recording anything other than students' legal names.

The first week of graduate school was my first introduction to transition-related bureaucratic headaches and the corresponding stress of having to explain my gender identity to strangers. For my in-person classes, I spoke to my professors before classes began and asked them to update their class lists accordingly. For my online courses, it was more complicated since the learning management system pulled student profile information, including display name, directly from the registrar's database. If I wanted to be addressed correctly, my only option was to out myself to all of my classmates at the start of the semester and hope that they remembered despite the course site displaying the wrong information. None of my classmates were actively malicious, but they still only called me by the correct name about half the time.

Before the start of my second semester, the registrar announced the introduction of a preferred name field. I immediately rushed to update my information, but the excitement I had felt quickly died as the page errored every time I tried to save. When I reported the issue, I naively assumed it would be resolved within a few days. Instead, I was informed that the registrar was already aware of the problem, but since it was not one of their priorities, they had no estimated timeline for a fix. In the meantime, they recommended I continue speaking to my professors individually.

Unfortunately, the professor for my online course that semester was less than understanding. According to him, remembering anything other than what he received from the registrar and the course site was too confusing, and he refused to even try. Since the registrar had added the new preferred name field option, he felt it was no longer his responsibility, and if it mattered that much to me, I should convince the registrar to fix the problem.

I spent the first two weeks of classes circling from the registrar to the professor and back with no progress on either front. Finally, I turned to the school's IT department in frustration and asked if they could possibly help. Officially, the answer was no, but unofficially, the answer was yes, since the person I spoke to was sympathetic and had the necessary credentials to quietly go into the back end of the system and make the change manually. The good news was that my name finally displayed correctly. The bad news was that the change was overwritten every time the system updated against the registrar's records, so I had to reach out to IT every couple of months and ask for it to be corrected again. As of the time I legally changed my name six months later, the preferred name field still had not been fixed.

This example is only one of many I could have chosen. It is a moment that is memorable, not for its exceptionality, but for its familiarity. I could have just as easily shared the story of the library head who never once got my pronouns correct in nearly five years of working together, or the scramble to make it back from break on time because the nearest gender-neutral bathroom was halfway across campus.

I am not alone in my experiences. According to a recent survey conducted by my current institution, 80% of staff overall felt that they belonged at said institution, but the number dropped to 61% for genderqueer and nonbinary staff.[1] Similar trends held across all of the questions asked—only 34% of genderqueer and nonbinary staff believed the institution would respond appropriately to reports of discrimination or harassment.[2] Extensive research has shown the need for academic institutions to create more inclusive policies to support transgender students, but as this survey and other studies show, universities still lag in implementing the necessary changes.[3]

In a perfect world, the situations I encountered would be non-issues. In a perfect world, neither individuals nor institutional structures would present roadblocks to non-cisgender individuals. In a perfect world, my

1. The options for gender identity given in the survey were: male, female, transgender, genderqueer or nonbinary, another identity, prefer not to say, and unsure.

2. Harvard University, "Final Report: Pilot Pulse Survey on Inclusion & Belonging," 2019, https://pulse.harvard.edu/files/pulse/files/pilot_pulse_survey_ib_final_report.pdf.

3. Brett Beemyn, "Serving the needs of transgender college students," *Journal of Gay and Lesbian Issues in Education*, 1, no.1 (2003): 33-50; Robert D. Brown et al, "Assessing the campus climate for gay, lesbian, bisexual, and transgender (GLBT) students using a multiple perspectives approach," *Journal of College Student Development*, 45, no.1 (2004): 8-26; Jeffrey S. McKinney, "On the margins: A study of the experiences of transgender college students," *Journal of Gay & Lesbian Issues in Education*, 3, no.1 (2005): 63-76; Jaime M. Grant, et al., *Injustice at every turn: A report of the national transgender discrimination survey*. Washington, D.C.: The National Gay and Lesbian Task Force and the National Center for Transgender Equality, 2011, http://www.thetaskforce.org/reports_and_research/ntds.

professor would have respected my name and pronouns, and the registrar's system would have allowed me to enter them.

As we all know, the world we live in is far from perfect. Within this flawed system, non-cisgender individuals rely on both individual and institutional actions to help break down the roadblocks that create unsupportive and unwelcoming environments. When both pieces exist, then one can temper problems caused by the other. Robust systems that support self-identification can push back against individual resistance, and individuals can help find workarounds for structural limitations.

For non-cisgender library students and staff, every issue we encounter is another roadblock that costs us time and energy we could be spending elsewhere. When we lack support from our institutions and colleagues, then we face those barriers alone, and one person can only do so much. When our institutions and our colleagues respect our identities and our needs, then there are fewer roadblocks in our path, and when they do arise, we are not navigating them alone. Instead of spending our time and energy fighting the structures we are working in, we can devote that space to the LIS work that brought many of us to this profession in the first place.

Bibliography

Beemyn, Brett. "Serving the needs of transgender college students." *Journal of Gay and Lesbian Issues in Education*, 1, no.1 (2003): 33-50.

Brown, Robert D., Brandy Clarke, Valerie Gortmaker, & Rachael Robinson-Keilig. "Assessing the campus climate for gay, lesbian, bisexual, and transgender (GLBT) students using a multiple perspectives approach." *Journal of College Student Development*, 45, no.1 (2004): 8-26.

Grant, Jaime M., Lisa A. Mottet, Justin Tanis, Jack Harrison, Jody L. Herman, & Mara Keisling. *Injustice at every turn: A report of the national transgender discrimination survey.* Washington, D.C.: The National Gay and Lesbian Task Force and the National Center for Transgender Equality, 2011, https://transequality.org/sites/default/files/docs/resources/NTDS_Report.pdf.

Harvard University, "Final Report: Pilot Pulse Survey on Inclusion & Belonging," 2019, https://pulse.harvard.edu/files/pulse/files/pilot_pulse_survey_ib_final_report.pdf.

McKinney, Jeffrey S. "On the margins: A study of the experiences of transgender college students." *Journal of Gay & Lesbian Issues in Education*, 3, no.1 (2005): 63-76.

About the Author

Kai Fay (he/him or they/them) is a queer, trans, autistic librarian at a large academic research institution. They started working in libraries as an undergraduate student worker in 2010. After completing their MSLIS degree in 2016, they started in their current position preparing physical library materials for digitization. Their other main areas of interest are trauma-aware pedagogy and the intersections between cultural heritage and book history. They lead regular workshops on those topics for groups ranging from kindergarteners to college undergraduates and educators.

No Gender, No Title

Notte A. Gherl (she/they)

Keywords: library school, public libraries, queerphobic policies, gender expression, genderqueer

The county I work for recently changed their branding. Granted, we needed it; now, instead of the artwork that was probably as old as I am that we had for our logo, we have a clean and simple icon that makes us look like a knockoff hotel brand. It's not the best we could have done, but it's certainly an improvement. As part of the rollout of this new county image, we were instructed to change our email signature to a uniform, unified format. Use the prescribed font, text must be in black, and you absolutely may not include your pronouns. An email went out to answer questions about the change, and it specifically stated that pronouns may not be part of our email signature; everyone had to match everyone else.

I was pissed off by this.

It's a small thing to be pissed about, but after all the time I have spent working here and not once witnessed any events or statements that endorsed or even acknowledged LGBTQIA+ diversity, I think I'm a little bit entitled to my feelings. They could have let us have this one thing, a small nod to gender diversity, to being inclusive, or even just to acknowledge that some people have gender neutral names and you can't guess how they want to be referred to if your only contact has been through an email. But I guess pronouns would mess up the aesthetic or whatever, so they're out.

I'm not out at work. It didn't seem to be an issue of much concern when I first got hired, and I thought I was only keeping my sexuality quiet. I was, and am, very, very single, so it wasn't a pressing issue in the first place, since I didn't have to decide whether or not to talk about my partner to my coworkers. I figured I would stay quiet until I worked out how the system viewed LGBTQIA+ issues. After all, it probably couldn't be too bad if they touted diversity as one of their core values. I kept thinking that until a month or so after I started, when I had a quick programming meeting with my supervisor and branch manager. My branch manager told us she would be happy to see any programming with LGBTQIA+ content, but we would have to sneak it in because it could not be overt. She didn't elaborate on what that would mean, but it was clear that nothing could be explicitly LGBTQIA+ inclusive. Later, I learned that one of the librarians had had to fight with administration in order to have an outreach event at Pride. That was within the first year of my hiring, so I quickly decided that it would be best to keep my identity to myself.

For most of my life, I thought I agreed with everyone else that I was a girl. Turns out we were all wrong about that one, which was kind of a shock. As I write this, I'm about a year into realizing that, actually, gender is something that happens to other people, so I'm still figuring a lot of things out about myself—a gender deconstruction zone, as it were. It wasn't until COVID hit and we all got sent into lockdown that my gender identity started demanding attention, and I began considering that maybe I wasn't as much of a girl as I had previously thought. I spent my time in lockdown contemplating how much of my gender performance was a result of fulfilling social expectations and how much was for me. The answer ended up being a mix of both, with an emphasis on the former. So I readjusted my sense of myself and started figuring out what that meant for me. When the county reopened and we were sent back to work, I had to put any gender exploration on pause so I could play the socially acceptable feminine library worker once again. That wouldn't last long, but I'll get to that in a bit.

Some time after I realized my gender didn't align with what I had previously thought, I began going to school for my Master of Library and Information Sciences to become a librarian. I was wary of being out at school because the library world is small and library circles tend to overlap, but after my first semester I had come across a couple of out nonbinary people in the school. I really wanted to be out in some area of my life, and as long as I was careful and quiet about it, I figured it would probably be fine. So I began introducing myself with my pronouns in my classes and school meetings, put my pronouns in my Zoom name, and absolutely nothing happened.

I mean that. Nothing happened. One of my classmates messaged me privately because we had the same (she/they) pronouns and we added each other on Instagram, but other than that, it was as if I hadn't done anything. Which wasn't necessarily a bad thing. My anxiety had been expecting a mob with pitchforks a la *Beauty and the Beast*, so not encountering hostility was comforting. But on the other hand, I wasn't really acknowledged and there wasn't any effort put into changing how I was addressed.

In one of my classes, the professor called me a lady. She apologized when I corrected her, but I had my pronouns in my Zoom name, so I shouldn't have had to point out my lack of gender. A classmate referred to me as a woman even though we'd been in three classes together, so he should have known better. I corrected him, too. Not once has someone used "they" to refer to me. I know that's a small thing, and "she" is one of my pronouns, but the fact that it's there does not mean I want it used exclusively. I even specifically said in a couple of classes that they could feel free to "mix it up" and not use one exclusively. No such luck. If I look feminine and sound feminine, I guess I must be a girl.

Now that I'm a year into my gender exploration, I've noticed that I'm a lot more sensitive to anyone assuming gender than I used to be, and it happens a LOT more than I'd realized. The number of times I get emails addressed to "Ladies" grates on me. My coworkers, as delightful as they are, have a tendency to use a lot of gendered language, so I get addressed as "lady" and "girl" pretty frequently. They're not aware of what they're doing, and it's not as if I've corrected them, so I don't blame them entirely because, again, I'm not out at work. They haven't had the experiences that I have, and they haven't had the pressure from administration to educate themselves and be more inclusive in their language. But every time I hear that aimed at me, or see that in my inbox, I die a little on the inside.

For a time after lockdown ended and the library reopened, I was very concentrated on pretending to be a woman at work, and I spent most of my time not at work trying to get out of that gendered mentality. This didn't leave me much time for really exploring what gender meant to me. At some point after the great gender awakening, I finally gained the confidence to start playing around with clothes that fit my identity a little better, so I did some gleeful online shopping in the men's section and was bold enough to wear some of it to work. The anxiety that prefaced my first day at work wearing men's jeans cannot be described, but when no one batted an eye, I got bolder. I bought more and more over time and wore it all, and no one remarked on any of it. I was absolutely giddy with how I was getting away with my gender subterfuge until the very next time someone called me a lady.

The only two bright spots in all of these gender assumptions finally came after I got my hair cut short. I was finally living my gender-ambiguous dreams, and it must have leaked out a little, because the security officer got me in a quiet moment and asked me what my pronouns were. I had to lie to her to keep myself safe, but I absolutely fell a little in love with her then.[1] She doesn't know it yet, but we will have an outdoor Fall wedding and I will wear a blue suit. The second time came from a library patron who approached me from behind and called me "sir" before seeing my face and realizing they were wrong. It was my very first time being misgendered in the other direction and I rode that high for the entire day.

---

1. Would being openly queer hurt my chances at promotion? Are my coworkers queerphobic and would that change how they treat me? Would the administration offer any protection? There are too many unknowns.

This is not to say that everything is fine now—that I present the way I want to and I'm secure in my gender identity. I still get dressed every morning with the intention of looking at least a little feminine so I don't attract the wrong sort of attention. It's a painful hassle to find the right combination of clothes that make me happy but still scan as "girl." I still spend a decent amount of time away from work trying to mentally distance myself from the gender role I play at work, but now I can do it while occasionally seeing a reflection in the mirror that sparks joy. And, unfortunately, it also means that sometimes I can go to work and be uncomfortably conscious of my chest all day because I'm displaying too much femininity in the name of safety. Not all breakthroughs have been happy breakthroughs.

As frustrating as my work and school-related gender problems are, I think I'm coming at this with some sort of privilege. I spend an extraordinary amount of time online in queer virtual communities, so I'm constantly surrounded by people who get it. They know that "she/they" does not mean I have a gender and they know that they shouldn't use "she" exclusively. They're comfortable with using "they" as a singular pronoun. It's a wonderful environment to live in, because I can be myself and I don't have to correct people or wonder if I'll have to explain what a gender is and why I don't have one.

Coming from that sort of background and comparing it to my experiences at school and work, it's understandable that I would be frustrated. The library world, as supposedly progressive as it is, and as inclusive as it claims to be, is lagging behind on queer theory and terminology. I recently watched a wonderfully done two-part webinar from ALA on LGBTQIA+ inclusion in the library, and the presenter spent the first twenty-five minutes of the first webinar explaining gender and sexuality and pronouns just so their audience would understand what they were talking about.[2] Out of all the webinars that I've watched on inclusivity, this was unique because not only did they make sure their audience was

2. Jessica Jupitus, "Creating A Safe And Welcoming Library For The LGBTQIA+ Community: Part 1," Webinar from ALA Publishing eLearning Solutions, May 11, 2021.

educated, but they went beyond having a Pride display or pronouns on their lanyard. It was the very first webinar I've ever attended that really considered what queer inclusion could look like—how to have inclusive programming and how to address that with the public in ways that keeps participants safe, rather than just paying lip service to the idea of inclusivity, which is what most of the other LGBTQIA+ webinars that I've attended have been like.

The experience was refreshing. On the whole, I've been unimpressed with library treatment of LGBTQIA+ people, especially anything outside the confines of sexuality. Pronouns in your email signature are well and good in that they normalize pronoun sharing, but it makes anyone who uses pronouns outside of she/her or he/him stand out, even from just an email. It makes some people confront the decision of whether they can afford to out themselves via their email signature. It's such a small thing, but it's a notable barrier for the very people it's supposed to be granting inclusion to. In a system like mine, that so very clearly marginalizes queer identities to the point of pretending they don't exist, normalizing pronoun sharing is a slap in the face, because it does absolutely nothing towards inclusion unless you also accept and normalize the idea that a person may not always fit into the traditional idea of gender and may, in fact, have a gender identity and pronouns that do not align with how they present.

Let's also keep in mind the privilege that I have in being a white, cis-passing person. I'm somewhat comfortable still presenting as a primarily feminine person. On most days, it doesn't bother me to be called "she." My legal name isn't great, but I don't hate it. Hell, I can even wear a dress sometimes without feeling like disintegrating. On the whole, I could continue masquerading as a woman and I'd only occasionally be miserable. Sure, being called "lady" or "girl" makes me uncomfortable, but it's not putting a round peg into a square hole, it's putting a round peg into an oval hole. I'm not a circle, but I'm vaguely reminiscent of one. This could be a lot worse for me. The nonsense that my county administration and library system have been churning out is only a mild inconvenience to me. It makes me angry, but I can roll my eyes, shrug my shoulders, and get on with my day secure in the knowledge that they're in the wrong and I'll be out of here as soon as that diploma gets put into my hand.

I know it's still bad and I shouldn't be telling myself it could be worse. It could be a hell of a lot better, too, and that's what I should be expecting. But I say these things partly because I think they're true—it certainly could be worse—and partly because that's the mindset I've adopted to get through each day.

This is not a good mentality for me to be in. I should not have to continuously expect the worst from my organization. I should not have to be counting the days until I can leave. They're not even coming after me directly! It's just some vague entity seven pay levels above me making queerphobic decisions that limit how I identify myself in my email signature, which subsequently makes me feel uncomfortable about being myself at work because I fear repercussions that may or may not come. I can't speak up to combat those decisions or the environment they create; I'm on the very bottom of the food chain, and it would probably require coming out to make my point. Dealing with an organization that didn't want to be seen at Pride doesn't make me feel super confident about my chances of being heard. The point I am getting at here is that I can survive this because even though these stupid rules affect me, I'm not miserable, but I shouldn't have to be at a point where I can consider that a bright side. I still feel helpless and invisible because of the rules that are in place. The rules shouldn't exist. They're discriminatory. They're narrow-minded. They force me to play a role that I find uncomfortable because I feel I have no other choice. They influenced the way I wrote this article and the identifying details I left out. Even though I'm legally protected, I don't entirely trust the powers that be to play by the rules, and that's unacceptable.

I don't have a neat way to wrap this up. I don't have a hopeful note to end this on. The library world has become progressive, but it needs to do more. I should not have to eclipse myself to feel like I belong in my workplace. I should not have to consider the dangers of dressing the way I want every morning. I should not have to have a debate with myself about whether or not to share my pronouns. I should not have to correct people who know my pronouns and therefore should know better. I'm tired and the library needs to do better.

Bibliography

Jupitus, Jessica. "Creating A Safe And Welcoming Library For The LGBTQIA+ Community: Part 1". Webinar from ALA Publishing eLearning Solutions, May 11, 2021.

A Nonbinary Experience of an LIS Program: Advice for Faculty

Zara Offner-Hernandez (they/them)

Keywords: LIS education, nonbinary, navigate, inclusion

I never asked for my existence in a body to be a radical act. Yet, I find myself in a Trans, Nonbinary, Queer, and Disabled body which I have come to love.[1] I love my body despite the inherent radicalization it faces from cisnormative (cisgender + normative) approaches to the world. I no longer fear the radical existence which envelops my identity, nor do I discount the nuanced pieces of me as a student of private universities, as poor to lower-middle class at best, as a graduate student of Library and Information Science (LIS), and a thousand other things. My inherently Trans nature, which now defines much of my interactions, has always been a part of me, even before I knew of its rebellious existence. It is important to look at my development before exploring the issues I have encountered in my LIS program.

I grew up on the riverbanks of the St. Croix, attended an Assemblies of God church, and spent summers camping in the north woods and never really fit in with the boys in those spaces. I knew that some of them made my tiny heart flutter, but I wasn't sporty, nor did I enjoy stereotypical masculine pastimes like sporty video games, hunting, or

1. Trans, Nonbinary, Queer, and Disabled (along with Gender Diverse which is used later) have all been capitalized to respect each of these experiences as representative of communities with shared experiences, distinctive cultures, and ongoing histories.

fishing. What I loved was the riverbed. I scooped up crayfish and let the water trickle out of my hands. The winter brought ice which, though solid, was still in a transient state—moving with the current or melting with the sunrise. It took me years to realize that I was like the water, shifting and changing. My gender flows like a river, which is only caught in your hands for a fleeting moment. I am neither man nor woman, I am genderless and multigendered. Undisturbed, I could wander in unending whirlpools like tendrils, connecting the world back to the sea.

Over time, the surrounding towns have encroached on the St. Croix River and affected how the streams run. Water is not caught in hands—it's caught in buckets, canals, and concrete made by an assemblage of techno-social constructions. Rivers are not redirected in a day but over years of natural wind-whipping, erosion, or through human interference. For Transgender folks like me and Gender Diverse people, the systems created by our present society shape us and our experiences in education in restrictive and harmful ways.

Valuable conversations about the issues Trans and Gender Diverse people face are filtered, buried, and censored by social constructs. This causes a great loss of diverse perspectives and wisdom to the strawman arguments propping up cisnormative social constructs. LIS graduate programs exist within this context and are inherent contributors to harmful impacts, unless there is critical reflection on the part of instructors. I argue that LIS faculty need to take a critical reflective lens to their course content and readings with Trans and Gender Diverse learners' safety in mind.

Issues and Impacts

My program peers, in general terms, have been adept at questioning the consequences of library policies on Trans people. They are excellent at identifying when Trans voices are left out of LIS narratives. My peers practice dedicated care for Trans people by using Trans-inclusive language, modeling pronoun sharing, and providing constructive feedback to each other about precision of language. My instructors have been welcoming and happy to facilitate respectful discussions on gender constructs as they impact library sciences in theory and praxis. These discussions are in addition to our ongoing discourse on antiracism, decolonization, and universal equity. This context is what keeps me in my program. The dedicated care and drive to improve are attractive and elusive in the general landscape of the world. I treasure such hard to come by qualities.

In stark contrast to my peers and instructors has been a plethora of binary-centric course materials which preclude my existence as a Non-binary Trans person. These texts have framed Trans existence as an issue of social debate, rather than a matter of life and death for many of the students reading these materials. When Trans people are treated like a topic, a freakshow, and a debate, I can feel my own focus and determination deteriorating, my passion for learning receding, and my mind disengaging.

From my perspective, poor representation in course literature of gender as a binary, or Trans peoples' existence as social debate, typically rests on a sort of false dilemma fallacy in which the existence and agency of Trans people is made equivocal to the opposition, which frames Trans people in terms of the following: *do they exist?* If they do indeed exist, they must be depraved, and if they are depraved then their agency must be restricted. What I would like to see in place of texts that uphold this false dichotomy is a body of work that treats Trans people as whole persons with agency whose existence is not up for public debate.

One particularly poignant memory of a negative textural portrayal fixated on a limited number of potential research examples. The posed study comparisons were framed as men vs women, boys vs girls, and male vs female. These poorly crafted binary examples reinforce the erasure of my Nonbinary identity and harm the multifaceted possibilities of results researchers could otherwise glean. I am a lover of qualitative studies and the immensely powerful narratives they can distill into concrete forms, but how can I continue to produce and participate in these studies when I cannot see people like me represented in the frameworks of the work?

Even more egregious was the text's continued treatment of what it deemed the *issue of homosexuality*. While I am indeed Queer, the historical and practical overlap between Queerness and Transness pits my Trans body against the text. Gay rights, marriage equality, and the overall existence of Queer people were made out to be quaint qualitative studies in opinions of the public by the resource. Through this trivializing framework the text made a clear stance of indifference to respecting the identities and rights of Trans, Gender Diverse, and Queer folks' collective liberation.

Though my peers and professors model a culture of Trans inclusivity, careless texts have impacted my mental health and wellbeing. Graduate education is difficult enough without the compounding pressure of textual Transphobia pushing me toward burnout. My personal experience with these texts is that they reinforce binary notions of gender and effectively negate my Nonbinary identity while framing a decades-long collective struggle for liberation as a matter of charming debate.

Further, about a year into my LIS program I attended a Zoom meeting with a familiar faculty member and two staff. Needing a moment to myself, I muted my mic, turned off my camera, and went to another room. Upon my return and before I could rejoin the conversation, there were multiple instances where the wrong pronouns were used to refer to me and nobody corrected the errors. Those staff and faculty held no ill intent, but the circumstances still caused harm. It was particularly jarring to witness the disconnect between my positive experiences with these people and how I was talked about in my absence. Faculty and staff mentors need to understand that this type of disconnect can stunt, if not ruin, their rapport with Trans and Gender Diverse students. To err is entirely human, but to be an ally is to correct these mistakes. Even if this was not an intentional jab, Trans identities must retain respect, even without a Trans person's presence.

I am unable to connect this instructor's actions to a certain set of experiences. However, I would argue that there is a certain level of influence from text and media in their life that utilizes a binary approach to the world and gender. This is paralleled in the binary-centric content of my courses, which has the potential to set my peers up for similar harm in their future with Trans and Gender Diverse folks.

Binary structures in class literature reflect the system that surrounds us. The result of this parallel is that Trans and Gender Diverse people cease to exist in the academy when systems only allow us to function within engendered binary expectations. I am reminded of these over-simplified binaries in unexpected and curious ways. For example, at the county hospital where I currently work, there is a flock of pigeons that are structurally constrained to sections of the campus. Diligent observers will notice tree-like structures on skyways that branch out and short spikes that add texture to any flat surface a restless pigeon may seek for respite. The operative binary is that there are spaces where pigeons are welcome and spaces where they must be deterred from occupying. The issue for the hospital as a system upholding this binary is that the pigeons come anyway. Seasoned nurses often pass by the feathered intruders actively playing with the anti-pigeon architecture. They continue to infiltrate these spaces and subvert the norms of the organization. All too often, Trans people are required to operate like those pigeons. We are made to subvert and skirt around structures that are built to exclude us, and it is exhausting work.

Support for Trans people must extend beyond kindness. If a person's respect for Trans identities does not continue after they've left a room, does not include correcting others, and does not investigate anti-trans structures, then it is not respect at all. By breaking binaries and systems of transphobia, faculty, staff, and peers can become accomplices in commanding the dismantling of anti-trans architectures around us.

Forward Together

Pressing my investigation on the structures supporting the context of my LIS program, I reflected on Trans-positive courses that did not use texts which reinforced transphobic/binary-centric approaches. Were there Trans or Gender Diverse voices in the content? For many courses, yes. I directly studied the experiences of Trans librarians in the academy within a course on academic libraries. Professors would include books with Trans authors or characters on book lists. When professors purposefully integrated gender diversity through high quality materials, I was able to feel a sense of space in the program for me and others like me. Trans folks' materials need not be segregated to their own specialized book lists; seeing these items incorporated in common librarianship practices opens platforms to Trans voices and contributes to the end of their othering.

To expedite the end of othering for Trans LIS students, an overall "Transing" of library science is in order. For me, Transing library science means dismantling personal and communal patterns of binary thinking. This process must result in LIS programs that are not just non-exclusionary, but proactively Trans inclusive. Additionally, this process will need input from Gender Diverse folks to fully encapsulate a rebuke of cisnormativity.

Library work and librarianship are inherently interdisciplinary, meaning we are already positioned to integrate multiple frames of knowing. For anyone seeking to understand Trans epistemologies without burdening Trans students, I would recommend literary immersion in Trans histories, reading modern Trans writers, and watching Trans-centric media that doesn't focus solely on transitioning. To take those resources a step further, become an accomplice in Transing LIS by integrating Trans histories/epistemologies into the curriculum. Most Trans people learn about their own history, if they can access this learning at all, through personal searches and discovery later in life. By bringing Trans truths into the LIS program, we can perpetuate a growth of Trans narrative dissemination that supports Trans people in the moment and through the future work of LIS graduates. More input is needed from Gender Diverse people to fully develop this process into a universal effort towards inclusivity and safety.

The most important process in Transing LIS education is critical reflective practice. It took time for me to contemplate my own experience and to identify the highs, lows, and whys of my education; instructors and staff of LIS programs will need time to search thoughtfully, think wholistically, and interrogate the ideals they are upholding. My recommendations for anyone having a hard time starting this critical reflection is to engage with peers, and especially learners, in group critical reflections. If your institution has access to qualified in-house consultants for Trans inclusivity or can bring in outside eyes, I recommend connecting with these resources early, often, and as a standard practice.

Conclusion

At face value, my time as a graduate student has been filled with positive experiences. My peers affirm and support me, and I can see myself in numerous Trans colleagues. My student documents, ID, and logins all use my chosen name. These are all small blessings to Trans students who are navigating daily hostility and erasure.

To be Trans is to be a walking act of fluid rebellion against binary thought cycles and rigid systems of narrative control. Bringing issues faced by Trans students to light is one means to end the requirement that existence, let alone education, must be a radical act for Trans people. Trans folks as a community were not born into the wrong bodies, we have been born into a wrong system that constrains and drains us—a system of othering that seeks to make us a sideshow or *topic* rather than full human beings.

It is particularly important to remember that kindness and easy system changes are only a start to a deeper process of dismantling harmful structures and Transing LIS programs. More conscious work is needed to instill a sense of space in LIS for Trans students. Acts of harm toward Trans students, whether overt or in theoretical frames, need to be met with apology, change, and learning. LIS faculty must take a critical reflective lens to their teaching, take on unmatched diligence to avoid perpetuating anti-Trans frameworks, and put Trans learners' safety at the forefront of their minds.

This may all be my sole experience, but I hope it serves to spur critical eyes to action. My gender is like water, my Transness a river—it gives life, it spreads, it changes. The only way for Trans people to continue to find space in libraries is for librarians to adopt a similar fluidity. My parting invitation is to join me in Transing LIS programs and subsequently transforming our libraries.

About the Author

Zara Offner-Hernandez (they/them) is a graduate of the Masters of Library and Information Sciences program at St. Catherine University in St. Paul Minnesota. Their areas of interest span from the nexus of student health and libraries; to critical Disability studies; to best practices in information literacy instruction. They hold a B.A. in American Sign Language Interpreting and live, work, and play in the Minneapolis area with their partner and beloved fur baby Norman. If you are looking to connect with them or find out more about them, please reach out using their website: sites.google.com/view/zaraoffner-eportfolio.

Gender Class at Zoom University

Viola (they/them)

Keywords: non-binary, LIS education, online learning, Zoom

"Give me thy hand / And let me see thee in thy woman's weeds."
Twelfth Night, 5.1.285-6[1]

I guess I can't say starting grad school remotely during a global pandemic gave me nothing, because it gave me the sort of despair that turned into the courage to text my best friend and say, "Hey, I think I'm non-binary."

She texted me back to say, "Amazing! What pronouns feel good now?"

"I think she/her still," I replied, in what is now known as famous last words.

I am a thin, white, able-bodied, AFAB (assigned-female-at-birth) non-binary person. I come from a white family who started their lives as refugees-turned-immigrants and are now living as upper-middle-class white Americans. I am what cis people think non-binary people look like. I use they/them pronouns. I am not going to tell you my name, but I will tell you that I had not heard the word gay until I was in high school, and I had not met an out trans person before I came to college. No one had told me I was playing with gender when I learned to love theatre, where my being skinny and flat-chested, paired with amateur to semi-professional theatre's chronic lack of men, meant I spent my

1. William Shakespeare, *Twelfth Night, Or, What You Will*, ed. Barbara A. Mowat and Paul Werstine (New York, NY: Simon & Schuster Paperbacks, 1993).

formative years in wigs and sports bras, hanging out with the tenors and tricking the audience. (I have often been known to joke that Viola of Messaline, from Shakespeare's *Twelfth Night,* made me trans.) I will never forget the first time someone refused to believe I had played a role, because they were certain it had been played by a boy. "It was," I didn't know how to say.

I texted my friend that I was non-binary a few weeks after I was admitted to my Master of Science in Library and Information Science (LIS) program. I applied out of a combination of passionate belief in the transformative power of libraries, my own memories of relying on public libraries for Internet access and freedom from an oppressively conservative community, and a stricken and terrifying desire to have some idea of what I was doing with my life. As I was starting to come out to the people I trusted most in the world, it also seemed like the sort of crunchy granola, accepting environment where I could live the newest, most authentic iteration of myself without fear or comment.

It is now the summer after my first year, the quiet time of dread when I am slowly processing that I am going to have to do all that again. I am writing this chapter to tell you that the program, and by extension our field, was not accepting. It was traumatizing.

It was hard for me to see how much of LIS's persona of hyper-acceptance was a facade until I attended my online orientation. I had worked in libraries before; I had felt victimized by librarians before, as a scrappy, difficult, too-loud youth in the restrictive public libraries that I relied on for my Internet access. But I always thought those were outliers. The pandemic was a low point, though. Grad school was shaping up to be another low point, in the way people had warned me my twenties might be—the in-betweenness of it all, the constant search for disappearing jobs, the relentless comparison of my messy apartment to the house that my friends had just bought. I decided that I needed to do something to make myself happy in an uncomplicated way, that if I was having this fresh start, however qualified, I was going to use it to be the version of myself I most wanted to be. When I joined the Zoom call for orientation, I added they/them at the end of my name.

I had never been visibly trans before, and I had never had an opportunity to examine the reactions to it. I was one of the lucky and privileged ones in my program who got an assistantship with the university I attended. Because of this job, I could observe people's response to my gender in the classroom, in my team meetings at work, and in library all-staff meetings. It was not uncommon for me to be the only person with pronouns in their display name, a trend that only became more dramatic when I left the classroom and entered meetings in my university library.[2]

I hadn't expected it to be so acutely frightening to be the only person with their pronouns in their display name in a sea of Zoom squares. It *felt* like the sea, like I had stepped off an unseen ledge and was in the deep end now. In some all-staff meetings, I stopped putting my pronouns in my name. It was no longer worth the discomfort of identifying myself in a digital space full of people who perhaps were trans with me, or who perhaps were helpful allies, or who perhaps did not care, or who perhaps were scoffing at me from behind their blank screens.

It was the not-knowing, the lack of all social cues, that was the hardest to bear. We were all the same blank squares. Zoom stole my gender presentation from me. No one could tell that, outside the Zoom classroom, I was dressed like a tenor in *The Pirates of Penzance*. They only saw the hair I broke down and cut short in September to cope with my gender dysphoria, and whatever it was in my face that made them think I was a woman. I kept looking for the place I could put my pronouns, a way I could cut my hair, some clue that would make everyone realize what I was, that would make them believe in my identity. I never found it. It doesn't exist.

There were social ramifications for this that were upsetting, like how I was still misgendered even with my pronouns now slapped beneath

---

2. I have a secret footnote for you: none of us can say with absolute certainty that someone is not trans. Plenty of people are not in positions to share this. Plenty of people are trans and use pronouns that don't out them as such. You don't know. Sometimes they're still figuring it out. So this chapter is not an indictment on anyone who did not share their transness with me; it is only a reflection of what it felt like to be on this side of the screen, looking at the sea of faces, knowing that anyone out there could hate me for it and I would never know.

my face, or how I started getting asked to join diversity committees. (I hadn't planned on being on committees. I don't know if they always knew I was trans. They might have just asked me because I have short hair.)

But there were also boring, tepid difficulties that had only to do with the technology we were using. I always joked that Zoom was made by cis WASPs (White Anglo-Saxon Protestants). Zoom was not ready to accommodate my very long name, a name that I am proud of because it speaks to my family's origins and journeys. Zoom had a tendency to chop off the end of it, so when people with names like 'Matt Smith' got their whole name visible, I would often have only my first name showing. This meant putting my pronouns at the end of my name was useless, because Zoom would cut them off. During "Zoom University," I experimented with jauntily sandwiching my pronouns between my first and last names, offset with quotation marks: First Name "they/them" Last Name. My friends and I joked that I looked like a character from *The Godfather*. It increased the amount my last name was cut off, but I decided that if Zoom was going to make me pick, I would prioritize my pronouns. With that victory over technology achieved, I then discovered that people would still misgender me, even with my pronouns between my first and last names—the opposite of invisible.

Although, like many, I failed to retain much information from my Zoom classes, they did give me plenty of time to notice trends in how people chose to share their pronouns. My program put a lot of pressure on anyone they assumed was cis to share their pronouns, on the assumption that A) their gaydar was spot-on, and B) doing so was helpful for trans students. As a result, as much as a quarter of the class (many of whom had self-identified as cis allies) would have pronouns of all types by their names. Those same people, who congratulated themselves on their allyship in class, would lecture me in our cohort's Discord for not being trans the right way if I didn't agree with all their takes.

"Zoom University" has not made our classrooms worse at gender, because they were already an inhospitable place to me. But it did give me time to contemplate how the public reception of my gender and pronouns changed in a digital space. I met wonderful librarians who did not put pronouns in their names, but supported me in ways I found humbling and inspiring. I also attended classes full of self-professed allies who would put their pronouns by their name but would bully trans students outside of class. This was oppressive in the context of LIS's constant self-identification with the good, the liberal, and the liberating. I felt like our field, and by extension my classmates and professors, demanded my gratitude for the little it was doing.

I decided early into my program that I was not going to become attached to my identity as a librarian, to this program, or to most of my classmates. I was going to get the piece of paper I needed to work the jobs I wanted. I had to take these classes and get this degree. And then it starts again, I guess, in another workplace that I will have to learn how to navigate. I acknowledge that my privilege has shaped the way I experience this—the privilege that is my ticket into this field and a system that is deliberately constructed to let us be this much, go this far, but no further—but I will not be grateful. LIS does not get my gratitude.

Bibliography

Shakespeare, William. *Twelfth Night, Or, What You Will.* Edited by Barbara A. Mowat and Paul Werstine. New York, NY: Simon & Schuster Paperbacks, 1993.

Section 3:

Public Libraries

A Conspicuous and Wondrous Bloom

Nathaniel Heyer

Keywords: transition at work, coming out at work, public libraries, patron interactions, library instruction

It is January of 2020, and I am thirty-four years old—a chubby pencil-necked boy in a tie, only six months into my medical transition. I'm standing at the head of a dazzlingly bright new classroom in my freshly renovated suburban public library, poised to begin a computer class. It's three minutes past the hour, and I have just finished distributing handouts to the small group of adult students who have assembled, when in strolls a patron I have not seen in over a year. She's a tall, slender beauty of some indeterminate middle age, astute efforts with a makeup brush, time well spent in the salon chair, and a chiseled physique courtesy of years of healthy living making it impossible to tell exactly where in the seasons of her life she falls. I search my brain for her name, and it comes after a long beat. Susan.[1]

"Ah, *crap*," I think, as I watch her notice me. She stops dead in her tracks and blinks, slowly at first, and I wonder for a hope-filled second if she will simply see me as I am, a newly minted guy, and thus fail to make the connection to my old self. But no. My heart sinks as I watch recognition and then curiosity ignite with a ravenous whoosh across her features. With her canted head, deep squint, and quirked lips, she

1. Not her real name.

might as well have a neon red question mark hovering over her head now, pulsing.

I feel a flush creeping into my cheeks as I try not to make eye contact. If I acknowledge her too directly, she will undoubtedly take it as an invitation to make a comment or ask a question, and the jig will be up with *everyone* in the room. The four others present are a mix of new and returning students. The two first-time attendees know I am a man from what they see and hear of my rugged skin, nascent whiskers, dapper attire, and deepened voice. The other two are regulars who have watched the changes happen incrementally and are thus frogs in a pot, bizarrely oblivious to what is unfolding directly before their eyes. These latter folks see only the image of me that they have stored in their memory banks, a feminine form imposed over the masculine one I have crafted through my painstaking presentation choices and months of weekly testosterone injections.

That some of the students in my classroom think I am a woman is frustrating and uncomfortable, but it is a delusion I allow to persist for practical reasons. The fact is, I am not the type of person who comes out as trans to responses like "I always suspected" or "well that makes sense." It is instead always a shock when I reveal my truth to those who have known me in any capacity, whether we have been acquainted for thirty years or three.

I was never a tomboy as a kid. I was far too bookish, nerdy, and stereotypically gay to climb trees or play sports. Gender meant nothing to me back then. It was irrelevant noise amidst perilous trials of abuse, neglect, and poverty. I spent the first fourteen years of my life tacitly agender, and it was good. When first puberty finally laid its marks upon my body, I shuddered and writhed in agony, but had no words to speak of my experience to anyone and no one to speak them to. The shame and loss I felt was all-encompassing. I did not know that trans men or nonbinary people existed. I did not know what dysphoria was. I did not know that I could be anything other than what everyone told me I was, and so I drifted far from my body, watching everything in my life as if from outside myself, going through the motions.

In college I began to awaken, began to piece the fragments together, but by then I had fallen in love with a straight man. The role of girlfriend and later wife to a partner I could not bear to lose made extreme denial the only course available to me. I thus lived in high femme drag every day of my life during my twenties. I painted my nails moodily, grimaced my way through an hour-long hair routine in the morning, applied makeup onto features made somber and blank by dissociation. I got married in a big, beautiful poofy dress and $200 updo. I went to crunchy granola birthing classes, and nursed my baby for thirteen months. I performed a soaring rendition of "strong feminist trailblazer," "body positivity champion," and "woman having it all" that could well have garnered me an Emmy, had I been on TV. I was pretty, smart, indomitable, put together, and kind. I was a vision of a shining star—in my career and everywhere else. Everyone in my life thought they knew who I was. I thought they did too. I thought this tortured falseness was just what it was like to exist in the world.

So nowadays, when I come out at age thirty-four, even open-minded people and vocal LGBTQ+ allies shake their heads in complete shock and disbelief. Some cry. Some interrogate me. Many cannot accept it. Many, I must come out to over and over and over again because they can't absorb the truth. Many are angry, and feel betrayed. It is devastating to come out.

I love being a public librarian—love answering questions, love helping people find their way during hard times, and love creating opportunities for entertainment, personal growth, social cohesion, and joy in a stressful world. But all of the pleasure I have taken in my library career for nearly a decade has in this last six months come to an abrupt and screeching halt. I come to work now filled with dread at the questions that will be asked of me, instead of excited to field them, because all too often, they will be unanswerable, or achingly personal. I come to work simultaneously afraid of who does and who does not know about my identity, caught between the equally oppressive forces of a need for privacy and a need for validation. I come to work embarrassed by the physical signs of my conspicuously late ascendancy from unfinished child to seasoned adult, which presently includes acne, a cracking voice, and a look which reads "awkward teen boy" rather than "thirty-something tech wizard."

I also come to work feeling totally overwhelmed, knowing the sheer volume of people who are going to be looking at and interacting with me, and wondering when my transition will reach a tipping point that cannot be overlooked. In my role as an adult services librarian, I work the reference desk, conduct outreach activities, run programs, and teach classes. The population I serve in this capacity is 85,000 strong, and a large number of those folks come through our doors on a regular basis. I am a familiar face to a great many people as a result. On top of that, I have been employed at this library for years. During that time, I have amassed a coterie of regulars and devotees. People go out of their way to check in with me, chat me up, take my classes, attend my events, and seek me out personally to answer their reference questions.

In other words, I am *known*. I am a public figure. I am not just transitioning in front my own mirror, friends, and family—a harrowing enough challenge for anyone to endure. I am metamorphosing rather, on a stage, in front of a very large audiencc that weeps, gapes, and protests as I strip off the poison-laced masks they have mistaken for the truth and thus come to love.

So, for now, while I can, I let some of that audience exist in a blissful state of ignorance. If people do not notice my transition, I do not make it a point to draw their attention to it. When people ask me about my voice, I let them believe their own theory that I have a cold. I ask to be called by a one syllable, gender-neutral take on my birth name and dissemble genially when asked why. "Oh, it's just what everyone outside work calls me, so I decided to change it here, too." I carve out elbow room through diversion and omission to pace myself as best I can, coming out to one person at a time—in my office or away from the floor of the library whenever possible—knowing all the while that soon enough, I will not have this unpleasant luxury. Puberty is like a glacier, after all. It moves too slowly to be seen by the naked eye in the moment, but it leaves the landscape behind indelibly transformed. There will come a day when I will no longer be hidden in plain sight.

The cognitive dissonance inspired by my desperate need for that day to come, paired with my fear of the pain and excruciating vulnerability that will immediately follow, is like being a fraying rope at the center of a game of tug of war: I am trying very hard not to come apart under the strain.

Meanwhile, I have little support among my colleagues. As a whole, they are well meaning and kind people, but they have known me too long and are afflicted by the same incredulity and shock as everyone else I've come out to. No matter how many times I correct them, the she/her pronouns continue to fly fast and furious, landing like little blows every time, especially now that the physical impact of my testosterone injections, bound up chest, and massive wardrobe changes signal so clearly exactly what it is I need them to understand, acknowledge, and respect. I am being called "sir" now by new patrons and strangers, more and more, and it is a profound relief. Far too often though, a patron will approach another service point before reaching me and be directed by a staff member there to "see the lady at the Information Desk over there," fingers pointed directly, and unmistakably, at me. Other times, a staff member will lead a patron to my office, and say, "[Feminine birth name] will help you." And there I sit—a boy, obviously. And the patron will just blink stupidly, or shuffle awkwardly, or turn to the other person with an inquisitive "What in the hell are you talking about?" look on their face. My colleague will then flush and stutter, roll their eyes skyward and gesture wordlessly with their hands to convey irritation or helplessness, or simply walk away without another word, leaving me to clean up the mess.

It's mortifying—this entire process, and I am so alone.

On days when I can't bring myself to remind someone who should know better yet again to gender me correctly, or when I have an opportunity to come out, but just can't find the energy or work up the nerve, I cloister myself instead in the bathroom to text message my therapist or another support with shaking fingers. Sometimes, crushed by anxiety and dysphoria after a long day of harrowing near misses with folks who don't know yet, and misgendering by folks who do, I blast violent metalcore at ear-splitting volume all the way home, screaming and roaring out the jagged rawness of my feelings, despite the deleterious effects of such exertions on my still delicate and squeaky new voice.

Today though, in this classroom on a sunny winter day, I can't retreat, or take my time, or seek reassurance, relief, or counsel. Today, I can tell, I will have to reset the mental caches of five patrons in one go, refresh five pages, cycle five dials, and start the estimation of my gender afresh as a group, ready or not. Because, you see, Susan is going to ask a question. It's absolutely inevitable. Having quite obviously noticed the evidence of my transition, I can see she is burning up with curiosity, vibrating like a small child trying to sit still at a desk on the last day of school.

So, I take a deep breath and get ahead of her. I introduce myself to the class and I add, as nonchalantly as possible, "and some of you don't know this, but my pronouns are he/him. Alright then, let's get started!"

I see the bright red question mark over Susan's head transform at once into a bright yellow exclamation point, and then the same blazing mark goes up over the head of every other person in the room. Bang, bang, bang, BANG. "*Yes*," I think grimly, as I begin to talk animatedly about Windows File Explorer, watching their brows leap or knit as they each realize the implications of what I have just said, "Oh yes, I am a transgender person. I see that you all see it now. I see your estimation of me changing, your unquestioning acceptance of my manhood suddenly falling through my clutching fingers like sand or your faulty perception of my womanhood evaporating through your clutching fingers like smoke. Yes, yes, this just got very awkward indeed. Yes, I know. Bear with me friends, I will impress you anyway. You will get what you came for."

And so, I lead my class. They all soon forget that I am transgender, and then for nearly two blissful hours so do I, because the work is joyful and because I am so well suited to it. Here I am, a gay man and consummate nerd at the head of a classroom, authentically myself and thus at the absolute top of my game. I am a sure-footed dancer in a tailcoat and my students are my partners, following where I take them. As I twirl and tango them through concepts and skills, winning their trust (and laughter) along the way, I draw upon *everything* that I am—charismatic and funny, cheerful and bright, flirtatious and disarming, yes, but also fiercely protective and uncompromising, analytical and serious, strong and decisive. I have spent long decades painfully dissecting my flamboyance away from my masculinity, allowing only what is colorful and pretty about me to show and burying the rest, because that is what has been demanded of me. But now, I know better. Now, I am whole, and growing more so by the day. And so, surfing a wave of prowess and elation, I forget to be self-conscious. I forget how fraught questions have become in my workplace. I throw my arms open wide to my students, creating a safe space, a temple to learning, as any good librarian does.

Unspoken, but unmistakable, I fill the room with a mantra that cycles around and around: "You can trust me. You can learn this. You can be vulnerable enough to admit what you do not know. You are allowed to have your information needs met. You are safe in this space. I will protect you."

My students thus learn what they were hoping to, and some of them even more—the blockading forces of their fear and self-loathing smoothed away. When I reach my final presentation slide, I hover in a moment of quiet, watching as they emerge from a state of deep and collective concentration like suns dawning over the horizon. Ah, but then there is Susan—always a step ahead of everyone else. She comes to herself so quickly, I can almost hear a crack of thunder. Her gaze sharpens and, within me, a spell breaks in response. I am tossed again into a hyper-awareness of my gender and transition, and brought back to the memory of having come out at the beginning of class.

I scan the room, wondering if anyone else has remembered yet. I am relieved to see in their body language and blinking faces that they have not. They are too busy thinking to themselves, pleasantly: "Well I'll be darned. I am at the library, and… I can't believe it, but I think I actually know how to use this software now! Isn't that something?" Grins erupt. The mood is festive. Kudos begin to fly.

I have a script for this profusion of gratitude. "Aw shucks guys," I say teasingly, reining them in when it all becomes too much. "I'm glad you enjoyed the class. The best thanks is to tell your friends and family about the work the library does to help bring folks up to speed on technology. People really think we're going to go the way of the dinosaur, while meanwhile, we're needed more than ever—isn't that silly? Good thing you know better." I smile at them encouragingly. "Now, can you all do me a favor and fill out this survey?"

As I pass out half page questionnaires and yellow golf pencils, I do my best to pretend that I do not notice that Susan is studying me. "*Is she even blinking? My god,*" I wonder, groaning silently. Her undisguised curiosity makes me want to cringe—for me or for her, I'm not sure. My self-consciousness feels like a knife biting into my flesh. I'm so unbelievably, overwhelmingly *aware* of my body and presentation in this moment, so aware of the ways these have changed, and also of the ways they have not yet. I am profoundly aware that I am not who Susan thought I was and that she really, really wants to talk about that fact with me, right this second.

I assess the situation in the fleeting moments bought by her attention turning reluctantly to the survey. "Hmm," I wonder, "Is it possible to somehow shuttle all the other students out of the classroom before Susan begins talk—ah, nope." She has finished her survey already and caught my eye for a microsecond, and now it's all over. Here we go. This conversation is happening, and it is going to happen right now.

"OK. OK," I think, steadying myself. "I can do this. I shouldn't have to, but whatever. C'est la vie. Being trans is a fucking pain in the ass." I unleash the full intensity of my gaze on her; then, finally, my wolf eyes smacking into her hawk eyes defiantly and holding steady there, I'm ready to do battle.

Today, though—today, I needn't have worried. Today, it goes differently than usual. Susan isn't awkward, embarrassed, or hesitant as she speaks to me. She doesn't reference and then linger on her own discomfort about my transformation. She isn't struck down by grief or personal offense at my identity and choices. She makes no desperate plea for me to continue to lie to her.

Instead, she says, eyes twinkling merrily, "*You* are looking *well*."

I am so surprised, I nearly burst out laughing. I tuck my metaphorical tongue firmly into my cheek, swallow my amusement, and follow her lead. "Why yes, I am very well, thank you."

My lips twitch with mirth at what is passing between us, unsaid, and I think for a microsecond that maybe she will leave it at that until the others leave the room, but before I can take in another breath, she is making her move. Quick as a flash, she notches an arrow, draws back her bow, and releases. Her question—the one she's been desperate to ask for nearly two hours—finally flies free. And when it lands, with a resounding *thunk*, it is as demanding and intensely personal as all those that have come before, but also not what I've been expecting at all.

"Are you happy?" she inquires, leaning in, huge beautiful eyes like moons as she waits for my answer.

In the room around us, her classmates fall silent. Those who were packing up their things, stop. The air is pregnant.

I let the moment stretch as I think about what she has asked me. I realize all of a sudden, that despite my constant angst and anxiety about transitioning on the job, the knitting together of my soul with my body is absolutely, hands down, the best thing that has ever happened to me—even here, even now in this room where I have just taught a class under such trying circumstances. It occurs to me, for the first time while at work since beginning my transition, that I *am* happy, that I am in full and wondrous bloom. I have until now simply failed to notice and revel in it. So I say, speaking as much to myself as to her and all the rest of the world, my voice clotted with emotion, "Yes, I am very happy. I'm happier than I have ever been in my entire life." The truth rings out like the resonant "bongggg" of a monstrous bell, and I sense that everyone assembled has been touched by it.

Susan overflows herself then, overjoyed like a stream swelling in springtime with mountain water. Her words come in a breathless cascade, her face beaming. "I can tell! Oh my god, you just look so *relaxed*. You look so completely, unbelievably relaxed. Do you have more energy?" I can't get a word in edgewise, so I nod, dumbstruck by this unexpected flood of affirmation. Her pitch hitches a tad lower, marveling, "You look so *good.* I just cannot believe it! You *move* different. Your voice…" she is shaking her head in disbelief, "I was so surprised when I came in here! You *shocked* me!" She clutches mock pearls with dramatic flair, and smiles. "Thank you for saying something."

There is a pause. My tongue feels like it is stuck to the roof of my mouth.

"Oh," she says, realization dawning, "Oh! That can't have been easy." She looks at the other people around the table, all now quickly gathering their things again urgently as the awkwardness falls heavy around the space. Her gaze has an uncharacteristic softness to it when it returns to my face—an unvoiced apology putting a furrow in her brow.

According to the tenets of liberal discourse about emotional labor, I have in this moment an opportunity and every right to teach Susan a lesson about appropriateness and discretion, to drive home her nascent self-awareness about the deeply uncomfortable bind her entitlement put me in with a public slap on the wrist, but I just can't help myself—I forgive her instead, my shoulders rising into a tiny absolving shrug, my half-cocked smile magnanimous. Because the thing is, it's all beside the point now. What matters to me in this moment—what makes me laugh with abandon as we flirt and playfully parry our way through the rest of our conversation—is my utter relief and pleasure at not only having been truly *seen,* and how good that felt to me, but also in the impact that *seeing me* has clearly had on Susan. In her expression of unbridled wonder at the fundamental rightness of my transition, I can see that I have blown her mind, changed her perceptions, and thus taught her something valuable.

Simply by being visible and showing up to do my job as my whole and unbridled self, I have taught her that yes, transgender people can be happy and accomplished and established. Yes, we can be neighbors, teachers, and friends. Yes, we can be professionals at the top of our game. Yes, we can be gay (or bisexual, or queer, or straight). Yes, like all humans, we can present a mix of feminine and masculine characteristics. No, you cannot always tell who is carrying the toxic weight of dysphoria just by looking. No, transition is not a cause for sorrow and fear, even when it comes as a great surprise. It is instead full of life and renewal. It is inspiring. It is beautiful. It is a seedpod exploding.

I feel elated by this exchange and its impact, and the good that my visibility has done, but I am also at the very edge of my tolerance for intensity. I am relieved when Susan says her goodbyes and heads toward the door.

With her departure, the classroom has emptied out but for one man, who remains stock still in his seat, a faraway look on his face. I give him a moment. I am just taking a breath to shoo him out when he snaps to attention, startling me.

"Yes!" he says suddenly, as if I've asked him a question just by looking at him, "Your happiness is all that matters." He says this like it has never once occurred to him before and as though long minutes have not passed since Susan asked me the question that has yielded this delayed conclusion. He smiles at me then, a nervous little flash filled with discovery and chagrin, and then shambles out of the room without another word, the weight of a deep thought balanced on his age-shrunken shoulders.

I watch him go, my eyebrows high on my face. I think to myself that apparently more than one mind was blown today, and that his was perhaps the one that needed it the most.

It is all too much—the responsibility and weight of it all, the fear and anger and resentment—and the unexpectedly pleasant resolution. As I drift back to my office, absently toting my laptop and paperwork, I am overrun with exhaustion and the unstoppable banging and clanking of my mind's gears spinning. Until today, I have felt only burdened by the interplay between my vocation as a public educator and my gender transition. I have wanted to crawl under a rock and hide. I have thought about quitting, forsaking a much-loved career, my passion for the work be damned. I have resented the questions I have been asked about my transition, and my own knack for answering them so effectively and patiently. I have hated my own fortitude, courage, and grace in the face of the uphill battle to come out, because I have been so bound up in the cost of this daunting task, and not the reward. But somewhere deep inside, the spark of my interaction with these patrons has kindled a cleansing fire today, and what I find in the void left behind is acceptance.

No, I did not choose to be here, naked and soul-bared this way before tens of thousands of people, but that is the position I find myself in. No, I did not choose to be trans, nor to be talented at teaching and answering questions—but I am those things anyway. No, coming out will not always—or even often—be met with such positive and joyful energy, but now I know what is possible. For me to be wholly authentic is to be a transgender man, and gay, and a teacher, and a performer, and a deeply informed expert, and to permit myself to take pleasure in these aspects of my identity when they yield positive experiences, and to grieve when they do not. It is to approach the present moment and coming out with curiosity instead of prognostication and judgment. I am exactly where I am supposed to be, doing what I am made to do. And this experience, I finally begin to understand, of being known, of educating, and yes—of becoming visibly myself in the glare of the spotlight—is not just a burden, but also a *privilege*. It is not wholly good nor wholly bad, but rather a paradox, a crucible, an opportunity to grow and help others grow.

"Perhaps," I think, invigorated and hopeful about my career for the first time since beginning my transition, "I can find it in myself to shine again. This time, for *real*."

About the Author

Nathaniel Heyer (he/him) is a gay transgender man, polymath, public librarian, writer, educator, library consultant, urban farmer, spreadsheet ninja, and father of one who lives and works in Upstate New York. Nate studied Fine Art at Alfred University and completed his Masters of Science in Library and Information Studies at Florida State University. Nate is passionate about educating community members and library staff about technology, information literacy, and LGBTQ+ issues. He lives in a ramshackle old house with great bones and a near endless supply of head-scratching peculiarities. When not wielding a paintbrush, nail gun, or shovel, he is working on his first book, a memoir of trauma and transition.

Holding onto Dreams

A.E. Baker

Keywords: coming out at work, public librarian, nonbinary

I've never been able to remember my dreams. I do sometimes remember those few moments of half-consciousness upon waking where I think, "that was wild, cinematic, stressful, dramatic," but the content of the dream never really sticks. My brain can only hold onto the slight residue of emotion, but not the plot itself.

At some point I read that dreams are just random neurons firing and your brain rushing to make some sort of meaning out of nonsense, but lately I've been wondering if my inability to hold on to dream worlds has any correlation to how dreaming in the metaphorical sense is such a struggle for me.

I am an excellent planner. I am a "get shit done" kind of person. I have a Virgo moon. But dreaming big is not my strong suit. I learned intimately about the work I have to do in this area when I was asked "What does liberation look like in the next six months?" Everyone's answers blew me away. Abolish the police didn't feel like a six-month kind of thing. There were so many big dreams and honestly, I couldn't even begin to answer that question. Which is fine. I learn more by listening anyhow.

So much of the good work I have done is because I have attached myself to dreamers. I use my skills as a doer in service of the dreams I find beautiful. I think that's why library work appeals to me so much. While the reality can be messy, the dream of the public library is a beautiful one. Communities making a space to share and learn and grow that anyone can come to? That's a big dream and one that can be hard to actualize. This is true everywhere, but especially in conservative communities.

A few years back at my state library conference, there was a panel about drag storytimes that was carefully named in the agenda to be about meeting room policy so as not to catch flak from politicians. The room was full-to-bursting and the conversation focused around two directors' ardent defense of their meeting room policies when outside groups used library space to host drag storytimes. The main issue, they both explained, is that their community thought the library was running the program. There was talk of fielding community hatred, defending equal access to public space, and the political ramifications of these controversies.

I want to say that I remember all the specifics of this conversation, but mostly I remember feeling like my skin was on fire, like I couldn't quite get a breath, like I wanted to scream "WE ARE RIGHT HERE" and also sink through horrific hotel conference room carpet at the same time. I did manage to speak up during the Q and A and asked something like, "So, what programming are any of us offering LGBT+ families at our libraries?" and I don't remember any of the responses because literally all of them were bullshit. I remember leaving that conference room and briefly trying to process with two queer colleagues. Our talk centered around serving our community and LGBT+ people being part of that community.

What we didn't talk about, what I don't even think I had the ability to even name at the time, was how deeply alienating and dehumanizing it is to always be thinking about how to better serve a community when it's politically toxic to even acknowledge that you and people like you are part of that community. When those librarians asked "Is my community ready for this programming?" they didn't recognize the implicit question felt by the queer people in that room: "Is this community ready for you?"

The trouble with attaching yourself to someone else's dream is that it isn't yours. What happens when you turn out to be the kind of person the community doesn't want working with its children? For so long, I thought transitioning would mean giving up the work I loved. My first American Library Association (ALA) conference was a time that not only expanded my mind about queer librarianship, but also left me devastated about the reality of my life at home. The following are some vignettes from that event interspersed with some moments at home where I was able to imagine just a little bit more.

I was coming out of a women's restroom stall in the Dallas Fort Worth airport when my friend yelled "Oh my god, oh my god, OH MY GOD!!!!! Gay marriage is legal. The supreme court just ruled!" She grabbed me and we both started crying as the stream of people moved around us, used to ignoring displays of affection in airports. I remember both of us glued to our phones, waiting for the layover, eager to connect with all of our loved ones at home. I remember boarding our flight bound for San Francisco and longing so desperately to be home. I needed to keep crying and keep being held. Instead, I was preparing for my first ALA conference (funded by my grad school) which also happened to coincide with 2015 San Francisco Pride.

Sitting on the train from the airport, I felt such a profound sense of unreality. I had never dreamt gay marriage would be legal in my lifetime. Even as there was chatter about the court case, it felt impossible to me. We came up from the BART and saw a giant rainbow flag on a street lamp. B snapped a picture and shared it with the caption #lovewins and tagged me in it. I didn't post anything. I felt like I was in a different country. There were rainbow flags absolutely everywhere, and at twenty-five, I had not yet experienced big city rainbow capitalism. I was confused. I was like, is every business owner in San Francisco gay? I knew more gay people lived in cities, but a city celebrating pride rather than merely tolerating it was outside of my experience entirely, let alone companies using it as a marketing tool.

I was grateful to get to the hotel and out of the sea of city people going about their busy lives like the world wasn't completely different. I sat staring at my phone in the hotel lobby and looked at pictures on Facebook of people in the streets with tear-streaked faces. I wanted so desperately to be home.

As a very queer person, home has always been deeply complicated for me. These mountains hold me and are my refuge, but I've also wanted to run away from them more than once. By 2015, I had realized my transness and also realized the near impossibility of my transness as a children's librarian in a very conservative, right-to-work state. My job was a dream. I bounced with babies and toddlers. I made giant hobbit feet out of cardboard with shy teenagers coming out of their shells. I went to schools and farmer's markets and festivals with Legos and potato stamps and told families to come play at the library. I loved it so much. Beyond the day-to-day joy of this work, my director had said more than once that she was planning for me to replace her when she retired. I always smiled and politely deflected saying, "Thank you for thinking of me" and "We'll see; I have a lot to learn," meanwhile thinking there was no way in hell they'd let me be a county department head—not the real me at least. I didn't even know if the real me was possible, never mind employable, but I was pretty sure I knew the answer.

I was raised Pentecostal, so my ability to pretend to be something I'm not is one of my finest tuned skills. For a long time, I didn't realize there was a difference between being something and pretending. In 2015 I was playing the role of new library school student, full-time children's librarian, and newlywed to my high school sweetheart in what appeared to be a heterosexual marriage. Presentation wise, I was very femme. I understood gender was performative, and like the perfectionist overachiever I am, I was very good at my role. It was all strategic to me. I remember asking my mom to help me pick out a purse so I could go to a conference and look like a "real woman." The rationalization I was surviving on was, if gender is fake, then I can just fake it. If I had successfully faked speaking in tongues at church and a whole-ass wedding I didn't really want (my partner needed healthcare, so why not), then I could carry the right purse and wear the right clothes and smile politely when storytime mothers asked me when I planned to have kids of my own.

Prepared with my "real woman" conference purse, B and I left our hotel for the exhibit hall grand opening. Even on the short walk from our hotel to the convention center, there must have been forty rainbow flags, and I remember being stunned. I now know this is pretty mundane for a city in June, but at the time it felt miraculous and otherworldly. At this point, I hadn't even made it to my nearest big city's pride because it always happened on a Saturday in June (a.k.a., inescapable summer reading workday). Walking into that exhibit hall for the first time was also a wild experience and an immediate sensory overload—so many people, so much stuff, and no sense of order whatsoever paired with "Ma'am, may I scan your badge?", "Excuse me, Miss," "Pardon me Miss." Polite, yet small and never-ending irritants I was used to, but not with this frequency or volume.

B and I made plans to meet back up later and went our separate ways. I moved from booth to booth, touching and looking and trying to not stay in one place long enough for people to talk to me. I happened upon the GLBT pavilion and zine space, which were one and the same. There was a big white wall that held an extensive zine library and several tables with zine-making supplies, as well as a handful of artists and zine makers selling their work. I spent the rest of the afternoon reading silently, full of awe and gratitude for so many people creating such honest writing. I didn't have the energy to be perceived and play my regular roles, but I felt like I spent that afternoon in conversation. I read nonbinary poets. I read anarchists whose ideas I didn't have the context to understand yet. I read a Latinx trans person's rage at everyone who read them and their partner as white lesbians. I thought so much about what it meant to be seen. I watched so many visibly queer and trans library workers visit that space and talk with authors or talk about putting this or that "in the collection." My understanding of the possibility of queer librarianship was shifting, if not for myself, then for the world more broadly.

As a child, I didn't really dream of my future. The now required so much tending, so much attention, so much energy, that I didn't really think about what kind of life grownup me wanted. At other times, I was certain there wouldn't be a grown up me. The child that made choices about my career, my home, my marriage, only had the context to understand survival. Running away to the big city is an ever-present narrative that queer youth hear over and over as a solution to their impossible-feeling lives. Since survival was my goal, I knew that option wasn't the best one. Paying rent felt hard enough, and I knew a city would be worse. Leaving whatever sparse safety net I had constructed for myself felt needlessly risky. And for what? Some hope of a liberal paradise? As sheltered as I was, I knew bad stuff happened everywhere. I want to say I was inspired by seeing the possibility of keeping my career and living a more honest version of myself, but all I felt was stuck and so, so sad. Every move towards a more honest future felt impossibly hard, whether that was running away or staying put.

I felt like I was going to vomit and turn my whole body inside out. I sat, heart-near-to-exploding, waiting for her to look up. When she finally did, she took a deep breath and the first thing she said was, "How would you feel if this was read aloud at a county commission meeting?" In a way, I was relieved. I spent so long not transitioning because of fear for my job and to hear that fear verbalized by someone else was validating. "I can't give this to the staff, and there is no way I can protect you if you want to share this letter." I had basically copied a coming out letter from the Internet. It was not spicy. It was corporate and to the point. "Do you want to keep working here?"

"I would like to if I can, but I know that may not be possible," I said.

"Maybe you're right." she said. "I don't think you can keep doing what you're doing. You know how parents are."

I said, "I understand. Thanks for your time. Thanks for trying. Thanks for thinking about protecting me. Thanks for not instantly firing me."

She never again brought up the possibility of my taking her place when she retired. We both knew that ship had sailed.

Over the next year, I moved into adult services and kept the same name, even as my body changed. Every day at the desk I just agreed to people's reality of my gender with each new transaction. Ma'am, sir, miss, bud, brother.

"Have a nice day!" I'd say in my cheery customer service voice.

I started doing Tech Time, which was mostly alright. Sometimes I would sit with three or four older folks, bobbing back and forth as I helped them delete files or set up emails or other basic tasks. They would talk about me and to me but not quite hear each other, as I silently hoped no one would notice their disagreement on my pronouns. I asked my boss again if I could change my name, if I could work on getting folks to change to a different pronoun now that I was less in the spotlight. I had given up on using they; he would do, not really great, not right, but good enough. Again, survival was the goal, not some pipe dream of authentic self-determination. She said I would have to change my name and gender marker legally before I could ask other people to refer to me differently.

I didn't really feel great about changing my gender marker to "M", but I did want to use my real name at work. Plus, it was around the time of Trump's inauguration and every trans person I talked to was preparing for the possibility of that option ceasing to exist. I realized your legal gender doesn't exist to make you feel good; it can just be functional. It, too, could be about survival. So I did the thing.

Through what felt like a million one-on-one conversations with every person I worked with and served, I came out with nothing in writing other than a name change order sent to county HR. It took two years, but most everyone at my job eventually started using he for me, except for my boss who used she at least once a week for the rest of my time there.

I really didn't expect my first ALA conference to have such a queer focus. Partially, I think that perspective came from being closeted and deeply depressed, but also partially because it just was? I would like to attribute it to the city and the timing, but all I experienced of SF Pride was a couple of hours on Saturday when I snuck away to see the parade.

I stood streetside for an hour and the only thing I saw was people in Apple shirts walking to that "shut up and dance with me" song. I don't know if they were employees or just got a free t-shirt to be there, but I quickly concluded that this wasn't the best use of my limited time in the city. At the conference, I seemed to be moving from one session to another that shattered my view of what was possible. I want to say this was a magical time of broadening my worldview and being inspired and seeing new possibilities, but mostly what I felt was the impossibility of my life. I had never been so acutely aware of how fucked my situation was. I attended the Stonewall Book Awards and in the signing line, I learned one of the authors had lived near my hometown. She signed the book and said "You'll have to put this signed copy in the collection!" I didn't know how easily I could do that without casting suspicions on myself, but I thanked her for her time. I attended a storytime interest group and service to queer families dominated the conversation. I sat in silence absorbing, but feeling the impossibility press on me like a weight. A sweet person with purple hair asked me if I wanted a cookie and passed a box filled with rainbow and genderqueer flag decorated sugar cookies. I went and cried for a while in my first gender neutral bathroom after that, next to the exhibit hall with the temporary sign velcroed over the conference center's existing women's restroom sign. Another great place to cry at conferences is in film screenings.

Mostly, I managed to seem like a person who was not on the brink of a mental breakdown. My traveling companion, B, had no idea of the turmoil I was in. I remember only one moment when my cover slipped. I was at a poster session where a sweet dyke in a rainbow lanyard and cardigan from some urban library was giving a spiel about increasing programming for LGBT people by some wild number, and the crowd was asking reasonable questions about funding and buy-in from administration. And I was struck by how mundane it was. Like, it wasn't the most beautiful thing in the world. It was just business as usual. It was just presenting your work on a poster at a conference. There in my real woman conference purse and dress, my tears came and I couldn't stop them. I was quiet and off to the side and ready to run away when that librarian saw me and asked "Are you okay?" I just said, "All of this feels so impossible for my community" and all she said was, "I'm so sorry." I was of course mortified but also relieved to have been seen, to be given a chance to be even a little bit honest about where I was.

On the plane ride back home, B was excited to share with me about a session she went to about improving accessibility for trans patrons. She talked about removing gender from card applications and having "alternate" name fields, so people could put chosen names down, too. She worked at a local community college and thought those changes would be easy to implement. She shared all she had learned about how hard and alienating it is for trans students. She asked me, do you think you could implement this at your library? Thinking not just of card applications but also of my own life, I said, "No, I don't think I can."

But here's the thing about me. I am a doer. Even if I can't believe in a dream, I can do the work. I made a proposal for those very things and submitted it to my director who never took it any further. I think I transitioned much in the same way. I did it, not believing it was possible. I don't know that I would have made the same choices I did if I lived somewhere else. In many ways, I feel like I traded my real woman conference purse for learning how to tuck my shirts in to create a more masculine waistline, not because I wanted that, but because I want the safety it affords.

Lately, I've been working on letting myself want things. I've been working on recognizing where shame and fear shape my desires. I've been working on dreaming my own dreams. Earlier this year, I applied for a new job and got it, after thirteen years at my library.

Sitting at my desk I realized that I didn't coach my references on which pronouns to use for me, and two out of three regularly use "they". I want to say I was cool as cucumber and boldly thought, "Good. I don't want to work for anybody that isn't okay with that," but my reaction was just panic. My reaction was, "You blew it." My reaction was "Of course they don't want you." My reaction was "Of course they don't want the toxic liability that is your existence as a nonbinary trans person," even if they are fine with trans people.

But I didn't pick up that phone out of bravery, but out of the "maybe they just won't notice" hope that trans people are all too familiar with. When they offered me the job, the board chair said, "What pronouns do you use? Your references used different ones," and that good, nice question we want cis people to ask felt like a trap. I said "'they,' preferably, but 'he' is fine in conversation" (not because that's true but because I need an out sometimes). And he did the thing everyone is supposed to want, which was to email the board and say exactly what I said to everyone so I wouldn't have to. The website announcement used my real pronouns. I put my pronouns in my email signature two weeks ago for the first time, and I am utterly terrified.

There's a public library one town over that has a librarian that uses "they" pronouns. I only know about them because they post on the library's social media and every time I see it, I tear up. I know that seeing a director at an information organization in our state and (reading between the lines) knowing they are a nonbinary trans person is going to make the world feel bigger and more possible for my trans and gender non-conforming colleagues, but the emotion that's easiest to access for me is fear. Everything in public librarianship has taught me that my identity is a risk, a hindrance, and something that needs to be dealt with quietly. Now that I am experiencing the normalization of queer existence I viewed at that first ALA conference, what's more present is "How would you feel if this was read at a county commission meeting?"

And yet, being this out feels like a dream I never thought possible for myself. I didn't plan for it or expect it when I applied for this job. So many parts of my life, body, relationships, and community are so much more beautiful than I ever dreamed was possible. I think representation is important to imagining, but there is a powerful kind of knowing that comes from feeling something. Feelings have always been the parts of dreams I could keep hold of.

I am so grateful to have the opportunity to be in movement spaces where I can practice liberation, which is this concept where we try to live, move, and be in relationship in ways that model what we are working for. It's one thing to say you are working towards liberation, and a totally different thing to be in a space where you know what that feels like in your body (even for just a little bit of time).

I didn't know this life I have was possible, and that reminds me that there are so many futures I can't even begin to fathom. The impossibility of my present makes me more able to believe in things that feel impossible. Imagination is a realm of political struggle, and I think that carving out spaces where we can experience the impossible feeling of showing up as our whole selves is a key tool in that struggle.

In a way, this book is a space like that for me right now. I don't know what anyone else is writing yet, but my guess is that this book in your hands is full of honest stories from trans library workers. When you put it down you may not remember all the words, but I hope there are some feelings your brain can hold on to. I hope they stick with you and you can use them as fuel when you start to do impossible-feeling things.

Embodied Multitudes: Resistance and Healing Beyond the Margins

M. Reed (el/elle)

Keywords: Indigenous migrant experience, gender fluid and queer, white supremacy culture, trauma, healing through decolonization

> "Stop. We greet you as liberators. This 'we' is that 'us' in the margins, that 'we' who inhabit marginal space that is not a site of domination but a place of resistance. Enter that space. This is an intervention. I am writing to you."[1] - bell hooks

For as long as I can remember, I have always embodied multitudes. Throughout my life, I have consistently gravitated towards fluidity. I have never felt aligned with categories, rigid rules, or constraints. Now, as an adult, I believe this to be an ongoing act of resistance on my part, perhaps a spiritual gift from my ancestors. You see, even in my spirituality, I am empowered by a collective—refusing to restrict myself to one deity. Moreover, I write to you, the collective, about my journey; a tale I have never tried to articulate for lack of words—but right now I choose to meet you here in this space—in the margins, a place of resistance. Join me.

As a child, gender identity was not a topic of conversation. I only understood the distinction between comfort and discomfort. I

1. bell hooks, *Yearning: Race, Gender, and Cultural Politics* (Boston: South End Press, 1990), 152.

understood that I felt liberated when I wore certain clothing and absolute torture when I wore other clothing, but for most of my childhood I had no autonomy over clothing choices. On top of this, I had eczema for most of my life which kept me in chronic pain and limited my clothing choices. I often hid painful broken skin and flare ups under long sleeves and pants year-round. This is a part of my story I have never talked much about but now find so powerful to unpack. For many of us familiar with chronic pain, it is so important to have our stories shared and validated. My personal journey with eczema, which I later learned became topical steroid withdrawal syndrome (TSWS), is as much a part of my personal expression as my gender fluidity. Now, having healed from TSWS over the past four years, I can experiment more with my gender expression year-round in ways I never thought would be possible.

Along with gender fluidity, I also identify as queer. Like my gender, I did not vocalize it until later in life, because I experienced and witnessed it as an aspect of my essential self and neither notable nor necessarily nameable. I simply believed that everyone found beauty in others, regardless of gender, until a group of peers approached me in high school to ask me if I was a lesbian. I also experienced consistent bullying from a sibling for "*dressing like a boy*," and my mother was perpetually disappointed in my lack of interest in certain clothing items.

Late in college I began hearing conversations about nonbinary and gender nonconforming identities and they/them pronouns. I often felt a bit perplexed, because I only saw these identities represented by white hairless androgynous bodies. I thought because I deviated from this type of body and was typically seen as femme presenting, I was not allowed to identify as such. It was not until I heard Alok Vaid-Menon share their story on social media that I finally felt something like acceptance, recognition of myself in another, and validation.[2] There I was: a brown, immigrant, hairy, queer, gender nonconforming poet. I felt at home.

For me, to identify as queer *and* gender fluid is to exist beyond the margins, to embrace the endlessness of space. I revel in the defiance

2. Alok Vaid-Menon, "The Complicated Reality of Being Trans and Indian-American," HuffPost, October 4, 2018, video, 4:24. https://www.youtube.com/watch?v=j-k1riPzf9c.

in its lack of clarity. I find the vagueness and expansiveness liberating in a world where I am constantly asked to specify my "otherness" for the comfort of *others*. To be queer and gender fluid is to express comfort with myself as I am, no matter how similar or different from the previous day, and to embrace the present without judgement. I simply am, and that is sufficient.

That said, I also understand the conflicting necessity to be thoroughly specific in describing my lived experience, but I do so in this chapter to provide context and not for the comfort of *others*. The purpose of this detail is to counter notions of a unified experience for people who look like me and, therefore, may be similarly racialized and oppressed. I choose, then, to specifically name the traumas I have experienced. These include the traumas of imposed gender norms, homophobia, medical racism and harm caused by doctors, racial bullying at school starting at age six, growing up in a home where domestic violence and emotional abuse were daily occurrences, being forcibly separated from a sibling, being undocumented in the US for a portion of my childhood, racism by immigration officials and United States Citizenship and Immigration Services officers, racism by educators, parental abandonment, emotional abuse while living with distant relatives, poverty, and sexual harassment. The manifestations of these traumas have been self-harm, substance abuse, suicide attempts, depression, disordered eating, and codependency. I have received out-patient and in-patient care for many of these issues, but I did not start healing from them until I began to acknowledge their origins. I disclose these experiences because they all contribute to who I am today and what it means to inhabit my personhood. Sometimes they make my work difficult; at other times, they are indispensable assets.

My career in the library and information science (LIS) field began with a job as a short-term contractor at a public library in a major metropolis on the east coast. I was fortunate enough to have had supportive supervisors in my role and I found my work fulfilling, challenging, and rewarding. However, the amount of emotional labor I performed in that role was enormous. I worked with vulnerable populations and saw many of my past traumas present in their lives. One program I worked extensively on required working with an immigrant population that was predominantly white. That experience was challenging, as my expertise and knowledge were frequently questioned by some of these library patrons at a certain branch. At this same branch, I also witnessed library patrons challenge the head librarian, who is an immigrant woman of color. In these examples, I believe these behaviors were rooted in racism and sexism.

My second job at a public library almost drove me out of the profession. I now know to understand this institution as containing the "characteristics of white supremacy culture."[3] During my time as a part-time LIS worker, I often felt overworked, devalued, ignored, silenced, hindered, unsafe, and unsupported. During a professional development day, I expressed anxiety and concerns over an ever-increasing workload despite the lack of training I received. The library director informed me that such was the nature of the department I worked in and it was common in the library world.

While trying to work on various projects, I experienced pushback from a white woman colleague who often dominated what were supposed to be open discussions in project meetings and who would not follow through on tasks, which halted my workflow. I eventually gave up on those projects. This person is one of those self-proclaimed allies, so many of whom are white women, who frequently reveal themselves as the opposite. You know the type, the kind that hoards control and power and is heralded as the library superstar. It apparently hardly ever dawns on these people that if they relinquished a portion of their power (never mind all of it), more could get done and even more effectively. Another white woman colleague joined our department to only add to our workload without ever contributing any help to our ongoing or upcoming projects. I see her behavior as trying to build up her career on the backs of those with less power, a form of extraction, and purely capitalistic.

3. Tema Okun, "White supremacy culture characteristics," last modified May 2021, http://www.whitesupremacyculture.info/characteristics.html.

It took vigorous therapy and having a support system in place to find the courage to quit that position. At the end of my time there, I was burnt out, suicidal, and afraid. I even had a hard time speaking up in social settings with friends, because I had become so accustomed to feeling silenced and invisible. Shortly after, I was fortunate enough to be offered a new contract position at a wonderful organization which is BIPOC led and centered. Since starting that position, I have experienced genuine support and proper onboarding. I have never once felt like I was thrown into a new work task or project and expected to sink or swim. I believe that adequately preparing and training LIS workers is a true indicator of an organization's commitment to valuing and retaining their employees. I also believe that genuine support looks like humane workloads, check-ins, follow through, and trust. Without these essential components, harm is caused and for those of us with a history of trauma, that harm is experienced much more intensely.

I also believe that mentorship is essential for BIPOC and gender diverse LIS workers. I have been fortunate to work with two mentors. One is also an immigrant, and another has many other similarities with me. I have found their guidance and support to be fundamental to my continuation in the LIS field and ongoing education. As a first-generation student, graduate, and LIS professional, I am constantly encountering new experiences and opportunities. My mentors help to demystify processes and aspects of the field. Prior to mentorship, I found scholars I admired, read their CVs, and pieced together what I could for applications, proposals, and scholarships. However, again, I emphasize the importance of a collective. When necessary, I reach out to numerous scholars, friends, and mentors for feedback and guidance. I have learned that reciprocity is important in these relationships as well and remember to offer my support in return.

I am now at the point where I prioritize my healing and health over any profession. Through meaningful ways of healing, I actively work to unlearn colonialist ways of thinking and internalized capitalism. One way I am healing is through caring for plant relatives and learning traditional medicine and foodways from my family. In this practice, I also burn daily offerings for my ancestors and ask them to teach me how to become a better relative. I strive to remain teachable, to learn from the land, and to recognize our healing as one and the same. It has been challenging growing up and living away from my community, but these daily remembrances help me feel connected and grounded.

Finally, I am inspired by the ongoing work of those LIS workers and scholars who exist within the margins. I believe those who came before us have done the work and we, in turn, continue their work. I recognize that the rate at which things change continues to be contingent on interest convergence.[4] Yet, as we find the language to express ourselves, as we share our stories, and as we support each other on this journey, may we find the freedom to expand beyond the margins.

Bibliography

Bell Jr., Derrick A. "Brown v. Board of Education and the Interest-Convergence Dilemma." *Harvard Law Review* 93, no. 3 (1980).

hooks, bell. *Yearning: Race, Gender, and Cultural Politics*. Boston: South End Press, 1990.

Okun, Tema. "White supremacy culture characteristics." Last modified May 2021. https://www.whitesupremacyculture.info/characteristics.html.

Vaid-Menon, Alok. "The Complicated Reality of Being Trans and Indian-American." HuffPost. October 4, 2018. Video, 4:24. https://www.youtube.com/watch?v=j-k1riPzf9c.

About the Author

M. Reed is a gender fluid librarian and archivist.

4. Derrick A. Bell Jr., "Brown v. Board of Education and the Interest-Convergence Dilemma," *Harvard Law Review* 93, no. 3 (1980): 523.

Standing Out

Jayne Walters (she/her/hers)

Keywords: public libraries, trans woman, coming out at work, role model

Coming out as trans is different for everyone. All of our experiences are different, and all of our journeys are just as varied. Nobody really knows what to expect. All I could do was assume how people would react. All I could do was hope for the best. Really, that's all any of us can do. We never know where our transition will take us.

When I first began my transition, I was asked a number of times about blending in, which is more commonly referred to as "passing." It's an obnoxious question and for me, frankly, it's damn near impossible to blend in. I'm a 6'4" blonde woman. I stick out. Even when I'm not wearing heels, I'm a big woman.

In the early days, when it was very clear that I was transitioning, I had a number of people asked questions. "When will you be done?" "Have you had surgery?"—lots of very invasive and personal questions. Some people who knew I'm married asked if I was going to stay married. As if this changed who I was attracted to and whom I love. There are so many misunderstandings about transgender people and people often only rely on media to inform them.

My manager was not one of those people. After I told her that I was trans, she went home that night, did a ton of research, and then came in the next day with questions. Not about my choices, medical or personal, but about what she could do for me. Did I want to transfer to a new branch and start fresh as the real me? She had a number of other very sweet and thoughtful questions.

I decided that I would stay. My reasoning was that, as a juvenile librarian, I had grown very fond of all of my kiddos in the local daycares, schools, and the neighborhood. I knew them. They knew me. I wanted them to know the real me and to help show them that trans people aren't the boogiemen of the restrooms. I wanted to de-mystify and shatter some of the stereotypes for the people that lived in the neighborhood.

It wasn't long before the questions came. But in that mix of inappropriate questions, I started to get ones that I wasn't expecting at all. "My cousin is like you and my sister doesn't accept her. What can I do as her aunt to help her out?" That was the first one and I'll never forget it. It floored me. I was being looked to for answers on how to support other trans people. I tripped over that one quite a bit with lots of "ums" and "uhs," but told them that the fact that they were asking was a huge step. Embrace her. Accept her. Hopefully, your sister will come around, but as long as she knows she's got her auntie…you're helping her.

Then I got messages from other staff in the library system. "How did you come out to HR? I want to, but I'm scared." "One of my staff's kids just came out trans. Is it okay if they email you and talk to you?" "One of my staff came out to me. I want to make sure everyone uses the right pronouns." "Could you read this letter I want to send to the rest of the staff? Should I send a letter to the rest of the staff?" "I don't know what to do and I don't want to mess up."

I was even asked to read over a foundation grant to make sure the language was inclusive. I was asked to help with the library application forms and how to navigate legal names versus names people are using. Most recently, I was asked if the trans daughter of one of the library employees could come in sometime and meet me. It was the mother that, nearly two years prior, I had told her manager, "Yes. Have them email me. I'd be happy to talk to them." They wanted to bring their daughter in to see a trans woman in a professional position.

I jumped into doing presentations on creating diverse story times, creating safe spaces, basic 101 information on the LGBTQ+ community, and so much more. I discovered a passion for it that I never thought I would have, because I had never been able to be my true self. By embracing all of me, I found my voice and I used it to try and help others be embraced, empowered, and not just accepted, but celebrated.

Helping to create the LGBTQ+ Committee in my library system was a dream made real. It also became another thing for people to reach out to me about. How could they help? How could they join? How could they create one in *their* library system?

The workshops and presentations began to result in people asking me to present rather than me having to beg to be part of their conference. Word of mouth is what led me to write an article for *Library Journal* about some of my experience as a trans library employee.[1] That led to trans and non-binary folks in other library systems reaching out to me about how to come out at work, what to do about name changes, how to handle coming out to the community they serve, and so much more.

As an audience member at the American Library Association convention in DC, I attended a talk on LGBTQ+ picture books. During it, I stood up and mentioned briefly about how awesome my manager had been and that one of the books mentioned in the talk was in our library system. I gave a little plug about Inter-Library Loan so that people knew where they could get it if their library didn't have it. After the talk, a woman came up to me and asked politely if she could get a picture with me. Another woman was standing off just a little and waiting to talk to me as well. I thought they were both there to just ask me again for the name of the book mentioned or which library system I was with.

Both wanted pictures with me, one for her daughter who was just starting college and had recently come out. Her daughter was afraid that, by coming out as trans, she would ruin any chance of a career in education. She wanted a picture with me to show her daughter that whatever career she wanted to go into, that being trans won't stop her.

---

1. Jayne Walters, "Trans and Nonbinary Library People Are Everywhere: Trans + Script," ed. by Elsworth Carman, *Library Journal*, September 28, 2020, https://www.libraryjournal.com/?detailStory=trans-and-nonbinary-library-people-are-everywhere-trans-script.

The other woman was also a mother who wanted a picture with me to show her little girl that she had met a trans librarian because her daughter is trans and loves the library.

It's been a rollercoaster of a ride. All of these great things and sprinkled through it are the nasty bits. Purposefully being misgendered. Jokes being made by patrons. Slurs from other patrons. Frustration from coworkers about having to answer so many questions about me. They didn't need to answer a single one with anything other than, "Ask her."

I've also experienced a shift in some patrons who were horrible at first. Once they got to know me, their views changed. One patron refused to acknowledge that I even existed and would ignore me when I offered help. Eventually, however, she would only ask for me when she came in and even bought me a piece of jewelry. She said, "You're always wearing such pretty sparkly things; I saw this and I thought, Ms. Jayne would love this." And I did love it. But I loved the fact that she thought of me like that even more than the fact that she got it for me.

I never know what the question is going to be when someone says they have a question for me. "Do you play basketball?" "My daughter is about your height, where do you get your dress shoes?" "How tall *are* you?" "Are there any queer support groups in the area?" "How do I come out to my folks?" "Where do you get all your pretty dresses?" "Where's the bathroom?"

Most recently, I had an elderly gentleman come into the branch. I knew him vaguely from a number of community partner meetings. He came initially for our CEO's tour and to talk to her. When he was done, he approached me and said that he had some questions for me and that he wanted to know if I'd be willing to sit down and talk to him. He doesn't quite "understand what all the LGBT and all the other ones mean." He'd always admired my work in the neighborhood and would really appreciate it if I would help him. I agreed, and asked him whether he wanted books or DVDs on the subject matter or if he just wanted to talk to me, or both. Because I could always do both. He just wanted to talk to me. He "knew guys growing up that when they later left school and ended up with another guy. Well…we all thought, well, yeah, of course he did. Why is that a surprise to everyone else?" But things have changed and there's more than just Gay and Straight. There's so much more. I'm happy to educate and advocate.

It's a very odd and wonderful journey I'm on and while I had originally just wanted to be me, I never knew what that would mean for the people around me. My choices, big and small, have impacted and influenced people in my life. Some of them I've met and others I have not and possibly never will. I never would have imagined that finally facing who I am and striving to be myself would cause people I've never met to reach out to me for guidance, insight, support, or to thank me. I'm forever in a spotlight that I never sought.

While I knew I would never really blend in, I never would have guessed how important it was for me to stand out.

Bibliography

Walters, Jayne. "Trans and Nonbinary Library People Are Everywhere: Trans + Script." Edited by Elsworth Carman. *Library Journal*, September 28, 2020. https://www.libraryjournal.com/?detailStory=trans-and-nonbinary-library-people-are-everywhere-trans-script.

About the Author

Jayne Walters (she/her/hers) is an accomplished librarian. Within months of gaining her MLS, she was promoted from a Children's Public Service Assistant to Branch Manager of the West Indianapolis branch of the Indianapolis Public Library system. She has worked in libraries for over twelve years. Her writing has been featured in *Library Journal* and Jayne is proudly the first openly transgender manager in IndyPL's history. She is a member of the IndyPL Equity Council, a founding member of the LGBTQ+ Services Committee for the Indianapolis Public Library, and serves on the Indy Pride Board of Directors. She has spoken at several conferences on LGBTQIA+ issues and can be seen in a number of Indiana State Library webinars. Her passions include LGBTQIA+

representation in juvenile literature, making sure libraries are accessible and equitable for the community, and making libraries a safe and welcoming environment for the staff and the public at large.

I'm Not

Alex Byrne (they/them)

Keywords: masculinity, non-binary identities, public trans narratives, trans (in)visibility, perceived men in youth services

Working in Youth Services means I can relate a lot of things to picture books, because there are picture books on most subjects, identities, and situations. This works well when you're recommending them to children and their grownups, but sometimes feels a little awkward around other adults who aren't similarly steeped in Youth Services and the picture book hoards that public libraries have in their locations. So, when I came across Pam Smallcomb's 2010 picture book, *I'm Not*, it gave me a framework to describe how I feel about my own relationship to the big trans umbrella.

At its core, *I'm Not* is a book about two friends: Evelyn, an alligator with a very outgoing and confident personality and definite opinions on everything, and the unnamed narrator, a different-hued alligator who is pretty shy and makes a lot of comparisons to Evelyn about all the things she isn't. I identify pretty hard with the narrator in this book, because it's a lot easier to see what you aren't when you have a friend who is supremely confident and has opinions about everything and everyone they come across. The narrator describes Evelyn as "not one single bit ordinary," and her choices in fashion and actions certainly reflect that. The Evelyns of the trans community look the part, unabashedly, publicly, and everywhere they go. By being loud, proud, and changing their presentation in visible ways to fit their internal image, they set the popular perception of what a trans person looks like. We need more visibly trans people to help show others that it's possible to live as a visibly trans person. But in the same way that the unnamed narrator looks at Evelyn and primarily sees what she lacks, compared to someone who's much more visibly trans, it can really feel like I'm not.

Physically, I look like a cis white dude. I dress like one, too, in men's fashion choices, and like other dudes, I complain about how difficult it is to find clothing that actually fits my proportions, looks good on me, and feels comfortable, because being Tall and not Big is relatively inconceivable to clothing manufacturers, it seems. I don't have any outward signs of being non-binary, save for when I'm wearing my pronouns upon my person, and I'm not trying to make my figure, form, or silhouette look more androgyne. I'm fine with my presentation, and even if it means I get misgendered by other people, there's still value in being someone who looks like a dude and works in Youth Services—if for no other reason than as a way of making people stop and think again about what stereotypes they may have internalized about who engages in programming for children. Among the many commandments of Scroobius Pip in "Thou Shalt Always Kill" is the admonition not to assume that someone who looks like a man and plays with children does so with a sinister purpose.[1] Some men are genuinely good around children, or perhaps they work in libraries or education. Yet another way I can say that I'm not, and it is "I'm not," not "I'm not like them," because "I'm not like them" almost always implies I'm *better*, and on that, I can assure you I'm not.

I choose not to identify as a man because masculinity is built on a shifting philosophical core, which comes out in more or less toxic forms depending on how threatened masculinity feels in any given situation. If the central tenet of masculinity is "don't be womanish," there's never any solid ground to build an identity on, and instead, it requires someone who wants to be a man to constantly be checking to

1. dan le sac vs. Scroobius Pip, "Thou Shalt Always Kill," recorded November 2007, track 11 on *Angles*, Sunday Best Recordings, compact disc.

make sure the men around them agree that they're a man and haven't slipped into some not-man status. It's a system rife with opportunity for a man without morals and with a large ego to declare that he is the sole arbiter of what masculinity is, and everyone who wants to be a "real man" should fall in line with him. Not-men become acceptable targets, and the in-group mentality reinforces toxic tendencies. If being a man means I have to perform toxicity and yoke my identity to someone that I think is a repulsive human being, then I'm not.

Making a choice about your identity brings its own problems. In *I'm Not*, Evelyn has more than just a strong personality, she has opinions about everyone else, as well. Through the book, she redecorates the narrator's living space, changes the narrator's outward presentation, and assigns her roles to play in their pretend games, without asking the narrator if it's okay to proceed. Evelyn assures her that "your ceiling will look dreamy in orange!", "you are scrumptious in pink!",[2] and assumes that the narrator's lack of objection is sufficient permission to go forward. The narrator says she's not a decorator or an artist, so she lets it happen, believing that Evelyn's opinion is the better one, because, well, Evelyn *has* one. Outside the world of the picture book, there's a lot of Discourse about what qualifies as falling underneath the trans umbrella, with very strongly held opinions about what is and isn't trans. Excluding the unqualified and the hostile still leaves lots and lots of opinions to sift through. Some of those opinions have been enshrined in law or procedure (usually because of the unqualified and the hostile), and many concern themselves with whether someone is legitimately trans if they don't conform to a particular narrative or don't do specific things. It's easy to fall back on "if you're not cis, you're trans" as a bedrock argument for your own legitimacy, but seeing so many people making changes to their presentation, undergoing therapies and surgeries, and being much more obvious about their transitions or their trans selves makes me wonder if I'm only pretending. If my claim is "the current definitions of masculinity are terrible, toxic, and I want

2. Pam Smallcomb, *I'm Not* (New York: Schwartz & Wade, 2010).

no part of them," does that really make me trans, or does it mean that I'm really in the man category and need to do work toward expanding and reforming the definition of masculinity until it can include me? In the book, Evelyn takes on the role of a circus performer, an artist, an Antarctic explorer, and the Queen of England, all with appropriate costume selections for those roles. If the standard of what it is to be trans requires very outward and public presentation that matches the identity inside, then, like the narrator, the best conclusion I have about being trans is that I'm not.

If I go looking for things that are common experiences among people under the trans umbrella, one of the things I end up seeing is that the community comes together to provide support for those who are experiencing oppression in their lives. There are enough stories of harassment and discrimination to fill our social media, article, and discussion spaces, but I'm not likely to end up getting strong pushback or harassment from anyone, because I'm not changing my presentation, I'm not really all that fussy about correct use of my pronouns by the public, and I'm not stuck at a worksite where co-workers are loudly, obviously, and deliberately misgendering people to be jerks and confident they won't be disciplined for it. I'm not saying that you have to be discriminated against to be under the trans umbrella. That's a trash take like "only people who have been abused by the public are 'real' library workers." That said, sometimes I wonder if the privilege of not being visibly trans in my presentation stops me from being fully able to understand the trans experience. Perhaps, after talking about why I identify the way I do, I sound like someone who's pretending and playing at non-binaryness, since it would be simple enough, if I decided to, to go back to identifying as a man and pick up where I left off. Popularized trans narratives talk about people who know they're trans in their guts, and have known forever, to the point where it's painful to continue staying closeted. Those narratives are the easiest for binary cis people to understand, even if it's only a small portion of the possible space under the trans umbrella. But, as the refrain goes, representation matters. It's hard to imagine the umbrella includes you if you don't see someone like you in it already. A lot of the narrative energy is (rightfully) being put into telling the kinds of stories that will make it easier for people who are more visibly transitioning to get to the place they want to be and live their lives fully and unapologetically. This doesn't leave a lot of narrative room for people who are pretty sure they're not cis, but who aren't necessarily interested in binary transition or significant changes to their presentation.

Because it's a picture book that's ultimately about friendship and celebrating what makes someone unique, *I'm Not* doesn't end in a down space as a story about someone who has low self-esteem getting run over by her outgoing friend with very little sense of boundaries. In the last few pages, Evelyn admits that she's not all that great at spelling, karate, or making cookies, and she's afraid of the dark. The narrator is good at all of those things, and not at all afraid of the dark, so "I'm not" becomes a positive thing and a way of showing that the narrator has different skills and abilities than Evelyn, and that they're valuable things. The full ending is that Evelyn needs a friend who will stick with her through everything, which, y'know, given Evelyn's trouble with boundaries and tendency not to check in about what other people want, could mean trouble for the narrator. If we explore that facet too much, though, we wreck the nice metaphor and lose the happy ending. We need supportive people, but good supportive people are the ones who will tell us when we're in the wrong or we're not behaving well.

So how do I turn my own narrative of not into something more positive? I'm not bad at using the proper pronouns with people once I know what they are. I'm not confused or deluded or any of the other adjectives that people throw at children (or adults) to insist they're wrong about themselves. I'm not going to back down from the idea that more people who look like me should be doing work like mine, without being shunted into other places that people think are more "appropriate." I'm not insisting that because I went through a long process to get where I am, that everyone else has to, as well. I'm not the worst at messing with people's expectations of gender and who does what work in libraries.

I'm not. And that's a good thing.

Bibliography

dan le sac vs. Scroobius Pip, *Thou Shalt Always Kill.* Recorded November 2007. Track 11 on *Angles*, Sunday Best Recordings, compact disc.

Smallcomb, Pam. *I'm Not.* New York: Schwartz & Wade, 2010.

About the Author

Alex Byrne (they/them/theirs) is a Youth Services Librarian in Washington State. They're not great at writing bios. They're not bad at getting toddlers to dance. They're usually around on Twitter @HeofHIShirts. They're not the swiftest at updating their usernames.

Transphobia and Healing in a People-Pleasing Profession: Reflections from a Public Library Employee

Cal the Saprotroph (they/them)

Keywords: burnout, codependency, coming out, accountability, allyship

The interstices of my identities that inform the perspective represented here can be found by reading my bio at the end of this chapter.

In Fall 2018, I realized that I had an abusive relationship with my job. Being the first person to come out publicly as trans at an institution is challenging as it is, but I was also codependent. I derived my sense of worth from being a library employee, and believed the lie for a long time that if I just said my truth in the right way, fawned my way into favor, morphed myself into a palatable, inoffensive, unproblematic, productive, and helpful (and ultimately, unrecognizable) version of myself, that someday I'd be granted dignity, worth, acceptance, even love.[1] To quote

1. This chapter uses "fawning" to refer to a trauma response (or typology) to Complex PTSD, along with fight, flight, and freeze. The term was first coined as a trauma response by Pete Walker in 2013, who provides an accessible definition: "Fawn types seek safety by merging with the wishes, needs and demands of others. They act as if they unconsciously believe that the price of admission to any relationship is the forfeiture of all their needs, rights, preferences and boundaries." Pete Walker, "The 4Fs: A Trauma Typology in Complex PTSD," http://pete-walker.com/fourFs_TraumaTypologyComplexPTSD.htm.

Alok Menon from a moving interview, "It's an elaborate form of begging. It's about saying 'Goddammit, see my humanity[...]!'"[2]

This essay was an extremely messy one to create. I've been up and down, revisited traumatic bullshit I thought I was done with, doubted whether I should share this publicly or not, filled pages with completely unedited and incomprehensible righteous ranting, edited viciously, and re-started and re-envisioned this essay multiple times. My intention in sharing this narrative is to be fully honest with others and with myself, to have my story witnessed, to let others with similar experiences know that they aren't alone, and to connect with other people trying to survive and heal from systemic trauma.

Introspecting on experiences I've had with Public Library System (PLS)[3] is challenging, because I am at once both very much still an employee of the library who daily navigates systemic harm and the ways the library evades responsibility for that harm, and at the same time, on the other side of the worst of that harm in some ways. Writing in this way is my attempt to make meaning out of something that so often feels meaningless. I believe in fungus—in transforming shit into connections and information. But I also believe in accountability. Part of transforming is acknowledging the ingredients you're working with.

What Happened?

Writing about trauma is hard. It requires an incredible amount of effort for the target of mistreatment to dredge up painful memories, to relive trauma in the body and psyche, and to share those experiences in the open. It's even more upsetting to know that this is the only way many people will believe them, and to know that they are making themselves open to scrutiny, gaslighting, rejection, pity, and any number of other

2. Alok Menon, "ALOK: The Urgent Need for Compassion," *The Man Enough Podcast,* podcast audio, July 26, 2021https://www.youtube.com/watch?v=Tq3C9R8HNUQ.

3. I've anonymized the name of the library system I work for with this generic name/acronym as a stand-in.

reactions that are likely to impact how people treat and think of them. It breaks my heart to know that these are the lengths—lengths to which I myself thought I had to go—to feel acceptance or peace. I still have to remind myself daily that I am powerless over what other people think of me, and I become freer the more I remember that. So, I'm sharing my story in a way that feels safe for me right now, and without trying to prove myself. This is one way I'm reclaiming agency and autonomy over my life after being denied these opportunities by the HR Department of PLS where I earn my survival under capitalism.

For the first two years of my employment at PLS, I worked mostly by myself. I spent a lot of time in my own head, worked two jobs, and slowly realized I was not a girl/woman. I started changing my appearance and, without any evidence of trans competence from colleagues, signage, institutional documents, branch displays, or recognition of trans holidays and observances, became hyper-aware that I could not come out without educating nearly every person I interacted with on a daily basis. This resulted in my becoming hypervigilant and over-analytical of the most minor of social interactions.

I started to notice a lot of gendered microaggressions and was bullied via stonewalling by my peers. For example, co-workers went out of their way to effusively compliment me when I dressed femininely, but stayed quiet or ignored me and acted evasive when I dressed masculinely. One co-worker in particular, who held the same entry-level classification as me, gave extremely clipped and dismissive responses to simple questions that I asked about our workflow during the day. The amount of attention she gave other staff in my classification was very different from how little she spoke to me, even casually. It brought me back to the bullying I experienced in elementary school, and I started to doubt my perceptions constantly. Every time I felt insulted, I would ask myself, "Are they just having a bad day and I'm being too sensitive?" "Am I not friendly, approachable, palatable, or 'normal' enough?" The more unsafe and powerless I felt in the face of harm being done to me, the more I attempted to control others' perceptions of my performance and worthiness as an employee. I took every training available to me, gave copious feedback, took on additional work, read through and commented on institutional documents—all as an entry-level employee. A common saying in Co-Dependents Anonymous is "Codependents make great employees." I derived my sense of worth and value from my job performance.

I transferred to escape the discomfort. When I was asked why by curious co-workers, I lied and said it would save me money on transportation (it cost the same). Unfortunately, the new branch I worked at was staffed by people who were just as inept about gender diversity (and sometimes downright hostile towards trans people) as the previous one. I also started substituting across PLS, often working six days a week and not uncommonly working multiple weeks without days off. I talked to everyone and anyone who would engage me about social justice issues, became involved in the union, and started to see the disparate social climates between branches. I discovered allies, met other closeted queer staff, built some confidence, and became increasingly desperate for understanding from my colleagues and the dizzying number of supervisors and administrators who had more power to affect policy than me. I was also working in a toxic retail environment to survive financially, and while I had joy, acceptance, love, and even celebration of my identity working with queer-positive salespeople, it became increasingly painful to go to work at PLS and feel the stark lack of these things. I eventually planned to come out during LGBTQ+ History Month via a Trans Voices display at my home branch.

After I created a display with a colleague (the one colleague at that branch I felt safe enough with to work on this project), and I sent an accompanying "coming out" email, I received a call from HR that a patron had complained about the display to our director, and that an unnamed coworker had shared my email outside of PLS. Nothing came of the complaint or the leaked email, but the fact that it was shared to *anybody* without my consent severely damaged my trust in the library system I had worked so hard for. It damaged my trust in the HR department's processes for amending or preventing interpersonal harm—the library's commitment to upholding the confidentiality of the person who forwarded my email meant that I never knew for certain who had violated my privacy, and without knowing the details of the investigation, my anxious mind ruminated on the worst possible scenarios. It damaged my trust in my direct colleagues—the preservation of (the leaker's, not my) confidentiality meant I suspected everyone. It damaged my trust in the managerial team that did nothing to prevent me from having to work with this person in the future. In short, this incident damaged my trust in the culture of a system that looked away when they saw harm being done. Supervisors and administrators showed that they cared more about their public image and in following written protocols of confidentiality than they did in tangibly making things better for employees targeted for discrimination.

I continued to transfer to different branches, and abuse from my colleagues continued to escalate. I continued to receive micro and macro-aggressions, continued to apologize when I corrected people on my pronouns, and my co-workers continued to undermine my work. I continued to vacillate between firmly insisting to managers (and managers of managers) that I needed help from the library at a policy-level, and I continued to fawn to them and the most egregious abusers, lest I be accused of being a nag or of being too intolerant of other viewpoints. I continued to be told in increasingly non-specific terms that PLS had plans for trans inclusion, but those plans continued to disappoint and miss the point. While I waited for those plans to come to fruition, abusive colleagues continued to work without apparent discipline, and they continued to create hostile environments for both staff and patrons.

Some Emotional Impacts

Exhaustion. Isolation. Growing bitterness and resentment. Self-doubt and gaslighting. Cognitive Paranoia. Burnout. Panic attacks. Deepened codependency.

The effect that these emotional impacts had on me was that my lens narrowed to one of survival. I learned to protect myself by denying and suppressing the immensity of pain I felt—not just from the harm of abusive colleagues, but from the even greater pain of the cavernous silence and hollow language of the people whose job it was to prevent it from happening again. At the lowest point, which lasted several months, I had a minimum of weekly panic attacks on the way to work and in the parking lot. I over-performed my masculinity to (unsuccessfully) curb misgendering.

My patterns of codependency deepened. I attempted to control work relationships by trusting people that I viewed as "queer-safe" or in a position to effect change, far too quickly, and placed unrealistic expectations on them. I bonded with the emotionally supportive people who got me through that time, and then eventually shifted the source of most of my self-worth to gaining the approval of *those* people, again attempting to control others to sate my inner anguish. I was paralyzed by others' view of me, constantly torn between the pride I felt at speaking up for myself and the intense shame that someone might be hurt or think poorly of me if I did so too forcefully.

I became distrustful of everyone, even the people who *could* help and were trying their damnedest to defend me and change library policy. I sank into and became stuck for years in the belief that I was alone and that only I could fix things. I was hyper-critical of people who were helping me, and extremely patient and understanding with the people who stood in my way. In early 2020, I listened to a podcast that named "cognitive paranoia" as a psychological effect of trans-incompetent workplaces on transgender employees.

> JENNICA: [...] we asked transgender employees whether they felt like they were forced to act in a traditionally gendered way or whether they were denied access to the appropriate bathrooms at work or if they were misgendered by co-workers and what we found was that those transgender employees who reported higher levels of this treatment adopted a type of mindset referred to, like you said, as cognitive paranoia and this is where they reported feeling three different things. So they reported feeling more hyper vigilant in their work environment, so you're just being a little more on edge you just can't really relax. They also were more likely to ruminate and have these repetitive thoughts about those

> interactions that they were just experiencing with co-workers. [...] And then they were also more likely to assume that the intentions of their co-workers were more malevolent and sinister.[4]

A chord resonated within me when I heard this. I started to realize that maybe I held unrealistic standards for myself to relax, trust, and be open with my co-workers, even the ones who were willing to fight for me. My fear wasn't something I was imagining and needed to force myself to get over.

Ways I Resisted and Fungal Alchemy

I hate to think of myself as a victim, even if it is sometimes an accurate word to use. Even in the darkest times, I resisted, and I'm grateful to myself and to those who supported me (even when I was painfully myopic about my struggle and experience) for the ways I learned to survive in a system that would never volitionally make room for me. I maintained—and continue to maintain—my dignity by taking my power back and trying to turn shit into meaning in myriad ways, like learning to trust my own perceptions, leaning into the collective strength, experience, and support of PLS employees, and learning to set healthy boundaries with others (and then, with myself).

One small thing that helped me realize my power again was the act of documenting my workplace experiences. After complaining about my experiences to union stewards, they suggested that I start documenting everything, in case I ever needed to build a case to show that I was experiencing a pattern of transphobic behavior. I kept email chains that denied my requests for trans competency and institutional support, staff-wide emails with problematic or questionable language and content, and recorded in a private drive all the times someone said or did messed up shit to me.

---

4. Jennica Webster, "The Gayly Grind," *Nancy,* podcast audio, March 5, 2019, https://www.wnycstudios.org/podcasts/nancy/episodes/nancy-podcast -gayly-grind

Documentation began as an act of self-defense, but as time went on, it became an act of self-affirmation. I stopped wondering if I was just being too sensitive, because the simple act of writing down my experiences somewhere no one else could see them allowed me to stop censoring myself before I could even name what was happening to me. I started trusting myself again. As my body of evidence, my self-confidence, and institutional competency grew, I recorded my experiences with dwindling frequency. I had enough support from my colleagues and direct supervisor that I no longer felt the same need to build my own defense, and I came to trust my gut without having to write anything down. I also learned to trust my gut about which colleagues made me feel safer at work, rather than simply believing those who said that they were allies. I remembered that "ally" is a verb.

Another way I resisted was by talking to anyone who would listen to me about social justice issues during the time that I was working as many shifts as possible to earn a survivable income. Slowly, I started to open up to other branch-level staff about what I was experiencing. I leaned into the camaraderie I felt with colleagues who also felt unsupported, mistreated, and helpless; we corroborated each other's experiences, fought against the siloing and isolation that keeps power in the hands of the few, and broke the silence that allowed system administrators and policies to gaslight us into thinking we were a workplace committed to diversity and fairness. I made friends, shared in righteous anger, and got a fuck of a lot queerer. Over time, it became easier to be frank about what happened to me without making excuses for the people who had harmed me; I became less and less apologetic about how it might make others or PLS "look bad."

For many years, my resistance took the form of appealing to people with power and going through the "proper" channels to change the work culture and environment. Navigating these systems gave me a sharper ability to argue with tact and humility, and a greater fluency in corporate jargon, which I could then translate for other branch-level staff that I would organize with in the future. Now, I know that respectability politics are utter bullshit, and that it's unreasonable to expect a person telling the story of their own trauma and oppression to do so calmly or palatably. I also taught myself to empathize with hurtful people as part of my fawn response/survival skills; I eventually learned to extend this empathy toward myself when I am hurtful, and in doing so I was forced to understand that empathy for others cannot ever be extended if it excuses or downplays the impact of harmful behavior. I cannot have love for myself and others if I allow harm to go without consequence, even if I understand why it happened.

One example of "going through the proper channels" was the crusade to get our communications department to print pronouns on nametags. Some of the more senior staff had language proficiencies printed on their nametags in a size and placement that made sense for pronouns to be, but when I asked the communications staff to do this, they claimed to have discontinued printing language proficiencies for "branding purposes." I used the branch label maker to put my pronouns on my own damned nametag until, years later, they finally started including optional pronoun fields. I continued using my own DIY nametag, though, while I sent back at least three nametags that printed my pronouns so small that anyone reading them would need to be uncomfortably close to my chest. In hindsight, I have to laugh with equal parts of spiteful joy and bemusement when I think about how much work they made for themselves after I had presented them with a reasonable and easy solution years prior.

Throwing myself into developing my professional skills was another way that I worked within the system to protect myself. I took every training and attended every conference I had the means to, both because I wanted to be seen as indispensable, and because it would get me the promotion and subsequent raise that would allow me to work less and reclaim my time. I gained SO MANY professional skills during the time that I was over-performing, and eventually I became so confident in my abilities as a library employee that I felt relaxed enough to choose work that I myself deemed valuable. To this day, I continue to use work resources to develop the kind of skills that I would want regardless of where I work.

With the emotional support of trusted colleagues and friends, as well as some financial freedom, it became easier to set healthy boundaries for myself. I learned that I could say "no" to working without days off or at branches with stressful work environments that would trigger physical symptoms like chronic pain. I stopped giving my energy to work conflicts that I knew through experience were not a good use of my precious skills and resources. I picked my battles. Rather than continually fighting PLS as one angry voice, I shifted my tactics toward building pockets of joy, places of respite, and the connections with my colleagues that would allow us all to live to fight another day, together.

And Now?

After I moved around and tested the climate at branches across the county for about four years, I transferred to a branch where I felt psychologically safer, and where I was better supported professionally, emotionally, and physically (accommodation-wise) in my day-to-day small scale work environment. It wasn't until things started to improve for me at work that I realized how damaging so many of my experiences had been and how much energy I had wasted trying to convince others of my right to dignity. Joining the Trans and Gender Diverse LIS Network in 2021 and working on this essay were also instrumental in this realization; I didn't think that I could ask for greater-than-basic trans competency from my institution until I connected with other gender diverse LIS workers and got out of my silo.

Blessedly, this realization freed me from looking for healing in the place where I'd been harmed. I have better workplace boundaries, namely that my well-being will always come before my job. I am starting the process of healing from the ways I give my power and sense of self to people I know will hurt me, and I am learning what it can look like to seek my own approval first.

I continue to spend the bulk of my energy at work attempting to make lasting cultural and institutional change, but I now do so as one of many on a library-sanctioned team, with my personal focus shifting to address the manifestations of white supremacy culture in myself and in the library. Hostility toward gender diversity still exists at PLS, but a more accepting staff culture, stronger organizational response to discriminatory behavior, and years of therapy have allowed me to move out of survival mode and stop feeling like I have to put all of my effort into defending my existence. The longer I work with others, the surer I am that no one person can effect change the way I had been attempting to do. I learn more, do more, and persevere when I share the struggle with folks who have different tools and experience than I do.

With all that said, the struggle continues.

The seedling of this essay was an article I wrote for the PLS newsletter in 2021, in recognition of Trans Day of Visibility (TDOV). I wrote a very short, very abbreviated, and very generous account of the PLS's improvement around trans inclusion since I came out. I felt fairly confident about this—until praise started rolling in. I got dozens of responses from people I didn't feel particularly close to—including several managers—thanking me for my "strength and bravery" and saying how much they enjoyed my piece. My autonomic response was swift and visceral. My skin *crawled*. I was already deeply uncomfortable when people gave me praise and recognition, but particularly so after sharing this story. Why was I being thanked for something that should never have happened to me in the first place? Was I being thanked for my ability to endure abuse calmly and palatably?

Mostly, I felt sick to my stomach because I realized how untrue my TDOV piece was. So much had been left out, and I worried that I'd given the impression that everything was all better now. It wasn't all better. Just because I'm not still bleeding doesn't mean there's not a wound still in need of healing. I had hurt people I loved, including myself, as a result of the stress caused by repeated institutional failings that PLS has had *years* to rectify if they were to take cues from peer library systems with regard to trans inclusion. I was a stranger to myself, and am only now starting to realize the extent of that estrangement in therapy and in Co-Dependents Anonymous. Even after finding a community of colleagues that I truly trust, I still struggle with feeling alone; most of us are all too tired and too afraid of failure, of being labeled difficult, of having professional opportunities denied to us, and we are too burnt out to be able to organize effectively. Even after management changed, after the long-time staff unwilling to change their behavior quit PLS, even after hiring practices were amended to mitigate bias and more gender-diverse staff were hired, I am still bitter and resentful when people point out how far PLS has come, particularly when people thank me for continuing to work to improve the library's equity, diversity, and inclusion policies in spite of having endured traumatic work experiences.

That TDOV piece and the ensuing recognition pointed me toward the realization that progress that people make institutionally—not just at the library, but in any institution, including the colonial project that is the United States—cannot create meaningful or substantive healing without first acknowledging and addressing the harm that was done. The piece felt dishonest, because the people who thanked me were complicit in the culture that left me feeling alone, afraid, ineffectual, and trapped. People with privilege have learned many ways to shirk responsibility, including focusing on the positives to deny their participation in creating the damage in the first place. Sharing the abbreviated and palatable version of my story in the way that I did was another iteration of my fawn response, and the discomfort that came afterward helped me realize what I really wanted by doing so.

What Does It Take to Heal?

After re-opening the library in 2021 following closures due to COVID-19, a patron said some garden-variety homophobic shit to me about the rainbow face mask I was wearing while on the desk. I very quickly told him that he couldn't talk like that in the library, chalked it up to "not the worst I've dealt with," took a break to self-soothe, wrote up an incident report, and let it go. I was shocked when, less than eight hours later, I received an email response from department heads that the patron would be banned from the library for six months due to harassment of staff. I had never seen this swift or severe of a punishment for bigotry, and cite it as clear evidence that PLS is starting to implement policies that uphold the values they claim to have with regard to supporting marginalized staff. Changes *are* happening.

At the same time, I want more. Every time I see evidence of real, actual institutional change, the hungrier I become for real justice and repair. It's much easier to place consequences on patrons that administrators will never have to see in person than it is to hold themselves and their immediate colleagues accountable. If I heard them say "We hear you, and we want to do better," that might be a start, but I still don't think I'd believe it.

I want to hear from each person responsible, "I made excuses for abusive and transphobic staff, as well as the people who protected them. That was not acceptable then just as it is not acceptable now." I want to hear "I didn't take you seriously, and it caused you to suffer needlessly." I want to hear "You should never have had to work so hard to advocate for your own dignity and safety." I want to hear, simply and sincerely, "I am sorry for the things I did."

What I really want is true accountability. I want them to acknowledge—publicly and formally—what has happened under their flawed leadership, because to not acknowledge it is to pretend like it never happened; this is another form of gaslighting that re-opens the wounds I and so many of my colleagues are still recovering from. I want the security of knowing that this will never, ever happen to anyone else at PLS again. It can't and will never be enough to simply change behavior and policy without acknowledging the harm that administrators and policy-makers have caused; the progress that we make today will be tenuous and easily swept away at the slightest threat.

When I sit and imagine what this would look like, though, I realize that as much as I want apologies, I won't wait to get them before I start healing. Besides, so often when people apologize to me, it's to absolve themselves of guilt rather than to actually make conditions for me or other trans people any better. So, I'm not writing this to appeal to systems, or to the people hoarding power. My story continues to be true and I will continue to heal, regardless of whether my abusers ever take responsibility for their actions and inactions. I'm writing this to be seen, to "comfort the disturbed and disturb the comfortable,"[5] and to connect with other people who still suffer silently or alone—you are absolutely not alone, and your story deserves to be heard, too. I write to destroy, to connect, to share information, to transform, and to provide nutrients for the people that need it.

Bibliography

Koinuma, Ari. "Art Should Comfort the Disturbed and Disturb the Comfortable." *Ari Koinuma* (blog), March 2, 2017. https://arikoinuma.com/blog/2017/03/art-should-comfort-the-disturbed-and-disturb-the-comfortable/.

Menon, Alok. "ALOK: The Urgent Need for Compassion". *The Man Enough Podcast.* Podcast audio, July 26, 2021. https://www.youtube.com/watch?v=Tq3C9R8HNUQ.

Walker, Pete. "The 4Fs: A Trauma Typology in Complex PTSD." http://pete-walker.com/fourFs_TraumaTypologyComplexPTSD.htm.

Webster, Jennica. "The Gayly Grind". *Nancy.* Podcast audio. March 5, 2019. https://www.wnycstudios.org/podcasts/nancy/episodes/nancy-podcast-gayly-grind.

About the Author

Cal the Saprotroph is a white, queer, non-binary transmasculine millennial from a working class/former military family. They have worked in libraries for twelve years and used to tape hand-written call numbers on their picture books as a child. Cal the Saprotroph lives with chronic pain, mental health challenges (including neurodivergence), and patterns of

5. Ari Koinuma, "Art Should Comfort the Disturbed and Disturb the Comfortable," Ari Koinuma (blog), March 2, 2017. https://arikoinuma.com/blog/2017/03/art-should-comfort-the-disturbed-and-disturb-the-comfortable/.

codependency. They invest a lot of energy in personal healing (mental, physical, and emotional), and do their best to apply those lessons toward community, societal, and institutional healing. They are in the recovery program of Co-Dependents Anonymous and are a divine and flawed human being. They currently believe in the revolutionary power of mushrooms to heal the world, love in everything, transformative justice, and not taking anything too seriously.

Isosceles Triangle Out of the Box

Mondo Vaden (he/they)

Keywords: intersectionality, DeafBlackTrans, gender euphoria, DEI

Part 1: The Before

Since a very young age, I have been a reader, and everything that I learned about life was a direct result of voracious literary consumption. I was also diagnosed from age six with profound sensorineural hearing loss.[1] This has resulted in my developing ideas about masculinity and femininity directly from books. I was not able to gain information from auditory hints like my peers, who had access to media and society without the need for constant accommodations. I didn't know captioning was available until later in my childhood. Once I did, I was able to gain further information about the world from media, although I still missed out on tones and nuances in language. I'm still not entirely aware of how much I miss in relation to context clues and socialization.

I was often confused by what was expected of me. As someone assigned female at birth, I was supposed to be a young lady, a princess, a perfect daughter, but I was quietly struggling with constant confusion because these feminine archetypes did not feel quite right to me. Juxtaposed with what I saw in the media about my assigned gender, I

1. Profound sensorineural hearing loss means unable to detect sounds quieter than 90dB. Things need to be at least as loud as a lawn mower for me to hear them without a hearing aid. I identify as Deaf and Hard-of-Hearing with English and Sign bilingual skills.

resonated much more with the teen boy heartthrobs of the 1990s more than the graceful, lady-like heroines I was told to emulate. Culturally, my parents (a martial artist and a law enforcement officer) were both very traditional and conservative, and my perception of their views on gender had an effect on me. In addition, as a child of divorce, I had a different view of femininity and masculinity. Words such as "strong" or "sensitive" were not inherently connected to gender for me. I saw those societally gendered traits as being equally available to anyone, male or female, and I chafed at being held to feminine standards.

My life experience is not unique in having a blend of influences and information regarding gender and sexuality. Cisheteronormativity is a big reason why many trans people have a long journey to realizing they're trans or otherwise queer. Trying to fit in a square box when you're a triangle is often a losing battle until you learn to accept that you're a triangle and find environments that are supportive of triangles. In a cisgender dominant world, when I didn't know trans people existed, I didn't know I existed. As such, I didn't know I was trans until well into my adulthood. Throughout my life, I measured myself against cisgender standards of behavior and appearance, which I always fell woefully short of reaching. To this day, trans people, binary and nonbinary, share this fight to be acknowledged and have their gender identity recognized and seen.

My strong positive memories of libraries started in childhood, when I would visit family during the summer. They would take me and the other kids in the family to the library to partake in summer reading events, where we would have a free meal and check out books to read. Those times were a big wonder for me, because I would get to choose a free book to keep. It was one of the few times where I could choose whatever book I wanted, and the book selection was not segregated by gender or the concept of boy books and girl books. I also remember winning a summer reading team game against a boy because I knew more about cars than he did; I carried this event in my memories as a badge of honor, as proof of my masculinity. This experience was the start of libraries feeling like a safe space for me, and I consider it fundamental in my personal development of associating libraries with being a force for good.

In high school, I ended up spending a lot of time at the library as a library intern. I would shelve books, help check them in, and work on displays, as well as chatting up my fellow students about books. It was very similar to a typical library assistant job. I was always in the stacks and looking at all the science books, with a particular focus on the ones about biology and human sexuality. I was having a lot of feelings in my own body that I didn't have terminology for at the time, and I couldn't accurately apply what I was reading to my own life. The human sexuality section at the library covered much more than our sex ed classes. Because I attended an all-girl Catholic school, we were not well informed on sex education. I remember classes focusing on the perilous and forbidden nature of premarital sex and abortion, and the complete erasure of same-gender relationships. This dogma carried into school policy, where an abortion was grounds for expulsion, and two girls would not be allowed to attend prom together. There was little to no discussion in relation to queerness. We were taught that marriage was exclusively between a man and a woman. It didn't help that I lacked accommodations that could have potentially allowed me the comfort to ask more questions in class. (My accommodations were a seat near the front of the class and extended time for test taking.) The implications of this subliminal programming on my mind didn't really hit me until later, as I reflected on my own gender journey.

My experience supplementing my high school's sex ed curriculum with books on biology and sexuality from the library motivated me to pursue a biology degree in college. There, I spent my free time poring over the available articles and research in my dorm room for insight on queerness. What *is* gender? What *is* sexuality? Why do people feel different ways from each other? While navigating my grueling major, I spent more time than ever trying to figure out the mysteries of gender. I couldn't figure out why I felt like I could be a better man than my peers and why I was so determined to prove it. The final paper for my

English writing class was an attempt to look at gender scientifically and to explore the differences between men and women. I look back on it and laugh, because that paper was so binary and still gave me no real answers! My accommodations had finally upgraded to Communication Access Realtime Translation (CART), a service where a person transcribed my lessons, and I still knew nothing further. I was also working in my university library at the time. This again allowed me access and time to explore the library and again pore over the available books relating to human sexuality.

A few years after I graduated college with a BS in biology, I applied for graduate school to pursue a Masters of Library and Information Science (MLIS) and a career in medical librarianship. As a result of a series of deeply traumatic physical and sexual experiences, including abusive relationships and an ableist and racist work environment, my mental health had declined substantially. My tenuous emotional state, coupled with not getting into the school I applied to, led me to pursue an Associate of Science in Library Science at a local community college in an attempt to boost my GPA. As part of this education, I worked as a volunteer intern for a medical library and greatly enjoyed the experience. Eventually, I realized that my pursuit of medical librarianship was based on a desire to use my biology degree, and that my real goals of pursuing clarity of self and empowerment for all through information science were just under the surface. I eventually began working for my local library system as a volunteer helping assist staff with programs, then became a shelver focused on getting the books out and creating displays. I worked my way up to becoming a library assistant in title, mirroring my high school intern position but with a much greater range of responsibilities. I was able to create my own programs and connect with my patrons, while advocating on equity, diversity, inclusion, and accessibility committees for changes designed to make library policies more inclusive. I continued to learn about myself, reading anything I could get my hands on that might get me closer to understanding, closer to things making sense. Then, in 2019, everything changed.

Part 2: The After

That year heralded my realization that I was trans nonbinary. I recognized that I deserved to live my life as ME, beyond the limitations of other people's expectations. My self-actualization went on to deepen and enrich my understanding of and love for myself. My self-advocacy skills grew.

After coming out in my personal life, I felt that it was time to do the same at work; I felt increasingly stifled by being called exclusively by she/her pronouns there, especially now that I knew that I was experiencing gender dysphoria. I began wearing more masculine work clothes and eventually I let my immediate managers and coworkers know in a mass email that I would be using he/they pronouns going forward. They respected my pronouns and they were very supportive of my right to be out at work.

Although my gender identity was accepted at work, I experienced discrimination from upper management around receiving pay benefits for my bilingual usage of American Sign Language (ASL). I had applied to get a five-percent pay increase for my use of ASL on the job when I was first hired in 2018. I was finally tested nearly three years later, in late 2020 (a process which has taken under a month for my spoken language peers), with an organization I had suggested back in 2018. Due to systemic ignorance of nonverbal languages, and against the recommendations of our union, the Human Resource Director, with the support of the CEO, declined both my five-percent bilingual pay increase and back pay for the extensive bilingual work I had already done. Despite a conversational standard for employees whose bilingualism was in spoken languages, they wanted me to have a test result similar to that of an interpreter, which was not made clear to me until four months after submitting my results to our Human Resources department. Despite already serving the needs of our Deaf and Hard of Hearing patrons, my bilingual skills were undervalued compared to spoken languages. My organization had effectively used me to develop a testing process that would discriminate against any future Deaf employees who were bilingual in English and ASL. They had not had a Deaf employee pursue bilingual pay prior to me, and their mistreatment of my situation makes me think that they are unlikely to get any others.

These conflicts compounded my mental health issues and made me question my experiences, especially once the library made an effort to hire an attorney to prove that they were not being discriminatory. Was this because I'm Black and libraries are, by nature, centered on whiteness, with accompanying ideas of propriety? Was this because I'm Deaf, and due to being deprived from learning ASL during peak language acquisition years, my usage of sign was not considered professional enough by hearing people who had no framework of understanding prior to my self-advocacy?[2] Was this because my neurodivergence affects how I operate in a way upper management does not understand? Or was this because I'm trans and they just don't want to pay me because I make them uncomfortable, and they're trying to push me and my ideas out? These questions and more formed in my mind. The more I talked to my colleagues and peers, the more I was confused. I couldn't understand why I was being made to jump through hoops for years in a process that takes less than a month for my hearing peers. The social difficulties I faced due to language deprivation and other components of my disabilities made it difficult for me to determine who to trust. I no longer knew where the line was drawn between paranoia and actual discrimination. I could not understand why I could be paid to use my verbal voice to communicate and to express needed insights to this system as the only visible Deaf employee, but could not be paid for using my nonverbal language and lived experience. In order for me to meet their criteria, I would have had to go back to school for ASL, and the library had already established that they did not provide tuition reimbursement

2. I and many other Deaf and Hard of hearing adults were mainstreamed in hearing schools, and the onus was on learning to speak. Due to systemic oralism, many of us use Pidgin Signed English (PSE) and/or Signed Exact English (SEE) in addition to ASL, and we do not sign at an interpreter level without extensive training due to missing the linguistic window in childhood that would have made native fluency easier.

for language learning. As I was already in school for my Masters of Library and Information Science (MLIS), I did not have time to start an additional program anyway.

I began to wonder whether the marginalized identities that informed and influenced my uniqueness were making me a target. I was starting to doubt that I was ever going to feel safe and okay in my own Black trans disabled body. I found it to be an increasing struggle to remain mentally well, because I wasn't sure if I had a place at my job, and I no longer had the support of my birth family. Communication and socializing during the pandemic were impossible, and my mental health was beginning to be impacted by the treatment I was experiencing since HR also was responsible for my accommodations. I considered going back in the closet because the stress was becoming too much, but I became determined to survive the pandemic and live my truth, no matter how uncomfortable people might be with the impactful discoveries I was making about myself.

At the beginning of 2021, I got a massive shock when I discovered that a particularly virulent transphobic book that questioned the humanity of AFAB trans people like me was part of the library collection. I had to sit with this and evaluate it on a personal and professional level. How did this book get on our shelves? Why did we request it, and why were there so many copies? How could I get it off the shelves without stirring up the timeless censorship debate? What could I do to protect trans kids by preventing their parents from receiving inaccurate information from a library resource that denied their personhood? How could I, as a trans library staff member, navigate the fact that this book existed? How could I avoid taking the existence of this book personally when it represented all my worst fears about the ways my family and other people view me, in the secular, religious, and political spheres?

Despite the concerns of myself and other staff members, our organization argued to keep this book on shelves. They neglected to inform me, the staff member who initiated and pursued this conversation, that this incident was deeply impactful on many levels in our organization. They went on to include this incident in their application for a national award. I received no named credit for my contribution to this, internally or externally, and my individual work and its impact was credited to the generic term "Public Services Front Line Staff." Soon after, I realized that my organization needed to develop a deeper understanding of and more empathy for intersectional trans issues after hearing a horror story about a Black trans woman who was harassed by another library employee for using the women's restroom. In conjunction with my library's Equity, Diversity, and Inclusion team, some coworkers and I began to develop a Radical Gender Advocacy training and discussion.[3] We planned for this training to use my own lived experiences as well as literary excerpts as tools to help facilitate discussion about inclusive practices. Unfortunately, this training never took place, as I was removed from the committee after going on medical leave. I began to realize that my work and self-advocacy as a Black, trans, disabled person was being used for clout by my administration, rather than to spur the radical changes I hoped for to support our marginalized communities. As I grew conscious of this, I began forming connections with other trans and nonbinary coworkers and built a community outside of work that was dedicated to making such radical changes a reality.

My experiences made me realize that, as library staff, we need to create and develop our roles in community care for our patrons. There are so many people, amongst both library workers and patrons, experiencing multiple forms of marginalization while having trouble finding support. I know that using my voice and ability to research could be useful in support of those whose lives are impacted by intersectional marginalization and this something I can do for my community. I am capable of inclusive, intersectionality-informed digital librarianship. I feel like I can breathe, now that I know my focus, and my drive, and my *why*. I do believe that change isn't something that can be carried out by any one person.

I do not know many people who are Deaf, Black, and trans. I do not know any other people who are Deaf, Black, trans, and working in

3. Radical Gender Advocacy is the act of challenging the dominant mindset in support of those who are marginalized by their gender.

libraries. I don't know what the future holds, but since coming out, it has finally begun to feel like I have one. I hope to help clear the way for other people marginalized on multiple fronts to find their way forward, and to inspire those in positions of privilege to advocate for inclusion, accessibility, and equity so that people like me have a chance at being who we are. I want people to see that it's possible and to see that changing the world isn't as unattainable as we think, and to see that, by living loudly, we can save the world a little bit every day.

I hope to be an inspiration for people to live that loudly.

Epilogue

One day, I was working the front service desk when a young teen came up to me. This person smiled, and asked, "What are your pronouns?" I said, "Well today my pronouns are "she," but most days I use "he/they"!

The teen's jaw dropped. "I use 'she/they' but my partner uses all the pronouns!"

It took everything in me not to cry behind my mask as my heart exploded with complicated emotion.

Like me! There are non-binary teens out there like me! There are non-binary teens out there in 2021 with accepting family and using all the pronouns! There are non-binary teens who use the library and know their librarian is non-binary too! The fact that this teen comes in with their family and makes a point of saying hi to me and asking my pronouns fills me with gratitude. We need real world representation of a world where people get to be themselves, even if it's outside of the binary, outside of cishetero standards of respectability.

About the Author

Mondo Vaden (he/they) is a poet, activist, and DeafBlackTrans Intersectional Librarian by day, and drag king Mondo Millions by night. He spends his free time gardening and dancing. He is fortunate to live in his favorite city with his loving girlfriend and dog.

Transgender Circulation Blues: Service Positions in Librarianship and Transphobia

Remy Biggs

Keywords: circulation, management, community service, and social justice

To start, I'd like to give my frame of reference: I am a white, gender-nonconforming neutrois lesbian with multiple disabilities, both physical and neurodevelopmental. I have medically transitioned (have had top surgery, take testosterone); I "pass" about 50/50 male and female—even though I consider myself genderless.[1]

I worked in circulation and reference in central and northwestern New York for the better part of three years. Lots of librarians dread it—I happened to love it. Many do not understand that circulation work is just as much a service job as it is a "library" job—circ workers interface with the public to an extent that interiorized librarians do not, or at least not to the same extent. As a circulation librarian, your job is intrinsically tied to the immediate needs and wants of the people who come to see you.

1. I put "pass" in scare quotes because I think the concept is frankly arbitrary and unhelpful most of the time. However, since the subject in this article is interacting with cis people, I feel it's something I need to bring up. I use the term "pass" rather than "perceive" or a similar verb because in my gender presentation in professional situations, I frequently take that binary understanding and represent myself accordingly. To me, that subject is not centered around how I'm perceived or read as, which is passive. It's about the image I specifically perform while in professional spaces, which is male roughly half the time and female the other half or so. I feel the distinction is important, because by focusing on the cisgender gaze and using passive verbs, I feel it ends up objectifying something and removing my agency from an image that I very much take an active role in cultivating.

The best thing about this role is having your finger on the pulse of the community, and being a face that people recognize. The worst thing about this role, in my experience, is *also* that you are the face of the library for all intents and purposes. As much as you are beholden to the expectations of your library, you are also beholden to the expectations—to some degree—of your clientele. What does this have to do with being transgender? Well, to be visibly trans is always a fraught experience; to be visibly trans and in a position of servicing others only amplifies that.[2] This is to say that being a trans person working in a front-facing position at a library presents its own issues, and was the ultimate reason that I had to quit my circulation job.

I had to quit not because of the *transphobia*—I experience it nearly every day and in all sorts of contexts. I quit because the structures in place at the libraries de-prioritized the kind of assistance I needed and relied specifically on carceral solutions that centered police presence, which invariably made things worse for everyone involved. I don't feel like it's particularly constructive for me to center this piece on the traumas I have experienced as a front-facing employee, so that's not what I'm going to do; I'm writing this specifically in order to give cisgender circulation managers an idea of what they should do better—marginalized people working circulation already know the different ways that people can act poorly, but maybe managers and supervisors don't understand how they abet or perpetuate that kind of thinking based on the "protective" actions they take (or don't take).

Much of what I dealt with was micro-aggressions: comments or behavior that were indirectly transphobic, and/or said from a position of ignorance. Most of the time, it is really easy to divert or de-escalate with someone who just doesn't know better—injecting the correct terminology into your response is usually welcome, and rare are the people who will ignore or behave in a hostile way when learning a new word that they didn't know before. Like any other type of cultural competency,

2. To be "visibly trans" is something that will vary situationally; it's important to be aware that based on other factors about a person's appearance, demeanor, or background, their gender may be policed by others more or less.

this is also just something that needs to be felt out on a person-by-person basis. Typically, barriers to assistance were ensconced into the architecture and hierarchy of the library itself—when asking for help, circulation supervisors were "a shout away," but typically stayed in their office across the building and *away* from the situation.

It is necessary to understand that it is, frankly, impossible to completely educate the transphobia out of most people. *I* am still unlearning decades of transphobic indoctrination, and I am trans—for people who do not have that vantage point, it is even more difficult; not impossible, but difficult. This is not to say that education is a lost cause, but more that gendered expectations of others are so normalized and so commonplace that, from the perspective of a small public library, it would be tantamount to trying to singlehandedly teach your community about the falsehoods of Newtonian physics.

I say all of this because, while you cannot fix your *community* (meaning it is impossible to shield your transgender coworkers from transphobia from your patrons), you *can* change your library. You *can* change your work environment. Like most problems in librarianship, the solution is found somewhere within collaboration, open communication, respect, and solidarity. It is going to look different for every community, for every library, and for every circulation environment.

Above all, what circulation heads need to know is this: if a front-facing employee comes to you with concerns about how patron(s) react (or may react) to their gender presentation, you should do several things. First, you must not dismiss those concerns. It is exceedingly difficult for the average trans person to speak to authority figures about things of this nature—if it has reached the point where they are asking you for help, it has already probably happened enough to affect their life on a regular basis.

The second thing is understanding that calling or using the police or security detail is not the fix that it seems. At the height of it, we had a few patrons who would come in to harass myself and other marginalized circ workers, so one of my supervisors suggested that a police/security detail be put in front of the desk whenever I was on staff. This produced an even more negative effect: not only were fewer people coming up to the circulation desk whenever I was around, but these officers were a) not necessarily trained in de-escalation, only confrontation, and b) due to the history of police violence against those marginalized by our society (in my case, transgender people), this just made things far worse for my mental health. Usually, the only thing that's really needed is more open communication, and to be flanked by two people armed to the teeth made that communication almost completely impossible.

The third and final thing you need to do is sit down with this person and determine a plan of action if transphobic situations transpire. It can be as simple as keeping your door open. It is variable depending upon what kind of people are in your community as much as it is variable on the person who needs the support—and for what reasons.

Like any other issue related to library management, taking care of your workers is just as important as taking care of your patrons. Circulation management in particular is made complex by the focus and continual attention of the public. Public attention for transgender people is frequently a mixed bag, in that the hypervisibility that is afforded to trans people can sometimes cause escalated tensions and, in worst cases, violence. It is important to be aware that while you cannot educate every single person who comes walking through your library's door, you *can* put safety plans in place in order to help your trans employees when things get uncomfortable. When any marginalized employee is facing harassment, it is important to not dismiss those concerns, to not over-rely on carceral or escalatory practices like police presence, and to maintain an open and supportive line of communication with your employees.

About the Author

Remy Biggs is an early career librarian and historian living and working in Rochester, NY. Remy's life as a librarian is focused mainly around disability advocacy and accessibility in libraries—some of xer projects involved creating accessibility kits for students at Syracuse University with neurodevelopmental disabilities to use at the library, and working with Project ENABLE to create content for training public librarians to assist patrons with disabilities. Xe is currently creating an accessibility literacy guide for another institute at Syracuse University.

Call Me by My Pronouns (and I'll Call You by Yours)

Ari Mahrer (they/them/he/him)

Keywords: nonbinary, pronouns, public libraries, presentation, transmasculine

In May of 2016, I was a twenty-two-year-old lesbian peering over the precipice that marked the end of my undergraduate education and my free fall into adulthood, equipped only with my impending gender identity crisis and a creative writing degree clutched in my sweaty hands.

I had come out as bi many years earlier, until it became clear without my having to announce it that "lesbian" was a much more fitting label—at least out of those I was familiar with. I was a girl (as far as I knew), and I was only attracted to girls, therefore I was a lesbian. Fine. Even once I began meeting people in adulthood who identified outside of the binaries I was used to (gay/straight, man/woman), it took a long time before I even considered the possibility that there was more going on with me than homosexuality.

I do sometimes wonder if part of me had long suspected, maybe even at one point known, that I never was and was never going to be a girl or woman, at least the way it's long been defined in Western culture. But even if that were true, I completely lacked the knowledge and vocabulary to even begin to understand it.

At the very least, I knew it had something to do with my profound aversion, which bordered on phobia, of my breasts, which I nearly disfigured my spine trying to hide when they first appeared during the hellish years of puberty. I knew it had something to do with the fact that, as a small child, I felt intensely drawn to and fascinated by, not just certain boys in my life, but also boys in my favorite movies, TV shows, and computer games—Harry Potter, Calvin from Calvin and Hobbes, and Pajama Sam, to name a few. They all shared a quality of boyishness that stirred something inside of me, some recognition of my own self.

When I think back to myself in early childhood and the way I related to these characters and to my friends who were boys, I am able to recall a truth I knew as a child, but which became obscured over many years of gendered socialization: I had a clear and distinct longing to *be* them.

But, like many people, even those raised in liberal, progressive areas like me, I was hardly aware that transgender and gender diverse people even existed until adulthood. Even then, my understanding was extremely limited. Transgender to me still existed in a binary frame; it meant people such as Laverne Cox or Caitlyn Jenner, women who were assigned male at birth. And trans men may as well have not existed at all. I had never seen one on TV or in movies, let alone in real life. For most of my life, I truly felt that transgender people had nothing to do with me.

But to be transgender means so much more. To be transgender, I learned not all that long ago, means to identify as any gender identity aside from, or in addition to, the one assigned to you at birth. Given the complex nature of human consciousness, it makes all the sense in the world that someone would not identify with one of the two narrow and prescriptive gender labels. The word "transgender" is an umbrella term that includes not only binary trans folk, but nonbinary genders such as agender, genderfluid, genderqueer, bigender, or several at once, though not everyone who falls under these labels self-identifies as trans. For hundreds of years, Western culture has denied and erased gender diverse identities in favor of a strict gender binary, so it comes as no surprise that many trans and gender diverse folks spend much of their lives without this knowledge and without a community to learn from.

According to Gender Wiki, the word transmasculine is "a term used to describe transgender people who generally were assigned female at birth and identify with a masculine gender identity to a greater extent than with a feminine gender identity. Usually transmasculine people try to appear stereotypically masculine in terms of their gender expression in order to create social recognition of their dominant masculine identity."[1]

I can't remember how I discovered this word. But when I did, something inside me woke up. *That* was me. Or, at least it was more me than anything else I knew at that point.

Around the time I began learning about transmasculinity and gender diversity, I was approaching my college graduation and the B.A. degree in creative writing I had spent four years working towards. It was time to get a job, and I decided I was far too anxious of a person to try and make it as a "writer" (to be honest, I didn't even really know what that would look like). So, I began spending nights poring over lists of careers I was desperately unprepared and unqualified for, from occupational therapist to statistician to cartographer, settling briefly on one before zipping manically to another. I can't remember exactly how I ended up landing on librarian, but I do remember the calm that settled over me when I did.

Looking back, I think I decided to pursue work in libraries because to me, a person who benefits from multiple privileges, they felt safe, like a place I was allowed to just *be*. But, like many others, before working in a library I had a stereotypical and inaccurate understanding of what it meant to be a librarian. I had internalized the perception of librarianship as a highly feminized profession, and I briefly worried I wasn't "librarianly" enough to pull it off, struggling to picture myself flitting about the stacks in a tight bun and glasses.

But of far more concern was the thought that pursuing librarianship would be foolish and impractical; that I would be beginning a career at an institution on the brink of obsolescence, breathing its last gasp, forsaken after years of begging the world to love it as it once had. I went online to get a sense of the practicality of a master's in library and information science, and nearly got cold feet after reading dozens of grim prophecies from doomsayers and pages of testimonies from

1. "Transmasculine," Gender Wiki, https://gender.wikia.org/wiki/Transmasculine#.

overworked library staff driven to the edge by chronic budget cuts. It's true—libraries are often underfunded and the challenge of keeping up with an increasingly digitized world is ever present. But it's clear that there is a place for libraries. And even still, I hoped that libraries had a place for me.

I ended up applying for a part-time library assistant position at a library I had grown up going to. I had never had a real, "adult" interview before—my previous jobs included scooping ice cream and babysitting—and I realized I didn't have anything to wear. I had just moved back home after college, and my mom kindly offered me access to her wardrobe. I begrudgingly chose the least frilly blouse I could find, some slacks, and a pair of black flats. I hadn't dressed in such feminine clothing since *maybe* high school, and I felt so uncomfortable and ridiculous I wanted to crawl out of my skin.

After years of working part-time in various public libraries and resenting the highly gendered sartorial expectations of the American workplace, I eventually landed a job as the Circulation Supervisor at a small public library in Marin County, California. Marin is one of the wealthiest counties in the U.S., and it is also where I happened to grow up. It isn't exactly known for its diversity, so by the time I began transitioning, I had already gotten used to feeling a certain degree of isolation. Still, I've been profoundly lucky to have been treated with kindness and acceptance, both by my coworkers and by our patrons. That privilege is why I eventually felt safe enough to transition, beginning with changes like wearing clothes exclusively from the "men's" section—button-down shirts and baggy-ish corduroys—to bigger changes like cutting my hair, and eventually getting top surgery.

By the time of the surgery, I had begun thinking of myself as non-binary, but hadn't made any changes to my name or pronouns—at least not officially. My first step was to sneak my pronouns into my work email signature, which ended up being a sort of testing ground for trying on different pronouns to see what fit. First, I wrote "Pronouns: All", thinking it was a clever but ultimately benign way to signal my gender nonconformity. As a nonbinary person, I figured people could use any pronoun for me and technically they wouldn't be wrong (although this is certainly not true for all nonbinary folks; it's just how I felt at the time). This shifted to she/her/they/them, which still gave everyone permission to change nothing but was a bit more decisive, and eventually just they/them.

I wonder if anyone tracked this progression. I never said anything to anyone. I figured, I'll just leave that there, and people will do what they will. But I wasn't ready to make an announcement. In all honesty, I didn't want to feel like I was inconveniencing anyone, and I didn't feel entirely sure myself. And as I've learned, there isn't much built-in space for this process of self-discovery; people are expected to accept their assigned gender without question. I mean, c'mon, first the gays, and now this?! We gender nonconformers were, to put it lightly, not part of the plan as conceived by the architects of Western culture.

I am acutely aware of the fact that I benefit greatly from the privileges awarded to white people, and that this certainly influences my experience in the world and in libraries. I am fortunate that the worst I have to endure is the sort of amusing experience of watching a well-intentioned person tripping over themselves as they become visibly bewildered by my appearance, realizing their framework for categorizing people into man or woman is failing them. Several times I have been called both "sir" and "ma'am" within the space of one interaction, because the person is unable to land decisively on a gender for me. But this is the worst it gets. Overall, in work and in life, I am given the space to continue my journey in peace, even if that means leaving one day with tits and coming back two weeks later without them. I truly am grateful for this.

Still, I waited a long time before explicitly requesting that my coworkers change the pronouns they use to refer to me from "she/her" to "they/them." There are several reasons for this, among them the fact that I still felt (and feel to this day) very much in the thick of my journey of self-discovery. But at the root of my hesitation was the fear of inconveniencing not just other people but myself. I dreaded the thought of being in a position of needing to correct people when they inevitably used the wrong pronouns, of doing the work of finding a balance between self-advocacy and letting things go. I didn't want to put myself in a position of being misgendered and having well-intentioned people struggle to refer to and interact with me, but I have found that as long as people are able to use language they're comfortable with to refer to me, I can present however I like and it changes nothing. They can still place me in a category that they're familiar with. Only once I insist on the words are they challenged to perceive things in a different way, perceive me a different way, and only then can I feel seen. So, I insisted on the words.

I spoke to my coworkers individually, letting them know of my new pronouns and briefly explaining the reason for the change (part of a reckoning with my gender identity, etc.) and letting them know I'd be happy to answer any questions they might have. I had planned for it to be a short and simple request but found myself quickly veering off-script before they even had a chance to respond. I ended up almost apologizing as if I were asking too much of them, saying things like, "I know it's a big change" and prematurely excusing them for their inevitable slip ups. Why was it so hard to just let them know? I didn't feel ashamed, so what was this impulse to put myself down?

The process of incorporating unfamiliar language—particularly when it has to do with identity, such as the singular "they/them" as pronouns—into our vocabulary is bound to be challenging and uncomfortable, sometimes even painful, for many people, including those of us driving the change. But it's a necessary process. For a growing number of people, myself included, "they/them" are the words that help us to feel seen. For me, using these pronouns allows me to reject, explicitly and formally, being placed in a binary, in a framework that I do not and have never consented to. They allow me to not be a woman without being a man. And right now, they feel like a way to move closer towards the me I have always been.

This act of becoming, of wrestling with something as fundamental to identity as gender, has been deeply unsettling, disorienting, and confusing. I've spent my whole life up until this point trying to be the person I was told I was, trying to get to know Anna, to make her someone I was comfortable being, fighting the parts that resisted, medicating them so that I could just feel OK. I am still in the process of unknowing who I thought I was and who I tried to be, and of knowing who I am. I am trying to be OK with that, to allow myself the process and to accept the in-between-ness I must live in in the meantime. But it is not always easy.

While in my MLIS program, I have been lucky enough to meet other trans and gender diverse students who have inspired me to lean into my own identity, even if it was, and still is, far from fully formed. Early on, I felt comfortable enough in my classes to begin indicating my interest not just in queer issues but in trans and gender diverse issues in particular, using assignments in several courses as a way to explore them within the context of library and information science. For the culminating assignment in one of my classes I wrote a twenty-page paper on the transgender information community, and I was happy to see that there were other students who chose similar topics.

Through my program, I have become excited about the future of libraries. I've had the opportunity to see firsthand the emergence of a new generation of information professionals who are genuinely passionate about social justice issues and ready to fight against the erasure and exclusion of marginalized communities. And this isn't just within LIS—in all fields, new professionals are embracing diversity and entering the workforce with a drive to improve spaces for those left in the margins and to challenge the existing power structures that led to this marginalization. It's encouraging to see something as simple as the inclusion of someone's pronouns in their work email signature or in their online student profile become more and more common. Even a change as seemingly small as this is an indication of something larger, of a shift in our cultural assumptions towards a new understanding of gender and its place in our society. As public places, many libraries have acknowledged their obligation to contribute to this shift, and to be safe and welcoming spaces for all—patrons and staff alike.

I want to be clear that I am not interested in romanticizing libraries. While I believe strongly in libraries and their mission to provide equitable access to information, it is impossible to extricate the origins and existence of public libraries in the U.S. from the country's history of violent colonialism and deep social divides. As a profession, librarianship has real work to do when it comes to contending with their troubling diversity statistics. For decades, libraries have maintained a predominantly white, cis, middle class, heteronormative, and able-bodied workforce, all the while claiming to hold diversity as one of their core values, declaring that "if libraries are to be their best, their services and staff must reflect both the people they serve and the larger global community."[2] This is why the visibility of non-dominant identities in these spaces, and all spaces, is so important. People, even strangers, have a profound effect on one another even if it isn't immediately apparent, and I know that every gender nonconforming person I have seen at school, getting coffee, or just walking on the street has contributed to the worldview I hold in which I am able to be me, whoever that may be.

Working in libraries as a public-facing staff member has given me the opportunity to do that for someone else. This is what I remind myself on particularly lonely days when the feeling of not being seen is most acute—I have to believe that there are people who see me.

In P. Carl's book "Becoming A Man," he speaks about W.E.B. Du Bois' concept of double consciousness.[3] He says that to be trans is to live in double consciousness, to inhabit multiple selves at once, and to hold the many truths, sometimes conflicting, of two lives in one body. An important part of this, I believe, is finding spaces and people that have room for this type of existence. Libraries have been one of these spaces for me. For that, I'll be forever grateful.

Bibliography

Carl, P. *Becoming a Man: The Story of a Transition*. New York: Simon & Schuster, 2020.

---

2. "Diversity Counts," American Library Association, https://www.ala.org/aboutala/offices/diversity/diversitycounts/divcounts; "Core values of librarianship," American Library Association, 2019, January, http://www.ala.org/advocacy/intfreedom/corevalues.

3. P. Carl, *Becoming a Man: The Story of a Transition* (New York: Simon & Schuster, 2020).

"Core values of librarianship." American Library Association. 2019, January. http://www.ala.org/advocacy/intfreedom/corevalues

"Diversity counts." American Library Association. https://www.ala.org/aboutala/offices/diversity/diversitycounts/divcounts.

"Transmasculine." Gender Wiki. https://gender.wikia.org/wiki/Transmasculine#.

About the Author

Ari Mahrer lives in the Bay Area with their partner and two cats. They graduated from San Jose State University's MLIS program in December 2021.

Luck of the Draw: Coming Out, Transition, and How a Supportive Work Environment Helps

W. Arthur Maurici (he/him/his)

Keywords: public libraries, social transition, transition at work, patron interaction, supportive work environments

While working in a public library, I came out to my supervisor by friending him on Facebook. I was newly out and having a terrible time navigating how to disclose my transness to people in various areas of my life. In most areas of queerness, *coming out* is rarely a one-and-done thing. I had approached my recent job interviews by staying closeted, using my legal name and she/her pronouns—because it seemed easier. The longer I was there, however, the harder coming out seemed, so I decided to let the internet do it for me. I had already created a profile using my actual name and I proceeded to add my supervisor as a friend. I had no idea how this was going to go, though I had a good impression of my supervisor and thought that, even if I didn't come out at work completely, at least someone would know.

One thing I've always found daunting about coming out is that, particularly for trans people, it's not just disclosure. Sure, telling people is hard, but there are so many steps after if, say, you want to change your name, your gender markers, etc. This is something that has caught me up many times over the years and kept me from coming out to others. Using Facebook to come out, even just to one person, gave the process an ease it had never felt like it had before.

It was, of course, still terrifying, but it was a step that I knew I needed to take.

The next day, when I came into work, my supervisor asked to speak to me. He told me that he'd seen my name on Facebook and wanted to come in and change my name on everything—nametag, mailbox, etc.—to William (my first name), but of course he knew that he needed to consult with me first. We talked a bit and he told me to let him know if I wanted to socially transition at work. It still felt daunting and like more than I was ready to handle, but after a few days of thought I decided to take that step. Knowing my direct supervisor had my back made it seem just manageable enough that I felt I could do it.

Our library director—with my permission—handled most of my coming out for the rest of the staff. He told them my name and pronouns, and for the most part, that was that—I was out at work and my social transition had begun. It is always a process, of course, but I had many allies at both of my part-time jobs. I was a different kind of nervous about coming out and socially transitioning at my second job. At the time, I mainly worked with children and I wasn't sure how parents would react. My direct supervisor there helped put me at ease as she knew the area better than I did and having her support gave me the courage to begin my social transition there as well.

Coming out and socially transitioning at two jobs was a step I needed to help me push my personal transition forward. The support of my coworkers and supervisors also helped keep me going, even when the process was daunting or the hoops felt impossible to jump through.

But along the way, I was lucky:

- My coworkers and supervisors—some of them straight, some not—were supportive and willing to step in when necessary.
- The library clerks would use he/him pronouns for me as a subtle correction after a patron misgendered me.
- Our director spoke to a patron who was making me uncomfortable.
- I vividly remember crying in the back office for a few minutes after insurance denied my request to start testosterone. Then, after

taking a deep breath, I asked the clerk on duty if it was okay if I could call them to sort it out. She said yes and stayed at her desk while I made the call, dealt with what had hung insurance up, and got the approval.

- When I had top surgery, my coworkers put together a food chain for me so I wouldn't have to worry about cooking.

It was not, of course, all good all the time:

- A patron, upon seeing the name *Arthur* on my name-tag, inquired if I was named for Bea Arthur because she was the only woman he knew of named Arthur. I informed him that I was not a woman. At some point, I cannot remember if this was the same day or later on, he followed me upstairs to where I was shelving to tell me to watch a TV show because there was a trans person in it.
- Another patron assumed my job title—Page—was my name rather than the name on my tag.
- A third patron, after I'd started working as a desk aide, was insistent that I should tell him my "real name." When I said it was Arthur, the name on my name tag, he disbelievingly asked, "Your parents named you Arthur?"
- Someone I knew from another area of my life came in and used the wrong name and pronouns. Living and working in a small city, it somehow never occurred to me to worry about that happening. Luckily, that person has since shifted their language, but at the time it was jarring and unpleasant.
- Yet another patron at my other job was surprised I was a man based on the color of my pants—red skinny jeans.

I cannot stress enough how lucky I was to be in two work environments that allowed me the space and support to transition socially and medically to the degree I wanted to. The relationships I built with my coworkers and the support I had from my supervisors were a great asset to me on my journey. I knew that the people I worked with were there for me and would support me. The fact that I was working in libraries at the time helped reinforce my love of working in this field and of libraries in general.

But I recognize my privilege here.

In a perfect world, all library work environments would be as accepting, supportive, and open as mine have been over the years. Unfortunately, we do not live in a perfect world and, while I got lucky, there are many trans and queer people who do not. In detailing some of the ways that my coworkers in libraries have supported and helped me, I hope to show ways that allies can step up.

Coming out and transitioning (to whatever degree one wants) are hard enough on their own, but trying to do so in unsupportive environments exacerbates the difficulties so much. Theoretically, libraries should be open and welcoming places for everyone, including queer and trans staff. Frustratingly, this isn't always the case; cis allies in library spaces must be aware that they have blind spots and be willing to put in the work to make these spaces better for their queer and trans staff.

About the Author

W. Arthur Maurici is a queer trans man who has been working in libraries cumulatively for about ten years. He has worked in public and academic libraries and is currently pursuing his MLIS at University of Maryland's iSchool, with a concentration in Archives and Digital Curation, that he hopes will enable him to participate in the preservation of queer history. Arthur is working with Dr. Pollock of Simmons University on a chapter for "Grabbing Tea: Conversations in Queer Librarianship." In 2021, he moderated a panel for the ASIS&T conference and, also with Dr. Pollock, presented a panel for LACUNY's 2021 conference. Outside of libraries, Arthur writes short fiction, does some voice acting, and is fond of fiber crafts (crochet and cross stitch, to be specific).

A Rainbow Sticker on Every Door: A True Story

AC Hunter

Keywords: public libraries, Australia, casual contracts, non-binary

The thing about memory is that it's a story. Autobiography has always bordered the divide between fact and fiction. Memory is less a recording and more simply the impression left on us. It's a truth ignored by the cataloguing librarian, because how else would anything get classified—it's not practical to be esoteric when assigning call numbers. What I'm writing here happened, but time makes skeletons of us all, eventually, and stories need flesh to live. So this is a story, my story, based on real life events.

Our story begins in November, 2017 in a very particular place and time. Two significant things were happening in Naarm (Melbourne). The Australia Marriage Law postal vote came to a close, ending relentless and sometimes brutal weeks of public debate about legalising gay marriage in this country. And I, AC, had finally managed to land a job back in a library after six years out of the industry, this time with a different name and new pronouns.

I was enthusiastic about the new job as a library technician, even though it was a contract of 0-35 hours a week with no guaranteed hours. I had decided I wanted to be out at work as non-binary, a change from my previous job as a receptionist. Months before, I'd talked to a trans librarian at a party who worked for my new employer while transitioning. Although I didn't ask about their experience as a trans worker specifically, the fact that they enjoyed their work and encouraged me to apply left me hopeful. I believed I had found somewhere that was supportive to take what was, for me, a significant step.

All outward signs from the library service and the city council that runs it affirmed my belief. There were rainbow stickers on the front doors of all their libraries; the council took part in Pride events and spoke up in support of same-sex marriage and the LGBTI+ community in press releases.

So, I submitted my CV with my dead name in brackets (for continuity as all previous employers and legal documents used that name). In the interview I made clear that I used AC and the interviewers and people who trained me followed suit easily. It had gotten off to a good start. This was reassuring because, while I was managing the stress and excitement of getting a new job, homophobic and transphobic opponents of marriage equality were conflating same sex marriage with gender diversity: running ads and media scare campaigns about "radical" sex education in schools forcing students to be gay and fears about boys being allowed to wear dresses to school (as though this is a bad thing). It was a time of heightened visibility for a trans and queer person and here I was taking steps to out myself to a group of strangers who were my new colleagues.

Things started to go wrong at work when my email address came through with my deadname in it. I told my manager, whose first response was—"Was that a problem?" Yes, yes it was a problem. She suggested taking it up with IT. After a couple of false starts, I figured out how to do this and got an email with my actual name on it. The same was not true of my pay slip, since the council's payroll system could only use legal names—something to look forward to every fortnight.

After a couple of weeks, I had almost finished training and would soon be doing my first desk shift unsupervised. The desk roster came out and I was appalled to read my deadname on it. Trying not to freak out and to remain calm, I emailed the person who organises the roster and explained that my name was AC and could they please use that. They replied that there were other people in the organisation with those initials and it would be too confusing to use that name. I wrote back, re-affirming that this was my name and it was not appropriate to use my legal name. Eventually, towards the end of the day, she wrote and said she would use "Ayecee", and I, feeling defeated and shaken, agreed to it. I went home and cried. Between the undercurrent of transphobic rhetoric in the public and how difficult and inflexible my new colleague had been, I was exhausted. The next morning, well-slept and ready for battle, I emailed her again. I suggested that she use A-C, with a dash, so there would be no confusion it was another person's initials. To my relief, she agreed.

That afternoon, the results of the marriage equality postal survey were announced. Sixty-one percent were in favour of legalising gay marriage. Co-workers and patrons at the library were excited and people seemed happy with the results. I was not as excited as most. There were still thirty-nine percent of voters who believed that myself and people like me don't deserve the same rights as heterosexual folk. Also, the result didn't take away from the weeks of homophobic and transphobic attacks. It was an empty win.

As I stayed on at the library, I began to find allies. I discovered that there were many out queer people working in the library service and more with loved ones who are queer or trans. About four months into the job, at a staff meeting, I brought up that it was discouraging for people who don't use their legal name to have it on their library card and received excellent support from one or two fellow Library Technicians. Management looked into it and our IT administrator pointed out that you can easily add a legal name as an "additional name" buried deep in the library user profile in our system but still searchable. While library users still needed to show identification to join up, the name on the card could be whatever the user preferred—it was a simple solution.

I worked at the library for almost a year. Halfway through they ended my contract, only to reinstate me two months later when staff shortages had made the workplace unsafe. I ended up resigning in November 2018, since I was moving to a different country and a job with regular hours.

A few days before my final shift, a library user approached the desk and asked to change the name on their library card. This trans masculine person had a birth certificate with the new legal name they had recently changed officially, and I was more than happy to help. I discovered they had only joined the library a week before and that whoever signed them up had told them their library card needed to be in their legal name. Even worse, the library worker who signed them up had added an incorrect binary gender to their record, an option that was no longer required. I apologised to the user and promised to report what had happened to management. I encouraged them to complete a feedback form; they ended up writing for a while on both sides of it before adding the form to the feedback box.

I wrote a strongly worded email to the team leader of that library, the customer services manager, and cc'd in the Diversity rep from the Occupational Health and Safety committee (a fabulous and unswerving ally). I didn't have a shift for a few days and when I got back there had been a long string of emails in response. Members of management went so far as requesting advice from the council legal team (an expensive endeavour). The IT administrator again pointed out that using a preferred name wasn't a legal issue and was easily accommodated in the library system. The emails petered out as it became clear that getting legal advice was unnecessary and that this was an issue about certain staff lacking knowledge and skills to work with trans library users. I finished my work there without learning what the organisation was going to do about it.

I left that job with mixed feelings about my experiences as a trans non-binary staff member. My sense was that my employer had a desire to be seen as inclusive, and there were attempts to do this, but that pockets of resistance existed—like inflexible systems and some hostile co-workers. These barriers to change persisted without a commitment to do work thoroughly in an ongoing, consistent way. One-off diversity training, so divorced as it is from the reality of day-to-day interactions in the workroom and library floor, is little more than box ticking. The learning process requires feedback. It is pointless to claim inclusiveness without acknowledging there is more to learn, seeking out constructive criticism, and working to address issues. In fact, promoting a library service as inclusive and safe when it's not is dangerous to the health and wellbeing of trans staff and the communities it serves. The additional emotional labour and hurt it creates goes unrecognised and produces cynicism and burn out for staff and leads to access and safety issues for library users.

The challenge to library services is to properly resource the necessary changes, some of which I'll spell out here:

- All employee systems—financial, HR, and otherwise—need to be upgraded to allow for people who use a name other than their legal one.
- Diversity doesn't work if those in your diverse workforce are all at lower pay grades and your diversity isn't reflected in management where decisions are made.
- A library service is only as trans-friendly as its most transphobic staff members. Find these people and work with them to reach a level of professionalism where their individual beliefs do not impact trans co-workers and library users.
- Increasing work insecurity and casualisation of library staff means being seen as different or challenging norms is discouraged. When the number of hours you are offered each week, or having your contract extended, is dependent on your standing with management, fear of losing work and a paycheck results in self-censorship and pressure to not "make trouble." Libraries should offer secure employment with regular hours and structure our organisations in a way that prioritises this.

When I reflect on these suggestions, I feel like I'm asking for crumbs when what I really want is a fair share of the cake—for everyone. Transphobia is a normative attitude to bodies that intersects with ableism, racism and classism. In the library space it speaks to a desire for social cohesion through conformity. We need to question the reinforcement of the status quo in our institutions, how hierarchy has entrenched resistance to change, and how capitalism prioritises cost efficiency over the wellbeing of staff. We need meaningful action to address the whiteness of our institutions. We need to acknowledge our place on the stolen land of Indigenous peoples and complicity in genocide, and work towards justice and healing. I don't just want a rainbow sticker on the door or my pronouns to be respected; I want libraries to be at the forefront of the radical change we need everywhere.

About the Author

AC is a queer and trans non-binary librarian of Scottish, Irish, English and Carribean African descent. Born in Ōtautahi (Christchurch, Aotearoa/ New Zealand) on the lands of Ngāi Tahu Iwi, specifically the rohe (territory) of Ngāi Tūāhuriri. Now residing in Naarm (Melbourne, Australia) on the lands of the Wurundjeri Woiwurrung of the Kulin Nation. AC is a radio producer with 3CR Community Radio, a stencil and print maker, and an organiser within the nuclear free movement.

What's A Gender Like You Doing in An Institutional Bureaucracy Like This?

Hypatia Jones

Keywords: transphobia, coming out, urban libraries, children's services

Getting involved in the library and information studies (LIS) profession feels, at times, like both a natural fit and a terrible mistake. There's an adage about how knowing the way sausage gets made makes one's appetite suffer. I went into this profession because I wanted to make a difference, because I loved books and the power of stories, because libraries had been a refuge for me growing up, and because I wanted to extend that same safety to others. Many of my colleagues, especially fellow children's or youth services staff, feel the same. And to be fair, I know that I *have* made a difference, that I have touched families' lives and made (hopefully) lasting change in my institution. As I write this chapter, I'm reminding myself not to be too pessimistic, too dour. I want to encourage others who share this work, particularly at the intersection of trans and gender nonconforming (TGNC) identities and LIS. I want other trans folks to know that they are not alone in this profession, that there is (or can be) space for them, and that the trans LIS people I know are thrilled at the idea of having others like us joining the ranks.

At the same time, I am tired. I've only been a full-time public librarian for five years and I am utterly exhausted. Part of it is from struggling against vocational awe, which Fobazi Ettarh describes as "the set of ideas, values, and assumptions librarians have about themselves and the profession that result in beliefs that libraries as institutions are inherently good and sacred, and therefore beyond critique [...] thus requiring absolute obedience to a prescribed set of rules and behaviors, regardless of any negative effect on librarians' own lives."[1] Part of it is the weariness of bringing my trans activism to work and feeling the burden of being the only out person in my branch, and one of the only out people in my entire system. Part of it is loneliness, too, because while I've built community with TGNC and allied colleagues, I am reminded time and again that our institution as a whole, and perhaps the LIS institution at large, is happy to forget about us.

A bit about myself: I am an assigned female at birth (AFAB) genderqueer demisexual who also identifies more broadly as trans and queer. Not so long ago, I identified as non-binary as well; however, I'm uncomfortable with some of the implications of "non-binary" as a label for myself, particularly being used in lieu of the older, sharper, and more direct "genderqueer." I'm white, coming from a small, rural community in the Southern United States. I'm disabled, fat, neurodivergent, and religious, but not Christian. I finished my library degree in 2015 before moving from my tiny town to a large metropolis in 2016, where I live and work today. I'm thirty-something, married, no kids.

Growing up in a conservative, Christian area of the country in the 90s/00s was difficult. Gay people were evil. Trans people didn't exist. I didn't understand the formative queerness in my childhood, but it plus my untreated autism and ADHD and my fatness made me a social outcast and a target for bullies for most of my school years. I found a refuge in books. More specifically, I found a refuge in the library. The school librarians sometimes felt like the only adults genuinely happy to see me. And while it was years before I finally read books about trans or queer characters, at least the stories didn't seem to mind that I couldn't figure out how to make myself fit in the real world.

---

1. Fobazi Ettarh, "Vocational awe and librarianship: The lies we tell ourselves," *In the Library with the Lead Pipe* (2018), https://www.inthelibrarywiththeleadpipe.org/2018/vocational-awe/.

I had funny ideas about the world, as I'm sure many of us do while growing up. I knew that the environment I was raised in—my school, my church, my friends and their families—were often intolerant and hateful. I sat in multiple sermons condemning queerness and nonconforming gender roles. I remember one day in high school, running out of English class in tears because the teacher stopped our lesson on Oscar Wilde to mock his sexual orientation. I knew the world couldn't be only like this, that there were other parts of the country that were more liberal (whatever that meant to a sheltered teen from Appalachia). In my head, "other parts" meant "big cities." Conservative pundits and preachers ranted about ungodly places like Philadelphia, New York City, and San Francisco, so I thought, of course, that's where I need to be.

Getting accepted at a large urban library was a dream come true for me. I wasn't even able to come out as cisgender queer in my hometown, but now I thought surely, I could present as queerly and transly as I wanted without anyone batting an eye. Instead of being in the closet, I imagined introducing myself with my real pronouns and maybe even asking to be called Mx. I imagined making displays with books like *Gracefully Grayson* and *George* for Pride Month, which of course would already be well celebrated at my new branch. Maybe most importantly, I wouldn't have to fight. I wouldn't feel alone. Because libraries, as I had been told over and over during grad school, were for everyone.

I don't know that I can accurately describe the pain and betrayal at uncovering transphobia and queerphobia in my branch. I hadn't yet worked up the courage to out myself to my coworkers before the assistant manager dropped the t-slur in front of me. My first Pride Month display in the children's room was challenged by my manager. My acknowledgement of being in a same-gender relationship was met with awkward silence and fumblings about my "you know, uh, partner?" when other coworkers had chatted openly about their straight significant others. Once, during Women's History Month, another coworker sabotaged a display I'd made by removing all reference to trans women and girl activists.

I also don't know that I can overstate how bad it was for my mental health to hide my gender identity and to downplay my queerness. Maybe I didn't need to; maybe I could have pushed more and called out more and made space for myself. But these sorts of attitudes rarely exist in isolation from others, and my coworkers held equally heinous attitudes about race, religion, immigration, class, mental health, home status, and ethnicity. I felt that I had to pick my battles—that I could only be *so* different and I was already visibly fat and disabled and was already known to be queer and not Christian. It hurt to pretend to be cisgender, but my logic was this: as an adult, I could handle being constantly misgendered and working in a transphobic environment. What are a few more years of trauma when my whole life had already been informed by such? However, the families I served, who were marginalized in different ways than I was, needed to have a safe space where library materials and programs reflected their own lived realities. I wanted each child who walked through the library doors to feel the same sense of refuge and ownership of the space that I had as a child.

I mentioned at the beginning of this chapter the concept of *vocational awe*. What I've just described, enduring a toxic work environment "for the greater good," is an example of how vocational awe hurts library workers in general, and marginalized library workers in particular. I didn't want to rock the boat and potentially interrupt necessary service to our patrons. Now that I'm no longer a new professional, I can make different choices. I do make different choices, and I hope that other LIS staff will make the best choices for themselves in a similar situation.

Now, that said, not all my experiences at the first branch were bad. I worked in a neighborhood with a high number of unattended kids in the children's room, and so I was in a unique position to answer those frank and sometimes embarrassing questions kids have about… well, everything. Such as:

Am I married?

What did I mean I wasn't married to a man?

Did I know that's gay?

Did I know that *I* was gay?

What's up with all the rainbow books on the display over there?

Why did I get mad at them for calling each other f*g but not shithead?

Because I was willing to have open conversations about almost anything, kids started talking to me. Some of the older ones shared concerns about their own identities, or the identities of other people in their lives. Some told me that their church or family had said something queerphobic and wanted to know what I thought. I don't know that these conversations would have happened in a library without unattended children, because kids often clam up around adults, and adults usually have way more problems than kids about queerness. Every single child I spoke to about using queerphobic or transphobic language eventually told me that this language was used *against them* by an adult in their life. This includes one child who eventually asked, very timidly, what would happen if he were transgender. I don't think he would have felt comfortable enough opening up to me if I hadn't built trust and respect between us over the years and treated him, and the other library kids, like what they did and who they were was important.

Eventually, I got out of that first branch and started working at another location in the same system. I knew I couldn't have a repeat of my previous experience being in the closet, so on the second day on the job, I told one coworker that I was transgender and to use they/them pronouns for me. A bit later, I told the manager and a few others the same. I changed my email signature to include pronouns; I started wearing a pronoun button with the genderqueer flag on my work lanyard. And, while I didn't come out to every coworker explicitly, I stopped being in the closet. I came out—or at least unlocked the door and let it swing open.

I realize that I am incredibly lucky to have been able to make that choice. I finally had supportive coworkers and bosses. Diversity, Equity, Inclusion, and Access conversations were becoming more and more common in the system, especially around queer and trans identities. Being white and AFAB also affords me certain protections and privileges that can soften my experience of transphobia. According to the National Center for Transgender Equality's 2015 U.S. Transgender Survey

Report, transgender people of color are at greater risk for experiencing discrimination, living in poverty, being unemployed, and living with serious health issues like HIV. Additionally, AMAB (assigned male at birth) transgender individuals experience the compounded effects of both transphobia and misogyny that put them at particular risk.[2] Julia Serano first coined the term 'transmisogyny' to describe the particular struggles that she and other trans women face.[3]

However, as many queer folks know, coming out is rarely a one-and-done event. In some ways being open about my trans identity has meant facing purposeful (or at least thoughtless) misgendering rather than simply mistaken misgendering. I've had to ask myself many times: Is it worth my time and energy to correct someone who calls me she, or calls me a lady, or Miss? What if the other person is upset, confused, or otherwise makes their reaction my problem? Would it hurt *more* in the long run to correct a coworker only to be misgendered again than it would to just keep quiet and allow assumptions to pass unchallenged?

I ask myself questions constantly about what I owe other trans folks, particularly in my profession. Should I be more forceful about my pronouns and gendered language to set an example for how to treat other trans staff? Am I "one of the good ones" that doesn't upset cisgender folks and thus reduces possible harm to myself and others? Am I selling myself out by avoiding conflict and accepting the slow, slow, *slow* pace of institutional change, or am I being realistic about how things work and what I myself am able to accomplish in my position? I'm afraid I have more questions than answers, and that most of the answers I do have are largely unsatisfying. I have to teach my colleagues, bosses, HR, and the union how to treat trans people, and I shouldn't have to. I had

---

2. Sandy E. James, et al, Executive Summary of the Report of the 2015 U.S. Transgender Survey, Washington, DC: National Center for Transgender Equality, 2016, Accessed October 31, 2021, https://www.ustranssurvey.org/reports.

3. Julia Serano, "Trans Feminism: There's No Conundrum About It," in *Excluded: Making Feminist and Queer Spaces More Inclusive* (Berkeley, California: Seal Press, 2013), 43-47.

to deal with existential crises about gendered bathrooms at work for years, and I shouldn't have had to.

And yet, *someone* has to do this work. Someone has to make it incrementally easier for the trans professionals who come next. Someone has to make trans patrons less of an afterthought in library planning. Someone, multiple someones, have to challenge the notion that libraries are inherently safe and diverse spaces that operate without a single bias or stereotype. Because, for all the struggle it's been to be trans and in LIS, I also genuinely love (most of) my job and I'm proud of what I and my allied coworkers have been able to accomplish. Despite everything, I'm still attracted to this notion of "libraries are for everyone." So often that's an empty phrase, or used to ignore the very real moral crises at the heart of LIS. Maybe, though, it doesn't have to be. I think about the very best of what libraries are and can be, and I think about the very worst experiences I've had working in them, and it seems to me that, while the gulf is wide, it doesn't need to be unbreachable.

So, what are some concrete, practical ways to challenge transphobia in libraries and to better support trans patrons and staff? My biggest advice is to find your people, whether other TGNC folks or cis people, who are willing to be accomplices in creating change. Some of the most disheartening times in my life have come from feeling alone and isolated, but there have always been more of us around than one might think. The TGNC employee resource group I facilitate is a few years old, and we're still getting new members who thought they were the only trans employees in the system. I've seen members come out professionally and begin social, legal, and other aspects of their transitions because of the camaraderie and support our group provided. We've tackled projects like curating TGNC material lists, developing employee training around trans etiquette and respect, and presenting at conferences. Plus, there are positive effects on mental health that come from connecting with other like-minded people. Just having a safe place to vent about the experiences of being a trans staff member is enough to make such a group worthwhile.

Luckily, we have some degree of institutional buy-in thanks to a growing interest in diversity topics in our system. Every institution is different, and I know that what is possible in my large urban library system is different from what I could have achieved in my local library back in Appalachia. That said, I've routinely been surprised at how much support our group has gotten from upper management and central services. There are people who have told us no, so we've either kept asking or did it ourselves. We asked for a mandatory sensitivity training on TGNC issues and were told no, so we created an optional training instead that over 120 staff members attended. Within months of our DIY training, our group was asked to provide feedback for a mandatory sensitivity training that was now back on the table.

I've dealt with a lot of doubt and uncertainty since joining this profession. I've also been surprised and humbled by where I've found support. I've been disappointed at what I couldn't achieve and delighted at what I could. What gives me focus and hope is the idea that, together, we can build something amazing. I think of how paltry my first Pride Month display was in 2016 and how hard I had to scramble to find enough titles to fit the shelf. Compare that to the treasure trove of TGNC picture books, nonfiction, and middle-grade titles that are in our collection now—not to mention the more broadly queer-aligned books. I think of how frustrated and isolated I felt at my first branch and how optimistic I am now with the TGNC employee resource group making measurable change in our workplace.

Bibliography

Ettarh, Fobazi. "Vocational Awe and Librarianship: The Lies We Tell Ourselves." *In the Library with the Lead Pipe* (January 10, 2018). https://www.inthelibrarywiththeleadpipe.org/2018/vocational-awe/.

James, Sandy E., Jody L. Herman, Susan Rankin, Mara Keisling, Lisa Mottet, & Ma'ayan Anafi. Executive Summary of the Report of the 2015 U.S. Transgender Survey. Washington, DC:

National Center for Transgender Equality, 2016. Accessed October 31, 2021. https://www.ustranssurvey.org/reports.
Serano, Julia. "Trans Feminism: There's No Conundrum About it." In *Excluded: Making Feminist and Queer Spaces More Inclusive*, 43-47. Berkeley, California: Seal Press, 2013.

Section 4:

Academic Libraries

I Remember, or the Transmigration of Hazel Jane Plante

Hazel Jane Plante

Keywords: academic libraries, trans women, transition at work, coming out, transphobic events

I remember telling my supervisor A that I was trans.[1] We were in a Starbucks in the middle of the crappy mall at the base of our campus. I told her that I didn't know how this would play out. I said that things were starting to bubble up for me, so I thought she should know, in case I felt the urge to shift things overnight. I talked a lot. Years later, I barely recall this meeting. I'm seeing it filtered through a thick gauze, most of my words mercifully blotted out.

When I finally stopped talking, A said she'd do her best to support me, that she'd never been through this before ("Same," I said, laughing), and that if she made any mistakes or misspoke it would be out of ignorance, not lack of care. Then, she apologized for second wave feminism and said she was more surprised to learn that I was an angry child than she was to learn that I was trans.

I remember wearing a huge hat on my commute to work for months. My face seemed ravaged and was strewn with stubble. I needed to keep my skin as shielded from the sun as possible so the painful, pricey sessions of laser could do their smells-like-burnt-popcorn magic. Suddenly, I

1. To anonymize folks, I will assign them consecutive letters of the alphabet.

flash on all the times Le Tigre's "Deceptacon" gave me a jolt of you-can-do-this-for-a-few-more-months energy as I walked with that enormous floppy hat and my unshaven, sunburned-looking face from the SkyTrain station to the entrance of the mall. Only now, several years later, do I realize that a Decepticon is a type of Transformer. Decepticons are the villains. And now I'm wondering why I chose that particular song for the three-minute-long walk from transit to work. Maybe it was its spunky, catchy refrain shouting that everything was all right. I probably needed that frenetic reassurance because things sure as shit did not feel all right. But I was game to let Kathleen Hanna lull me into phantasmal all-right-ness for a spell.

I remember going for a fancy lunch with my ex/bestie/roommate B shortly after sending an email to my library colleagues informing them that I was transitioning. In a summer dress at the upscale restaurant, I scrolled on my phone through replies from colleagues, bracing myself for the worst. The messages were mostly lovely, with a few clumsy-but-inoffensive replies thrown into the mix. To be sure, the Venn diagram of my overlapping privileges positioned me for one of the smoothest transitions imaginable: I was a white trans woman working in a feminized profession at an academic institution who transitioned mid-career. I thought of gender-variant folks I knew who'd transitioned in workplaces that were far less welcoming, including trans femmes who worked as plumbers and mechanics. I felt lucky and embarrassed.

I'd also transitioned the same day on social media. Most of my friends already knew, but this was a pretty massive shift for the wider circle of people in my life. I kept feeling the pull to refresh my phone, bracing myself for linguistic Molotov cocktails or laugh react emojis. I ordered an overpriced burger and a Sazerac. B had helped with my transition in countless ways. At the time, I couldn't fathom all the ways my transition affected her. I still can't. When our drinks arrived, we probably said something and clinked glasses.

That entire day is a blur, but I do recall feeling more relieved than jubilant. Like a good Virgo librarian, I'd spent over a year putting dozens of dominos in place so I could send out that work email (subject line: "transitioning"). I'd answered blunt and barbed questions about my gender to access the care that I needed. I'd threaded my way through physical and virtual labyrinths to get to the right gates and said the right things to change my name and my gender marker on every official document. I'd waited like a good girl for each glacial change. I'd combed through best practices on transitioning at work. Some of these "best practices" left me aghast. I recall one document from a major company that suggested having a staff meeting where an employee's new gender identity would be announced.[2] This was framed as a way to allow colleagues to ask questions and voice concerns. There was the suggestion that the transitioning employee might want to make a video introducing their new self. I imagined dozens of my colleagues crowded into a room on the sixth floor of the library, sipping coffee and eating slices of cake with (sickeningly sweet) pink icing, watching an oversized, overly-femme version of me telling them my new name and pronouns, making an awkward joke or two. Then, I saw someone from admin floating the question, "So, how do you feel about working with Hazel?" No. Just, no.

I remember going for coffee with my friend C, a faculty member who I'd bonded with over the years while collaborating on creative in-depth research-related projects for her courses. When I told her that I was trans, she exhaled deeply. "Oh, my god," she said. "I thought you were going to tell me you were dying. This is good news." We hugged.

I remember asking my new supervisor D and my previous supervisor A, both of whom I really liked and trusted, if they would help me transition. "Yes," they both said in an instant. I don't remember how it happened or who suggested it, but I added another member to my small transition team: E, who was my dean. We held a few furtive meetings so I could talk through my transitioning timelines and the inventories

2. I don't think this odd gender reveal party involved explosives and colored smoke, but I could be wrong.

I'd made of the dozens of things that needed to be done. In the end, I decided to take a two-week vacation. I would send an email to colleagues after one week of vacation. E offered to send a follow-up email shortly after my message affirming both the library and the university's support for my transition. That would give my colleagues a week to adjust to the news and allow other folks time to make the remaining changes on the transitioning inventory (e.g., updating my name throughout the website). Then, I'd return to work.

C told me she imagined me strutting into the entrance of the library with a wind machine, Beyoncé-style. I laughed. I told her that I wanted none of that: no wind machine, no 'It's-A-Girl' cards signed by my colleagues, no one blasting "Man! I Feel Like a Woman!" No, thank you.

I remember resisting asking the colleagues on my tiny transition team to use the right pronouns (she/her) for me. I hadn't changed my "gender presentation" (what a fucking phrase) yet, so I felt like it would be too much work to ask them to address me as a woman. The Smiths song "You Just Haven't Earned It Yet, Baby" ran through my head regularly.

I remember bracing myself when I entered the women's washroom near my office for the first time. This is easy to remember because I still brace myself every time I enter a women's washroom or any gendered space. So far, I've been lucky, but I'm always aware that this time things could go sideways and I may be met with vitriol or violence.

I remember wondering how I could simply be myself but also always unambiguously telegraph my femininity to strangers. (Forget Fermat's Last Theorem; this is an actual conundrum.)

I remember attending a day-long symposium on gender and sexuality in librarianship the day after I sent my "transitioning" email to colleagues. I still remember what I wore to the symposium: a long black button-up top made of rayon (it's so hard to iron, friends!), blue jeans, and stylish blue-and-cream Fluevogs. I bought the Fluevogs the day before (i.e., the day I transitioned). As I walked from my apartment in the West End to the downtown campus, it started to drizzle. I'd never really walked in heels before, and these shoes have a short 1.5-inch heel.[3] I felt wobbly in my shoes, but I also felt wobbly in my body and in my femininity.

Two female colleagues at the symposium told me that when they read my email about transitioning the day before, they'd cheered and high-fived. I don't remember how I responded. I probably laughed.

That night, I went out for drinks and fell in with a few cool, smart librarians who worked at North Carolina State University (NCSU). A month earlier, North Carolina had passed an awful anti-trans bathroom bill. These librarians told me that everyone they knew thought the bill was bullshit. We talked a bunch, drank a bunch. They invited me for a late dinner. I hesitated and debated (are they just asking me cuz I'm a baby queer trans girl and their state is fucking with my shit?) and eventually agreed to go (they seemed genuine; plus, they were bright, funny, queer, and—okay, I'll just say it—kinda cute).

One of the NCSU librarians had to fly to Seoul, Korea, the next morning, so she'd told us she was going to turn in early. When she heard that I was going to go for dinner and more drinks, she changed her plans. "If she's going," she said, hitching a thumb at me, "I'm going, too." At that moment, I felt like a cherry blossom that had finally burst from its tiny bud. A couple hours later, I wobbled home. At one point, I slipped on rain-slicked cobblestones and almost fell. But, no, somehow, I managed, just barely, to stay upright the entire night.

I remember being misgendered by a TA at the start of a research skills workshop. I thanked the TA for introducing me and told a roomful of students that I was, in fact, a woman.

---

3. I just measured the tapered heels. As I type, the shoes are fairly glowing on the table in the afternoon light. I imagine these gorgeous shoes pulling a Pixar, coming alive, glowering at me, their tongues wagging, "Why don't you love us? You knew we were a tad pinchy when you bought us. Our official name is Promise, but we might as well be called Sexy Librarian." I might reply, "Oh, gosh, you're so cute (and, yes, subtly sexy!), but you've given me blisters. Plus, there's a global pandemic. I'm sorry."

I remember foregrounding my transness and my pronouns in communications with profs and TAs whose classes I visited. For at least a few years, I worried about being misgendered every time a prof, TA, or student started talking about me. (Let's be real: Every time I'm in front of a class I still wonder if I'll be misgendered.)

I remember being on a hiring committee at the campus where I worked before transitioning, the one with the crappy mall. I went to a coffee shop I used to frequent. I was dressed in a blue blazer with white polka dots, a crisp white button-up, blue-and-white polka dot pants, blue-and-cream Fluevogs, and a short blonde dyke-style cut.

When I placed my order, the barista behind the counter said, "That's such a great look. You look like Bowie when he was super cool and not trying too hard." "Aw, thanks," I said. At the time, I wanted to crawl into a broom closet, curl into a ball, and weep because all I heard was "he."

I remember being given a prize by my elementary school librarian Mrs. F. There was no ceremony. We were in her cramped office, and she was just giving me something small, like a bookmark with tassels or a scratch-and-sniff sticker. But I was so excited. Like, super-duper excited. I was maybe eight or nine years old. I started flapping both my hands, like you might do if they were soaking wet and you wanted to dry them lickety-split. Mrs. F looked at me flap-flap-flapping my excited hands and said, "I used to do that when I was a little girl." I felt dumb. I felt numb. I bit my tongue. I stopped my weird, girlish flapping.

I remember being at a three-day-long workshop for managers. I wasn't a manager and didn't want to be a manager, but I had been part of a team at the library who worked with the woman running the workshop, and I liked and respected her. I felt like I could learn from her. And I wanted to learn how to make meaningful changes without being in a leadership position.

There were about thirty or forty people in the workshop, about a dozen of whom were from my library. On the first day, we went around the room, each of us explaining what we wanted to get out of the workshop. What I wanted to say was this: "I want to figure out how to top from the bottom." But that might be a bit much for a breezy, sunny Wednesday morning with everyone quietly sipping coffee and nibbling on pastries and cut fruit. I imagined myself making hand gestures to explain "topping" and "bottoming." And, uh, no. That language was far too queer. In the end, I said something about how I worried that I was seen as a squeaky wheel, a noisy killjoy. I said that I wanted to make a more melodious squeak, to make the kind of noise that might make my colleagues think, "Oh, I like the sound of your squeak."

Later, one person approvingly repeated the phrase "melodious squeak" to me while we filled our lunch trays with watery soup, iceberg-lettuce-based salad, and they-all-taste-pretty-much-the-same wraps.

While getting a coffee refill, a colleague who was once my supervisor dead-named me. "Hazel," I said. "My name is Hazel."

"Oh, right. Oops."

"Sorry."

"It's still hard for me to remember."

"I get it. It's okay."

I remember prominently and purposefully referring to myself in the third person in classes and in consultations, to signal my pronouns. "Maybe later," I'd say, "you'll be wondering, 'What did she say? What did Hazel say?' She showed me how to do this magical research thing. So, this two-minute-long video will totally remind you of how to do this magic thing." (I still do this. All. The. Time.)

I remember meeting with someone in HR to share my experiences being a trans faculty member and transitioning at my university. She told me she was unaware that there were any trans faculty members at my institution, which has over 1000 faculty members. She was gobsmacked when I showed her my extensive transition-related checklists and timelines. Before then, she had no idea how much work it is to transition in a system that sees gender and identities as fixed.

Coda: More than five years later, my computing ID, which is required to log into every system at my university, is still derived from my dead name. I've been offered a new computing ID, but I have to be prepared for it to break each time I log into a new system. (There are over a hundred different systems, and there's no inventory of all the separate places your computing ID is stored; I still come across at least one or two new systems with my dead name each year, most recently while using a professional development form and a survey tool.)

I've suggested ways of making transitioning more seamless, but I've been told on different occasions that a) we're moving to a new system soon, b) this is a priority, and c) I just need to be patient. It's not like my computing ID is displayed prominently in the upper right-hand corner of some of these systems or like researchers see it when I log into resources during workshops and consultations. Oh, right, it is super visible in all those places. To quote that cartoon meme dog drinking coffee surrounded by flames: "This is fine." It's not as if that cute doggo thinks about quitting their job on the regular.

I remember standing outside a university auditorium when I overheard a couple of students talking about "pounding" energy drinks to stay awake for this class. Clearly, "Introduction to Human Sexuality and Sexual Behavior" was not the intellectual fuckfest these bros were expecting. And now, here I was, a just-out queer trans femme librarian, waiting to deliver a scintillating hands-on session to 200-300 first-year students on information literacy.

I remember sobbing in my office because anti-trans events kept happening in libraries and universities, and now one was slated to happen at my university. I'd done everything I could behind the scenes to elucidate how utterly fucking deplorable this event was and how it would hurt people I love and care about, how it would hurt me. I contacted every person at my institution who could cancel this event. I used my sharpest language to marshal my strongest arguments. I also made myself vulnerable in my messages, because I know these noxious events are anything but neutral; they normalize, legitimize, and amplify hatred and violence against people with complicated genders, especially racialized trans femmes.

Every person with power who deigned to reply to my messages said their hands were tied, that the event, as unbalanced and unfortunate as it was, had to go ahead. I wondered how I would react the next time I saw the high-up administrator who often said hello to me at queer events, who had replied to my message by stating that this unfortunate event could not be canceled. I wondered if I could resist yelling unfortunate words at her. I wondered how it would feel to spit in her fortunate face.

I remember a colleague asking me quietly if I was acquainted with imposter syndrome. I nodded. She confessed that she suffered from it. "Same," I said. "I even feel like an imposter in my gender sometimes." A wave of worry flowed through me. I should not have said that aloud. My access to femininity already felt provisional. I should avoid admitting that gender is weird and messy and just pretend that I wanted to play with Barbie dolls as a kid.

I remember accessing a therapist through a program that would be covered by work. When we met, I listed a few challenging things going on in my life and told her which one I wanted to discuss. About ten or fifteen minutes into the session, she said, "Hazel, that's a nice name. What was your name before?" I told her that was an awful question to ask, that it was something she should never ask a trans client. She was surprised, thinking it was a harmless question. I told her my current issues were not related to my gender. I steered the session back to the issue that I came to discuss. A little while later, she wondered aloud if some of my problems were related to my genitals.

I remember agonizing over how much or how little to include in my "hey-I'm-trans" message to colleagues. In the end, I decided to aim for brevity and levity.

Here is what I sent:

Dear colleagues,

I'm sending this message to let you know that I'm transgender, and I'll be transitioning at work.

My new name is Hazel Plante and I'll be going by female pronouns (i.e., she/her/hers). My email address is now hazel_plante@sfu.ca.

I recognize this will be an adjustment for many of you. Honest mistakes will be made (especially initially) and that's okay. There's no need to walk on eggshells around me. Really. I'm the same person I've always been.

My transition probably won't affect most of you, aside from adjusting to my new name and pronouns. (If you didn't know me before receiving this message, you may not need to make any adjustments whatsoever. Well done.)

Last year, Harvard Business Review published a brief article called "What to Do When Your Colleague Comes Out as Transgender" that seems appropriate to share. (And I can't resist sharing a not-appropriate-for-work-but-I'm-on-vacation-so-why-not segment from Last Week Tonight with John Oliver on transgender rights [warning: this video includes quite a bit of cussing, but it's also surprisingly informative].)

I'm currently in the middle of a short vacation, but I look forward to returning to work at the start of May.

Thanks,

Hazel

Looking back, I still think this message works. I avoided justifying my transition, which was a sad staple of so many "hey-I'm-trans" sample work emails that I saw in some "best practices" guides. I emphasized that this wasn't a big deal. And I linked to a couple of resources—one practical and factual, one incisive and hilarious—that might be helpful.

Now I find myself drawn to the following sentence of my message: "I'm the same person I've always been." Here, I seem to be reassuring my colleagues (and myself) that things won't change. Several years later, I recognize that so many things have shifted. And it hasn't been a jostling—like how luggage shifts during a flight—so much as it's been an unmooring, a razing, a fumbling, a slow-fast/embarrassing-liberating/ public-private bursting. At times, it has felt closer to transmigrating than transitioning.[4]

I'm reminded of a Philip K. Dick novel called *The Transmigration of Timothy Archer*. And now I'm wondering what colleagues who have known me for a good stretch of time would say if they were interviewed for an oral history project called *The Transmigration of Hazel Jane Plante.*

I remember another librarian at my university telling me they were sorry they'd have to miss an event being held at the library to celebrate the launch of my first novel, *Little Blue Encyclopedia (for Vivian)*. I was gobsmacked, because they'd recently publicly applauded the decision by Vancouver Public Library (VPL) to allow a notorious transphobe to hold an event at the library.

Here's the comment my colleague posted in the comments section of an article on VPL being banned from Vancouver Pride, which is a copy of a message they sent to VPL director Christina de Castell:

> Dear Christina,
>
> A quick note to say I applaud your position on this matter. You are spot on - however offensive the event may have been to some, it is a completely legitimate example of the library's necessary committment [sic] to the exercise of free speech and intellectual freedom, as you say – and Pride is out of line in their critique of the Library's stance and in 'banning' VPL from this year's parade.
> Many senior academic and institutional representatives have in recent years caved in to this sort of illiberal, censoring, 'deplatforming' pressure – it is especially evident on North American campuses. Your position – which was no doubt difficult to take and maintain – is courageous and sane and absolutely the correct one.
> Thank you and best wishes.
>
> [my colleague] [5]

4. If this sounds over-the-top, I will mention that people have grieved me, while I'm alive. And I've understood. All of this is to say that "transitioning" is an all-too-tidy word for a messy, ongoing process.

5. All comments from this article, which was published in July 2019, have since been removed. I still have a copy because at the time I linked to and

I remember signing copies of my novel after a well-attended, delightful launch at a local bookstore. One of the people in line was the chair of VPL's board when the library rented a room for a transphobic event. My body jolted into panic mode. Should I refuse to sign her book? Spit in her face?[6] She was no longer the chair of the library board, so I told myself that publicly haranguing her would do no good. I'd just be a hysterical trans girl. Plus, I'd recently learned that she was tight with a friend of mine, a trans woman I adore. I signed her book. It's the only copy I've signed that didn't end with "love, Hazel." For what it's worth, I withheld "love."

A couple of weeks later at the same bookstore, she approached me at a launch for a book by another trans femme writer. She came up to me after a friend of mine wandered off to look at books or pee or something. The ex-chair of VPL's board told me that she was sitting in a chair on the other side of the room, reading my novel and fangirling. I don't recall how I responded. But I know that I didn't cause a scene. There were no accusations. There was no spit. I didn't even tell her that she never replied to an email I sent to her and her fellow board members less than a year before, trying to persuade them to cancel this transphobic event.

Here's what I sent:

> Dear [chair of the library board and future fan of my novel] and other VPL Board members,
>
> I'm emailing to convey my concerns over VPL's decision to rent a meeting room for Meghan Murphy's upcoming talk, "Gender Identity Ideology and Women's Rights."
>
> Meghan Murphy is a well-known proponent of transphobia. It's not coincidental that she strongly opposed Bill C-16, which added gender

---

quoted the comment in an email to A, my former supervisor, because this comment prompted me to reconsider whether or not to hold a launch event for my novel at my library.

6. Before writing this piece, I didn't realize how much I want to spit in people's faces. (Note to self: Think more deeply about spit.)

identity and expression to the Canadian Human Rights Act and the Criminal Code. She testified against it and published several pieces on its perceived anti-feminism. Before Senate, she argued that women are oppressed "solely due to biology" and has stated repeatedly that trans women are men, both of which are clearly untrue and, equally clearly, transphobic.

I'm a trans woman (and a librarian), and I have no desire to "engage constructively" in an "open dialogue" about whether or not I deserve to exist. From past experiences, engaging with trans exclusionary (so-called) radical (so-called) feminists only leads to harm. Anyone familiar with Meghan Murphy's stance on gender identity knows exactly what she will be saying at this event.

I understand that the organizers of this event have promised "not to contravene the Criminal Code of Canada and the Human Rights Act of British Columbia during the course of their rental/program, and [that] this statement [was] included in [their] rental contract." If this event goes ahead, I'm interested in knowing how VPL plans to ensure that the event doesn't contravene the Criminal Code of Canada and the Human Rights Act of British Columbia, which the organizers have apparently promised to do.

If VPL is serious about community-led librarianship, it should do more to consider the safety and voices of those in trans communities. Transphobic and transmisogynistic views such as those held by this speaker feed directly into physical and verbal violence against trans people, and the decision to continue allowing this talk negates whatever positive effects have resulted from VPL's external programming and internal consultations around trans inclusion.

While it is possible to claim that offering a platform to someone does not constitute the endorsement of their ideas, the fact remains that this event will take place at VPL, and it will be perceived by many patrons as being part of VPL's programming slate, a fact that Murphy is clearly relying on.

The booking of public meeting rooms for controversial topics often brings up debates on intellectual freedom and free speech. However, if VPL truly wants to be a safe space for trans folks, our safety should be prioritized. VPL's meeting room policy allows for it to refuse or cancel bookings, so I would encourage you to do so to support those most affected by this decision.

Thanks,

Hazel

I remember that, while writing my next novel, the narrator started describing how trans women "are too good for this world. It isn't safe enough for us. It's killing us. It's especially awful for Black and brown and Indigenous trans women. They deserve safety. They deserve love. They deserve to live with ease. They deserve joy and pleasure. They belong in a world that is good enough for them." I think my narrator is right. In fiction, I'm often trying to write into a world that I wish existed, a world where I can breathe deeply and feel at home. It would be lovely if I felt at ease around librarians and if I felt at home in libraries. At times, I felt that way before transitioning. Sadly, as a visible trans femme librarian, I feel neither at ease nor at home.

I remember in my initial proposal for this chapter framing it as a 'stroboscopic piece' that would display an array of emotions related to being a trans librarian.

Oh, I've just located my submitted proposal. Here it is:

> For my chapter, I will share a kaleidoscopic collection of snippets related to being a trans femme librarian at a university in Canada. Some snippets will stem from before I transitioned. Some will involve transitioning. Some will fall on the 'after' side of the transitional fence. They will run the emotional gamut: positive, negative, mundane, bizarre, funny. I'll be using the "I remember" constraint, which was first used by Joe Brainard in his memoir I Remember (1970). Essentially, my piece will be a series of work-related, trans-specific memories, each of them beginning with the phrase "I remember ..." This structure (or, perhaps, 'stricture' is more apt here) will afford my piece a strobe-like effect that will allow me to tumble through a series of memories (not to worry: there will be a method to my weirdness) and help convey some of the emotional jumble that being trans in the workplace (and the world) can have.

While writing the first draft of this piece, I realized how much anger I have. There are far fewer positive, mundane, bizarre, and funny memories here than I thought there would be. But I think my anger is healthy and legitimate, because I feel forsaken by my institution and my profession.

And now I'm wondering if I should cut the reference to spitting in the face of a queer administrator at my institution. It feels like TOO MUCH. And I'm thinking about all the things that I left out of this piece because they felt like TOO MUCH. The trans lady doth complain too fucking much. I should be quiet and happy because I'm allowed to be here. It's as though an unspoken message thrums below the surface. *You have the audacity to exist, and we're letting you live. We even let you transition. You're welcome. Isn't that enough for you, Hazel? (Okay, sometimes you're not welcome, but you're still a lucky duck.) I mean, who do you think you are? (Don't ever forget how lucky you are.) What more do you want? (You are so bloody lucky.)*

About the Author

Hazel Jane Plante is an academic librarian, cat photographer, and writer. Her debut novel *Little Blue Encyclopedia (for Vivian)* (Metonymy Press, 2019) was given a Lambda Literary award for trans fiction. She also releases music under the name lo-fi lioness and helms the podcast t4t, which is about writing while trans. She currently lives in Vancouver on the unceded ancestral territories of the xʷməθkʷəy̓əm (Musqueam), Sḵwx̱wú7mesh (Squamish), and səl̓ílwətaʔɬ (Tsleil-Waututh) Nations.

Thirteen Books

Avi Bauer (he/him)

Keywords: transmasculine, law libraries, passing, disclosure

The law library where I work houses over five-hundred thousand volumes. Of those five-hundred thousand volumes, there are a total of thirteen books in our catalogue that include the term *transgender people* as a subject heading. Of those thirteen books, only two are classified under the call number **HQ77**, which is one of the few places in the Library of Congress Classification (LCC) that explicitly name transgender people. Or, well, close. The actual heading is:

- Social Sciences – The Family. Marriage. Woman – Human sexuality. Sex – Transsexualism. Transgenderism

That LCC uses the terms "transsexual" and "transgenderism" and classifies them under "human sexuality" is a conversation worth having for multiple reasons, but not here. I am more interested in the fact that, of the remaining eleven books on transgender people in our collection, six are classified under four different call numbers that refer only to sexual orientation, not gender identity:

- **HQ76.8:** *Social Sciences – The Family. Marriage. Woman – Human Sexuality. Sex – Homosexuality. Lesbianism – Gay rights movement. Gay liberation movement. Homophile movement*
- **KF337.5.G38:** *Law – United States (General) – Community legal services. Legal aid. Legal services to the poor – Legal services to particular groups, A-Z – Gays*

- **KF3467.5:** *Law – United States (General) – Social legislation – Labor law – Labor standards – Employment and dismissal – Discrimination in employment and its prevention – Particular groups – Sexual minorities. Sexual orientation discrimination*
- **KF4754.4:** *Law – United States (General) – Constitutional law – Individual and state – Civil and political rights and liberties – Particular groups – Sexual minorities*

The remaining five are filed under a variety of call numbers that have nothing to do with gender or sexuality at all. The closest we get from this group is:

- **KD7975:** *Law – Law of England and Wales – Criminal law – Particular offenses – Offenses against the person – Sexual offenses*

Again, there are conversations worth having about the choices we make when we classify, and the ways our classification systems constrain and shape those choices. But that aside, this is all to say:

It is hard to find transgender people in the law library.

A story: I have been working here for almost a year. Although the hair on my chin has been growing in, it is still sparse, and I keep my face shaved carefully clean. There is a student notorious for flirting with the female staff at the desk. He asks me what I am doing over the weekend. I stumble with my words, mutter something about being busy with housework. I wonder what he sees in that moment, or who he sees.

I am trans. That much is perhaps obvious. Strangely, it is less obvious than it used to be. Introducing myself used to be a practice in coming out, every "Hi, I'm Avi, I use he/him pronouns" met with some mix of surprise-confusion-amusement-approval-disapproval-concern. My face, my voice, my stature stood out enough from the acceptable box of "people who use he/him pronouns" to tag me immediately as some kind of gender Other, an outsider outlier.

These days, I still introduce myself the same way, but the response I receive now is flavoured by a new shape of surprise. As always, there are those who do not understand why someone would introduce themselves with their pronouns. But now I am also met with those who do not understand why someone *like me* would introduce themselves with their pronouns. "Hi, I'm Avi, I use he/him pronouns." *Well,* these people think, *obviously.*

It's the *obviously* that gets me. Since when have I become an Obvious that is not an Obviously Other? If gender transition is a journey, when did I arrive? Have I arrived? The answer, more and more often, is yes.

I have been working here for a year and a half. I have started to experiment with letting my facial hair grow in, and it is doing so with patchy gusto.
Two of my coworkers are chatting near the desk, discussing their personal dislike for tall-heeled shoes. I pipe up, joking that I could never get the hang of anything higher than an inch as a teen. They both pause, staring at me as though I had sprung suddenly and fully-formed from the invisible, irrelevant ether. I suppose that to them I have.

To the surprise of very few people, probably, a Jesuit law school is a decidedly gender-conforming space. (It's a very White space, too. And straight. And Catholic, although that one's a gimme.) Even in the library, men wear neutral colors, young women wear their hair long. In a weird way this helps disguise my gendered Otherness. If the expectation is that masculine equals male, all I have to do is put on a boring button-down and a pair of slacks and boom! That must be a dude, or why else is he dressed like a guy?

I do like causing trouble from time to time by breaking rank and wearing florals or doing my nails. But interestingly, the overwhelming cis-straight-White culture comes to my rescue. No one calls me out on my occasional flamboyance, because (1) generally, people are decent, and (2) it would be a much larger disruption of the Culture to acknowledge the deviance than to pretend it does not exist. An unofficial Don't Ask, Don't Tell, if you will.

To clarify: I work with lovely people who are nothing if not supportive allies. I even get compliments on my brighter outfits from time to time. But between this self-reinforcing gendered culture and the newly-gendered shape of my body, I find myself in a strange position. Almost without noticing, I have answered the questions Nordmarken poses in his autoethnography of the transmasculine journey: "Will people still stare at me when I am absorbed back into a sea of normative-appearing masculinity? When my gender ambiguity becomes less than it appears? How will I be in the world, if people become able to see me?"[1]

The answer, much as Nordmarken found it for himself, is surprisingly boring. Patrons greet me as they did, coworkers chat with me as they did. I check in serials and upload articles to our repository, as I did. But now I do so without the unspeakable arrow of Other pointing at me at all times. In many ways, this is a relief. But it is also a worry.

Here is my shameful secret: I do not know how to be trans without my body doing the talking for me. For years, my queer activism has been built upon the assumption that by merely existing in the public eye, I offered an educational resource for curious allies and a spiritual haven for the similarly gender-troubled. While canvassing or hosting workshops, I never had to prove my Queer Credentials. People simply looked at me, and heard me introduce myself ("Hi, my name's Avi, I use he/him pronouns") and they Knew. These days, though, I have run into the prospect that I have to explicitly tell people that I am trans for them to know it, rather than it being an assumed unspoken Known.

But how does one go about disclosing such a thing? What are the rules of verbally challenging an observer's assumption about my body?

I don't know. I've never had to.

I have been working here for just over two years. My facial hair has mostly grown in, and I have recently purchased my first pair of clippers.
A participant in a workshop I am hosting asks a question related to transness. I respond, describing my own experiences, but several members of the audience look confused. I realize with a start that nowhere in my presentation did I mention out loud that I am trans. With an even greater start I realize that lacking that explicit disclosure, my participants had assumed I am cis.

1. Sonny Nordmarken, "Becoming Ever More Monstrous: Feeling Transgender In-Betweenness," *Qualitative Inquiry* 20, no. 1 (2014): 43.

Why bother with disclosing my trans status at all? There are perks to letting others assume what they will. As my body has become newly visible in its maleness and invisible in its unremarkableness, I no longer have to Be Trans In The Library—I can just be, in the library. Nordmarken puts words to the experience: "This is the shape, the articulation of gender normative, White male privilege. Belonging is what this configuration of privilege feels like. The energy moving through the eyes: a way of looking that communicates inclusion, camaraderie, comfort. An ease in the taking of me as one of them."[2] If belonging is the benefit of staying stealth, why disrupt it?

There is something to be said about the power and value of being visibly trans, especially in as conservative a community as a Catholic school. Something about Queering spaces by being queer within them. Something about demonstrating to our student patrons that yes, there are trans people out in the world, and they are happy. Silin is one of many who have presented arguments encouraging us to consider the opportunities presented by integrating our identities with our educational work: "How is pedagogy changed when we dismantle the wall between private and professional experience? What risks do we take? What goals do we achieve when we open our lives to public inspection?"[3] Accordingly, many others have challenged the so-called coming out imperative, such as Rasmussen: "When coming out discourses are privileged, the act of not coming out may be read as an abdication of responsibility, or, the act of somebody who is disempowered or somehow ashamed of their inherent gayness [or transness]."[4]

Once again, we find a debate that is worth having, but not here. Setting aside these matters of pedagogy and discourse, I am still left with

2. Nordmarken, 44.

3. Jonathan G. Silin, "Teaching as a Gay Man: Pedagogical Resistance or Public Spectacle?" *GLQ: A Journal of Lesbian and Gay Studies* 5, no. 1 (1999): 96.

4 . Mary Lou Rasmussen, "The Problem of Coming Out," *Theory Into Practice* 43, no. 2 (2004): 146.

the question: I have worked so hard to be perceived as male, so why does being perceived as cisgender leave me with a foul taste in my mouth?

There may be no singular, perfect answer to that question, but that does not mean there are no answers to be found, partial or imperfect as they are. One such answer may be derived from the central term that sits at the heart of Nordmarken's description of passing: *privilege*. The benefits of (White) male privilege are manifold. To be heard; to be respected; to be deferred to; to be thought of as competent. They may play out in subtle ways in a majority-women space such as the library, but they are ever present. For example: like other types of libraries, law libraries are staffed primarily by women, somewhere in the range of 68% as of 2018.[5] But the balance is inconsistent as one moves up the ranks. At the law library director level, the percentage of women is closer to 57%: still a majority, but a much slimmer one.[6]

It would be so easy to accept privileges such as these as the just rewards of having "achieved" my gender, to allow myself to settle unreflexively into the "natural" order of things. But what is seen cannot be unseen, and privilege is a harsh spotlight. So, what to do about it? If only it were so easy as to simply decline. *No thank you, I have tasted your wine and it is bitter to my tongue.* Instead, I must learn how to disrupt it how I can, call attention to it when I can. I have some practice; after all, I have been White my whole life. But these new dimensions of unfairness are a new terrain, one I must first map before I can attempt to dismantle. In the meantime, what is left is a sticky feeling of impotence, of having been handed ill-gotten gains. To paraphrase a trans musician in similar shoes: now that I have a voice, I find I can't stand it.[7]

5. Jamie J. Baker, "The Intersectionality of Law Librarianship and Gender," *Villanova Law Review* 65, no. 5 (2021): 1011.

6. Baker, 1011.

7. Quinn Christopherson, "Erase Me," recorded May 2019, track 1 on *Erase Me*, Bandcamp, audio track.

I have been working here for two and a half years. I have slowly grown practiced at taking care of my beard, and tend to keep it at a carefully trimmed stubble.
A patron is struggling with one of the scanners. I happen to recognize the issue and am able to help them resolve it. Two coworkers observe and joke that they should clearly start sending all tech issues my way. I laugh along, unsure how to bring up that there are at least two women in our department who use these machines much more than I do, who I would consider to be much more obvious experts. I wonder: Does masculinity always taste like tongue-tiedness?

A second piece of the answer might be found in another term taken from Nordmarken: *belonging*. Like privilege, belonging can serve both as a benefit and a cost of gender passage. Belonging's role as a benefit is obvious: its absence indicates isolation, rejection, the weight of Other pulling us back from genuine connection. Belonging as a cost, though, is perhaps more subtle. It may, in fact, do us better to refer to benefit-as-cost by its synonym: *assimilation*.

As an American Jew (at a Catholic institution, no less), I am intimately familiar with the double-edged sword of assimilation. To assimilate is to enter into a community fully, to be accepted as one of their own—but to be accepted at the expense of what makes you unique. For many, this is a trade worth making. It comes with safety, job security, reduced scrutiny or harassment. But I am privileged (there's that word again) to be in a position where I can question the value of the trade-off.

To put it bluntly, I am tired. I've had my fill of being erased, of invisibility and illegibility. I fought my way out of one closet and through years of intelligibility to arrive where I am. Why should I be expected to feel satisfied with what amounts to a second, shinier closet? Who I am today is the culmination of so much work, so much time and patience, so much love. It seems an awful shame to swear all of that effort to secrecy just to secure belonging to an already suspect category.

Which leaves us with the same question as before: how am I supposed to disrupt these suspect categories all by myself? As I've said, I enjoy wearing the occasional feminine flair—but I can only experiment with my presentation so far before dysphoria or misgendering has me running back to the relative safety of gender conformity. Do I start wearing a white-pink-blue pin on my lapel as a signal to those in the know? Do I add it as a line in my email signature, where identity is already digitally abstracted? Do I simply start introducing myself as trans, self-outing as declarative? ("Hi, I'm Avi, I use he/him pronouns, which I'm telling you because I'm transgender.") And to whom should I be out: my coworkers, other university staff, our patrons? Does my being out serve them, or only myself? Does it matter?

Here is a simple truth: I don't know. Navigating the strange terrain of being out as a passing trans man is hard, and confusing, and terrifying. I am only just relearning to push back at the normative culture that I used to flaunt simply by being, and the learning curve is steep.

Maybe I will figure it out someday. Find the perfect balance between visibility and belonging, acceptance and subversion. Or maybe I will be seduced by the siren call of conformity and give in to the voice in the back of my mind that tells me to relax now that I've "made it." I find that unlikely, though.

Here is a simple truth: it is hard to find transgender people at the law library. Why make it harder?

A story: It is today, May 2021. My beard, short and well-kept, scratches at the inside of my face mask where no one can see it.
I pull all thirteen books with the subject heading "transgender people" in our stacks, which when put together take up less than the top shelf of my cart. We could fit all of them in a single display for Pride next month. I could bring out the small trans flag I keep hidden away on a shelf in my office. Maybe one or two of the handful of graduates studying for the bar will stop to take a look, but likely not. It will be a small display.
But it will be there.

Bibliography

Baker, Jamie J. "The Intersectionality of Law Librarianship and Gender." *Villanova Law Review* 65, no. 5 (2021): 1011-1035. https://www.villanovalawreview.com/article/18978.

Christopherson, Quinn. "Erase Me." Recorded May 2019. Track 1 on *Erase Me*. Bandcamp, audio track. https://quinnchristopherson.bandcamp.com/track/erase-me.

Nordmarken, Sonny. "Becoming Ever More Monstrous: Feeling Transgender In-Betweenness." *Qualitative Inquiry* 20, no. 1 (2014): 37-50. https://doi.org/10.1177/1077800413508531.

Rasmussen, Mary Lou. "The Problem of Coming Out." *Theory Into Practice* 43, no. 2 (2004): 144-150. https://doi.org/10.1207/s15430421tip4302_8.

Silin, Jonathan G. "Teaching as a Gay Man: Pedagogical Resistance or Public Spectacle?" *GLQ: A Journal of Lesbian and Gay Studies* 5, no. 1 (1999): 95-106. https://doi.org/10.1215/10642684-5-1-95.

About the Author

Avi Bauer is the Digital Initiatives & Scholarly Communication Librarian at the Boston College Law Library and an MLIS student at Simmons University. In previous lives he worked for the Yes on 3 transgender rights campaign in Massachusetts and studied Mechanical Engineering and Women's & Gender Studies at MIT. He's not sure how those led to librarianship, but is glad he got here.

My Name Is Max

Max Bowman (they/them)

Keywords: self-deprecation, coping, isolation

In discussing my career in libraries, there is a specific phrase I regularly employ, one meant to obscure, and make light of, the conditions that result in feeling as though a place isn't meant for you. The phrase is this: "A lot of my career is fueled by spite." I've said it hundreds of times, but right after the words make their transition from private thought to public discourse, I register the unease that admission causes, and I quickly say, "Spite isn't exactly the right word." But isn't it? Upon seeing the call for proposals for this book, I knew that I wanted to participate. The parameters were broad and I'd been searching for a project that would allow me the opportunity to explore how spite, anger, exhaustion, and exasperation came to be emotions I associate with my time in academia. In the proposal I submitted, I asked for a space to be unapologetically indignant and angry; over time, I've learned to embrace these emotions because their impact in my life is one of movement. I hadn't predicted that by the time I actually sat down to write, I'd be unable to channel anger, bitterness, or any of the emotions that usually propel me into some kind of action. I'm exhausted, and for me, exhaustion doesn't manifest as a rallying cry. It manifests as getting by. This isn't the chapter I'd intended to write, or wanted to write, but I'm done fighting it; even though I can't seem to summon that familiar frustration, I still have things to say.

How We Get By

In early 2021 a friend reached out via Twitter to share an observation about a panel I'd participated in; they were the moderator, and they'd asked a question relevant to the panel's topic, which was all about logistics work. I'd answered, moved on, and thought nothing more of it. Months later, they were rewatching the recording and the way that I spoke about a recurring incident struck them. Though I couldn't remember the specifics of my answer, when they told me what it was about, I immediately knew what they were referring to. In answering a question about providing library services and forming relationships with people we never meet, I'd illustrated that point by recalling the overwhelming number of times that I'd been referred to as "Mr. Bowman." In my answer, I said, "A lot of it was helping people all day long that we never saw, as I can attest to being called Mr. Bowman [insert laughter] so many times, no one ever knew who we were..."[1]

I am intimately familiar with how my affect changes when I'm describing incidents that have caused me some discomfort—I laugh in an attempt to make sure everyone else is at ease. This downplaying of my own emotions to ensure the relative comfort of others is a technique I've perfected because it's self-preservation. Unless you've spent years trying to hide or diminish your own discomfort for the sake of others, the distress is nearly invisible. Even though the event I'm describing was over in an instant, my friend and colleague, who also identifies as non-binary trans, recognized my discomfort because, as they put it, "you laughed in this funny-not-funny way that I am very familiar with, and I turned the recording off there 'cause I had to sit with that for a Real Long Time."

This conversation between my friend and I occurred nearly a year ago, but even now, I can remember every part of it. I can remember

1. Max Bowman et al. "Logistics: The technologies and people that manage our stuff," panel talk at the Access 2020 Annual Conference, streamed live on October 19, 2020, YouTube video, 4:09:10, https://youtube/Asqx7-iRlE4?t=11087s.

what I was doing, where I was sitting, how it made me feel, and that's of note because these days, after a seemingly minor head injury earlier this year, I've struggled with both long- and short-term memory. But for conversations and events that evoke strong emotions, for better or worse, I can recall every detail. This exchange also happened to be especially relevant in those moments because I was grappling with complex emotions related to a series of recurring incidents that took place on the campus where I work.

In 2019 I accepted a position at a small private liberal arts college. I began my career in a similar setting and after years of working at much larger institutions, I was relieved to return to a campus setting where I would be able to go to the dining hall and actually put faces to names; I'd missed the familiarity that comes with working on a small residential campus. My start date was close to the start of the fall semester, so there wasn't much time to acclimate to campus before students arrived. When I began that semester, I was genuinely excited to make connections with students, faculty, and staff. I'd moved 800 miles from my home and my family, and aside from my wife, I didn't know anyone.

For the most part, everything in those first few weeks went well. I was making strides at work and getting to know my colleagues, but I was incredibly busy and I struggled to find time to leave the library. One day, despite the pile of work on my desk, I made the decision to take time to explore the campus; I wanted to meet people, and anyone who knows me knows that I can begin a conversation with anyone, anywhere. Talking to strangers is a skillset I come by honestly, and I was ready to practice it. I remember leaving the library that day and feeling encouraged. It was a beautiful fall day, the campus was gorgeous and so much of what I was experiencing—the cool weather, the early fall, the smell—was new to me. I'd only been walking around for a few minutes when I sensed that there was a commotion behind me. Someone was yelling a name, not mine, and it seemed like the person they were calling out to wasn't responding, because the person doing the calling out was getting progressively louder and their tone was growing more insistent.

A few seconds later, the person who was calling out caught up to me, and it was only then that I realized that they'd been trying to get my attention. They weren't calling my name, but they'd mistaken me for someone else. When they realized that I was not the person they thought I was, they were embarrassed and apologized. I, of course, said that it was okay, and we moved on. As I mentioned, I can usually begin a conversation with anyone, and I'd considered striking up a conversation right then, but I could tell the person was feeling self-conscious about our interaction and wanted it to end, which I understood. I continued walking through campus, visiting all the spots I'd spent the last few weeks directing students to and feeling relieved that I'd managed to give out the correct directions to places that I'd never been. I was deep in thought and staring at a campus map without really paying attention to the people around me when, again, I thought I heard a person yelling out a familiar name, though still not my name. For the second time in less than half an hour, I'd been mistaken for someone else. This time I turned around well before the person approached, and they, realizing their mistake right away, shouted a quick, "Sorry," and ran off.

At this point, I thought I recognized the name they were calling out. I'm hard of hearing, so I wasn't certain that I'd heard it correctly, but I took a chance and, eventually, asked a colleague if they knew of a person by that name. As it turns out, I'd heard the name correctly. I learned that this person was a staff member at another office on campus. In their role they had significant interactions with students, and though they'd only worked at the college for a little over a year, their position on campus was one of visibility.

I'm going to fast forward to the present day—I would love to tell you that those two incidents were isolated, but I can't. For the six months that I was on campus (before we transitioned to remote learning due to the pandemic), I would go on to experience similar incidents at least a couple of times per week. After the first few times, I tried ignoring it. I thought that if I kept walking and didn't slow my pace, people would realize that I wasn't the person they were looking for, but that didn't happen either. Sometimes when people are embarrassed because they've made a mistake, they become defensive, and that's something that I experienced. It's hard to explain, even to myself, because it doesn't seem logical that simply saying to a person, "I am not ___, my name is Max," would be cause for defensiveness, but time and again, it was. If it wasn't defensiveness, it was embarrassment, and in an effort to soothe the other person's embarrassment, I would often tell folks that I was regularly mistaken for this person, as in, "Don't worry, lots of people do it, you're not the only one," but never once did the other person offer reassurance. Just once it would have been helpful to hear, "It's frustrating that this happens to you so often."

This is the point in my story where I tell you that I don't look anything like the person I was so often mistaken for. In fact, I've never met them. I know a few things about them—they wear glasses, they use they/them pronouns, and it could be said that we dress similarly, at least that's what people told me as they backed away after realizing I'm not the person they thought I was. In the plainest of language: people saw a fat, gender nonconforming, visibly (to them) queer person and that was all they saw, and so, in an instant, I became someone else. The truth is, I hadn't allowed myself to acknowledge the impact that this was having until I had the conversation with my friend where they mentioned their familiarity with self-deprecating laughter as a coping mechanism. But this person, my not-so-lookalike, had been on my mind lately because I'd just found out that they'd left the college, and when I heard that information, all I felt was a sense of uncomplicated relief. It wouldn't last. As it turns out, that feeling of relief was emotionally costly; it wasn't the kind you celebrate, it was more the kind that accompanies you after you've outrun something.

Let me explain. I came of age in the nineties, so this is going to be a particularly nineties reference, but it's important—do you remember the Blind Melon video for their song, "No Rain?"[2] It's the one that opens with a small girl in a shiny bee costume, gold pipe cleaners for antennae,

2. Blind Melon, "No Rain," September 1, 2021 YouTube Video, 4:06, https://www.youtube.com/watch?v=3qVPNONdF58.

striped fabric on her head and arms, and she's wearing tap shoes, a thing you realize when she begins a short tap dance routine. In that opening scene she looks unencumbered—not exactly joyful, but, and please forgive this cliché, she's dancing like no one is watching. When the routine ends, there's silence, until someone in the audience, just out of view, begins laughing. The little girl bows her head, wipes her eyes, runs off stage and begins running and dancing through the streets of L.A. Throughout the video, you can tell she's trying to make connections, and though it's not going particularly well, she's undeterred. Finally, there's this scene—it's at minute 2:20 if you're following along by watching the video—she approaches these gates that are in fields of green grass best described as the Windows XP fields—she looks through the gates, and her mouth opens wide in pure joy and astonishment. What she's just seen in those green fields, with nothing but blue skies as the backdrop, is a group of people in bee costumes joyfully dancing together. The song lyrics evoke this togetherness, a promise of someone to always be there, and encouraging the listener to stay with them.[3]

For the majority of my life, I've been that bee. The middle of three daughters, the only one who didn't "act right," the only one who was fat, the only one who changed their name, their body, and the only one who silently craved acceptance from the people around them but refused to do all the things required to achieve it. So much of my adulthood can best be described as what I've come to call "the unraveling." I don't know who I am without all of the adjustments I make every day so that I can fit. I digress—what I want you to know is that I'm accustomed to being the only, and I've spent so much of my life saying silent prayers before I enter restaurants, bathrooms, classrooms, workplaces, parks, beaches, locker rooms, doctor's offices—you name it, and I can guarantee that I've made it holy, with all the prayers I've said: "Please, please let there be someone who looks like me in this place." So, when I say that the relief I felt didn't come without consequences, this is what I mean.

3. Winggo2382, "Blind Melon - No Rain – Lyrics," YouTube, September 23, 2009. https://www.youtube.com/watch?v=Miec205fvnE.

Along with the relief came guilt, isolation, and this nagging feeling that it wouldn't change anything. I am resilient, not by choice, but out of necessity. But even with so much rehearsed resilience at the ready, what I'd realized was that even if my not-so-lookalike's departure somehow miraculously changed my lot on campus and I managed to be seen as more than fat and queer, the events that took place over the last year and a half—all the offers of reassurance I'd given, all the awkward hellos and goodbyes they'd given, all the apologies I'd offered, all the backing away, all the relief that a person feels when they exit an embarrassing situation—had taken a permanent toll. I no longer wanted to meet people in those informal ways that usually fill me up. More than that, the sum of all those interactions is that they took from me the one thing I always understood to be a constant in my life: the reassurance that I felt from being in a space with people who looked like me.

I wanted to tell you this was the end. I desperately wanted this section to effortlessly swell and meet some grand conclusion and when it did, I'd tell you that I'd learned so much about myself through this process and that what I'd learned was far more valuable than what was taken from me. I wanted that. I needed that. About a month ago, I was standing in some random line on campus (could've been any line), in some random building (could've been any building), when a person brushed past me and said, "Good to see you..." and then they said a name that wasn't mine. It's only happened one other time since then—that's something.

What Do You Need from Us?

I'm glad you asked.

I've been asked some variation of this question, both personally and professionally, by a number of folks, and what I've realized is that when someone asks this kind of open-ended question, what they're really asking is, "When will my part be over?" For better or worse, transitions aren't a solo act; they require the participation of partners, friends, family, colleagues, and even strangers. When I change my name, my pronouns, my appearance, I am constructing a home for myself, carefully, quietly at first, but for it to be complete, I have to let you in. I hold my breath. I wring my hands. I hate that I need you to sign the papers, approve the changes. But this is the way it is—I need you.

Your participation doesn't end when you call me by my name or use my pronouns. It doesn't end when I stop correcting you, either because I don't want to, or I don't need to. It doesn't end when previous versions of my digital self finally merge with the tangible one I built from the ground up. I let you in; act like that means something.

I know that people make mistakes. I make mistakes. I can be gracious, just as I am grateful for the grace that has been extended to me. But some mistakes are more costly than others. Some mistakes come at points when I am already on the ground, having not had time to right myself since the last blow. What I need from you, from myself, our families, our neighbors, our collective workplaces is for us to *see* one another, to care for each other.

Where We Go from Here

The introduction for this chapter is based on the proposal that I submitted nearly a year ago. I expected this to be an opportunity to engage with anger, but it's turned out to be a chapter about the consequences of using deflection and self-depreciation as a coping mechanism. I have absolutely no idea how I didn't initially make that connection—a portion of the first line of this chapter reads, "there is a specific phrase I regularly employ, one meant to obscure, and make light of, the conditions that result in feeling as though a place isn't meant for you"—it's right there. As a trans person who works in academic libraries, on campuses where we are quick to tell everyone that they're welcome without knowing if that's actually true, without having asked anyone, and usually without having done much preparation, I want to be able to express anger and frustration, but I don't think there's room for that. And so, I get by. I hope that if I make you feel better, I'll feel better—instead, I just feel empty.

I wrote this chapter during an active pandemic—we're still in it, and I don't have any idea when or if this will ever be over. Throughout this time, I've seen a particular quote shared widely that is regularly attributed to Dr. Fauci, the Chief Medical Advisor to the President. The quote is, "I don't know how to explain to you why you should care about other people." Those aren't the words of Dr. Fauci, they're the words of Lauren Morrill who tweeted them in January, 2017 to express frustration about debates over the Affordable Care Act.[4] It's easy to understand why Morrill's words were applied to our current situation—from masking to vaccinations, all that's required of us to get through this pandemic is for us to consider one another, and yet I've never, ever felt more doubt about our willingness to do that.

I can't tell you where we go from here.

Bibliography

Bayer, Samuel. "Blind Melon – No Rain." YouTube. October 15, 2021, Video, 4:06, https://www.youtube.com/watch?v=3qVPNONdF58.

Bowman, Max, Gillian Byrne, Michael Campbell, Jordan Hale, and Dustin McMurphy. "Logistics: The Technologies and People That Manage Our Stuff." Access Day 1 2020. YouTube, October 19, 2020. https://www.youtube.com/watch?v=Asqx7-iRlE4&t=11087s.

Morrill, Lauren. "My Biggest Problem in These ACA Debates? I Don't Know How to Explain to You Why You Should Care about Other People." Twitter, January 13, 2017. https://twitter.com/LaurenEMorrill/status/819714138213642241?s=20.

Winggo2382. "Blind Melon - No Rain - Lyrics." YouTube, September 23, 2009. https://www.youtube.com/watch?v=Miec205fvnE.

---

4. Lauren Morrill, "My Biggest Problem in These ACA Debates? I Don't Know How to Explain to You Why You Should Care about Other People," Twitter, January 13, 2017, https://twitter.com/LaurenEMorrill/status/819714138213642241?s=20.

About the Author

Max Bowman has worked in academic libraries for over twenty years. They have a fondness for resource sharing, logistics work, peer support, and celebrating their colleagues.

Acknowledgements

Thank you to all the folks who helped me get through this chapter (and these last couple of years)—I appreciate you. Thank you to the Queer Thirst DM group for hearing me when I was in pain, and for providing the gentlest of guidance and support. Thank you to my wife, Lizzy, for reminding me that I am worthy of love.

On Being Seen, on Being Legible, on Being: A Black, Agender Perspective on a Career in Libraries

Adrian Williams (they/them)

Keywords: agender, non-binary, Black American, academic libraries

I remember lying in bed one night, around six years old, puzzling over a word that a fellow child on the playground had called me earlier that day. We had been in the tire tower during recess; they were sitting in its bowels and I was climbing past them to the top. His friend had asked him if I was a girl or a boy, and they had replied that I was a "tomboy." I don't think that in the moment, in the tire tower, that I'd paused to agree or disagree with that stranger child. I think I just kept on climbing. But later that night I remember coming back to that word tomboy and asking myself whether I was, indeed, a boy. I decided no, because I didn't feel like a boy. Then I asked myself if I felt like a girl, and the answer came again as no. When I looked inside for where gender might be there was instead a blankness, a field of gray lit by a pale sun. I was a not-girl not-boy, and because I didn't know what to do with that information, or what use it gave me, I put it aside for another day. There just wasn't anything I could do with it. I placed it in the back of my mind for the rest of my childhood and adolescence until, in late high school, I found an online community on tumblr.com and saw other users talking about a gender identity called non-binary and another one called agender. And all at once I remembered what I'd already realized about myself so long ago.

I knew I was Black much earlier than six. I only had to look at my skin, and at my parents, to know this. I confess that when I was growing up, I found myself much more resistant to my blackness than I was to my lack of gender. My blackness was something that other kids and teachers could, and sometimes did, see as a fault about me. My family tried to teach me to love my blackness, but it's a difficult thing to do in a society like ours that devalues blackness so, so much. It took me a while to embrace my skin and my culture.

Though I've always felt at home in libraries, it was not a profession that I immediately gravitated to. For a while, it felt like too obvious a career choice. Just because I loved to read didn't mean I would make a good librarian. But when I began to head into the latter half of my undergraduate studies and found myself in need of both work experience and a tentative career path, libraries presented themselves as a welcoming option. The actual, visible work of librarianship was about as mysterious to me as it was to anyone else who had only ever been a patron, but after looking more into it, it seemed like work I could do. It looked to be organization, helping other people with their research, helping people find books they were interested in reading, giving those patrons a public space to exist without obligation or fee. When I graduated with my bachelor's, I went straight into pursuing a master's in library science. A couple of months after the start of my first semester, I started my first academic library position as a staff member in the medical library at that same university.

In this first position, because it was a fairly small library with a fairly small number of staff, I did a good amount of everything. I did the cataloging and some of the e-resource management, processed interlibrary loan requests, and sometimes helped the librarians on reference and research assistance requests. From this miscellaneous work, I gravitated to cataloging and classification. Everything felt so well-defined. Every book could be put in its proper place with only some subject analysis and cataloger's judgement. Scope notes and used fors. Authorized headings and local notes. A few more years into my career as a cataloger now, I know that these subject headings are not as static and objective as I once thought them to be. I now recognize that these subject headings exist as reflections of the dominant groups that have created and maintained them. Furthermore, being institutionally-established things, these headings are inherently resistant to significant change, especially as they regard people-centered topics like ethnicity, gender, and sexuality. Nevertheless, cataloging is still a field that I feel fairly at home in. The work of bridging the gap between the language we have available to us in our authorized headings to the language everyday users will search by is work that I'm committed to engaging in.

I wasn't out as a non-binary person at the medical library. It was a small library, and though there were a few people there who I knew wouldn't have a problem with it, I'd heard enough of my supervisor's political opinions to know that she would. I wasn't at a stage in my life where I felt emotionally equipped to explain that part of myself and defend my existence. I was already doing so much work to be perceived as a peaceable Black person in an astonishingly white work space that it felt like too much to add another thing on. There's actually a word someone gave me the other day to help me articulate this: legible. There's already a fairly wide cultural divide between myself and many of the colleagues and managers I've had in my brief career in libraries. We've grown up in very different ways, and have very different ways of naturally approaching work-related problems. As a young professional seeking to learn and grow as much as I could in this first position, I needed to remain legible to my white cishet manager and coworkers, because if I didn't, I wouldn't receive the information and mentoring I needed to be able to move on to higher positions.

So, I wasn't out gender-wise, but I did take this first position as an opportunity to try out different styles of professional dress that I might be able to carry forward into the rest of my career. I'd always looked at more masculine fashions and wanted to try them for myself, but hadn't yet been able to make the jump to actually wearing overtly masculine things. The best I'd been able to do before then was to emulate what I often referred to as, "twelve-year-old boy trying his best"—graphic t-shirts, jorts, Henleys. Buying ties and then never having the guts to wear them outside of my bedroom. Boat shoes with skinny jeans. I never tilted too far to either end of the feminine-masculine spectrum, instead limiting myself to some safe, awkward patchwork of polos and ballet flats. But this library had a dress code, so I took the opportunity to try out different styles. I would wear a button-down shirt with straight-leg slacks on one day, a dress with flats the next. I can give partial credit to my former supervisor at this first position, who only complimented my appearance when I wore make-up or dressed femininely, with my full headlong tilt toward masculine presentation. I do not blame her; I somewhat understand her perspective. She probably saw me switching from slacks to skirts as me dressing up, and she wanted to acknowledge that in a positive way, so she complimented me. At the time, however, I just wanted to experiment with my gender presentation and remain unperceived while I did so (an impossible task, I now know). These interactions, however, did lead me to further question who I was from a gender presentation perspective, how I wanted other people to view me, and what compliments or comments I wanted people to have about my body. As time has gone on, I've gotten rid of my dresses, bought more button-downs and sweaters from the "men's" side of stores, and felt more and more like myself and who I want to become.

Certainly and obviously, one's gender is not wrapped up in what they wear, but finding a style of dress that brought me closer to how I wanted to be perceived did bring me some measure of confidence. It also made me more and more unwilling to continue letting people use pronouns for me that didn't fit. My friends, classmates, and professors knew to use they/them pronouns for me. I was studying at the same university for which I worked, and with the overlap between library science professors and librarians, it was becoming increasingly more difficult to compartmentalize and remember who knew me as they and who as she. Mostly to grow in my career and cataloging expertise, and partly to have a fresh start as Adrian the non-binary person, I applied for and was offered an open position as a cataloging associate in the main library's cataloging department.

I disclosed my gender to my supervisor at this new job for a couple of reasons. The first is that I knew I wouldn't be there for more than a couple of years at the most. I would be graduating from my master's program at the end of the year and interviewing for cataloging librarian positions after that, so I felt that any discrimination or negative attitudes about my gender could be endured for that relatively brief period of time. Other than the occasional misgendering, it was fairly easy to exist there as an agender person, especially since my job as a staff cataloger was fairly siloed and independent. I didn't have to worry too much about being misgendered to my face, because my job was so solitary that there were few people around to talk about me in my presence. Also, my supervisor there had a trans child that she advocated strongly for, so I had little to worry about from a management perspective.

Once I graduated with my MLIS, I began looking for librarian positions that would help me grow in my career. I applied to several places and ended up getting a couple of in-person interviews. The one that was more promising, more in line with the work I wanted to do and the type of library I wanted to be at, was ten hours away from my hometown. It was in Kentucky, a faraway land that I hadn't heard a single Black, queer thing about. I didn't want to go through the trouble of moving there and being so far away from everyone I loved before I knew whether or not it was safe for me to be myself there, so at the very beginning of the two-day in-person interview I told my would-be supervisor the name and pronouns that I use. My pronouns were used correctly for the rest of the interview, I was told where the gender-neutral bathrooms were without having to ask, and I was generally treated well. Despite the very small number of BIPOC there, it seemed like a good place to work, with projects I'd be excited to participate in.

I've been in this position for almost two years now, and I don't regret the decision to come here, nor to be as open as I've been. I've been able to meet a couple of other gender diverse people who work here and to speak openly about equity, diversity, and inclusion issues and equity opportunities our library system could take action on.

Occasionally, thinking back to my colleagues at that medical library and how kind and helpful they were to me, I regret not giving some of them the chance to know me. At the end of the day, I rationalize it in this way: despite the fact that (at the time of writing this) we're in 2021, a lot of people still aren't understanding of transgender and gender diverse people. Some may hide that intolerance or ignorance behind a gritted smile or neutral expression, but that doesn't take away from their bias against us. I was in my first library position and didn't want to damage my prospects by making the wrong people "uncomfortable." My parents are the survivalist type—keep your head down and stay out of the office politics types, smile and keep it to yourself types. They had taught me to prioritize my safety and security over my self-expression. I wasn't about to out myself unless I knew I could be safe doing so, or otherwise safely extricate myself from the situation.

I am not so much unlearning as reworking the rules I've set for myself on how to keep myself safe. I speak out more about equity, diversity, and inclusion issues at my current position than I ever have in my life. It is terrifying and fulfilling, and sometimes I don't do it right, but sometimes I do. The world in which I spend the majority of my time—which is to say, the public academic sphere—is progressing in uneven fits and starts towards treating transgender and gender diverse people better. Even still, when someone misgenders me and I find myself in the position of having to correct them, it feels like doing so is like asking to get punched in the face. More often than not, against my own self-interest, I don't correct people at all. It still feels terrifying and self-destructive. Do I remain legible to my colleagues, let them keep their misconception of me and in doing so protect my professional safety? Or do I fight for my inner self that deserves to be seen clearly as who I am?

There is also something to be said about being hypervisibly Black and invisibly trans, and the isolation that is both perpetuated by myself and by the people around me. Being trans in a roomful of cisgender people who have mistaken me as a cisgender woman has clued me into the fact that there are hateful and ignorant things that cisgender people will be perfectly comfortable saying as long as they don't think the type of people they're talking about are present. This is something that I've known on an intellectual, commonsense level for a while, but to experience it in the flesh is simply another thing. It's made me a bit paranoid, to be honest, of what my white colleagues are comfortable saying when I'm not in the room. But I have to push past this paranoia and this isolation to connect and be seen and do my work.

I'm still early in my career, but my hope is for it to be a long one. I hope that, throughout the rest of my time as a cataloger, I can learn more and do more to make our library catalog and other systems inclusive and accessible to the people it has not historically been inclusive to. Libraries have given me a lot in my life, and I love them. Part of that love is participating in the movements and initiatives that seek to hold libraries accountable for their past and present injustices. I have neither the stamina nor courage to be an activist, but I want to do what I can in my daily life and work to improve things for those that come after me.

About the Author

Adrian Williams is a cataloging librarian. Their interests include inclusive subject headings and classification, linked data, and the history of classification and controlled vocabularies. They spend a lot of time outside of work indulging in their hobbies, which include Dungeons and Dragons, playing music, and riding their bike around town.

Nail Polish Epiphany

Mark Bieraugel (they/them)

Keywords: non-binary, clothing, professionalism, gender expression, authenticity

Peep Scented Nail Polish 5 Pack!

Do they really smell of marshmallow Peeps? I nervously sniffed my brightly polished fingernails as I walked to my on-campus video interview, where I would talk about what it was like being a gender non-conforming person at my workplace. My university wanted individuals' experiences, mine included, to create a webpage full of written and video stories of a group of employees to show how inclusive we were. But back to my nails. My pink, purple, yellow, green, and blue nails should smell of Peeps, those super sugary marshmallow chick-shaped Easter treats. *Do they smell like sugar?* I inhaled deeply, almost dizzy from trying to figure it out. *Why is this so important to me right now?*

Walking faster now, up some stairs, and past some undergrads. *Am I doing the right thing?* Not about painting my nails Peep colors, but did I really want to be interviewed, on video, about being gender non-conforming at the university I worked for? No one was forcing me to do this. I chose this. To be public about myself, and not in a small way.

Am I ready to come out to everyone I work with? The campus community? Was I just doing this so our marketing department could show how inclusive my university was? *Why am I doing this to myself?* Wasn't it enough to just be, at that point, gender non-conforming? To not shout it out to anyone with an internet connection and a willingness to watch a video about me?

Yes! I had decided to go to the interview, so I was going. When I commit, I commit. So, with my Peep-smelling candy-colored nails, each a different color and impossible to ignore, I went to spill out a new part of my life online, publicly, and in bright, living color: my new, gender-non-conforming life out in public.

By performing my non-binary gender, do I become that gender? When I was a man, I learned to perform my boy/man gender from babyhood. I had a script and a costume. Although I struggled with traditional male behaviors such as "boys don't cry" and "men are stoic," I still knew the parameters of my gender even as I pushed to expand those parameters in different ways.

As a non-binary person, the performative aspect of gender seems even more apparent to me. I feel as if I'm making up my non-binary gender as I go along. I have some external, living models of non-binary people whom I watch to see how they act, speak, write, and dress. However, there is no overarching archetype, no standard model for being non-binary, no societal norms for non-binary intelligibility. If "identity is a slippery theoretical construct" as Maureen Goggin states, then living the theory is slippery as well.[1]

How did I get to a place where my nails were bright, my necklace was a long strand of pearls, and my blazer was a coat of many colors?

I was surprised as anyone to realize my new, non-binary gender in my mid-fifties. I always wondered how some people didn't know they were until much later in life, especially queer people who would come out in middle age. For me, I knew I liked men early on in life, and I benefited in the late 1970s and early 1980s, when I was coming out, from access to books and a more information-rich world about gay men. But in my reading there was practically nothing about gender. I rarely even thought

1. Maureen Daly Goggin, "Fabricating Identity: Janie Terrero's 1912 Embroidered English Suffrage Signature Handkerchief" in *Women and Things, 1750-1950: Gendered Material Strategies* edited by Maureen Daly Googin and Beth Fowles Tobin (New York: Routledge, 2009), 18.

of my gender, other than in relation to my sexuality. In fact, my gender was there, giving me a privileged status that I benefited from. Once I accepted that I wasn't a man, but was non-binary, I was able to see more clearly how I tried on, literally and figuratively, garments and ideas about being something other than man or woman throughout my whole life.

I'm still working out how to be non-binary and what exactly my gender is. What I do know is that my gender isn't female, and my gender isn't male—my gender is something else. I'm a gender maximalist. It feels right to be more. It is all the material stuff we add to our bodies which interests me: the clothes, the jewelry, accessories, fragrances. The things that customize us. I also want the freedom to act like I want, outside of our society's gender expectations.

One reason for my late-in-life realization was a lack of role models early on, a lack of seeing non-binary ways of living and of being. Of course, non-binary people were always about, living their non-binary lives, being and presenting themselves if they could. But I didn't see them, or if I saw them, I didn't see what they were as a viable option for me. I didn't have a good way of describing what I was, what I am, until recently.

The new narratives and the new gender identity tales being told allow for complexity, and at the same time, make a wide variety of experiences valid. Once I read some of those personal narratives, I realized there are more options for me to live a truer life. I'm on a different path, one that has a story arc but not an end point. Well, we all have an endpoint. In a way I'm already at my destination, in that I've embraced my new gender privately and publicly.

Mid-Day Bliss Out: A Nail Polish Epiphany

Is nail polish going to be the theme of this essay? Maybe.

An epiphany is a sudden insight into the reality or essential meaning of something, usually initiated by something simple, homey, or commonplace. My epiphany was caused by a bottle of dark purple Essie nail polish with the wonderful name of "Winning Streak."

It was early in September 2018, a few days before our library's spa day: The Mid-Day Bliss Out. To improve morale at our library, the administration started doing fun events, and our Mid-Day Bliss Out aimed to do exactly that. During the two-hour Bliss-Out, you could get a chair massage, sip on some fancy water with a raspberry in it, have your chakras read, and, most importantly for me, get your polished nails stamped. (Stamping is when you get a design applied to each polished nail.)

For some reason, I really wanted to get my nails done and stamped. I didn't question that want, I just sort of went with it. My coworker offered to polish my nails a day or so before the event.

What did it mean to have my nails done? I wasn't really looking at the meaning of it, but rather, how it felt. When I looked at my purple "Winning Streak" nails, it just felt right and glorious—like I had been missing something and my nails were a puzzle piece that moved in perfectly. *Click.* I felt whole.

In *Appropriate[ing] Dress: Women's Rhetorical Style in Nineteenth Century America,* Carol Mattingly writes that "gender, inscribed on and around women's bodies, was constructed largely in the visual impact created by their clothing and appearance. Second, gender aligned women by their location, a specifically assigned 'sphere.'"[2]

As a speaker and instructor in classrooms, I consciously choose my clothing, jewelry, nail polish, and fragrance, all to construct a gender that is unique to me. In working to manipulate my presentation, I also threaten the gender binary. This threatening leads to tension and the question of whether that tension should be addressed or mitigated. Or should it be ignored? I'm breaking cultural norms by my dress, or at least bending them quite a bit. Mattingly notes that challenges to gender norms in terms of dress engender fear, and also reprisals. In the 18th century, women's dress, at least for certain strata and races, was very codified, and "a rhetoric of dress was in place."[3] In the business and

2. Carol Mattingly, *Appropriate[ing] Dress: Women's Rhetorical Style in Nineteenth-Century America* (Carbondale, IL: Southern Illinois University Press, 2002): 1.

3. Mattingly, 7.

work worlds, including higher education, there is often an unspoken dress code, even if the organization doesn't have a written one. There are certain conventions and societal expectations for men and women, including how they express themselves through their clothing at work. Although the dress codes for women in the 18th century (and beyond) were restrictive, women worked within that regimented system to "construct the image they would project."[4]

Within the confines of the work world, I, too, am working to construct an image I want to project: an image that confounds, confuses, and forces people to consider their own gender expression against mine. Trying to project the correct gender expression for myself forces me to work to understand how attire affects not only myself, but others. At the same time, I realize that their reaction, be it positive, negative, or neutral, is beyond my control. There is no real guidance for non-binary trans people on how to dress, how to act, how to "be professional." I want to look right in my non-binary gender, but how does that fit into my gender journey?

Everyone has a gender journey, no matter what your gender. I first heard about a gender journey from writer and actor Jacob Tobia, a non-binary person. They note that everyone, including cisgender people, has their own unique gender journey in life. How we react to our gender, what we do with it, how we experience it, is specific to each of us. This essay covers a bit of my gender journey, with digressions.

Once I came out as non-binary, I started to look back at my life to see if there were any clues to my non-binary gender. Turns out there were:

- Kindergarten-8th grade: Colorful striped pants with matching socks, hung out with girls, roller-skating, wrote and directed backyard plays. Never wore blue jeans to school, but wore pants.
- High school: Came out as gay to a few, wore the brightest yellow pants ever for my senior photos, completely jealous of a pleated skirt worn by a student in chemistry class.

4. Mattingly, 8.

- My Roaring 20s: Lots of brooches worn on blazers, wore a skirt to a gay bar, dyed my hair platinum blond, changed name to Marq for a bit.
- Age 30-48, The Long Business World of Narrowing: Boring man-clothes and smells, tried to dress for success in the startup and business world. Yawn.
- The Last Ten Years: Academia, expanding, remembering, more perfumes, nail polishes, and pendants. New pronouns and a new honorific, Mx.
- Present and Future: Hand sewing clothes and someday wearing the skirts I sew. More jewelry, louder scents, and yes, capes.

Coming Out, Again, But in a New and Slightly Rocky Way

Coming out to my forty or so colleagues in the library as non-binary wasn't a quiet, one-on-one affair. I had to do it big, broad, and with slides.

I've worked at my current job since 2011—as a man. My gender was never in question. Nobody commented on my gender at all. So, it was with a big dollop of naiveté that I decided to come out at work, in a big way, as non-binary. Almost at the same time, my nails were Peep colored and I was being interviewed on campus about being gender non-conforming.

I'm all about doing a "two for one." I had an upcoming conference where I was presenting on how to create a more welcoming place for your non-binary coworkers. I decided, unwisely, to practice the talk for my coworkers at an all-library staff meeting. I wanted them to be welcoming to me and any other non-binary trans employees at the library or on our campus. So, it was a win/win: me practicing, them learning, and everything glorious. Until it wasn't.

I was very nervous before the talk, which wasn't a good indicator of my readiness. Also, I assumed a degree of prior knowledge about gender in my peers that I shouldn't have. Prior to the presentation, I was deep in reading about gender, non-binary employees, and work organizations.

I broke my cardinal rule of presenting: assume no prior knowledge. I assumed a heck of a lot, and that wasn't fair to my colleagues.

After my talk, one coworker asked something to the effect of, "Why is all this important? Why are pronouns important?" I honestly didn't really have an answer ready. Now, with more experience leading non-binary workplace workshops, I'd say that pronouns validate my gender, and with so much of our society invalidating my identity, your pronoun use is profoundly helpful in making me feel seen and supported. Also, how rude not to use someone's pronouns if you know them. At the time, I wasn't as schooled in all things non-binary and trans as I thought I was.

Later, I thought about how, when I came out as non-binary there wasn't really any response from my long-time coworkers. Crickets chirping. I didn't expect a gender reveal party, but I was surprised by their lack of a reaction. Were they embarrassed by my honesty? Unsure of what to say? I don't know.

I guess a null response is much better than a negative response. But a null or non-response really *is* more of a negative response. In the absence of a positive response, I often think my colleagues' responses are negative ones. I realize that there may also be gender evasiveness as well. This is similar to race evasiveness, in that the dominant demographic doesn't feel the need to talk about something that they don't think affects them.[5] It feels like many people are socialized to not talk about gender in society because of the privileges they have in their own gender. The dominant culture, cisgender people, evade their privileged status by not talking about gender. Also, some people seem to be uncomfortable discussing or even acknowledging gender. I know I certainly have this kind of gender evasiveness socialized in me, not to call out or comment on people's gender. To not call attention out of what I thought was politeness. Growing up, I was taught to not comment on differences between people. That is, if I noticed something different to

---

5. Helen A Neville, Germine H. Awad, James E. Brooks, Michelle P. Flores, and Jamie Bluemel. "Color-blind racial ideology: Theory, training, and measurement implications in psychology." *American Psychologist* 68, no. 6 (2013), 455.

say nothing, positive or negative. As an adult, I realize that silence can often feel more like condemnation than approval.

Learning from my awkward presentation to my library colleagues, I spent a lot of time prepping for my conference talk about creating a more welcoming space for non-binary library employees. That went well, and it felt like I was ready to be a more public non-binary librarian and speaker. I started to write more on LinkedIn about being non-binary and my gender journey and being non-binary, revealing more and more about what it is like to navigate the work world, and letting my broader network know what I was up to.

All of that posting on LinkedIn led a former colleague to suggest me as a speaker for the annual Pride celebration for Mojang Studios. (This company is based in Sweden and Redmond WA, makes the game Minecraft, and is owned by Microsoft.) Terrified but happy, I said yes.

Many years ago, while still a graduate student, I worked as a research contractor for Microsoft. While there, I learned about a job function that struck me as weird and strange: technology evangelist. How could those two words function together? What did this person do? It seemed to combine the profane and the sacred. I found out that technology evangelists work to change people's minds about technology and to convert them from using one type of software or hardware to another. They promote a certain vision of a technology landscape.

During my temporary return to Microsoft, via Mojang Studios, I was doing my own form of evangelism. Not technical evangelism, but non-binary evangelism. I was not trying to convert people's gender to non-binary, but rather to change their minds a bit about their non-binary coworkers.

Clothing and Work: The Intersection of Being Non-binary and Being Professional

"Clothing is a social language. It is the way we make our bodies socially legible to those around us."[6]

6. Emma McClendon, "Sweatpants and Anxiety in the Age of COVID,"

As my gender journey takes me off the road of maleness/manliness and into uncharted territory, I realize that, as I add clothing, accessories, and mannerisms associated with women, I am making my gender more and more difficult to assume. When I wear necklaces, get my nails painted, or wear a long flowing caftan to the pool, I move me away from the speedy and easy highway of how other people understand who I am, or at least what my gender is. There isn't a conventional, traditional model of being non-binary. I read of one non-binary person who dresses entirely in women's clothes some days and entirely in men's clothes on other days.

One view of gender expression claims that people are expressing their gender in non-traditional ways to have fun. I mean, yes, I think it is totally fun to match my handbag with my necklace to my blazer. But it is serious business making these choices to bend away from the binary. And the hot, hateful stares I get in the grocery store aren't fun. I don't express my gender for fun. I express my gender because it is who I am.

> Heteronormative culture dismisses queer rituals as "superficial" "phases," like "playing dress up." There's this enduring idea that play, that adornment, that glamor are redundant and inconsequential. That we must somehow evolve out of this presumably juvenile space toward... what exactly? Banality which masquerades itself as stability?[7]

At the center of it all is a desire to be myself. More Mark than people are used to seeing. Not banal, business-attired Mark, but me playing dress up in new ways. What does that mean at work? How can I work at being professional in my job, but still present in a variety of ways that may seem, for some or even many, to be totally unprofessional? For example, I have a tall, hairy body. When I wear skirts, I am not planning on shaving my legs. How do unwritten dress codes fit for me and

---

Tatter Journal, accessed July 12, 2021, https://issues.tatter.org/articles/issue-1/sweatpants-and-anxiety-in-the-age-of-covid/

7. Alok M Venon (@alokvmenon), "Queerness is not just our identity, it's about how we inhabit our bodies and this world..." Instagram, May 23, 2021, https://www.instagram.com/p/CPPT7qNLyaV/?hl=en.

other non-binary people? Can we, as non-binary people, wear anything that either binary gender might typically wear? In any combination? Infinite combinations of all the appropriate work clothes? What can I wear, what non-binary finery is suitable for work? I don't have the answer because I don't have any role models. There isn't any guidance or advice for those of us seeking to be taken seriously at work, but also to wear what makes us feel right.

Easing the Tensions About My Identity

I am passionate and a bit obsessive about the things I learn about and love. I bring that same passion to my newly found gender. For example, I don't have my nails polished with a discreet color, but rather with bright colors stamped with silver designs. My favorite silver nail polish is a dull tin-like liquid, the color of the Tin Woodman, called "There's No Place Like Chrome." I use my passions for handbags, fragrances, polishes, and designer sewing patterns to mitigate some of the tensions around my gender presentation.

I lean into those passions to show to people that I am having serious fun with making myself look like I want to, and that my fun is harmless to them—that my fun is maybe even a little interesting. I'm always oversharing about my latest passion, and within the framework of work, this type of sharing is legitimate small talk. Not everyone is obsessed by Japanese designer Issey Miyake's sewing patterns for Vogue, but when I make an article of clothing by them and wear it, I have a story behind it. That story, that narrative, is going to work towards someone's understanding of my gender. It comes from a true place: a place of learning and making and being proud and happy about who I am now and where I'm going to be.

Showing up as my more authentic self means being more non-binary, being more queer, being more over the top, and being more dramatic. According to Michail D. Kokkoris and Constantine Sedikides, "authenticity is linked to positive outcomes, such as job satisfaction, organizational commitment, and job performance."[8] Being myself is being vulnerable, because the work world isn't really used to things other than straight, cisgender men and women and their concerns. I don't need to be vulnerable in the workplace. I already am vulnerable just by being a bit of myself. Of course, I know people, my coworkers, are already silently judging me, but it gets a bit more personal when they judge my identity. I want to bring more of myself to my work, and I feel that I'm more focused and successful when I do. But, back to risk versus reward, is being more myself more rewarding than the risk of sly comments and dismissive looks when I show up looking all fabulous in hat, gloves, and a smart-looking dress and coat?

I don't like making trouble. I like harmony, not arguing, and certainly not confrontations. This puts me at a disadvantage in my evolving gender expression. All I want to do is wear what I want to wear and swan about feeling fabulous and correct. In public spaces, I wonder how I'll handle the trouble I cause by being my non-binary self. To dismantle cisgender, binary oppression, I'll challenge the status quo and subsequently be, as Butler notes, "*punished or maligned for its ostensible destructiveness*" for doing so.[9] It isn't as if I'm aiming to dismantle the binary, but my very actions, my gender expression, serve to criticize it and demonstrate another way of being. Or, if not criticize, then to open up the discussion of what it means to be something other than cisgender. Trouble makes me nervous, but I don't see how I can simply *be* without someone being disturbed, jealous, or angry about my existence—even though I aim for delight, frivolity, and a life full of caps, gloves, and stunning accessories.

As the saying goes, it's the journey, not the destination. As a non-binary person, I don't have a gender destination. Merrily, I go along. As shown in this small slice of my gender journey, I am working out the path, exploring new areas, uncovering new trails towards something.

8. Michail D Kokkoris and Constantine Sedikides, "Can you be yourself in business? How reminders of business affect the perceived value of authenticity." *Journal of Applied Social Psychology* 49, no. 7 (2019), 448, https://doi.org/10.1111/jasp.12596.

9. Sara Ahmed, "Interview with Judith Butler," *Sexualities* 19, no. 4, (June 2016): 484, doi:10.1177/1363460716629607.

Towards gender euphoria, a feeling of feeling right in how I am, wearing nail polish, skirts, clever hats. My journey is my own, but I've been inspired by so many folx. Now go and have your own fabulous gender journey, no matter what gender you are!

Bibliography

Ahmed, Sara. "Interview with Judith Butler."*Sexualities*, 19, no. 4 (June 2016): 482–492. doi:10.1177/1363460716629607.

Goggin, Maureen Daly. "Fabricating Identity: Janie Terrero's 1912 Embroidered English Suffrage Signature Handkerchief." In *Women and Things, 1750-1950: Gendered Material Strategies*, edited by Maureen Goggin and Beth Fowkes Tobin, 19-42. New York: Routledge, 2009.

Kokkoris, Michail D., and Constantine Sedikides. "Can you be yourself in business? How reminders of business affect the perceived value of authenticity." *Journal of Applied Social Psychology* 49, no. 7 (2019): 448-458.

Mattingly, Carol. *Appropriate [ing] Dress: Women's Rhetorical Style in Nineteenth-Century America.* Carbondale, IL. Southern Illinois University Press, 2002.

McClendon, Emma, "Sweatpants and Anxiety in the Age of COVID," Tatter Journal, accessed July 12, 2021, https://issues.tatter.org/articles/issue-1/sweatpants-and-anxiety-in-the-age-of-covid/.

Neville, Helen A., Germine H. Awad, James E. Brooks, Michelle P. Flores, and Jamie Bluemel. "Color-blind racial ideology: Theory, training, and measurement implications in psychology." *American Psychologist* 68, no. 6 (2013): 455.

Sawyer, Katina, Christian Thoroughgood, and Jennica Webster. "Queering the Gender Binary: Understanding Transgender Workplace Experiences: in *Sexual Orientation and Transgender Issues in Organizations* edited by Thomas Köllen, 21-42. Switzerland: Springer, 2016.

Venon, Alok M (@alokvmenon), Queerness is not just our identity, it's about how we inhabit our bodies and this world…" Instagram, May 23, 2021. https://www.instagram.com/p/CPPT7qNLyaV/?hl=en.

About the Author

Mark Bieraugel is white, college educated, and grew up in a middle-class household. For the past ten years, Mark has been the business librarian at California Polytechnic State University (Cal Poly) and worked as a paid research consultant through the local Small Business Development Center. Prior to their coming to Cal Poly, they worked for two years at Tacoma Community College and Edmonds Community College as a reference and instruction librarian. For the first ten years of their library career they worked at companies doing competitive intelligence and business research. Mark is a non-binary queer person, and their gender expression is a mix of traditionally men's and women's clothing and accessories. Combining a vigorous business background and an understanding of organizational culture, Mark has a unique and practical take on the challenges libraries face in diversity and inclusivity issues. Outside of work, Mark enjoys hand-sewing clothes, hats, and bags, hanging out with their husband and tuxedo cat Tinky, and swanning about in one of their hand sewn caftans.

Survey Headaches

Katherine Deibel

Keywords: survey, self-identification, academia, inclusive data collection, microaggressions

A climate survey to determine the campus's feeling of safety and inclusion after a violent incident
A climate survey to establish a baseline on diversity, inclusion, and equity experiences at a university
A research study to explore impostor syndrome across gender beyond the traditional binary

You would hope that these well-intended data collection efforts would do their best to be welcoming, inclusive, and safe. Yet, all too commonly, these efforts fail in asking the question "What is your gender?" Too many times, I have felt othered or outright excluded as a trans woman by the way that question and its answers are phrased. The same transphobic errors happen again and again and have left me in tears each and every time. I wish those were tears of laughter at the ineptitude of the researchers, but more often it's a reminder that trans people like myself do not exist in the eyes of the survey makers. In the act of asking a simple demographic question, a person can experience systemic hate and bias. And that experience of bigotry can drive a person away from participating in a survey, destroying the diversity representation we all claim to desire.

University of Washington Climate Survey

It was late August in 2017 when I sat down to fill out a campus diversity climate survey for the University of Washington (UW). As was a common and, as of 2021, still ongoing trend in higher ed, the university wanted to gather data on how included and safe everyone felt on campus. Admittedly, my answers were not going to be great. As a trans woman who had transitioned fifteen years earlier as a grad student at that university, I had seen a gradual slide away from what had been fairly supportive actions and polices. Notably that January, Milo Yiannopoulos had been brought on campus despite much outcry regarding his hatemongering, including the transphobic mocking of a University of Wisconsin-Milwaukee student in December. Thus, the university that said it embraces diversity and promises a welcoming and safe environment showed their true colors as the leadership argued the importance of protecting hate speech. They took back the promise of a safe campus. Staff were advised to leave work early to avoid the expected massive, and likely violent, protests. That former sense of safety and inclusion was further shattered that night with an actual shooting on campus. For me personally, I got to enjoy how the press's photograph of the shooter was taken only a hundred yards or so outside my office space in Suzzallo Library on the famous stairwells.

And then I read that first question: "What is your gender? Are you a: Man, Woman, Transgender Man, or Transgender Woman"? I bristled immediately. That question has so many flaws, including but not limited to its strict adherence to the gender binary. Personally, I reeled in pain and anger at the implicit othering. **REAL** men and **REAL** women are not transgender. If you are trans, you're not truly man or woman. Thank you so much for that EpiPen of dysphoria straight to my heart!! I closed the survey right then and never returned to it.

A part of me regretted doing that, not just because I knew that getting survey responses can be like pulling teeth. At that time, I had already announced that I was leaving my position as web applications specialist at the University of Washington Libraries to become the Inclusion

& Accessibility Librarian at Syracuse University. In less than a month, I would be taking on a much more active role in promoting diversity, equity, inclusion, and accessibility (DEIA) in libraries. I already had experience advocating for disability access but admittedly felt worried about my qualifications for promoting inclusion more generally. That diversity climate survey really interested me for my future work directions.

Syracuse University Climate Survey

Three years later, I found myself again looking at a diversity climate survey for the university I worked at. In Seattle, that survey was motivated, in part, by a transphobic asswipe guest speaker on campus and subsequent campus shooting the same night. Although not as violent a motivation as a shooting, Syracuse University (SU) had its own recent spate of hate. Multiple racist and antisemitic incidents motivated and spurred the need for massive inclusive change. Since everything must be data-driven, the university commissioned an external party to conduct a campus climate survey on diversity and inclusion. Despite serving on some institutional inclusion groups, I was not involved in the crafting of the survey. I did have some hopes, though, as the company chosen had a good track record of doing the same at other universities.

That did not happen. As has been my experience with these climate surveys, the first questions are always the demographic ones. In this case, there were two transphobic questions. First, the survey asked for my sex (as in male, female, or intersex). Then, it asked for my gender with a single choice between Man, Woman, Transgender/Gender-non-conforming, and a fill-in text option if your preferred response was not given. I learned later that, if you chose the Transgender option, the next page of the survey would include a question asking for clarification about your identity. To be perfectly clear, you only discovered this if you chose Transgender. There was no way to know that otherwise.

This is the other way gender survey questions turn transphobic. While the UW question othered trans status, this question instead outright cleaved away part of my identity. I identify as a trans woman. I am a woman and transgender. This question required me to deny one if I were to answer.

The whole of my gender identity is more than the sum of its separate parts. I am a woman. I am trans. Making me choose only one is to deny my existence. I cannot separate out my experiences of one from the other. And yet that survey, as far as I could determine, demanded I do exactly that. Asking me to choose only woman or only transgender diminishes me. And while I could have utilized the survey's fill-in text option, that itself comes off as othering as it still implies that I can't belong in either group.

I wish I had abandoned the survey then as I had with the UW survey. Instead, I reluctantly persevered due to my role as a DEIA advocate on campus. After all, I had encouraged the libraries' staff to take the survey. I ultimately listed myself as a Woman. But I could not sit in silence, so I immediately contacted the survey company and the campus's chief diversity officer about my concerns. I even apologized to members of the library staff I had encouraged to participate in the survey, since I had potentially exposed trans colleagues to the same abuse. I had to apologize and warn others.

Needless to say, I made waves that were not fully welcome. The dean of the libraries and the chief diversity officer responded. The survey company immediately responded in email in defense of their survey. A virtual meeting was arranged where I would talk directly to the survey people. The diversity officer and my dean would be there, too, alongside the interim head of the university's LGBT center. Although I cannot fully confirm it, I greatly suspect that I was the lone, uppity trans person in a meeting of cis people wanting to stem a crisis.[1]

1. I do want to clarify that despite their being cisgender (to the best of my knowledge), I absolutely hold no ill will regarding either the chief diversity officer nor the head of the LGBT center. I worked with both gentlemen multiple times fruitfully and with respect. Both even kindly reached out at times to make sure I was taking care of myself as I advocated for others. Still, fighting against the obstinance regarding trans rights in higher education, their cis allyship went unheard in their attempts to face and fight back against the embedded power and privilege of the status quo.

I reckon the purpose of that meeting was mostly to assuage me and prevent me from making more noise. They also stated they were hoping to learn from me as if I could speak on behalf of all trans people on campus. While I do have some social research experience, it is not in gender studies and is by no means strong enough to be advisory. Much of the meeting was a rearticulation of the survey company's defense against my objections, my responses to them, and their continued deflection of those criticisms:

- They mentioned how the survey's questions had been vetted by a major university's LGBT center. Given the rapid changes in trans rights advocacy in recent years, I asked how recent that vetting was and if a trans rights specific group could also be consulted. No response.
- I asked why both sex and gender were asked for and how that data would be used. I was repeatedly informed that they understood how a person's notion of their sex could change on a daily basis. Honestly, I am still confused to this day exactly what they meant. My only certainty is that it did not pertain to my question about how the data would be used.
- I continued to ask for details about how they would use the two sets of collected data. Would they use the sex or gender answers to split the responses into groups for statistical analyses? Would they somehow use both and perhaps operate perverse logic about them? For example, would some sick logic take a person saying male and trans man and "correct" it as having a female sex? Despite my queries for some transparency, I was told how much they understand the flexibility of sex and gender in some people's lives.
- The survey software itself was blamed for its lack of flexibility in that survey logic could not add the question until the next page. I pointed out several ways they could have addressed that issue, none of them unique to the software.
- Most importantly, they kept emphasizing that all the questions were optional. As they insisted, anyone could "...omit responses to any

> questions they feel uncomfortable with or would prefer not to answer." I kept reminding them that a campus climate survey's main purpose was to get insights about the comfort people at SU have around their diversities. If the design of the survey makes some underrepresented groups uncomfortable to answer questions directly relevant to their identities, how are their experiences to be represented? If I skip questions abusive to my identity, how do I get represented? How is that not silencing?

The conversation endlessly returned to the importance of science and statistical rigor and the problem with capturing small group representation. It came off to me as lip service. Here I was, providing comments and citations for how to better capture trans representation in surveys to address their expressed concerns. Instead, I was repeatedly informed of how their method was not harmful. And speaking of harm, at no point did I ever hear any acknowledgment of what I was doing. Despite the barrage of transphobia happening in society, I dared to out myself to these strangers and rationally discuss how to avoid the presumably unintended transphobia they had proliferated. I mentioned the emotional labor of doing that. I got thanked for providing some links. That's it.

That meeting ended with everyone agreeing the matter was resolved. I did not object. Agreeing to the meeting was a mistake on my part. It was never going to change anything. Afterwards, the dean of SU Libraries wanted to send an email to staff reassuring them about the survey. Fortunately, he asked for my opinion before he sent it. His first draft implied my concerns had been satisfactorily addressed by that conversation. He graciously dropped that point and only shared his opinion when encouraging staff to complete the survey.

The Subsequent Report and Blaming "Science"

I tried to put that climate survey behind me. It had been a major time sink and apparently not a good use of my work time, as I would later learn in my annual performance review. Unfortunately, as one of the leaders in DEIA efforts in the SU Libraries, I had to read about the report of the survey's findings. It was only the first public draft, but it was a doozy.

A part of me began my reading with a hopeful cursory scan for any mention of my concerns with the gender questions and caution about interpreting some of the gender results. Call it a mix of wanting some pride in and results for my hard-fought labors. There was no such discussion.

Then I began reading the report as I would the evidence section of any social science article. Quick scans of the sections revealed so many tired practices. The section labeled gender results only looked at a breakdown between men and women. No mention of data collection concerns. No mention of genders outside the binary. And, because I had to choose between woman or transgender, I was represented here among the cis women. I had no influence on the data about the trans experience.

So where was the trans experience discussed in the results? It really never was discussed. Any trans data was saved for later in the LGBT section, where all the LGBT survey responses were compared against the data of the heterosexual responses. Despite the fact that every Trans 101 diversity training goes over how gender and sexuality are distinct aspects of identity, here we had a survey in 2020 placing trans people as a sexuality! Why was it done? Apparently, it improved the statistical power of the data if you combined these two smaller groups into one. It was SCIENCE! Not good statistical science, admittedly, since you should only pool data if your research framework has valid reasoning for it. Instead, the unique experiences of trans people compared to cis people gets completely washed out. The statistical power is stronger, yes, but it's no longer truly representative of the cultural experience of trans people on campus.

But then there was a footnote. The footnote had nothing to do with the limits of the study when it came to gender or trans issues, but it did mention the word transgender. Ultimately, the entire footnote was removed from the final survey report, but I have chosen to replicate it here in its entirety. It does discuss several types of assaults. As a content warning, the following quoted text mentions transphobia, Islamophobia, and antisemitism.

> Microassaults are the "biggest" and most explicitly violent type microaggressions identified by Dr. Derald Wing Sue (2007, 2010). They are obvious. They are usually deliberate and on purpose. They can be subtle, but usually aren't. They usually happen when the perpetrator is anonymous, they are being supported by peers around them, and/or they know they can get away with it. There's no guesswork in determining if you were the victim of a microassault. They are characterized primarily by a verbal or nonverbal attack, meant to hurt the intended victim through name-calling, avoidant behavior, or purposeful discriminatory actions. In some instances, they can rise to the level of physical assault. A particularly heinous example would be attempting to grope a transgender individual to "check if they should be in the restroom." These are referred to as microassaults, because these are DEI-challenged interactions that take place at the interpersonal level, between individuals, or between individuals and the environment, for example when someone touches your hijab, or a swastika is placed on the wall. The term "micro" is in no means meant to suggest that these events are unimportant or minimal. To the contrary, they are just the opposite. That challenges often abound in small-scale ways should be taken very seriously by leaders hoping to create diverse, equitable, and inclusive environments.

I apologize to the reader for having to confront that block of text. Beyond its convoluted syntax desperate for editing, the sudden example of assaulting a trans person floored me on first reading. At least I was gracious enough to offer a content warning. That "attempted" gender-conforming grope is a **"micro"** assault. While the text states that this term is not meant to belittle the impact of said events, I cannot help but shudder at comparing an attempted sexual assault to the seemingly less invasive affronts of witnessing hate graffiti or having a part of religious garb touched. I do not intend to belittle any of these hate experiences but rather to note the difference in the level of description for each. The trans assault is made far more visceral by using the verb "grope" versus "touch." The trans assault is also the only example in which they give a justification or reasoning for the attacker.

Upon reading the report, I did take one action of advocacy. I emailed both the chief diversity officer and the head of the LGBT center with a list of these concerns. Moreover, I made clear that I did not wish to further engage with the survey company. I openly shared how I had felt as the lone trans person having to speak for an entire community. Despite what many others said about feeling like good outcomes coming from that meeting, I did not share those sentiments. I have even less faith that the questions will be rephrased better in future instances.

Fortunately, as I said, the footnote was dropped in a later edition of the climate survey report. I have no idea if my complaint had any sway in that editing decision.

All of Us are Fallible

I look at experiences like this and ask, how could we do better next time? I am not sure if that is just a part of my personality or a wannabe optimistic habit gleaned from years of various DEIA advocacy work. Often, one of the more common answers is to say that greater diversity will change things. Maybe that will happen, but too often it erroneously presumes that just one person can make a difference. Maybe that works sometimes, but we must recognize that singular representation is not a panacea.

For example, I have one other notable experience with a flawed gender demographic question in a survey. For a small study for a conference talk, a trans librarian aimed to collect data on perceptions of impostor syndrome among library technologists and analyze the results by gender. I admittedly found this to be an awesome idea for a research study, so I chose to participate in the survey.

The original version of the survey had three options for the gender identity question: man, woman, and trans. You could only select one. As I have explained, this forces a trans woman like myself to have to make a tough choice and cleave my identity in two for my experiences to offer data and research insight. I chatted in some public library forums about my frustration with the survey, and eventually through various conversations, I was connected with the researcher.

I wish I could say that the conversation went well; Twitter conversations rarely do. I do wish I had an archive of our exchange to try to understand where the confusion started. I do not know if I had made clear my own trans identity to them. I tried to explain that the setup of the answers created a transphobic situation, which was not the best tactic. I probably offered the solution of: cis man, cis woman, trans man, and trans woman. I got accused of being transphobic as the researcher defended that they just wanted a survey where their gender of "trans" was finally an option. My then go-to set of answers did not acknowledge genders outside the binary. I was transphobic and so were they. We both wanted the same thing: representation. It took some deep breaths from both of us to realize that. Changes were made to the survey and the study went forward with better data collection.

My point in sharing this experience is to remind all of us that even a singular trans person will do this survey question wrong. They had biases. I had biases. Their approach failed to represent me. I failed to represent them. We are all fallible. Moreover, we also should not pressure ourselves to take on that burden individually. When I had that meeting at SU regarding the climate survey, I regretted doing so because I felt so alone. We need to work together.

Asking the Question Correctly

The purpose of my sharing these experiences was to do exactly that. I wanted to share how a simple demographic question has repeatedly made me confront systemic transphobia as an academic librarian who just happens to be a trans woman. Pushing back on this is part of my DEIA advocacy, but that constant labor is emotionally exhausting.

I truly believe that educating people about how to ask gender demographic questions well is the way to achieve systemic change. However, this book is not the right venue for a detailed breakdown of how to ask about gender in a survey. This book is about lived experiences and not a guide to research methodologies. Still, I want to part with some advice based on what I have learned. Although I don't expect anyone to pick up this book for methodology advice, perhaps these words may inspire or remind a reader to do better and prevent some future trans frustrations.

At the time of this writing, more and more good practice guides are being written and shared, many online. To design a survey that respects trans people when asking for gender demographics, I would recommend starting with their current advice. For a start, though, here are a few key concepts that you will not go wrong with:

- Just ask for gender. For most demographic breakdowns, especially in library surveys, that will be more than sufficient. If you think you need more nuance, do some research into the concepts you need to explore, be they medical, legal, sociocultural, etc. Find recommended best practices that have been lauded by both researchers and trans and gender diverse people.
- Avoid mutually exclusive options. Let a person select multiple options and be prepared for the impact which that will have on your analyses.
- Avoid the binaries of man versus woman and cis versus trans. Gender is complex and you need to learn and respect that (like I had to).
- Offer a fill-in option, just in case. Also think about how those may impact your analyses. How will you process them, especially if you are going to conduct statistical analyses that require you to pool participants into groups?
- When presenting your results, openly discuss how the data was processed, pooled, and analyzed in regard to the varied identities captured in your study. In fact, be prepared to answer such questions when collecting data. Transparency about methodologies allows for deeper and better nuanced discussion of the findings and their relevant impacts.

Demographic questions in surveys may seem minor, but if they perpetuate systemic bigotry, you will fail to capture the responses of those you push away from participating. This is not unique to gender. We should all do better.

About the Author

Dr. Katherine "Kate" Deibel, PhD has had a varied career in academia working within and across many disciplines, including computer science, education, disability, comics, digital literacies, and libraries. After transitioning in her first year of graduate school, she earned her PhD in computer science and engineering at the University of Washington in 2011 with a multidisciplinary study of the social and technological factors that hinder adoption of reading technologies among adults with dyslexia. As an ardent advocate for usable and accessible technologies, she works and educates to ensure that library technologies are effective tools for both library patrons and staff.

Thank You for Calling the Research Assistance Desk, This Is...

L.E. Eames (he/him)

Keywords: agender, phone reference, academic libraries, library instruction, voice dysphoria

Choosing

At some point in grade school, we were assigned to ask our parents about the origin of our name. When I spoke to my mother about this, she responded:"I asked my college roommate what she would name a girl."

When I asked my dad, he responded: "Your mother wanted to name you Patricia, but I pointed out that your initials would have spelled PEE. Kids can be cruel about names, and we couldn't sign you up for a lifetime of bullying."

For my own part, I wanted desperately to be called Ashley in honor of my first childhood fandom: the Olsen Twins. When I asked how to change my name, I was told that this was unthinkable. I would only be able to change my last name to match my husband's when I got married, but to change my first name was not only frivolous but legally impossible. A first name was forever.

I no longer remember what story I told for that assignment.

Unchoosing

I discovered that I was only subjected to this assignment by my all-girls K-12 school by a clerical error in October of 2016. All of the lecturing

I'd received for being unladylike was no longer a matter of shame but a matter of pride. Whatever name I chose now, if I chose to change my name, would finally come with a story. I was nonbinary. This was what I'd picked for myself.

In fact, I started with my name. I was content to keep she/her pronouns until a co-participant at a Theatre of the Oppressed workshop kept slipping up and using he/him for me and I found out that I liked it. Given the reins over my own identity for the first time, I chose my grandfather's name. My dad's father and I share a first initial and it felt like the fullest subversion of the story I'd been told about names. Not only was I taking on my own first name of choice but also making myself a "the second." I was reinserting myself into my own family history.

I could assert control over who I tell the world I am.

After the Classroom

"Dear Ms. Eames…"

I look back at my slides from the first-year rhetoric and writing classes. I definitely introduced myself as "Mx. Eames," right? I did. Good. But every email from a student I get addressed to "Ms. Eames" sends a chill down my spine with the feeling that I forgot to introduce myself correctly. That I signed my last email with my legal name as a holdover from the last email I sent my parents or a doctor or a bank. I didn't do any of that here, thank god.

But I know what I look like.

And sound like.

And that I can't change that because I can't be out at home. Not that I know what I could do to be more visibly agender and be visibly myself at the same time even if I could have access to HRT or top surgery. All I have is who I tell people I am.

> *"[Student],*
> *First off, you can absolutely call me by my first name. I'm not one to stand on ceremony..."*

"Dear Dr. Eames..."

Wait, where did that come from? Oh. The professor introduced me as Dr. Eames. That's when. I should correct them. What's the academic version of stolen valor? I don't have a Ph.D. and the only power on earth that could compel me to go through that process would be to earn that honorific.

But I know what I look like.

And sound like.

And this student has seen me on videos I recorded for their English class. They know, too. And they didn't default to a gendered title. I shift in my office chair.

> *"[Student],*
> *If you feel more comfortable calling me Dr. Eames that's fine, but you can absolutely call me by my first name. I'm not one to stand on ceremony..."*

On the Desk

"Good afternoon, ma'am..."

I flinch. I'm at home on our virtual reference desk. The student is still talking. Was that something about a course reserve? Or maybe a research question? Concentrate. *"...and ma'am I was hoping..."* There it is again. I pull it together. I find the course reserve they're looking for. I direct them toward similar resources to help with their midterm paper. But when they hang up, I practice picking up the phone out loud to myself. I lower my pitch each time.

But I know what I sound like.

And the patron knowing what I look like wouldn't help. I think to myself that this is why I keep "she/her" in my introduction. Because people see me as a woman. Especially in a library setting. But I also think about my supervisor asking which pronouns I'd prefer in my annual evaluation and how she was 100% on board with the fact that I'm shifting to using only he/him pronouns. And I think about how nice I felt when I read her write-up of my work over the last year using "he/him" pronouns throughout. No, more than nice. I think about how my discomfort with receiving praise was outstripped by my feeling that I was reading about myself—maybe reading about myself for the first time.

I can't correct this patron. They've already hung up. But I can practice lowering my customer service voice and hope that next time I won't get "ma'am"-ed.

"You know, I don't think I know your name. I'm [name]. What was your name?"

I'm at home on our virtual reference desk. This is a regular phone patron. We speak weekly if not more frequently. And I've never introduced myself. I open every phone call with "Research Assistance Desk, how can I help?" I don't say my name when I pick up the phone for a reason. I don't want to have this conversation. And I especially don't want to have this conversation with someone who I know is an older man.

"Oh... it's Larry."
"Larry?"

Does he sound skeptical? Or is he just confirming that he heard right?

"Yep!"

I'm trying to sound cheery. Of course, upbeat means up-pitched. I haven't trained myself out of that habit.

"Oh... Where'd you get that name from?"

He knows. He knows my name and my vocal pitch don't match up. He's confused. Is he upset? How is he going to respond? How am I going to respond?

"It's my grandfather's name."

That's the truth. I chose it for that reason. And I'm choosing not to elaborate on it the way I usually do when I feel like I might be unsafe. I'm choosing not to say, "It's short for Lawrence. Laurence is a woman's name in French." I'm choosing to introduce myself and I'm choosing not to equivocate.

"Oh, Larry. That's nice that you're named after your grandfather. Well, thanks a lot for all you do for me."

And he hangs up.
And I release a breath I didn't know I was holding.

About the Author

L.E. Eames (Mx., he/him pronouns) is an agender, academic librarian living and working in Colorado Springs, CO. He publishes under L.E. Eames so that, if needed, he can dive back into the gender closet—and because a friend once told him that his initials sounded like a gender-ambiguous, nineteenth-century children's book author, and he loved that.

A Queer Queer: Academic Librarianship as an Autistic Nonbinary Person

M.P. Green (they/she)

Keywords: disability, autism spectrum disorder, non-binary, academic libraries

Introduction

Increased attention to gender diversity is filtering down from general awareness into librarianship, particularly into academic librarianship. Awareness and appreciation of autism spectrum disorder (ASD) is growing as well due to self-advocacy groups, prominent academic figures like Dr. Temple Grandin, legendary actors such as Sir Anthony Hopkins, and even problematic pop culture figures like Elon Musk. Rarely, however, do we see discussion of the intersection between these two identities, and never within the context of academic librarianship, particularly at the faculty level.

Autism is a disability, and being a disabled librarian in higher education poses unique challenges. Adding a nonbinary gender identity to this recipe makes it all the more interesting. The icing on this cake is being born, raised, and currently living in a conservative (or "red") state where microaggressions, intentional or not, are frequent. The intersection of these identities impacts my career as faculty-level academic librarian at a mid-size, non-research university in a rural area.

Sharing my story is a way to inform and educate others. Anecdotal evidence often carries far more weight than data, numbers, and statistics.

I am not my autism, nor my gender identity, but a combination of the two. They are parts of me and affect others' perceptions and treatment of me, particularly in a higher education setting. This chapter is my message to students, the public, faculty, staff, and everyone who reads it. It is a plea for patience, consideration, and compassion.

This is also a reminder for all of us that any identity does not exist in a vacuum. A nonbinary person may also be Black, Indigenous, or a person of color. They may have a disability or financial hardship. There are many possible intersections and infinite issues that come along with those intersections. I hope that someday there will be greater awareness of these and other identities and experiences.

Definitions and Usages

In this chapter I will use a handful of terms that may be unfamiliar. These are my own personal definitions and understandings, which may deviate from standard usage. My definition of autism spectrum disorder (ASD) is derived in summary from the standard diagnostic manual. ASD is a social and communication disorder, a developmental disability. It is marked by "persistent deficits in social communication and social interaction across multiple contexts," manifested by traits that can include lack of social interaction or interest in it, little to no eye contact, or difficulty maintaining relationships, among other traits. ASD is also defined by restrictive, repetitive patterns of behavior which can include strict adherence to a routine, inability to cope with change, repetitive motor or vocal gestures, and more.[1] Autism is not caused by vaccinations, diet/nutrition, or other environmental factors. It is a genetic condition, present from birth to death. For people assigned female at birth (AFAB), masking, or learning to mimic the behavior of allistic (non-autistic) girls and women, is often adopted as a survival technique, an attempt at social preservation.

1. American Psychiatric Association, *Diagnostic and Statistical Manual of Mental Disorders*, 5th ed., vol. 20 (American Psychiatric Association, 2013).

I use the term AFAB to refer to myself as it is what is on my birth certificate. It is how I am consistently and constantly misgendered, and it serves as a reminder of my lived experiences being conditioned to behave as a female child and teenager. It is why I learned to mask my autism and go undiagnosed until age thirty-five; society conditions those who are AFAB to be social, to observe, to obey, and to perform. My status as AFAB is also important to consider in light of my chosen profession, a field dominated by white people who identify as women.

Another term I will use is nonbinary. For me, this term means that I identify as neither male nor female. Society at large may treat me as a female, but I do not identify socially as such. (I do legally, however.) When I refer to myself as nonbinary, I am indicating my lack of identification with female or male gender norms and expectations. My pronouns are they/them/theirs, but I acknowledge and sometimes use she/her/hers.

Finally, another note on my discussion of autism. Many (if not most) adult autistics with low support needs prefer to use identity-first language ("autistic person"). This is an effort to eliminate the societal stigma attached to autism and take pride in our unique brain type (roughly only 1% of the population). We typically see it, in spite of the struggles, as just one type of brain among many. As with any community, of course, there will be those who have differing beliefs and opinions. Some autistics want to be cured or may prefer person-first language ("person with autism"). While most of us disagree, we respect the rights of all people to choose their own labels. With these terms and definitions in mind, I would like to share my experience.

Autistic Librarianship

I generally keep my office door closed and turn harsh halogen bulbs off; my office is lit only by warm lamps. I will crawl under my desk, feeling a sense of shame. What grown adult does this? Yet the perspective from the roughly-carpeted floor soothes me. I find comfort in the curved lines of the computer and phone cords. Other days, when I am overstimulated or perceiving something unknown to me, or just plain exhausted from the weight of being autistic, I pace my office, flapping my hands, lightly pounding my chest, and rhythmically whimpering.

This autistic trait, which I share with most of my peers, is stimming, or self-stimulatory behavior. Most humans do it. It is clicking a pen, doodling during a meeting, biting fingernails, jiggling a knee when nervous. It is the mind's way of soothing, comforting, and easing anxiety or dis-ease. Mental illness and cognitive disorders increase the frequency of stimming. Autistic stereotypes bring to mind the hand flapping, shouting, recitations, et cetera.

Adaptation to an academic environment resulted in the development of socially acceptable stims: fiddling with a pen, jiggling my leg, and lately, clicking the pop socket on my phone in and out. I am highly aware that I would not survive in public librarianship or a staff position without an office. With an office and a door to close, my more destructive stims, the ones that might frighten people or give me scabs and bald patches, are hidden.

Tenure and promotion are not desirable options for me. My autism experience prevents the effort from being worth it and has even resulted in a contract not being renewed because my disability (undiagnosed at the time) required too much accommodation for that particular workplace. Two years in another tenure-equivalent position (all the while going through the autism diagnostic process) was enough to show it is a far too socially involved process for my deficits, my disability. Committee work, service to the profession, and other expectations are more difficult for me and require concerted effort.

The interactional expectations of librarianship are exhausting, and I find myself fatigued and burned out at the end of most days. I struggle to adapt to new workplace norms with every new position. Adherence to the norms of wider academic culture still eludes me, even after five years. Knowing the rules does not mean I follow them. In one position, peer review during the reappointment process was brutal, even in a more accepting and forgiving workplace. My nonbinary identity was respected, but my autism was not. There will always be negative or critical comments on my social interactions, no matter how hard I try.

Nonbinary Librarianship

Separately, I face barriers due to my nonbinary identity. In a woman-dominated field, I am regularly sorted, unasked, into a female role. The "F" in my employee records and my traditionally-female name seem to encourage misgendering. Sharing one's pronouns in a workplace email signature is only effective when people actually read the signature. I am grateful to fellow librarians who identify with their assigned gender and put their pronouns into that email signature.

I was born, raised, and have spent my adulthood in conservative, or "red," states, with one exception. Even in my current university setting with its diverse array of faculty, students, and staff, the rural setting wins out every time. Having been out as nonbinary at work for approximately three years now, I have observed a sharp difference in pronoun usage between my previous workplace and my current one. For most of my colleagues here, it is unintentional. For one in particular, it is purposeful. Yet every "she" or "her" from people who have been told my pronouns, or read my email signature, or seen my pronouns in a Zoom meeting is another cut of the knife, another reason I retreat.

Even in a higher education setting, the image of the librarian as a sweet traditional woman refuses to go away. If you are AFAB, forget it. You will be assigned a female role no matter your real gender identity. You will be treated as such by the overwhelmingly traditionally-gendered male leadership in most academic libraries. Humans in all career fields like a binary, and librarianship is no exception. Removing gender from ideas of professionalism and career advancement remains an elusive goal.

Queer Autistic Librarianship

The crux of this chapter is my experience at the intersection between autism and nonbinary identities in academic librarianship. Repeated misgendering results in time lost stimming so that I can calm down. It pushes me into an isolated space and reduces my contributions to the field and to my workplace. I am certain that if I was allistic, I would have more of an edge in recovering from these instances. I like to imagine I would be more apt to kindly correct misuses and promote the rights and needs of other nonbinary people in librarianship. I am certain I miss many of the microaggressions due to the deficit in understanding social cues. Subtlety is very often lost on me.

My autistic brain craves rigidity and structure, and when people do not follow my rules, such as using my pronouns, it is very often upsetting. Masking in order to perform well enough in academia drains me, so I generally choose to retreat, and feebly hope they see my email signature, rather than politely reminding them of my pronouns. My nonbinary identity is inextricably woven with the autism at this point and has become a (thankfully infrequent) meltdown trigger at times.

This interweaving, this intersection, blends with a third thread: academic librarianship, particularly when one holds faculty positions that very often entail tenure or promotion expectations. I am frequently frustrated that I cannot do more, but I am limited by autism and chronic health issues. It is draining and exhausting. I would be exhausted just as a nonbinary person in a binary-loving culture, but the autism adds an extra depth to the fatigue.

I have to be content with my limits, but I rarely am, unfortunately. What might be minimal effort for allistic and cisgender people is maximum effort for me. As I approach forty, I am finally learning to accept myself and my limits. Leadership is out of the question for me, but I can certainly co-chair a diversity committee (knowing all the while I am likely being tokenized for my autism and nonbinary identity). Socially-oriented service to the profession is a struggle, but I can certainly advance the field through book chapters, articles, and creative works. People are often surprised that I do not seek tenure or promotion. This is a boundary I have set for myself in order to do my best in librarianship. Unfortunately, this boundary is frequently not respected, whether by peers chastising me for not wanting more or rebukes from bosses who feel I only do the bare minimum.

Conclusion

At first glance, it seems that my autism is far more impairing to my career than my gender. Yet I cannot dismiss the role that being nonbinary plays in my experience. My gender and my autism are so tied that they feed off each other in my career. When colleagues do not respect my pronouns, my autism rears up. When I have a sensory overload or engage in stimming, I am no longer able to mask, and thus step out of roles assigned to me as someone people perceive to be female. While this space outside of the gender binary is my natural state, it is confusing for most and irritating for some. I hope my continued self-advocacy will inform others and widen their horizons, creating a safer world for disabled and queer folks.

Bibliography

American Psychiatric Association. *Diagnostic and Statistical Manual of Mental Disorders*. 5th ed. Vol. 20. American Psychiatric Association, 2013.

About the Author

MP Green is a health sciences/optometry librarian in Oklahoma with two awesome dogs. They hold an MA in Historical Theology (2011) and an MLIS (2016).

Boundary Setting as a Non-Binary Librarian and Facilitator

Amy Gilgan (they/them, she/her)

Keywords: non-binary, genderqueer, boundaries, facilitation, library instruction

Introduction

What does it mean to show up authentically as a trans librarian and facilitator? What boundaries do I need to have in place to take care of myself while seeing the humanity of everyone in the room? These are the questions I ask myself as a white, queer, non-binary instructional librarian from a working-class background. In this chapter, I reflect on the challenges of naming my trans identity in library spaces and facilitating discussions on gender identity as a non-binary person. I examine why, when, and how I share my gender identity alongside my racial identity.

My library instruction is influenced by my work as an intergroup dialogue facilitator and mediator. Intergroup dialogue pedagogy invites both the facilitators and participants to examine the ways in which their social identity development impacts how they see themselves and others.[1] According to Jackson and Hardiman's Social Identity Development Model, there is a stage of resistance in which folks with privileged identities experience cognitive dissonance between how they see themselves

1. Ximena Zúñiga, Biren (Ratnesh) A. Naagda, and Todd D. Sevig, "Intergroup Dialogues: An Educational Model for Cultivating Engagement across Differences," *Equity & Excellence in Education* 35, no. 1 (April 2002): 7–17, https://doi.org/10.1080/713845248.

and the impact of their social identity on others.[2] Using this framework of identity development, I am able to anticipate some of the types of resistance I may encounter from cisgender students and colleagues. Understanding the ways in which cisgender folks may resist learning helps me understand the boundaries I need to create in order to take care of myself while also seeing the humanity of the cisgender folks who are new to the work of trans allyship. This chapter will explore the strategies I use to authentically show up as a non-binary person while modeling consent and boundary setting.

This journey looks different depending on one's social identities, geographical location, and workplace. To imply that there is a particular way to show up authentically as a trans person in the workplace would invoke the "only one right way" aspect of white supremacy culture.[3] As such, I speak only from my own experience as a white, non-binary librarian. I identify on the trans spectrum as both non-binary and genderqueer, and I will use the term non-binary to describe my gender identity.

Facilitation Beginnings

My journey to anti-racist teaching and facilitation started in 2006 when I served as a member of the Community United Against Violence (CUAV) LGBTQ Speaker's Bureau. CUAV was founded in response to police violence and the murders of San Francisco Supervisor Harvey Milk and Mayor George Moscone in 1979.[4] The goal of the Speaker's Bureau, which ran until 2009, was to humanize LGBTQ people through the power of story and connection. CUAV trained LGBTQ volunteers to

2. Rita Hardiman and Bailey W. Jackson, "Conceptual Foundations for Social Justice Education," in *Teaching for Diversity and Social Justice*, ed. Maurianne Adams, Lee Anne Bell, and Pat Griffin, 1st edition (New York: Routledge, 1997), 16–28.

3. Tema Okun, "White Supremacy Culture – Still Here," Divorcing white supremacy, May 2021, https://www.whitesupremacyculture.info/uploads/4/3/5/7/43579015/okun_-_white_sup_culture_2020.pdf.

4. CUAV, "History," Community United Against Violence, accessed September 15, 2021, https://www.cuav.org/history.

speak on their experiences and answer questions in elementary, middle school, high school, and college classrooms. The components of the class sessions, which were called gigs, involved two co-speakers from different racial backgrounds sharing a brief overview of CUAV, ground rules for the session, and a short personal introduction involving their social identities. The students were then invited to ask the speakers questions. In terms of ground rules and disclaimers, the speakers would state that they could not discuss their personal sex lives, that they were speaking only from their own experiences rather than for the whole LGBTQ community, and that they had the option of not answering a question if it was too personal.[5] During my time on the Speaker's Bureau, I identified as queer but did not yet identify as non-binary. The practice of stating my social identities (race, sexuality, gender, class) and frontloading that I could not speak for all LGBTQ folks challenged me to constantly reflect on the intersections of my identities, especially my privileged white identity. This experience fundamentally shaped the way I show up as an instructional librarian and facilitator. I learned that, even in a situation where I was consenting to sharing my personal experiences, I could hold boundaries in a loving way. One of the ground rules was simply "If your question is too personal, we'll let you know."[6] Frontloading this disclaimer made it much easier for me to decline a question without shaming the student for asking. As I've developed as a teacher and facilitator, I think a lot about what boundaries I need to state up front so that I can be fully present as a queer and trans person.

Since my time with CUAV, I have continued to train in different modalities of facilitation and conflict resolution. In addition to working as an academic instructional librarian, I am currently an intergroup dialogue facilitator with Rise for Racial Justice as well as a volunteer mediator and conflict coach with SEEDS (Services that Encourage Effective Dialogue & Solutions) Community Resolution Center. I strive

5. Connie Champagne and Jennifer Daniels, eds., *CUAV Speaker's Bureau Manual* (San Francisco: Community United Against Violence, 2006).

6. Champagne and Daniels.

to help groups build spaces that nurture growth and transformation as a teacher, facilitator and mediator. However, I must not lose myself while holding space for others. As a non-binary person, I need to enter the space with awareness of what I will and will not share around my trans experience. One of the things I learned from my time with CUAV was to name that I was consenting to share some of my experience in that particular space, and that my consent in that space does not extend to all situations. In doing so, I am not only modeling consent, but also setting boundaries that protect me. When I maintain my boundaries around my trans identity, I can hold more compassion for cisgender folks who are at the beginning stages of building solidarity with trans folks. My boundaries are both an act of self-compassion and love for others. As Prentice Hemphill states, "Boundaries are the distance at which I can love you and me simultaneously."[7]

The Social Identity Development Model

The Social Identity Development Model, created by Bailey Jackson and Rita Hardiman, is a tool I use when planning workshops and discussions on gender identity with predominantly cisgender participants. Based on previous models of racial identity development, the model is generalized to apply to both privileged and marginalized identities within a larger context of multiple oppressions.[8] The model is comprised of five stages: naive, acceptance, resistance, redefinition, and internalization. The naive stage, which occurs in childhood, is characterized by a lack of awareness of power dynamics and how identity is seen by others. In the acceptance stage, one starts to become aware of social identity, but accepts the dominant societal structures as normal. It is at the resistance stage that awareness of oppression leads to a tension between self-image

7. Prentis Hemphill, "Boundaries Can Be Love," in *Holding Change: The Way of Emergent Strategy Facilitation and Mediation*, ed. Adrienne M. Brown, Emergent Strategy Series, no. 4 (Chico: AK Press, 2021).

8. Hardiman and Jackson, "Conceptual Foundations for Social Justice Education."

and how one exists within dominant power structures. This tension starts to dissolve in the redefinition stage as one begins to understand their identity in relation to oppression. The final stage, internalization, involves integrating the knowledge of power and positionality into the identity and acting in ways that challenge oppression.

When I apply this model to a gender identity workshop or discussion, I am most likely to be challenged by cisgender folks at the acceptance and resistance levels of development. Cisgender folks in the acceptance stage may be willfully ignorant or openly hostile to trans folks. Folks in the resistance stage have a desire to act in service of trans liberation, but may find it difficult to move beyond their discomfort. I have found that the majority of folks who self-select for a gender identity workshop or discussion are at the resistance stage, and that mandatory workshops are far more likely to be sites of open hostility. Recognizing these patterns helps me make decisions about what workshops I take on, ground rules, curriculum, and modality. This model helps me set boundaries while holding compassion for both myself and the participants. I consider the Social Identity Development Model when making decisions about how I show up in workplace facilitation, library instruction, and professional conferences.

Workplace Facilitation

As I have come into my non-binary identity, I have made choices about when and how to come out at work. My general practice is to state my social identities that I find most salient to my lived experience (race, gender, sexuality) openly in my professional bios as well as the social justice workshops I facilitate. In addition to library instruction, I have co-facilitated workshops on race and gender identity as a member of my university's Bias Education & Resource Team (BERT). BERT is led by the Dean of Students and comprised of staff and faculty across campus. The BERT workshops are primarily with students who work in campus housing. I have also facilitated a number of social justice workshops for faculty and staff in my roles on other university DEI committees. When I think about the boundaries I need to facilitate a workshop or discussion on gender identity at my place of employment, I start with these questions:

- Who is the audience?
- Have they been primed for the conversation?
- How closely do I work with them?
- Is the workshop mandatory or have the participants self-selected to be there?

In terms of my potential activators as a non-binary facilitator, the BERT workshops are generally lower risk for me than the ones for faculty and staff, since the sessions I've co-facilitated are part of a longer residential life employee training with social justice themes. Not only are the students more engaged in the workshops, but the cisgender students are generally at the resistance stage of identity development where they want to build solidarity with trans folks. The Student Housing and Residential Education staff are intentional about building trust between the student workers, and it is helpful for me to work with a group where accountability and repair are already established as norms. It has also been helpful to work with facilitators with racial and gender identities different from my own. This provides the option for one of the facilitators to step in when the other is a target of a microaggression from a participant.

Facilitating gender identity workshops for faculty at my institution can be challenging since I work more closely with them. I do not facilitate mandatory workshops on gender identity for faculty. Mandatory workshops can include those who are actively hostile to trans folks, and I recognize that I cannot simultaneously hold space for others and take care of myself in that context. When I facilitated a reading circle on the *Trans Allyship Workbook* for my university's Center for Teaching Excellence, it was important to me that the faculty members participating were choosing to be there.[9] Since the cisgender faculty members in the read-

9. Davey Shlasko, *Trans Allyship Workbook: Building Skills to Support Trans People in Our Lives*, Updated and expanded edition. (Madison: Think Again Training, 2017).

ing circle were beyond the acceptance stage of identity development, I was able to build relationships with them while holding onto myself.

Library Instruction

My pronouns have changed as my gender identity has evolved. At the beginning of each class, I introduce myself with my name and pronouns. Since the majority of my library instruction is one-shots, I don't always know the faculty members or classroom dynamics. While there are limitations to the trust and rapport I can create as a guest instructor, I can model the how and why of sharing pronouns. I use multiple pronouns, including they/them, and sometimes faculty struggle with which pronoun to use when introducing me to the class. When faculty members struggle with my pronouns, I recognize both the potential harm to me as well as the students who are witnessing it. After seeing Natalie Thoreson, a social justice consultant and facilitator, introduce herself as "pronoun flexible" at an advanced facilitation institute, I have adopted that practice as well.[10] I introduce myself in class and meetings by saying: "I go by they/them and she/her. I am pronoun flexible, but not all non-binary people are." By doing so, I am not only frontloading information to avoid pronoun confusion but also strategically coming out as non-binary. I choose to come out because I have both the privilege and social capital to do so safely. I recognize that this is not a viable option for all trans and gender diverse library workers. In my case, it allows me to model and connect with students while showing up with my whole self. As a result, trans students occasionally contact me for resources and I connect them to the appropriate campus offices and organizations.

Pronoun go-rounds, in which folks introduce themselves with names and pronouns, is another opportunity for me to model sharing pronouns as a non-binary person. Having volunteered with several anti-oppression

10. Natalie Thoreson, "Advanced Facilitation Skills for Navigating Difficult Conversations about Racism, White Privilege, and Oppression" (Pre-conference institute, White Privilege Conference, Kansas City, MO, April 27, 2017).

organizations, I am very used to sharing pronouns during introductions. However, I need to remember that this is a new practice for many folks. When I was teaching a for-credit summer course a few years ago, I asked the students to do an icebreaker activity that involved sharing their names and pronouns on the first day of class. One of the students earnestly asked me why we share pronouns. I responded by saying, "There are many different genders, and folks may use pronouns like they/them, he/him, she/her and many more. We share pronouns because we want to create a space where all gender identities are valued." This was a major "a-ha" moment for me. I was asking students to do something for which many of them had no context. I now make a point to briefly explain why I invite the sharing of pronouns before any go-round. Over the years, I've noticed pronoun go-rounds go sideways when teachers and facilitators do not explain why they are doing it. This is often due to a participant being flustered and confused by a new activity. Another consideration for pronoun go-rounds is that one could inadvertently encourage a student to out themselves in an unsafe environment. To avoid this situation, Davey Shlasko of Think Again Training and Consulting recommends stating that sharing pronouns is optional and that the group will just use the participant's name if they choose not to share pronouns.[11] I have adopted this practice alongside explaining the why of the go-round to not only support trans and gender diverse participants, but also to give grace to folks who may be thinking about pronouns and identity for the first time. By introducing pronoun go-rounds with an explanation and an option to use one's name instead of a pronoun, I am modeling for both the faculty member and the students.

Professional Conferences

In recent years, I have started to apply the facilitation skills I've learned from working closely with community organizations and student affairs professionals to my library conference workshops. I had an experience

11. Shlasko, *Trans Allyship Workbook*.

where I was facilitating a discussion on a different topic when one of the cisgender participants became distressed and started crying, stating they feared they had misgendered me. I have also been in spaces where cisgender faculty members discharge their discomfort about pronouns by laughing about it, which can negatively impact the trans and gender diverse folks in the room. These experiences made me wonder what skills cisgender participants needed to cultivate in order to actually absorb the content. The Social Identity Development Model helped me understand that these folks were in the resistance stage in which they recognize they have cisgender privilege and are experiencing discomfort around it. My trans solidarity workshops are designed primarily for cisgender folks in the resistance stage of identity development, with the secondary audience being trans folks seeking tools to engage with cisgender folks. In the pre-work for latest iteration of the workshop, I am explicit about the intended audience, and I introduce the Social Identity Development Model. By referencing the model, I am able to normalize the discomfort and name the harmful ways in which cisgender folks sometimes discharge it.

Since trans folks attend my workshops too, I am intentional about what I invite participants to share with each other. Unlike the courses I co-facilitate with Rise for Racial Justice over several weeks, my conference workshops are usually about an hour. One of the key components of intergroup dialogue is building the container for the conversation, and recognizing what that container can actually hold. A single workshop does not have the same scaffolding and relationship building as a multi-week course or dialogue. I do not provide discussion prompts that could allow cisgender folks to interrogate trans participants. I have the capacity to acknowledge the discomfort cisgender folks experience around gender identity, but I have limited capacity to process that discomfort with them. As such, I do not create space for cisgender folks to process or discharge that discomfort in my workshops. Instead, I invite participants to share what community means to them and strategies they use to stay present when called on harmful behavior.

At the beginning of a sixty-minute conference workshop on trans solidarity, I state that the session assumes racism and transphobia exist, and that I will not debate the existence of these oppressions in the session. By doing so, I am setting boundaries for the workshop. My workshops are designed for folks who want to do solidarity work, and I will not provide a platform for folks who seek to derail anti-oppression work.

Conclusion

As a white non-binary instructional librarian and facilitator, I am invested in holding spaces where folks can explore their liberatory potential. When I consent to sharing parts of my trans experience with cisgender folks, it is a gift, not an obligation. I approach this work from a place of love, and I know that there will be times when my boundaries are tested. My biggest learnings have been to get clear on my boundaries as a trans person, frontload them at the beginning, and show myself compassion by maintaining them.

Bibliography

Champagne, Connie, and Jennifer Daniels, eds. *CUAV Speaker's Bureau Manual.* San Francisco: Community United Against Violence, 2006.

CUAV. "History." Community United Against Violence. Accessed September 15, 2021. https://www.cuav.org/history.

Hardiman, Rita and Jackson, Bailey W. "Conceptual Foundations for Social Justice Education." In *Teaching for Diversity and Social Justice*, edited by Maurianne Adams, Lee Anne Bell, and Pat Griffin, 1st edition., 16–28. New York: Routledge, 1997.

Hemphill, Prentis. "Boundaries Can Be Love." In *Holding Change: The Way of Emergent Strategy Facilitation and Mediation*, edited by Adrienne M. Brown. Emergent Strategy Series, no. 4. Chico: AK Press, 2021.

Okun, Tema. "White Supremacy Culture – Still Here." Divorcing white supremacy, May 2021. https://www.whitesupremacy-culture.info/uploads/4/3/5/7/43579015/okun_-_white_sup_culture_2020.pdf.

Shlasko, Davey. *Trans Allyship Workbook: Building Skills to Support Trans People in Our Lives*. Updated and Expanded edition. Madison: Think Again Training, 2017.

Thoreson, Natalie. "Advanced Facilitation Skills for Navigating Difficult Conversations about Racism, White Privilege, and Oppression." Pre-conference institute presented at the White Privilege Conference, Kansas City, MO, April 27, 2017.

Zúñiga, Ximena, Biren (Ratnesh) A. Naagda, and Todd D. Sevig. "Intergroup Dialogues: An Educational Model for Cultivating Engagement across Differences." *Equity & Excellence in Education* 35, no. 1 (April 2002): 7–17. https://doi.org/10.1080/713845248.

About the Author

Amy Gilgan (they/she) is the School of Education Librarian at the University of San Francisco. They are a facilitator with Rise for Racial Justice, an organization that helps K-12 teachers build capacity for anti-racist action. As a certified mediator and volunteer conflict coach with SEEDS Community Resolution Center, they are passionate about transforming harm and the systemic conditions that cause it. Amy is white, queer and non-binary, and is also trained as a restorative justice facilitator.

METALLIC INGENUE: Reflections of a Trans Woman on Transition, Stealth, the LIS Field, and Heavy Metal

Larissa Glasser

Keywords: academic libraries, trans woman, coming out, disability, heavy metal studies

> Watch for what the religious right tries to do to your schools, watch for them trying to shut down cool record stores or cool college radio stations, and as Frank Zappa puts it, "Don't let them govern by telling people what they don't like, go out and tell them what you *do* like." Support these people![1]

It is not lost on me that five years ago was the first time I felt safe enough to hang a trans flag on my door. In 2020, the first thing I saw when I walked into a local Target was a T-shirt display, "Live Authentically" arrayed in the colors of the pink-blue-white trans flag. In June of 2021, I drove back from work and saw Pride Month being advertised on a huge electronic billboard, as big as any anti-choice or Chick-fil-A advert you might find during a typical highway commute. Sometimes I feel like all of this is a waking dream, because I thought trans people would always need to keep our heads down. Now we are a household word, even though most people continue to place us in the wrong context, use us as a political football, or see us as a shill of right vs. left. Trite, because we trace back as far as humanity itself.

---

1. Jello Biafra, "Tales from the Trail," *High Priest of Harmful Matter,* Alternative Tentacles Records (1989).

I cannot help but feel imposter syndrome as I write this, because although I've lived and navigated life as a trans woman for twenty-five years, over a generation of being out, I spent much of that time keeping my own head down, living stealth in the workplace. As of the Bostock v. Clayton County decision by the Supreme Court in 2020, we have employment protections at the federal level in the United States. Although we have made these huge strides, we still have a long way to go. But I have seen so much change; the genie is out of the bottle, and we are not going back.

Cultural output is key for the advancement of trans rights. I cannot reasonably encapsulate twenty-five years of my post-transition life and career in LIS within the framework of this chapter—suffice it to say I watched gay and lesbian rights develop during the twentieth and twenty-first centuries through news and entertainment media. The Defense of Marriage Act, *Will and Grace*, *The L Word*, and *Queer as Folk* paved the way for greater overall acceptance of queer people, with the caveat that it was mostly white- and cis-centric. Of course, this is an oversimplification—infinite factors come into play. But I never thought I would live to see anything change for the better. When I paid for facial electrolysis, E. valerate, and surgery completely out-of-pocket, I did so from a determination that I'd never go back to the way things were for me before. They were untenable, as they can be for anyone navigating dysphoria and I felt powerless to remedy that until my own transition.

One way I remember coping with my isolation during transition was to compartmentalize my life. When I was a young student, out but not "fully" transitioned, playing in bands gave me an outlet to be creative and feel safe. It's a strange paradox that although I'm an introvert, I've never felt stage fright. Perhaps it makes sense that I gravitated to an over-the-top, flash-bang genre such as heavy metal. I started as a new wave kid back when MTV was in full sway and well before social media. But then, not long after puberty, what became as equally clear to me as identifying as female was my identification with heavy metal music.

The genre of metal is consistently assertive, if vulgar and rebellious. As many words may have been expressed about metal as about trans people and our place in the drive for civil rights (and it is well-documented that both are global in scope and effect). There has also been persecution from the same sources: the religious right always needs a scapegoat for political ammunition and fundraising initiatives, and during the 1980s, metal was their target. During our current era, post-Obergefell v. Hodges, trans rights are the new scapegoat. And in the same way that censorship worked with the religious right and metal during the tail end of the Cold War, their legislative conspiracies against trans rights specifically target the young. I've seen this happen in cycles, and many have been hurt along the way. We don't need to brook that any longer.

I'd prefer not to add to the noise with extrapolations or theories about the universal and inevitable advancement of trans rights. The surge of visibility we have experienced in the past decade has brought forth many voices that are eminently more qualified than my own, in addition to the hot takes from dizzy unfortunates who would like to see all queer people fail. However, as one who transitioned within the field of professional academia more than a decade before the so-called "tipping point" indicated by the *Time* magazine cover story about Laverne Cox,[2] I hope I can offer a unique perspective as someone who split their personal and professional time in a way that felt empowering but utterly alone—when I was not at work, I dedicated my life to starting and maintaining a metal band.

I admit that I still feel completely alone in this. During the past few years, I've met many other trans people working as professional librarians, many of whom are storied, award-winning writers and scholars. Although trans folks will just have to see what comes next for us in the library profession, we now have more agency than ever before. Cultural output is key in maintaining the struggle for our rights. Show them what you DO like, because affinity goes a long way.

---

2. Katy Steinmetz, "The Transgender Tipping Point," *Time* (June 9, 2014).

Bibliography

Jello Biafra. "Tales from the Trail." *High Priest of Harmful Matter.* Alternative Tentacles Records (1989).

Steinmetz, Katy. "The Transgender Tipping Point." *Time*, Jun 9, 2014.

About the Author

Larissa Glasser is a librarian-archivist from New England. She writes dark fiction centered on the lives of trans women, library science, and heavy metal. Her work is available in *Transcendent 3: The Year's Best Transgender Themed Speculative Fiction* (Lethe Press) and *Tragedy Queens: Stories Inspired by Lana Del Rey and Sylvia Plath* (Clash Books). Her debut novella *F4* is available from Eraserhead Press. She is on Twitter @larissaeglasser.

Gender Inclusivity Trainings at Academic Libraries: Two Case Studies

Kylie Terra Burnham (she/they)

Keywords: gender 101, workplace training, allyship, transitioning, coming out

To the best of my knowledge, I was the first out trans employee at two libraries, both of which were academic libraries at upper-echelon, Northeastern US, liberal arts-style higher education institutions.

Being the first out trans person was sometimes amusing. For example, when I was about six months into my hormone therapy, my library got a new director. My body was becoming visibly queer but not yet visually assigned "woman" by others. For my own comfort and safety in a socially conservative area, I wore clothes that, like my body, signaled maleness as much as they might signal a queered gender. As I was starting to be quietly out at work, I realized that continuing to use the men's bathroom sent mixed signals about my identity to my coworkers who saw me go into or out of it. However, our only all-gender bathroom was a single-stall down two flights of stairs, in a patron-facing area that had no men's room; as the only or the most comfortable option for our male patrons *and* trans patrons of all genders, it was frequently in use. I casually mentioned this difficulty to the new director. While doing so, I noted that I wasn't comfortable being in the women's room (since I still presented so masculinely), and in response he said something which seemed to signal he thought I was a later-in-transition trans masculine person instead of an early-in-transition trans feminine person. He undoubtedly was trying to be affirming, and I found the gaff endearing.

Other times, it's been upsetting. For example, I found out that a week after starting a new job, my hiring manager outed me to another new hire who was coming from a different field, telling her that she wasn't the only one experiencing a transition. Not only was my so-called transition already as "complete" as I wanted it to be, it also wasn't a comparable topic of discussion. Clearly, there was a lack of knowledge that being out in one setting—such as during a job interview when diversity, equity, and inclusion are being discussed—does not rob someone of their right to out herself (or not) to her coworkers.

No matter what, being the first out trans staff member always necessitates education. At one library, I advocated for and conducted a gender diversity training co-facilitated by a nonbinary faculty member; this was so successful that the library decided to create a LibGuide from the content. At the other library, the Office of Equal Opportunity was brought in to do the training with nearly disastrous results that ranged from confusing *cisgender* with *binary gender*, to waving a magic wand "absolving" all in attendance from harm caused by mistakes, ignorance, and microaggressions. In this chapter, I'll briefly look at the reasoning behind the different approaches, what worked and what didn't, with the aim of building best practices for gender diversity training for library workers. My hope is that this can alleviate educational burdens which result from being the first (or second, or third!) out trans person working within a library space, by suggesting successful paths that libraries can take to promote and practice inclusivity.

My Positionality

Understanding the way identities and identity narratives structure our experiences (not unlike the way walls or mountains do, a social and narrative environment comparable to the physically built and grown environments around us) begins with knowing one's own identity and positionality; by naming the ways we categorize ourselves and the ways others categorize us, we shed a light on both invisible social structures and our personal growth edges.

My marginalized identities include being a Jewish trans feminine person who was raised rural poor, and who is a lesbian-leaning bisexual. My privileged identities are integral to my being able to be the first out trans staff member at two libraries, and to the generally positive treatment I received as such: I am a white, abled, American citizen who is book/test smart, college-educated, English speaking, thin, generally considered attractive, and seen or accepted as a binary gender. This is all important to state, in order to shape the ways you can understand and critique my experiences.

Coming out as trans is often not a one-time process, but is something one does again and again. I came out to myself when I was fifteen after finding a definition of transgender online. Contrary to the popular idea that trans people inherently know they are trans from early childhood, in my experience most trans people do not realize they are trans until they are teenagers or adults. I struggled without trans representation or access to trans adults and peers. In particular, at the time there was no positive representation of trans lesbians, who were often framed as sexual predators if mentioned at all, in a world where trans feminine people seemed to be typically conceived of as a subset of gay men. I felt like I would never encounter others like me.

My first professional library job was a continuation of my job as a student worker, on a team with Research Librarians, Educational Technologists, and Instructional Designers. While I had been demurely yet firmly out in college, after graduating I threw out the feminine signifiers, like clothing and makeup, that I had acquired. I buckled down to live my life pretending to be a man, which I thought would be safer and easier for me; I thought if I was out as trans, I wouldn't be hired or would have a difficult time at work.

Gradually, I realized I needed to be out (again)—for my own happiness as well as to be an example and create change. I started hormones (which wasn't an easy process, as therapists and doctors in the area refused to see me, stating ethical concerns due to a lack of prior experience providing hormone therapy). While I didn't make a big deal at work or have a formal coming out, I slowly opened up to having coworkers know I was trans.

Eventually, I left that institution out of a desire to move to a city. This happened to coincide with being on hormones for a year, just before my physical body changes began to signal "woman" to most people. After moving, I changed my name and pronouns before I got a new job. So while I've been the first out trans person at two libraries, in neither workplace did I undergo a period of social gender-related changes (in popular parlance, a "transition," a simplification that elides nuance and focuses on a before-and-after narrative which is not always descriptive of lived experience; I also want to clarify that my gender didn't transition so much as the way that people described it changed). As a result, my experience was undeniably an easier position than most trans people who do come out and transition at work.

Training 1: "Gender Inclusivity in the Classroom"

For context, this is about a teaching and learning lecture series hosted by an academic library at an institution with a somewhat conservative and traditionally hierarchical structure.

This training was initiated by me. It was part of a monthly, institution-wide peer learning and professional development workshop series organized and hosted by the library. I approached my supervisor and asked about doing a workshop on gender inclusivity. She was accepting of the idea, but not enthused. She told me I would need to get a faculty member to co-present and that it would need to focus on practical advice, not anything abstract. I think she may have been concerned about blowback from people or departments who may not have been friendly to gender inclusivity. If that was the case, I wish she had named that particular concern and included me in brainstorming solutions rather than creating an atmosphere of obstacles.

Through connections with the campus diversity center, I was introduced to a nonbinary faculty member who, like me, was only quietly out. They agreed to co-host the training. I then did some collection of data regarding trans patrons and community members, asking what experiences at our institution they found marginalizing or centralizing. Outreach to trans community members was done in partnership with the diversity center and through my own informal network. After reviewing the data, I crafted an outline script for the training—keeping in mind the directive to focus on practical tips.

The training itself was one of the most-well attended public events in our library, filling the space; in fact, we had to add extra chairs. It was primarily attended by faculty as well as by library staff in teaching and management positions. After my co-host and I took turns presenting from the outline, we had a lengthy Q&A. Feedback was resoundingly positive, though participants indicated that they wanted the more theoretical "gender 101" content I'd been instructed to avoid; most of the questions asked in the post-presentation Q&A reflected that as well.

A modified version of the outline script, incorporating feedback from participants, can be found at the end of this chapter in Appendix A.

What was good about this training:

- It was trans-led, by trans people who had offered on their own to do this work (and as part of their paid work with the organization, not as additional unpaid labor).
- It was general/preemptive, not in response to someone coming out.
- It centered feedback from trans community members solicited in advance.
- It created and utilized pathways for partnerships with other institutional stakeholders, such as the campus diversity center.
- It focused on tips for teaching; many librarians are educators, as are many of our patrons.
- It had ample time for generative questions and responses.

What wasn't good:

- There was resistance from library management to hosting this training, and to hosting it as part of our public programming, rather than active support and interest.

- There was pressure from management to focus on practical tips only and avoid background concepts about gender.
- It didn't delve into tips for workplace inclusivity, contributing to the false narrative that only young people such as students or external audiences such as patrons are trans.

Training 2: "Workshop on Working with Trans and GNC Individuals"

Context: a diversity training for library staff at a progressive institution with a generally decentralized organizational structure.

This training was initiated by upper-level library staff in response to a colleague coming out as nonbinary. Library management had reached out to the Office of Equal Opportunity (OEO), who sent a staff person to conduct the training. The training was optional but strongly encouraged.

I attended the training out of curiosity. To my dismay, the trainer, who was cis and seemed well-meaning, clearly didn't understand a lot about being trans. In addition to misinformation and misuse of terminology, the approach seemed focused on helping cisgender people feel safe and comfortable working with trans and gender-diverse individuals, rather than creating a working environment that is safe and accommodating for gender diversity and gender-diverse people.

As the training went on, I felt more and more disheartened and defeated, knowing that my coworkers were learning actively harmful information. I immediately let library management know, and the director worked with me to pass along feedback to the OEO. I ended up writing an 18-point list, which I've included as an instructive example of what not to do (Appendix B).

What was good about this training:

- It was promoted and encouraged by library management.
- It discussed specific situations related to the workplace, including trans people as colleagues or direct reports.

What wasn't good:

- It was in response to a colleague coming out, which can single-out or other a colleague, and can make colleagues hesitant to come out in a workplace if they think doing so might result in a similar training for their coworkers that would shine an uncomfortable spotlight on them and their identity.
- Information was incorrect and sometimes demeaning. While the cis participants I spoke with seemed to find it useful, in my assessment they left knowing less-correct information and less-inclusive practices than when they arrived.
- The training was only cis-led, without input from a trans co-facilitator or content creator.
- The trainer relied heavily on the experiences of a single binary trans person they knew, instead of utilizing broader knowledge, practices, and discourses explored by gender educators and people with historically marginalized genders.
- The trainer continually said things that were microaggressions and verbalizations of their own negative biases towards trans people, particularly nonbinary people, in the training.
- The trainer did not specialize in gender education.
- The training was framed around making cis people feel comfortable, as opposed to inclusive practices.
- The training assumed everyone in the room was cis. Non-cis people can still benefit from gender inclusive training, as we don't all have the same experiences or identities.

Conclusion

By being proactive about creating awareness of trans people and how to include us, you'll be making life easier and happier for future trans employees—who can then focus on doing work, instead of on educating their peers (and supervisors) about their own identities, or navigating being a worker in an environment that misunderstands or is hostile to them.

If your library doesn't have an out trans staff member, don't wait for someone to come out as trans or for an out trans person to be hired before taking steps to make your organization comfortable for trans colleagues (as well as trans patrons). Hire an external trans educator. Plan regular training or discussions around gender, marginalized genders, oppression, and inclusion. If you have a workplace book club, include books by trans authors. Consider opening trans inclusion trainings or discussions to patrons as a public program.

Get used to sharing your own pronouns if you are comfortable doing so, rather than asking for pronouns from others (see Appendix A for reasons why pronoun sharing should be optional). This could be done when interviewing job candidates, when introducing yourself while hosting public programs, in the name or pronoun field in video-conferencing software, and in staff bios on your website.

Figure out what goes into making a name change at your organization, and plan to make name and pronoun changes streamlined. What technical systems have name information? Ideally, it should be as simple for a trans colleague as for someone who changes their last name after marriage.

If you do have out trans employees or colleagues, check in with them privately about what you can do to make the library more inclusive. Do they want to take part in any of these initiatives, like figuring out which trans educator to hire for trainings? Trans coworkers didn't volunteer for gender education work simply by virtue of being who they are, but the way this work is done at your organization directly impacts them—and they should be included in a way that doesn't assume they'll do the work themselves.

Appendix A. "Gender Inclusivity in the Classroom" Training Outline (extended based on participant feedback and updated for this volume)

Background information

- **Gender** is a cultural social category, often involving behavior, presentation, identification, and social roles including labor division. People can have one or more genders, or none.
    - Which category someone is in can only be reliably determined by that person themselves, though many people and cultures often use shorthand to guess or assign genders based on cultural assumptions, associations, and expectations, which may be wrong or limiting.
    - The relationship between gender and the idea of self can be conceptualized in several ways; for example, you can think of your gender as something you *are*, and/or as something you *use* to navigate the world.
- **Sex** is a cultural way to interpret bodies and assign gender based on embodied characteristics called sex traits. (Note: Sexes are socially constructed categories.)
    - **Sex traits** are embodied characteristics that are given a sex value in a culture, and include genitalia, internal reproductive organs, chromosomes, and hormones, as well as facial features, body hair, skin texture, body shape, and many others. What sex values are used, which traits are given a sex value, and how that trait has to look or be for each value can change over time and culture.
    - People are often legally, socially, and/or physically assigned a sex at birth, based on their sex traits. Some cultures give preference to some sex traits over others when assigning sex; often, reproductive organs are considered the primary sex traits at birth, though in social interactions other characteristics (e.g., face, height, gender expression, etc.) are more

dominantly used to assign sex.

- In many cultures, each sex is expected to correlate to a gender.
    - In Western gender systems, people who are/use only the gender societally assumed based on the sex they were assigned at birth are **cisgender (cis)**; people who are/use one or more genders that are not societally assumed based on the sex they were assigned at birth may identify as **transgender (trans).**
- Dominant Western cultural paradigms have/allow/expect a binary of distinct, opposite genders ("man" and "woman") and so interpret bodies as a binary of distinct, opposite sexes. This is called the **binary gender system** or the gender binary.
    - In this system, the legally and socially recognized sex categories are "male" and "female." (Note that this is changing with increasing Western social, legal, and scientific acceptance of understanding bodies and genders in different ways. Some Western countries and regions, including some US states, have added a nonbinary option for legal identification documents.[1] However, at this point even these legally-inclusive regions commonly still socially enforce oppressive features of the dominant Western binary gender system described here.)
    - In the Western binary gender system, people are **assigned female at birth (AFAB)** and expected to be women or **assigned male at birth (AMAB)** and expected to be men.
    - Framing genders as opposites, in the binary system "male" is typically imbued with more valued associations and "female" with less valued or diminished associations.
    - In the Western binary gender system, someone assigned "male" is culturally expected to have only sex

1. While efforts to include nonbinary genders on legal documentation have some benefits, the author feels it imperative to note here her opinion that a more inclusive, less marginalizing, and less susceptible-to-surveillance change would be to not legally assign or record sexes at all.

traits given a sex value of "male"; someone assigned "female" is culturally expected to have only sex traits given a sex value of "female." When people have sex traits that deviate from these groupings (e.g., someone assigned female with facial hair, a sex trait currently given the value of "male" in the West) they may face social consequences including ridicule or exclusion; people may feel pressure to hide or modify particular sex traits to match the current cultural idealization of a sex category.

  - **Intersex** refers to people who have variations or combinations of sex traits which may not fit into the sex categories used in Western (and many other) cultures. People who are intersex are often non-consensually surgically altered at a young age to fit into culturally accepted sex categories as part of their sex assignation. Juxtasex or perisex are emerging terms for non-intersex people.
    - Note: Intersex people may or may not identify with the gender expected of their medically-assigned sex and/or the gender(s) expected of the sex traits they were born with (which may have had a mixed or unclear gender expectation). As such, intersex people may identify as cis, trans, or another term that clarifies the relationship between their gender and their assigned sex.
- A **binary** person has/uses one of the genders recognized in the Western binary system of "man" and "woman." Binary people can be trans or cis, intersex or juxtasex.
- Not all people are women or men. **Non-binary** (sometimes shortened to *enby*) people do not fit into the Western binary gender system.[2] There are many ways of being non-binary,

2. *Enby* refers to the sounds (in the English alphabet) of the initials for non-binary, NB. While *NB* is sometimes used as a shorthand to refer to nonbinary gender, *enby* is increasingly used instead. *NB* has a longer history of meaning non-Black, often when indicating non-Black People of Color. Using *NB* for gender not only causes confusion (note: people can be both non-Black and non-binary) but points to how racialization and the language describing race used by People of Color are often ignored or erased by the dominant white culture through which access to language and terminology is often filtered.

such as being outside or between the binary system's social categories, or by having/using multiple genders.

  - Some non-binary people feel affirmed or included by the terms trans or transgender, while some do not.

- Many cultures have genders other than "man" and "woman," such as hijra people in South Asia, fa'afafine in Samoa, femminielli in Naples, a variety of Native American third and fourth genders such as niizh manidoowag for Anishinabee people, and many others. Many people who are these genders do not identify as transgender or non-binary and may not fit within Western transgender or non-binary conceptualizations.
- People who are **gender non-conforming (GNC)** do not conform to expectations of their gender. People who are GNC may be trans or cis. People who are trans may see themselves as gender conforming or gender non-conforming.
  - Some ways people can be non-conforming are: how their body looks, the clothes they wear, the jobs and social roles they perform, their sexuality.
  - For example, dominant societal narratives assume women are attracted to men and only men, so queer women are non-conforming. Women are assumed to have long hair, so short haired women are non-conforming. Women are assumed to be short and small, so taller and bigger women are non-conforming. Men are assumed to have certain jobs and not others, so male nurses or ballerinas are non-conforming. Men are assumed to wear certain clothes and not others, so men who wear dresses are non-conforming.
  - A trans woman wearing a dress is conforming to cultural assumptions of her gender. A trans woman wearing a suit and tie is gender non-conforming.
  - What is or isn't gender-conforming often changes across time and cultures.
- There is no one way to look or act like any gender, to look or act non-binary or binary, to look or act trans or cis. You

can't tell someone's gender, or if someone is non-binary or binary, or if someone is trans or cis, just by looking at them (or hearing them, learning their name, etc.).

Pronouns

- Pronouns are words that substitute for noun phrases. Personal pronouns are words that substitute for a specific person's name or other identifying nouns. Personal pronouns do not have to be related to gender, but many languages with personal pronouns use a word tied to a person's gender to stand in for that person.
    - Personal pronouns are similar to a shorter name for a person. Using the wrong pronoun for someone because of your associations with how they look is similar to using a name for someone because you think they look like someone who would have that name.
- Don't assume anyone's gender or pronouns (just as you wouldn't assume their name). Use "they" as a gender inclusive pronoun for people whose pronouns you don't know.
- Share your own pronouns before asking for those of others.
- Don't make sharing pronouns mandatory. Trans students are often singled out in mandatory pronoun rounds.
    - Sharing pronouns can be marginalizing, dysphoric, and difficult for some people. Common issues include 1) people having to either out themselves or lie about their gender, and 2) people not feeling trans enough, non-binary/binary enough, or woman/man enough to claim their pronouns publicly.
- Consider asking on "get to know you" index cards during the first class.
    - Note: for a variety of reasons, not all people are represented by or affirmed by the personal pronouns used in English. Students at [university] have reported being affirmed when the option to choose "no pronoun" is presented and respected by faculty. In these cases, refer to the student by the student's

name.

- Do not assume that because a student told you which pronouns to use, they are out to their family or their employers. Ask before using their pronouns in those situations (if you do not know what pronouns to use in vulnerable situations, use their name only).
    - Letters of recommendation for students who do not want to be outed to potential employers/programs: Some students have reported feeling affirmed by recommenders who make it clear that they will change the letter later (to the student's correct name/pronouns) or use different pronouns/names for different letters if the student desires. If sending a copy to the student for their records, send one with the student's correct name and pronouns as well as the version sent to the employer/school.
- What to do when you have misgendered someone:
    - "If you accidentally use the wrong pronoun, apologize quickly and sincerely, then move forward. The bigger deal you make out of the situation, the more uncomfortable it is for everyone."[3]
    - If someone corrects you, it may be appropriate to also thank the person for the correction.
- When talking about a person from a time they used different pronouns, use the pronouns they currently use. In most cases, it is also inappropriate to out that person or indicate they used different pronouns.

Names

- Names can be a marker of gender. Many trans people are not affirmed by the name they were given at birth, and may go by different names. Misgendering and misidentifying someone by using the name they were given at birth is called deadnaming.
    - If you do roll call daily, can you get corrected names

3. "Tips for Allies of Transgender People," GLAAD, November 11, 2021, https://www.glaad.org/transgender/allies.

from students *before* your first roll call? For example, with index cards on the first day of class or via email.
    - Do not ask people for the name they were given at birth if you do not know it.
    - When talking about a person from a time they went by their deadname, it is incorrect and inappropriate to refer to them by their deadname.
- Ask all students for their common-use name. This may be difficult or dysphoric for some students, as can be class activities centered around student's names.

Language

- Avoid gendered generalities like "men and women," "he or she," or "ladies and gentlemen." Use gender inclusive generalities like "people," "students," "everyone," etc.
- Avoid calling a group of students "men," "women," "ladies," "gentlemen," etc., unless you know all students in that group are that gender or use that gendered term for themself (reminder: the only way to know is to be told).
- Adopt a gender-inclusive writing policy in your class, e.g., encouraging students to use "they" instead of "he or she"; describe people with non-gendered descriptors instead of assuming genders.
    - The MLA, APA, and Chicago Manual of Style have suggestions for how they approach gender inclusive language, and approve singular they in the context of gender diversity. The AP and a variety of newspapers also approve singular they.
- When speaking about bodies, say what you mean and what body parts you mean rather than using gender or sex as shorthand; e.g., "people with uteruses," "people who can get pregnant," "people who menstruate," etc. As well as including people with trans and non-binary genders, this also includes non-normative cis bodies and experiences; e.g., not all cis women can get pregnant, some cis women have beards or don't have mammary glands, etc.
- Actively look out for ongoing work by marginalized com-

munities on improving terminology around gender and sex diversity. Listen to marginalized communities when they critique current terms and propose new ones, and adjust your language.

Materials & Curriculum

- Articles, textbooks, videos, handouts, and other assigned or in-class content will likely not use gender inclusive language or represent gender diverse authors, thinkers, history, characters, or issues. This is marginalizing to gender-diverse students, who are underrepresented (often unrepresented) in course materials.
    - One strategy students have been affirmed with is having a class discussion on the underlying assumptions the author(s) have used, or by faculty drawing attention to and showing awareness of the gender exclusivity of materials.
- Use materials that represent gender diversity when possible. Include gender-diverse authors and topics as applicable to your discipline. Put the work in for inclusive curricula.

Appendix B. Feedback Given to the Presenters of "Workshop on Working with Trans and GNC Individuals"

Hi OEO Office,

I was at the first training for library staff called Workshop on Working with Trans and GNC Individuals. I wanted to pass along some feedback.

1. At the beginning, the presenter used the phrase "somebody who looks like me" to refer to cisgender (cis) people. While later the presenter acknowledged that there are trans people who pass as cis, and who one may not realize are trans, they started by implying that you can tell who is trans or not by their appearance.

(Note: the phrase "pass as cis" was never used, though the demeaning phrase "passes as male" was later in the training to refer to a trans man. A trans man does not pass as male—he is male. He may, however, be able to pass as cis, meaning people assume he was assigned the same sex/gender at birth that they are assigning to him now, i.e., they may assign male to him and not assume he was assigned female at birth. Note: there are cis people out there who do not pass as cis!)

2. When defining "sex," the presenter described it as "basically your plumbing." This is reductive and potentially essentializing. Best practices for gender diversity trainings include talking about sex as a spectrum, which contemporary science supports; sex is about how we interpret bodies based on sex traits which include, but are not limited to, "plumbing." This is more inclusive for intersex individuals on campus, as well as trans and gender-diverse people.

3. When introducing what transgender meant, the presenter used the "born in the wrong body" explanation. Justifying your existence can feel hard to do with complexities, and easier to do with simple statements that elide a lot of truth. Some historically prominent trans people used explanations like "I was born in the wrong body," and some trans people still do today when coming out to their families or other times a simple explanation is needed. However, this explanation is sensationalist,

locates transness in a particular relationship to the body (and specifically to genitalia), and doesn't describe accurately the experience of many, if not most, trans people (who do not feel they were born in the wrong body, but feel that their body was or is assigned gender inaccurately). Being transgender is not about one's body being wrong—and while many transgender people do modify their bodies to feel more comfortable in them, many cis people do too!

This "trapped in the wrong body" explanation is rooted in something comfortable and easy for cis people to understand or accept, not in affirming and representing trans people and their experiences. This explanation has also been the source of a lot of harm: on one hand, it has been used to exclude people as "not really trans" for not experiencing body dysmorphia or undergoing medical transition; on the other hand, seeing this simplification as the whole of the trans experience has been used to dispute the validity of all transgender experiences from a variety of angles, including feminist perspectives, religious perspectives, and medical and mental health perspectives.

4. The presenter referred to a trans person as "born with male parts." This follows some of the same reductiveness as point 3 above. Transness should not be reduced to genitalia. Additionally, many trans people do not get surgery and consider the body they have, and all their parts, to be in line with their gender. For example, many trans women would say they have a female body, regardless of surgery status.

5. The presenter seemed to be using the phrase "gender non-conforming" to mean "non-binary gender," and never used the phrase non-binary. These two ideas are different. A person who is gender non-conforming does not conform to some of the roles, behaviors, etc. expected of their gender in their current culture/time; for example, a man who is a ballerina or a woman who has short hair. A non-binary person is a gender other than the two we expect/assign in Western cultures (regardless of how they appear to conform to any gender).

6. The presenter used the term "cisgender" to refer to the gender binary/people with binary genders, which is not what cisgender means. Cis means "same" and cisgender means someone's gender is the same

as what they were expected to be based on the sex assigned to them at birth. Trans means "across" and transgender means someone's gender is different than the gender expected based on the sex they were assigned at birth. The gender binary means the Western binary system where everyone is categorized as either a man or a woman; a person whose gender fits into one of these two categories is a person with a binary gender. Put another way, all women and men are people with a binary gender; this is true whether the women and men are cis women and cis men or trans women and trans men. All cisgender people are one of the two binary genders, but not all binary people are cisgender!

7. The presenter said "using they is difficult" in reference to singular they. This is demeaning and disrespectful to non-binary employees and students of [university]. Best practices would generally not be suggesting using inclusive language is difficult, but would provide tools on how to shift to using inclusive language. Using singular they consciously for some people may take a mental adjustment, but it is not difficult, especially if one no longer thinks of that person as either a man or a woman. Additionally, we all use singular they in colloquial conversation frequently.

8. The presenter promoted a way for dealing with a name change within a department that was not best practices for inclusive, affirming name change processes. The suggested solution seemed rooted in the experience of cisgender coworkers, not the experience and needs of trans (and other gender-diverse) community members. Enacted at the [location] campus, the solution was for all staff to call each other by only their last name, for a period of time. This is not done for name changes made for reasons other than gender. This decision was touted as having been arrived at through consultation and agreement with everyone in the department, when the only voice that matters here is the trans person changing their name. It may have helped cis people not feel guilt for deadnaming someone, but it may not have helped the trans person feel comfortable in their work environment. It's possible in this particular case the trans person may have wanted this to avoid deadnaming, but in many cases it would be awkward or overblown, the trans person may feel

like the source of a burden, and it may prolong the adjustment period to the new name. If a Margaret decided to go by Peggy, or a William by Bill, would we do this? [The library's] gender diverse staff is an example of how an effective name change for a coworker can come about with a simple email to the staff, an email address change, and immediate staff use of the new name; while someone might say the wrong name the first few times, they quickly correct themselves until they adjust. This is also how we handle last name changes due to marriage.

9. The presenter used the phrases "origin pronoun" and "origin name." This is awkward terminology, especially given the cultural value of "origin" as truer or closer to the source. Best practice would be "the pronoun/name they used to go by" or something that located the focus on use by the person themselves. This also allows for nuance for people who use different names and pronouns at several points in their process (for example, from "he" to "she" to "they"). The origin or ending of the process is not relevant; what is relevant is what they use at this particular moment and/or the moment in question.

10. The presenter suggested trans people "will notice the little changes." This concept seemed to be for patting cisgender allies on the back. Making inclusive changes should have nothing to do with it being noticed, and there should be no expectation of noticing, attention, or reward of any kind. Additionally, little changes may not be enough—the absence of harm is not in and of itself help or inclusion. There was also no mention of the converse: that trans people notice the little microaggressions, results of not making changes or educating oneself, and that *that* is a large part of what makes a work environment unsafe.

11. The presenter passed out a handout on pronouns, and said the phrase "preferred pronoun." The presenter also made comments in response to a potential audience reaction, saying "everyone has a different way they want to see these" terms around pronouns. That is not true; while there is dialog in the gender diversity community on terminology, how to talk about pronouns is rather settled. "Preferred pronoun" is not best practice because the pronouns are not simply a preference and harm is caused if someone chooses (actively or passively) to use

the wrong pronouns for someone. This is not just a trans issue; we see this when cis people are derogatorily misgendered, "she" used to undermine or attack a man or "he" a woman. Instead, best practices are to just call them "pronouns," for example "what are your pronouns?" or to talk about use, "what pronouns do you use?"

12. The presenter said the younger generation is bringing up non-binary issues (again, not using the term non-binary), implying that non-binary genders are new or created by the younger generation, a common but not factual trope. While the terms non-binary or genderqueer may date back to the 1980s/90s, genders that don't fit in (or otherwise aren't part of) a binary male-and-female-only system have existed for all of human civilization and can be found all around the world.

13. The presenter prompted statements about the [the library's] bathrooms (even though all single stall bathrooms in [the library] are already all-gender and [library] employees had indicated, when asked, that we did not have questions or a need to talk about sharing bathrooms with gender-diverse people), which led to a story about how [the library] needs more bathrooms and the previously staff-only (all-gender) bathrooms had been turned into public all-gender restrooms. The presenter responded emphatically, saying "that sucks," that our staff bathrooms were "taken away" to become all-gender bathrooms, and that that was the wrong way to do it. Not only was this response factually incorrect, but implying that creating inclusive bathrooms "sucks," pitting staff bathroom users against gender diverse users (which ignores these two groups could have overlap!), and suggesting that we lose access or have it "taken away" to create an inclusive bathroom, are actively harmful things to do. A library employee pointed out that anyone could still use all-gender restrooms, so they are hardly taken away.

14. The presenter told a hypothetical anecdote about how the grandma who sees an all-gender bathroom is "never gonna donate" now. I do believe the presenter meant specifically multi-stall all-gender bathrooms. Even still, implying [the university] should care more about donations than gender-diverse employees does not make a comfortable and welcoming environment for gender-diverse employees and students.

The thought is also irrelevant to a training about working with gender-diverse individuals.

15. The presenter suggested the right way to address creating all-gender restrooms is to make the accessible restrooms all-gender. While this may be because the accessible restrooms are single stall, it isn't best practice to limit two marginalized groups of users to one shared bathroom. As long as there are limited accessible restrooms, the many gender diverse people who are able-bodied should not have to take space and time from disabled people (including disabled trans people) who cannot use non-accessible bathrooms.

16. The presenter could not adequately answer all questions, as a cis person without the lived experience and nuanced understanding a trans person would have.

17. The presentation seemed to assume the audience was all cis, and that only cis people need to learn about creating inclusive environments and working with gender diverse individuals. Because there are so many ways to be trans and gender-diverse, many non-cis people would also benefit from gender-diversity trainings or may only have a basic level of knowledge.

18. The presenter said, in reference to talking about singular they pronouns, that "English professors hate me." While I do not know or want to discount the presenter's experiences with English professors, the English professors I know are all among the first to promote singular they, to say it's grammatically correct, to speak about and validate its long history of use, to compare it to how "you" used to only be plural ("thou" was the singular second-person pronoun), and to push for inclusive language practices, of which pronouns are just one part. Even if the presenter's experiences with English professors have been otherwise, mentioning that in a training like this is questionable, suggesting there is something incorrect about the singular they by making reference to a supposed authority who we in academia respect. It suggests that they singular is new and not truly accepted (especially when coupled with the presenter's comments that they singular is hard to use). Instead, the MLA, APA, and Chicago style guides, as well as newspaper

style guides like the Associated Press and the Washington Post, and dictionaries like the Oxford English, Merriam Webster, and American Heritage, all include singular they as a personal pronoun (and document its centuries-long history of use). This is also supported by groups like the American Dialect Society and the National Council of Teachers of English.

Bibliography

"Tips for Allies of Transgender People." GLAAD. November 11, 2020. https://www.glaad.org/transgender/allies.

About the Author

Kylie Terra (she/they) is an educator and multimedia artist who has worked in library makerspaces for the past decade. She has a certificate in Learning Design and Technology from Harvard Extension School and an M.A. in Museum Education at Tufts University. In addition to her work in libraries, Kylie is a performance artist, writer, and book artist whose work often explores gender.

Classroom Disrupted: Being Trans and Disabled in Library Instruction

Debbie Krahmer

Keywords: academic libraries, information literacy instruction, disabilities, trans elder

Land Acknowledgement

The township of Hamilton, NY, where this chapter was written, was built upon the unceded ancestral lands of the Onyota'a:ká (Oneida) of the Hodinöhsö:ni´ confederacy. As a settler on this land and descendant of immigrants, I acknowledge the painful history of violence, dispossession, and betrayal that led to the colonization of these lands. I also recognize and honor the modern Indigenous experiences of the Oneida Indian Nation of New York. I am committed to combating the continued erasure of Indigenous experiences and cultures, as I continue to work towards ensuring justice and equity for all in my life and my work. I ask you to take a moment to consider these legacies before you continue reading.

Introduction

When I first started teaching at Colgate University, I was completely out as a trans person. Early on, I was invited to a sociology class to speak directly about trans issues. I have no memory of what I said, other than something about gender being an ocean and to not hold too hard to your assumptions. One event continues to stand out to me, even thirteen years after the fact. One of the students asked, "What is the best thing about being transgender?"

After years of advocacy and being asked to share the worst experiences of my life, it was the first time I was ever asked what was good about being trans. It disrupted my whole way of thinking, and it took me a long moment to find an answer. That question opened my eyes that day, and changed how I approach my differences—what advantages do I have because I'm different?

Teaching

My favorite library classroom isn't a typical computer classroom. It has twenty computers, but around thirty seats. The computer desks are set up in four L-shaped pods, making it easy to separate students into group-work or quickly identify the social groups in the classroom. In the middle of each pod is a round table with extra chairs that is perfect for working away from the computer (or fitting more bodies into the room, which happens more than I like to admit). It's a favorite of mine, mostly because there's plenty of space to move and bring along an extra chair, so I can work with students one-on-one without squeezing between seats or delicately deciding whose face my butt will be in when I bend down.

For the sighted students, the classroom comes with a terrific view. Two walls are nearly floor-to-ceiling windows, but there are automatic shades I can bring down to darken the space. When the shades are open, we're gifted with a broad view of the township—trees and old school buildings in one direction, and the lake and more trees and distant hills in the other. We're on the edge of town, but the thick foliage helps hide the houses away, making it a great place to work on homework.

The students come in at the front of the classroom. There's no sneaking in; you have to parade past the first pod and to the center of the room just to find a seat. The lecture station is at the front as well, but I tend to select a seat in the back, at least for the start of the class. Sometimes it encourages the students to sit at the front by virtue of the "teacher force field," which naturally repels students. Sometimes they sit around me and include me in discussions, and I feel like I'm absorbed into the class.

The students' reactions to me depend on how they see me. As a man, I have a boyish face; as a woman, my weight gives me an eternal-motherly appearance. As a professor, I'm seriously under-dressed in jeans and t-shirts. As a student, I'm oddly old-fashioned, layering a long sleeve shirt under my oversized t-shirt. I wear a black wedding ring and rainbow shoelaces, and I'm often wearing some sort of pride clothing to signify my queerness. I'm white and I'm fat—these things seem to be universal, regardless of who is looking at me. I'm wearing dark glasses, even though the shades are drawn and the lights are off. Am I blind? Or am I just weird?

When enough time has passed or enough students have filled the seats, I stand up and begin talking from the back of the room.

"Hi everyone. Welcome! I'm Debbie Krahmer. I'm the Accessible Technology & Government Documents Librarian. I prefer that you not use pronouns when you refer to me, so you can just call me Debbie or D." Depending on the format of the class or the quality of my vision that day, I might also add, "I wanted to let you know I have a visual disability" and then explain how it will affect some of the work we'd be doing in the classroom. On good days, it's hardly noticeable beyond the dark glasses that protect my sensitive eyes. On bad days, I frequently ask the students what they see. On the very worst days, my words slur and my eyes squint; I stand at the back of the room and rely on the students to be my eyes as we talk through and walk through any exercises.

It doesn't matter if my introduction answers any of the questions the students may have about me, or if it just brings up even more questions. My existence, much like the library classroom, is a disruption of the "norm," and I use that unease and ambiguity to my advantage.

Disruption

Disruptions are everywhere. They happen in technology, in the classroom, and in the crossroads of both (remember Massive Open Online Courses/MOOCs?). COVID-19 disrupted the entire world. A car breaking down will disrupt your schedule, as will a storm or traffic. A disruption can be a good thing, a bad thing, or just a thing that happens that you must deal with.

My sight is full of disruptions. Sometimes they're small, like flashes of light or sparkles of snow. Sometimes it's a blizzard that obscures the road, or TV static that causes words to dance and lines to glow. There's nothing from the outside that indicates when these visual artifacts are there. If you see me on a bad day, you wouldn't have any idea of what is between you and my image of you. They can be faded and indistinct, or dark and swimming. I'm not blind. It's all in my head (AKA neurological), but they're there just the same, an ever-present disruption to otherwise perfectly near-sighted vision.

My body is a disruption. I'm fat and ambiguous at best in my gender presentation. Among the affluent students and faculty at my university, I'm far outside the typical spectrum of body sizes. I have to ask for a seat without arms, and I test where I'm about to sit in order to avoid any weight-related pratfalls. I only started to medically transition in my forties, despite living as an out trans man for most of my life, but testosterone can only do so much when masculinity is a bit rounded and faded in my bloodline. I still don't pass except with a fleeting glance.

My name is a disruption. How the hell do you pronounce "Krahmer" anyhow? "Kr-ah-mer?" "Cray-mer?" I had promised myself as a child that I wouldn't change my name for marriage, so when I came out in 2000, I didn't bother trying to find something more masculine. Why should I? Just because Debbie sounds feminine doesn't mean it can't be my name. ("A Boy Named Sue," anyone?)

The library session, especially the one-shot, epitomizes disruption. The students are brought out of their regular classroom and into the library space. The professor is a bystander or completely absent. The content of the session may be related to the course or may seem completely unrelated. I'm not always made aware of how the class is usually structured, and even if I were, I wouldn't teach like their professor.

We, as librarians and as trans people, are disruptions, so we might as well use it. It leaves the classroom space open to anything.

Critical

I use the disruption of my difference to bring critical information literacy into the library classroom. I am visibly trans and I out myself as having a disability, so it is always relevant in my classroom to call out problematic subject headings or point out bias in the search results. I leverage my differences to break through some of the reluctance to discuss difficult topics in the classroom, usually by drawing attention to them in the first place.

My visual impairment creates a natural space to talk about how we can access information. How do I search for information when I can't see it? How can someone like me interact with this image? I bring up those times when I run into barriers and, by doing so, I invite students to think of how other barriers might come in. I've experienced this change in the classroom: a student describes a chart to me unprompted, or they introduce themselves and point out how we know each other, or they ask about whether the article can be downloaded as an audio file. It also opens the door to talk about access—if we weren't on a university campus, would we have access to these articles or these databases at all? What kind of students don't we see on this campus? Why?

My transness also creates a natural space to bring in discussions of bias within information organization. From my own lived experience, I can point out times when important information was obscured behind strange academic terms that a young transboy couldn't understand. We still use outdated phrases like "Female Impersonator" and "Illegal Aliens" in the library catalogue, and it's important to talk about it in the classroom. When the language hurts me, I bring attention to that feeling because sometimes the students will need to use that language in their own research.

A colleague of mine once challenged my support for critical information literacy with a question. It was something along the lines of "If I'm teaching someone how to drive, and I only have fifty minutes, and I spend forty-five talking about Henry Ford's antisemitism, do I then expect the student to be able to drive the car?"

My comeback in the moment was that, for many people, Ford's antisemitism is directly relevant to learning to drive, as relevant as knowing how to interact with police or what to do when your license says F while you present as M. I would bring up the topic, as appropriate, and if we needed to talk about it more, we would. If not, we can continue with the driving lesson.

Since that time, I've continued to turn this question over in my head and consider how to answer it. It's a somewhat ridiculous question to begin with—if you were teaching someone a skill, do you expect them to know how to do it if you spend zero time teaching it? If you bring critical pedagogy or antiracism into the classroom, does that then mean you can't teach anything else?

In most cases, librarians don't have the time to cover what we need to teach in a one-shot library session, let alone anything additional. But if we're already just skimming over the ideas in the classroom, what's the harm of bringing in new ones? It can take thirty seconds to point out a problematic subject heading and explain that it can take many years to get controlled vocabulary changed. There's a greater chance of doing harm to students by treating something racist or sexist as invisible. A student once broke down in angry tears because she just wanted her professor to mention Henrietta Lacks in biology, to recognize the harm done to Black women in the name of science. For myself, I'm still thrilled when a speaker at a conference describes an image on their slide without being asked or uses inclusive language when referring to people. These small opportunities to recognize and name things can mean more to students than pointing out the full text button on an article—and you don't have to give up pointing out the full text button in order to include them in a class.

It doesn't matter what discipline the course is in; criticality and inclusiveness are always relevant. Even when we're not studying humans, we are all humans doing the research. By virtue of my existence, transness and accessibility are already centered in my classroom. To skip over it or try to hide it as being non-relevant to the situation is losing an important part of myself that adds authenticity to my teaching. When I was younger, I had to cross dress and pretend not to be trans in order to get a library job. I was miserable, and I did a terrible job (of teaching and pretending). I know I must bring my whole self into the classroom in order to teach well. Part of that is acknowledging my difference, and that acknowledgement brings attention to other areas of difference. As a trans person, I can't see something harmful without wanting to address it, because I know how it feels to have my pain disregarded.

You can teach someone to drive while also recognizing them as fully human and acknowledging their lived experiences. It doesn't make them bad drivers. It makes you a good teacher.

Conclusion

I am supremely lucky to be trans and disabled. When you're already outside the "norm," it seems almost ridiculous to not take advantage of it. It is rare that I'm ever in a "safe" space to be myself, especially in America. But being out and loud can be its own protection. I'm visibly and openly different. If someone wants the same old thing, they can go to someone who looks more like them, or acts like them, or teaches like them. Our students, ourselves, our classrooms are unique, and every librarian should take advantage of that to experiment, and explore, and teach the things that energize them.

I'm scared every time I go into the classroom. After all this time of teaching, no matter how much I prepare, I never know what I'm going to find when I stand up at the back of the room. But finding those small spaces to make a difference, to teach what I want to teach, and reach out to students authentically, is what keeps me going. Every day I step out into an unknown, and I decide to embrace it, laughing, ready to see what happens.

About the Author

Debbie "D" Krahmer is a white, fat, trans, queer, disabled librarian who has been working in libraries most of D's life. I prefer that others refer to me as simply Debbie or D. I have a BA in Educational Media/Library Studies from Chadron State College and a Masters in Information Science and Learning Technology from the University of Missouri-Columbia. I was born and raised in a small town in Nebraska, and I currently work in Upstate New York. My passions center on accessibility, equity, and inclusion, as well as film and media. My office is covered with toys, which keep me entertained and help to open up conversations around neurodiversity. I'm married to a wonderful man, and orange is my favorite color.

650_0‡a Libraries ‡x Moral and ethical aspects ‡v Handbooks, manuals, etc.

jocilyn wagner

Keywords: ethical dilemma, hypothetical scenario, career trauma, dossier building, overcoming professional adversity

Introductory texts that a student of graduate studies in Library and Information Science (LIS) encounters in their first semester often pose tricky hypothetical job-centric scenarios and related ethical dilemmas. Many situate the reader in a no-win scenario that is akin to a traditional Star Trek *Kobayashi Maru* thought experiment with no single implicitly correct response. Perhaps these vignettes are designed to wield a cudgel of sophistry in an effort to scare off the easily intimidated. Perhaps they're designed to paint LIS as a profession in exciting, if unnatural, gravitas-laden colours for reasons known only to admissions specialists and too inscrutable to be easily stated here. In any case, the LIS campfire yarns I was exposed to succeeded beyond their intended purpose and have become forever lodged in the back of my mind as I go about navigating work at an academic library. Fifteen years later, with noted chagrin, I find myself narrating an eerily analogous and frightening yet true tale of my own LIS career woes. In order to better frame my narrative within the aforementioned context, consider the following fictional scenario: imagine you're a Library Head at a busy public library and you've just received a complaint from a male patron that one of your staff members was believed to be using illicit drugs in the restroom at work. However, when you approach the young Library Page, you quickly learn that they are, in fact, transgender and were simply taking their prescription testosterone. Having run out of the medication and needing to wait very nearly too long between doses while their doctor approved a refill, they had finally received a text message earlier that day that the refill was ready for pickup and had run to the pharmacy and back on their lunch break to retrieve it. Subsequently, they were able to take their medication just in the nick of time when they returned, but doing so necessitated injecting themself in the library men's room. Clearly the most ethical and cogent response you could give your staff member is simply to empathize with their plight and apologize to them for having their name dragged through the mud as it were. Of course, there are various other directions one could take with the situation, such as summarily terminating the staff member for violating protocol by having needles in the library and so forth. As you'll see, the scenario I just described is not unlike my own LIS transgender trial. Though to avoid being quite as pedantic and melodramatic as the haunting hypotheticals I've herein described, I'll lay it out for you straight up: my literary intention is to be merely a cynosure, a guide. Should you choose a career in library science, verily the possibility exists of encountering unexpected ethical dilemmas as an archivist or school media specialist. Additionally, if my experience is in any way characteristic, being trans or non-binary may gift you better odds still. You have been warned; here there be dragons.

My career misadventure occurred in December of 2013, just after finishing graduate school and a few years into the profession. The no-win scenario I found myself in: an accusation was anonymously lodged against me. "There have been complaints that you've been seen in the women's lavatory and staff no longer feel safe using it" should be my epitaph.

I'd finally secured a real job with benefits and the kind of excellent health insurance which, incredibly, would one day cover the costs of my bottom surgery (as well as some badly needed rhinoplasty). I was finally living as an out transwoman for the requisite six months-to-a year that was required at the time for psychiatry to pronounce me fit for hormone replacement therapy. I was lucky enough to find myself working in a building that boasted single-occupancy restrooms. As it happened though, those facilities were approximately eight flights up, through the stacks and into the South building from my desk in the basement of the North building (and at that, not necessarily designed for staff use). Just down the hall some twenty meters from *Acquisitions* was the North building's secondary, or perhaps tertiary, women's restroom (the freely accessible and open to the public writ large restroom a floor up from me being the more popular destination). As a secondary lavatory, one reserved for staff and even requiring a key for entry as it also housed our lactation room, occupancy was never greater than two or three. Given all of the above, I mistakenly believed it would be all right for me to use this restroom in emergencies while I was in transition—all my peers were professionals who outwardly professed to embrace diversity as one of the institution's core missions.

To be sure, I had actually worn nothing but traditional women's clothing and makeup to work for *ten months* when a complaint was filed that I was supposedly making women feel uncomfortable in the bathroom. It turned out that most people believed an official pronouncement from the library's administration that a transgender individual "is safe to share a restroom with" was needed for people to relax and accept my presence. I assure you, reader: regardless of its lofty status of being the foremost prestigious academic library in the state, one in which a commitment to diversity, equity and inclusion continue to feature readily in its mission statement, cultural acceptance of gender variance at my institution should not be assumed.

My supervisor was duly notified of the complaint against me and (for some inexplicable reason) a subsequent inquest was arranged for me.[1] Admittedly, *inquest* is my word not theirs, by which I mean "disciplinary

1. As the editors of this book pointed out, my inquest was without merit—a wholly inappropriate response and **should in no way serve as a template** for corrective action by a supervisor or administration. Recognition of a need for broad diversity training, creation of a general policy, and simply dismissing the complaint as ridiculous would all be considered acceptable responses.

meeting with multiple supervisors and human resources (HR) present and you in the hot seat." Honestly, though, I can't point to a more apt appellation for this most judicious use of our time.

When I learned of this coming inquest, I became despondent, taciturn, and terrified that my career was over. I even begged my trans-masculine ex-boyfriend at the time (a well-respected librarian) to come to this meeting with me as moral support and to demonstrate that gender variance was, in fact, accepted in Technical Services. I have little doubt that I nailed the coffin shut on our relationship that day but to me it made all the difference, and I probably still owe him a boon; but I digress.

My supervisor at the time would be another incredibly understanding and supportive presence at the inquest. I knew he would have my back, and he did. For this, at least, I'm grateful. By itself, unfortunately, these two champions sitting on my side of the table as it were, wouldn't be enough to erase all doubt of my culpability (though of what, I was still unsure). I have never studied law, but it was clear to me where the burden of proof lay. I needed to build a preponderance of evidence that the jury of my supervisor's boss, our HR representative, and that anonymous complainant couldn't ignore.

Thankfully, this episode arrived on the coattails of my decent-if-prohibitively-expensive LIS graduate education. I was a firm believer in the fact that any problem could be solved through project management, and spreadsheets are my métier. I thus produced a multi-colored, eight-tabbed spreadsheet of the "needed" documentation. The dossier I had in mind would verify in exacting clarity that I was indisputably female and would hopefully make the administration feel so foolish as to never put another soul through the ignominy of these proceedings ever again. With apologies to Jennifer Finney Boylan and all my gender variant role models and colleagues (and my later genderqueer non-binary self), for the purposes of this meeting, *gender* needed to be established as an easily verifiable and immutable fact. Presentation being everything, after digging through our supply cupboard, I produced a set of file folders I would frame the needed documentation in: lavender on the outside, lilac on the inside. I don't know who ordered those file folders, or when, but whoever you are I owe you a hug.

In order to establish proof of something that can't really be proven, I also needed to order these documents well. Courtroom television not really being my thing, I looked elsewhere for inspiration and instead borrowed another trick from grad school: keep pushing the labeled (if empty) tabs back and forth inside a spreadsheet until they seem to resemble a logical progression. In the end, I produced the following materials, which I printed out for all attendees and collated in those lavender file folders: a brief and forthright personal narrative; three very basic educational trifold handouts from Transgender Michigan; the clinical definition of *Gender Dysmorphia* from the then forthcoming DSM-V (thank you Internet Age); a timeline of all the "steps" I'd so far taken in my transition; a list of professional contacts the University's Comprehensive Gender Services Program had gifted me; a confirmation letter from my therapist at said program office; another from my newest doctor (in Endocrinology); a copy of my hormone replacement therapy prescriptions (the inquest was scheduled to coincide with my finally obtaining them); an expenditure report of my personal finances from the previous year (totaling something along the lines of $4,000 spent on clothes, shoes, makeup, the list goes on); and lastly, a list of the State of Michigan's legal name change requirements. After lugubriously flipping through this unending compendium, I felt certain that my claim of being a transwoman would be irrefutable. Thank you, *Library Administration and Project Management 7040* (as well as to my Buddhist Studies instructors in Japan for instilling in me an incapacity to dissemble).

I'd once had a ~~colleague~~ librarian tell me that she couldn't see me as female if I had a trace of facial hair. We clearly were making great strides with our diversity, equity and inclusion training. Of course, being an HR matter, I never learned the identity of the complainant that had accorded me the delight of this meeting, but if I had to hazard a guess it certainly would not have been that staff member. No sense in crying to the administration about the unfairness of the world when you can just browbeat those who don't subscribe to your ideology with microaggressions. To me, lodging an anonymous complaint of this nature was the work of the spineless and unfeeling; such a person wouldn't be sitting down on the opposite side of a table from me and painting themselves as "conservative transphobe" for the library to shun. No, instead I was given the task of proving myself to a group of colleagues who already wanted to believe me and probably wanted nothing more than to be out of there as quickly as possible. I began to think that, despite a civilized front, our HR interventions tend to fall back on drumhead discipline.

To put us all at ease with the difficult subject matter, HR had given a great deal of thought to the location of this meeting. The six of us were accommodated with a table in a narrow, windowless, former group-study room that the Science Library had given over to HR for staff meetings, probably because it lacked the needed technology for anything else. I was gratified to have skipped preparing a PowerPoint presentation.

Odd accommodations notwithstanding, HR did come prepared by extending an invitation to a staff member from our University's LGBTQ resource center. Although at first this unknown variable seemed intimidating, when the inevitable question arose, incredibly this representative stepped up to the task and was able to rattle off exactly under what legal criteria someone's gender was defined by the University.

Let us be clear: while the intended audience of our deliberations was not at the table and the words that passed among us that day were perfunctory in nature, the meeting itself *was* professionally and emotionally damaging. To date, this inquest remains the greatest trial of my professional career: one which lacked a definitive exoneration to my mind but, in truth, acted simply as a formality needed to put the matter to bed. Thus, I put it to you: If you, reader, were on the receiving end of a complaint about the gender expression of one of your staff members causing "duress," what steps, if any, would you take to mitigate the situation? Or is this (unfortunately less than hypothetical) scenario rendered moot by being non-sequitur to Library and Information Science?

At the time of this writing's publication, my inquest will have happened nine years ago. Said decade has seen a sea change in our diversity, equity and inclusive zeitgeist and no small amount of progress has been made in the ways human resources managers engage with staffing inequities. However, events like my inquest may still occur as long-standing institutional inequities are finally being openly challenged at all levels. Colleges and universities with far fewer human resources than mine must now grapple with and demonstrably embrace the growing numbers of gender diverse people seen in the latest generation entering the workforce. My sincere hope is for a reader of this monograph to have encountered it in pursuit of knowledge rather than out of a desperate need to defend oneself at the point of inquest. I would, in fact, very much love for this text's existence to be one of ready reference: to be lost in the *Z 682*s after occasionally doing a stint as bibliography fodder for this or that tangentially-related graduate essay. If, however, you have struck upon this text in your capacity as a supervisor or human resources manager looking for an easy solution with which to soothe patrons and others uncomfortable with your gender variant staff, consider this: the only policies that libraries need draft on the subject are those that protect and affirm transgender and non-binary lives.

About the Author

My name is jocilyn paris wagner. i could be described as an amateur photographer, a thirty-something librarian, an avid reader, and a lover of tea and horses. If, like a modern Candide, you wish to think a bit more pragmatically (my default modus operandi), i invite you to imagine a broadly educated human being who happens to be genderqueer, living in the United States circa 2022, and as a consequence, has managed to develop: severe irritable bowel syndrome, hypochondria, migraines, social anxiety, psychosomatic delusions, depression, insomnia, haphephobia, and a wicked haircut. Fortunately for you, tovarisch, said life has yielded haunting experiences as a transgender, non-binary, Library and Information Science graduate student and academic library staff member.

Section 5:

Archives and Special Collections

Trans Archival Practice: Cultivating Public Memory, Investigating Professional Binaries

Aiden Faust (he/him)

Keywords: transmasculine, coming out, community archives, academic libraries

This is a story about coming out in the workplace at age forty while standing for tenure as library faculty. It is also a meditation on false binaries in professional practice with the hope of identifying and ultimately dissolving them.

I currently serve as the associate director of an urban history archives in a small public university library. This work involves stewarding approximately 200 collections, including institutional records of the university itself, as well as a collecting repository on twentieth and twenty-first century Baltimore. Our records are primarily organizational, focusing on nonprofits, philanthropic groups, community associations, local grassroots groups, and quasi-governmental entities that have shaped modern Baltimore. It's easy for me to talk about the archives, because I'm passionate about its mission and I've devoted more than a dozen years of my life to advocating for its preservation and public accessibility. It's also a very convenient monolith to hide behind as a queer transman.

Disclosure in a professional setting eluded me for the first decade of my career in library and information science. I'd transitioned medically, legally, and socially before starting library school. For many years I asked myself, "What is there to say?" And the longer I said nothing, the more opaque the scrim between my personal and professional lives became. *Managing disclosure* sounded better than *closeted*. How could I be closeted as a trans person after coming out as gay at fourteen, helping lead the LGBTQIA+ student group in college, and thinking of myself as out and proud for so many years prior to transition?

Quite simply, I didn't have the words. Before transition, I never had to tell anyone I was queer. People looked at me, immediately saw my gender nonconformity, and came to their own conclusions. After transition, I became invisible. My lack of socially recognizable variance in gender or sexuality meant people treated me differently as I moved through the world. The complex phenomenon of passing began exerting enormous new pressures, as well as conveying enormous new privileges. It was too much to parse out so I kept it to myself, especially on the job. My queer life, no matter how superficially obfuscated it had become, still felt economically precarious to me.

Non-disclosure took an enormous psychic toll. There was simply no way for me to neatly untangle the threads of my personal history from one another. Being disowned by family at nineteen, putting myself through college, running with a wild art crowd, falling into the East Coast rave scene of the 1990s, washing cars and busing tables and serving coffee, liminal years spent working for cash only when bank accounts and photo ID seemed unattainable, drifting through apartments on the fringes of Baltimore's gayborhood while trying to find sympathetic doctors, surviving the "real life test" for hormones, and paying for gender transition out of pocket.... This was my personal history, and it seemed increasingly incongruous with my post-transition professional life. So, I simply withheld it all.

Collecting local community histories from the recent past, however, is not a career path well-suited to those who want to remain personally decontextualized. Traces of my own footprints through a quarter century of Baltimore queer life are woven through multiple collections in the archives I manage. Queer and trans friends, colleagues, and comrades began frequenting our research room, drawn in large part to the records of the local LGBTQIA+ community center. Art installations and classroom projects and book chapters began to be born from these archival holdings. My heart leapt in joy!

As more self-identified queer and trans researchers sought material in our archives, unmistakably quizzical looks from library colleagues began to accumulate. "Guilt by association" is an inside joke among transfolk—when we gather together, our trans-identifiable bodies materialize, seemingly out of thin air, to the cisgender gaze. The final push toward professional self-disclosure came when my staff began struggling with patron pronouns. The need to unmistakably articulate my own positionality simply emerged. And so, sixteen years after transition from female to male, and nine years into my work at the university library, I celebrated my fortieth birthday and finally brought together the pieces of my life in Baltimore—the place I call home, and the only home I've known.

The process of coming out professionally felt terrifying and risky. I was in the middle of a year-long review process for permanent status, which is the library faculty equivalent of tenure within our university system. I was direct, formal, and concise in how I went about disclosure, talking individually with my supervisor and then with each of my staff. The care and support I received from colleagues through this process was revelatory and galvanizing.

Now I have the immense privilege of working with LGBTQIA+ students on internships and independent studies in the archives, informally mentoring colleagues, and presenting to classes on local queer history as both an archivist and community member. I'm passionate about the need to build capacity for intergenerational continuity in queer communities, and I've found young LGBTQIA+ people yearning for our history, no matter how complex or fragmentary or downright problematic that history may be. Being able to identify that fragmentation and hold that complexity together, to draw it out through dialogue around the archives, is an active process of cultural work that constitutes the beating heart of community archives, in my experience.

The privileges inherent in being a white, middle-aged, masculine presenting, managerial class information professional with dual graduate degrees and tenured faculty status are unmistakable and real. These advantages made long-term identity management and planned disclosure possible. Coming out as trans within my profession was on my time, based on my own psychic needs, at a point when I felt emotionally and psychologically capable of taking on the risks I saw as inherent in that process. With humility and gratitude, I believe these advantages bring with them a social obligation to be visible, to show up, to speak up, and to be honest, in the hopes that these actions will create space and reduce suffering for others.

My story of identity and work reveals that the distinction I tried to make between professional and personal spheres proved unsustainable. The professional self versus the private self was revealed as a false binary. By integrating my own identity, including claiming a personal history, projecting a socially recognizable position, and articulating a broader cultural context for my work in local archives, a confidence previously unknown had room to manifest. To move through the world in a professional capacity as an openly transgender person is an exercise of political agency. For me, this entails performing cultural and intellectual work in the public sector—work that is generally undervalued, but that I consider a powerful form of capacity-building for community organizing and social change.

Why does this story matter in a broader professional context? How has my personal, relative experience informed my archival practice? In addition to being a healthier, happier archivist and being visible for students and community researchers, I've also found that bringing an explicitly queer transmasculine lens to archival work reveals certain dichotomies in our profession. These dichotomies operate in ways that circumscribe the liberatory potential of archives. I call them false binaries, and they are the focus of the rest of this essay.

This consideration of false binaries is really an open question, or series of questions. Where do we split ourselves off, as I tried to do, to make messy things more manageable? Where do we draw lines in the sand, us versus them, to make ourselves feel safer, or to make our situations feel less precarious? How do these binaries operate in professional settings, and whom do they serve? And, most importantly, how can we move through them to advance the conversations in our fields of information science, public humanities, archives, and cultural heritage? I'll briefly describe three such binaries operating in my own archival experience: historian versus librarian; university insider versus outsider; and state versus community control in archives. The discussion of each of these scenarios serves the goal of moving beyond them, of opening the possibilities of professional practice, and ultimately, of queering the archives.

The first of these dichotomies is rooted in professional identity—the archivist as historian versus the archivist as librarian. These are the archetypes that bifurcate the disciplinary foundations of modern archival practice. In the 1970s, university systems were still producing large numbers of newly minted PhDs in history who faced unprecedented job scarcity upon graduating. This cohort was predominantly male and included many who were the first in their working class "ethnic" European immigrant families to go to college. These young historians migrated into roles as archivists at a point when the national Bicentennial fueled public interest in archives and the federal grant monies flowed in ways unimaginable today. Bolstered by the democratic impulses in the new social history and its emphasis on the lives of everyday people, these historians filled repositories coast to coast with zeal. But, as the 1980s wore on and Reaganomics decimated public funding for historical and cultural pursuits, the archival profession began to shift increasingly toward library science to sustain itself.[1]

Librarians brought longstanding professional practices in standardized descriptive practices, data sharing, and automation through technology into the archival discourse. Union catalogs for finding primary source material across repositories paved the way to increasingly more powerful computerized search and discovery tools. The historian's preoccupation with archival acquisition and appraisal shifted to the librarian's concern

1. I've written about this previously here: Aiden Faust, "Social History in the Archives: Baltimore's Enduring Legacy," in *Baltimore Revisited: Rethinking and Remaking an American City* (New Brunswick, NJ: Rutgers University Press, 2019), 315–25.

with organization, classification, and accessibility. Emerging archivists today are, by and large, expected to earn master's degrees in library and information science. And with this shift into librarianship came a new professional culture: predominantly female, white, and middle class.

The professional divide between the historian-archivist and the librarian-archivist is riddled with intersectional tensions along lines of race, class, gender, and generation. Or, so the story goes. Is there a way to collapse these distinctions in archival practice? To what extent are archivists today trained in both information science and historiography? How can we design curricula and promote hands-on trainings that teach archivists how to employ the lenses of both historian and librarian? Can we acknowledge and embrace a hybridized professional identity? Do we train in both fields and learn to speak both languages before we can realize a professionally distinct archival identity? As libraries increasingly shift from print to digital collections and deemphasize corresponding physical collection management activities, how do ML(I)S archivists articulate the enduring value of their analog holdings? Is there a third turning of the professional identity wheel—from historian to librarian to a distinctly archival identity? At what point are we strong enough to stand on our own, distinct from either of our parent professions?

In the context of higher education, many archivists face another dichotomy between internal and external stakeholders. College and university campuses and services emerge as proprietary spaces for customers only. Even public institutions are privatizing their campuses with card-swipe-only access to buildings, online single sign-on for access to information resources, and budgets that prioritize programs that generate revenue streams. For whom is the public university and its library? How do library functions such as the federal depository for government documents and the archives as a collecting repository fit into this vision?

The shift toward privileging university insiders ("our students" and "our faculty") often comes at the expense of outward facing programs and initiatives tied to civic engagement. To categorize current students as customers inherently excludes the possibility that others may become prospective or future students. The myopia of a hyper-monetized business mentality in higher education creates a uniquely challenging scenario for a public archival program, whose mission it is to facilitate public research within its collecting scope. The intensity to which these pressures are felt within academia likely vary by school, with tier one research institutions providing greater support for a public research mission. However, research-intensive universities are also pressure cookers for grant funding to provide revenue streams and support doctoral study. Higher education's stated interests in civic engagement and community outreach look suspiciously like vehicles for sponsored research and philanthropic support.

In the current painful era of steadily declining funding from state governments for their own public university systems, archivists must make a case for their free, open, public-facing programs. This is where the binary is revealed: there is no insider and no outsider. To embrace *all researchers* as part of the university's functioning over time means building relationships that strengthen the fabric of the institution itself, its reputation, and its ability to attract and retain its stakeholders of all varieties. An emeritus faculty researcher becomes an archives volunteer and advocate. A community researcher matriculates into a graduate program as the result of their introduction through the archives. A local nonprofit worker is introduced to the campus through a public workshop in the library and joins the ranks of adjunct faculty. Student workers supported by campus jobs in the archives become alumni who stay connected and support their school's annual giving campaign. Building a web of relationships around the academic library and its archival program is an example of a long tail approach to sustainability. This is part of *transing* the archives. No insiders, no outsiders—the duality dissolves when both are held together.

Within the context of my own department, another binary challenge revealed itself in relation to collection ownership. State versus community control of the archives is at the crux of the matter. The first time I was called an agent of the state by a prospective donor, I was caught off guard. In the eyes of this longtime activist, our archives represented hegemonic control. It is true that we are state employees, working in buildings owned and operated by the state, as part of a historically white institution. The extent to which the archival program relies on external funding and maintains a degree of intellectual independence through adopting faculty status for its staff does not change the fact that we *do represent* the state's university system when we engage in outreach work in local communities.

In response to this critique and others like it, we've tried to adopt a variety of different approaches to the question of ownership. In the case of the records of the local LGBTQIA+ community center, the collection is on deposit. Only physical custody transferred when the board of the center sold their building, creating an emergency situation for volunteers who'd maintained the center's archive for years. In this scenario, the donor organization was adamant that all rights remained with the center, as a matter of queer ownership and pride. Archivists involved with the transfer also understood that community members had a desire to eventually retrieve the collection if a suitable long-term facility for their center could be re-established.

While the notion of supporting community ownership (particularly for historically marginalized and oppressed groups) is a laudable one, it also presents certain challenges. First and foremost, researchers are impacted by the limited rights for use that archives staff are able to convey. To procure these permissions, users are referred back to the center—a hand-off that relies on an active and ongoing relationship with center staff. The extent to which the archival program can justify staff time and supplies for processing the collection is also an open question in this rather tenuous arrangement. Queer activists' sustained distrust of government institutions is a very real factor in the way the issue of ownership plays out in the archives. But to what extent does an alternative arrangement involving only physical custody of community collections protect them long-term? Are trust and commitment necessary ingredients between collection donor and archival repository?

A more recent approach to the difficult question of ownership that we've employed is the community archives paradigm. In our community archives program, the aim is to support and facilitate local groups in preserving their own records *in situ*. No transfer of custody occurs. Community members are stewards of their own cultural heritage, and the role of archivists is to lead workshops, provide consultations, share resources, and teach preservation techniques that match the goals of the group. This approach is being used currently in a multi-year initiative with local historic Black churches. A non-custodial approach may ease community fears of appropriation and misrepresentation, but the viability of long-term preservation outside of traditional repository environments remains an open question.

In the case of ownership of collections, the development of more *both-and* approaches is necessary. Digitization and the creation of digital surrogates may provide some degree of shared ownership between donor and repository. In the case of digital material, Creative Commons licensing allows for content creators to maintain ownership while explicitly defining terms of free, public use. Engagement with legal practitioners is essential to review, revise, and author legal language that both reflects and protects the community histories we are committed to preserving. Skillful use of legal language is a familiar tactic from a trans perspective, since almost every aspect of our lives and ourselves must be defined and defended through these instruments.

In each of these binaries—archivist as historian/librarian; university insider/outsider; and state/community control—my goal is learning to acknowledge, hold, and promote *bothness* as part of a larger project of applying queer knowledge to archival practice in an academic library setting. Trans becomes a verb here, an act of moving through dualities rather than away from them. This way of being does not rely on a theoretical rejection of binaries. Rather, it is grounded in a bodily experience of moving from one social category to another, collapsing the boundaries between them and, ultimately, being able to hold space for both positions in unity. I am the female librarian and the male historian in equal measure. My actions represent both the interests of the state and the grassroots subcultural communities that raised me. I make no distinction between internal and external researchers in the archives, because public means everyone.

When both relative truths within the false binary are acknowledged, the limitations of each category are revealed to such an extent that the boundaries begin to dissolve and the power these concepts have over my daily experience weakens. Here is the liberatory potential of queer knowledge to create space for all bodies, all beings. This space is multifaceted: cultural, physical, social, political, psychic, spiritual, and temporal. It is simultaneously bound by time and timeless. The past, present, and future are unfolding together, contingent upon one another. From this perspective, archival work takes on a certain urgency. And from this sense of archival urgency, "I'm putting my queer shoulder to the wheel."[2]

Bibliography

Faust, Aiden. "Social History in the Archives: Baltimore's Enduring Legacy." In *Baltimore Revisited: Rethinking and Remaking an American City*, 315–25. New Brunswick: Rutgers University Press, 2019.

Ginsberg, Allen. "America." Poetry Foundation. https://www.poetryfoundation.org/poems/49305/america-56d22b41f119f.

About the Author

Aiden Faust is the associate director of Special Collections and Archives at the University of Baltimore. He received his MLS in archives and records management from the University of Maryland College Park and his MA in historical studies from the University of Maryland Baltimore County. His most recent publication, "Social History in the Archives: Baltimore's Enduring Legacy," appears in *Baltimore Revisited: Stories of Inequality and Resistance in a US City*, published by Rutgers University Press. His professional practice is informed by lived experiences as a queer transman in recovery, meditation student, flatwater kayaker, and avid gardener.

---

2. Allen Ginsberg, "America," Poetry Foundation, https://www.poetryfoundation.org/poems/49305/america-56d22b41f119f.

Getting the Trans Thing: Assigned Identities, Invisibility, and Anonymity

Gideon Goodrich

Keywords: non-binary, archives and special collections, ethical description, misgendering, cisnormativity

Introduction

It is hard not to be angry most days. As I write this introduction, I am sitting on an air mattress in an empty apartment, preparing to relocate for a new position and reflecting on my experiences at the University Libraries at Penn State. First, a bit of personal context: I came out as non-binary in 2019 during my last semester in graduate school, so the concept of being out and visible as a trans librarian was still new when I began working at the Eberly Family Special Collections Library. It was easy to feel like I'd done something wrong when I was repeatedly misgendered, even in cases where I specifically pointed out my pronouns. I was misgendered every single day, and it became an exhausting slog.

This chapter largely focuses on my experiences with cisnormativity.[1] I discuss how performative allyship impacted my daily work life, and how that mirrored other issues I encountered in accessioning and describing

1. Cisnormativity is listed in the Wiktionary as an LGBTQ neologism that falls into a group of terms attempting to get at societal assumptions about gender that avoid the "-phobia" or fear aspect of people's actions. "Cisnormativity," Wiktionary, accessed October 31, 2021, https://en.wiktionary.org/wiki/cisnormativity.

collections. Specifically, I will discuss assigning identities to figures in archival documents, and how I used my experiences to shape description decisions. As a result, it's a very personal essay and at times an angry one, yelled in the silence surrounding the trans experience in libraries and archives.

Performative Allyship and Forced Invisibility

I knew when I applied for a job at Penn State what I was getting into—I've previously lived in Blacksburg, a college town in conservative Virginia. Still, every Appalachian town has its own flavor, its own prejudices to navigate. I had hope, though, that perhaps work would be different—some of my future colleagues at least had their pronouns in their email signatures, something that once impressed me but slowly became more commonplace in the profession.[2]

I never planned on doing a grand reveal regarding my gender identity at work—while I wasn't out to my family at the time, I was out publicly, and I did everything in my power to convey that. I added my pronouns to my email signature and referred to myself using gender-neutral language. When the head of my department asked for a short bio so that she could introduce me to our library faculty organization, I made sure my correct pronouns were included. Questions came up and I answered them. A few colleagues expressed support and pre-apologized for any mistakes they might make and, for a while, things went well. Then I began to notice that colleagues seemed to misgender me regularly, and some never seemed to get the memo that I was nonbinary. I was trans, but seemed to conform to a gender expression that aligned with my assigned gender, and I was making no steps to transition in the expected manner. At the time, I thought, "No matter! It's not like I *actually* came out to the department." I hadn't been out when I interviewed for the position and it seemed that I needed to perform a grand coming-out ritual of some kind if I was to expect recognition.

---

2. As with many things in the digital space, when pronouns became a part of email signatures is difficult to pinpoint because so many university websites have changed the information on their site.

This idea is something I still struggle with. For example, in an earlier version of this chapter, I'd written a paragraph excusing the behavior of my coworkers because I wasn't "out" to them. However, my editor pointed out that I *was* out when I started my job and had followed every path available to me to inform my colleagues of my gender identity and pronouns. Nonetheless, they were ignoring them. The exceptions only proved the rule. There were people on my side who educated themselves and helped me educate others, but the vast majority of people I encountered on campus and in the libraries didn't seem interested in that effort. Information I made publicly available was ignored, and I took the blame for the failings and (in some cases) malicious ignorance of my colleagues. Through no fault of my own, and despite my best efforts, my queerness was rendered invisible.

While it took some kind feedback from my editor for me to really reckon with this reality and the anger that came with it, my experience began to really chafe when we switched to a "work from home" model of work during the initial COVID-19 lockdown. In a physical space, it was easier for me to excuse misgendering because I was used to feminine labels for my body; in the digital meeting space, however, it was hard to ignore the deep divide between those who respected my humanity and those who did not. Initially, my supervisor and I came up with a handful of solutions—she helped me develop language for correcting coworkers via email and encouraged me to add my pronouns to my name on Zoom, and I also shoved my pronouns directly under my name in every email. When I wanted to change my name at work, my supervisor helped me track down the forms required to do that.

I reintroduced myself as Gideon in October 2020, around the same time Penn State removed the ability to add pronouns to your Zoom display name. They added this feature again in February 2021 in order to "[continue] to create and maintain an open, safe and inclusive environment honoring gender and sexual diversity."[3] (The removal was an

3. "Canvas and Zoom: Adding Gender and Identity Pronouns to Your Name," Penn State University: Penn State News, February 18, 2021, https://www.psu.edu/news/campus-life/story/canvas-and-zoom

unofficial security measure, and it is entirely possible that adding the feature back in was the result of good faith work, but I'm nothing if not a cynic at this point.) I found colleagues referring to me by name almost exclusively in order to avoid my pronouns. Many continued to misgender me. When I began work on the diversity committee in 2021, a friend told me she'd had a conversation recently with a fellow librarian who "just didn't get the trans thing." During diversity week a month or so later, a librarian doing some basic work on trans solidarity mentioned that she "didn't think [we] had any trans colleagues."

I was exhausted and worn out. Still, when I wrote the first draft of this chapter, I made a number of excuses for my colleagues in the name of being kind. However, if I've had any revelations this year, they are that I want to be seen and understood, and I want to name the behaviors standing in the way of inclusivity and basic human decency. It was not too much to expect my colleagues to pay attention to what little signposting was available for trans employees. I gave everyone multiple chances to learn, to ask me questions, to see me. That they refused to do that is on them.

Queer Identities in the Archive

My personal struggles to demand basic recognition coincided with internal efforts to develop an inclusive description guide for archival description at Penn State. The guide was spearheaded by a graduate employee with myself and other archivists as consultants, and broadly tackled description for historically under-represented and under-described communities. My work on the guide as a whole focused on elevating queer histories in the archival collections we already had, as well as providing guidance on describing queer and gender diverse people in history.

This interest was driven by a number of things—namely, my own struggles with identity and language, and the difficulty of identifying queer people in archival collections.

-adding-gender-and-identity-pronouns-your-name/.

Language in queer spaces is ever changing. If I had come out in the 2010s, for example, I might have referred to myself as genderqueer rather than nonbinary, simply because genderqueer was the more popular and accepted term. The transition from transsexual to transgender reflects the struggle with the medicalization of trans and gender diverse people. And lesbian, as I learned through my description work, was considered an insult akin to sodomite in the early 1900s. The problem is that "when it comes to queerness, we have to be mindful of language as shifting tectonic plates beneath our feet. Language was a code; language was a shield."[4] In addition, there are complex and difficult discussions around creating a unified queer history to reckon with when tackling description.[5]

Many creators choose to remain in the shadows of history, even when it seems clear they were active in the communities they documented. The creator of the scrapbooks in the Early male tightlacing, corsetting, and cross-dressing collection at the Eberly Family Special Collections Library, for example, made sure there was no way to link them to their scrapbooks. The collection was brought together by a bookseller, and the creator was (presumably) a member of the male tightlacing community in the 1890s through the 1930s.[6] Each scrapbook was full of celebration and joy and highlights gender variant people and included rare, subscription-only publications about male tightlacers and female impersonators.

The scrapbooks all appeared to be made by the same person; however, nothing was signed. There were no personal stories in the scrapbooks themselves, only the stories of others. It is possible that some of the photos depict the scrapbooker—one of the photos was previously cropped to cut out the subject's face, but the scrapbooker mended the

4. Jeanna Kadlec, "A Brief History of Queer Language before Queer Identity," Literary Hub, Published May 13, 2019, https://lithub.com/a-brief-history-of-queer-language-before-queer-identity/.

5. Ben Miller, "The Life and Death of Modern Homosexuality," *The Baffler*, January 28, 2021, https://thebaffler.com/latest/the-life-and-death-of-modern-homosexuality-miller.

6. Early male tightlacing, corsetting, and cross-dressing collection, 10034, Eberly Family Special Collections Library, Pennsylvania State University.

photograph with adhesive and what looks like ink. In addition, an extensive hand-written history of tightlacing was included with the ephemera, and was housed with clippings, advertisements, and publications. As the accessioning and processing archivist for this collection, I faced a dilemma—what terms could I ethically use to describe the anonymous creator that would link them to our broader LGTBQ+ collections? There were a number of items that used specific, community-generated terms that were easy to integrate into descriptions of the material. Should I include the creator in the communities they documented, or refrain from mentioning them at all?

We'd faced a similar issue with another pair of collections—the Dr. Grace M. Henderson papers and the Delpha Wiesendanger papers, which had originally come to Penn State as a single collection. The archivist at the time separated the papers and obscured the long-term and well-known relationship between these women in describing the papers. When processing archivist Lexy deGraffenreid updated the finding aid, we wanted to include both women as important figures in Penn State University, but neither Henderson nor Wiesendanger labeled their relationship. In this case, we settled for including keywords related to queer history in the processing note (which would include the finding aid in keyword searches for those terms) to avoid assigning an identity based on modern language. This decision was based on a number of factors, not least of which was the fact that we were working with language these women simply didn't have access to in the early 1900s. As Jenna Kadlec noted in her article on queer language, if we use our modern understanding of sexuality to develop historical narratives, "we run the risk of anachronistic projections on writers and artists from past centuries whose conception of sexuality was different."[7] In addition, as someone who had their identity ignored on a daily basis, I argued it was unethical to do the same to the subjects of archival collections.

Engaging in a conversation with Lexy about Grace and Delpha helped guide my description of the early male-tightlacing scrapbooks;

7. Kadlec, "A Brief History of Queer Language before Queer Identity."

the identity of the scrapbooker should remain unknown, unless a researcher stumbles across identifying information I may have missed. Still, as I looked through the scrapbooks, I saw hints of their personality—personal drawings and splashes of humor, and a focus on the joy of tightlacing and cross-dressing, in particular—which led me to add a note on the matter of identity: "The creator took great pains to keep themselves anonymous, but was likely a member of the tightlacing movement in some form."[8]

My experiences with identity and recognition in my own work are on the opposite end from this scrapbooker. I've worked hard to ensure my identity is a part of the work I do, where appropriate and healthy; the scrapbooker, for their own reasons, wished to remain anonymous, and I am more than happy to grant them that.

A Conclusion of Sorts

In archival work, there is a lot of talk about silence in the archive—the gaps in collections that are glaringly obvious to the communities that should occupy those gaps. There are also gaps in professional literature that render the experiences of trans and gender diverse employees nearly invisible. When I started work on this chapter, I did so because a majority of the literature surrounding issues of gender and sexual diversity is written about patrons and undergraduates. While championing solidarity for transgender patrons is vital, especially in reference and outreach, it does reinforce the idea that these identities, and their related struggles, are faced by younger generations. This obscures and deemphasizes the struggles of trans and gender diverse employees; if trans people are always patrons, our cisgender colleagues are less likely to look for and confront cisnormative attitudes, misgendering, or other alienating policies in their own workplace.

8. Early male tightlacing, corsetting, and cross-dressing collection, 10034, Eberly Family Special Collections Library, Pennsylvania State University.

While I worked at Penn State University Libraries, I was misgendered every single day by patrons and colleagues alike. I used all of the tools available to me to make myself visible, to be "out" in all the ways expected of me, and I still had to explain and re-explain and justify my gender identity. On the other hand, my supervisor (curator for our LGTBQ+ collection area) began to bring in more material relating to trans and gender diverse communities, where I encountered the complex intersection between identity, assumed identities, and history. Ultimately, I was assigned a gender at work—one that reflected a comfortable binary—and so was able to inform our best practices regarding creators and subjects whose identities are unknown. As a result, the description guidelines at Penn State include the following provision for queer and gender diverse identities:

> Follow the individual's example of how they describe themselves. Only use names that the creators used to refer to themselves. This may mean deviating from Library of Congress name authority records. The humanity and dignity of the creator are more important than adhering to [existing] standards.[9]

My position at Penn State ended in October 2021, when I started a new position at another special collections library in the Big Ten, and I've found my expectations have changed. While my colleagues have been incredibly respectful so far, I find myself bracing for the other shoe to drop—waiting for someone else to confess that they "don't get the trans thing," or to stumble across some truly horrific descriptions of queer and gender diverse people in the collections I'll be working with. I am, however, done with being made to feel invisible.

Bibliography

"Canvas and Zoom: Adding Gender and Identity Pronouns to Your Name." Penn State University. Penn State News, February

9. Benjamin Mitchell, "Collections Services Manual: Inclusive Description Style Guide," ed. Lexy deGraffenreid, Gideon Goodrich, Racine Amos, and Kevil Clair. State College, PA (2021).

18, 2021. https://www.psu.edu/news/campus-life/story/canvas-and-zoom-adding-gender-and-identity-pronouns-your-name/.

"Cisnormativity." Wiktionary. Accessed October 31, 2021. https://en.wiktionary.org/wiki/cisnormativity.

"Early male tightlacing, corsetting, and cross-dressing collection," 10034. Eberly Family Special Collections Library, Pennsylvania State University.

Heinz, Matthew. "Transmen on the Web: Inscribing Multiple Discourses." In *The Handbook of Gender, Sex, and Media*, 326–43, 2012. https://doi.org/10.1002/9781118114254.ch20.

Kadlec, Jeanna. "A Brief History of Queer Language before Queer Identity." *Literary Hub*. Literary Hub, May 13, 2019. https://lithub.com/a-brief-history-of-queer-language-before-queer-identity/.

Miller, Ben. "The Life and Death of Modern Homosexuality." *The Baffler*. January 28, 2021. https://thebaffler.com/latest/the-life-and-death-of-modern-homosexuality-miller.

Mitchell, Ben. "Collections Services Manual: Inclusive Description Style Guide." Edited by Lexy deGraffenreid, Gideon Goodrich, Racine Amos, and Kevin Clair, 15. State College, PA, 2021.

About the Author

Gideon Goodrich is a reference librarian specializing in archival and special collections reference, as well as archival arrangement and description. A large part of their work focuses on radical empathy in archives and special collections and equity of access. They currently work as the Research Services Librarian at the Special Collections Research Center at the University of Michigan, Ann Arbor.

Reflections: An Indigenous Non-Binary Experience in Archives and Libraries

Skylee-Storm Hogan-Stacey (They/Them)

Keywords: non-binary, archives, public history, personal reflection, Indigenous

Introduction—Coming from a Place In-between

I wanted to come out when I was young. I remember early elementary school, grades one and two, where I had convinced half the school into believing I was a boy through presentation and lies by omission. I would use the boy's washroom, get short haircuts, and pick out the best batman shirts that the thrift store had to offer. At recess kids would stop mid-sentence asking me, "Wait, are you a girl or a boy?" I would shrug and state, "A little bit of both." This gender play became a problem when the bullying started coming from my peers and teachers. On a sunny day in May when I was in grade five, my mom took me out of school for lunch at the park. She told me it was time I "started acting like a girl"; she was hoping the bullying would go away if I presented as more feminine so, for around eleven years after, I did.

Libraries were a sanctuary for a fat, weird kid with a single mom and no money. I could take out endless books and CDs. On the weekends, I did some filing for my mom's company, and they commented that the file locating system I made was better than anything produced by the adults they employed with administrative degrees. I didn't know it yet, but archives would be my calling into the world of heritage, academia, and research. However, I saw very few queer, Indigenous, or gender-diverse representations in libraries, museums, or archives. My early experiences with them usually involved female-presenting staff with a male-presenting administrator or senior manager. Everyone was tattoo- and piercing-free and had natural hair colours. I was never sure if it was the right environment for me.

I began university as a mature student. I decided to travel to Sault Ste. Marie because a friend was going there as well. It was at Algoma University that I felt comfortable enough to start exploring my gender identity again. While I had cosplayed and cross-dressed for fun for many years, I was afraid to admit that I did not feel like a woman. Saying the word woman makes me physically uncomfortable, especially when used as a descriptor for my body or identity. I have never felt at home in that identity. I have never felt the comfort of a "sisterhood" or that cis women had my back. So when I began my academic career, I was battling with myself about how I should identify.

Coming Out

I have a high voice at times and have always been a fat person. Being fat comes with bodily curves associated with femininity. When I first self-identified as non-binary in late 2017, I felt pressure to fit the model of androgyny to validate my identity. I began living a lifestyle that contributed to rapid and unsafe weight loss. I felt that if I could look thin, have short hair, and minimize my body's natural curves, I could legitimize my non-binary identity and have others accept me as non-binary. But when I began connecting with the two-spirit community, I discovered that much of what I thought about gender performance had been formed through a colonial lens. My hair and body should not have to conform to colonial standards of what it means to be non-binary. The fact that I am non-binary is enough. What other people perceive as my gender expression is on them, not me.

I still struggle with this. My understanding of my gender identity and my Indigenous identity are still evolving as I learn more about myself, my family's history, and those in my father's community who are gender diverse, trans, and two-spirit and are advocating to be seen and respected within the community.

I was working with the Shingwauk Residential Schools Centre (SRSC) during this time of coming out. I was growing comfortable with what non-binary meant for me and had some highs and lows. But working in such a diverse environment with queer co-workers gave me a different experience than others I knew who were coming out in their workplaces.

Shingwauk Residential Schools Centre

My experiences in the archive were good. I started working with the SRSC at Algoma University in 2015, a short time before deciding to make my coming out official.[1] Working with the SRSC, I felt supported coming out. I did not feel like I had to come out; the demographics in that space were queer, and I felt that they could all sense it from me. Still, when giving tours or serving patrons, I felt pressured to identify as a woman because it required less stress and less explanation. I did not want to come out to strangers and worry about a potential reaction. While I know my co-workers and supervisor would have supported me, I did not want to make the session or tour about my gender; I tried to keep the focus on the survivors and the residential schools.

Dealing with visitors was already difficult due to the nature of the history I was presenting to them. But having teachers tell their students to "follow the lady" or "listen to the young woman" made me feel drained by the end of the tour or education session. Most of the youth were great and did not ask me questions about my gender, but when I started presenting as more masculine or androgynous, kids would often ask me if I was a boy or a girl. In most cases, I would laugh and say I was a girl, or I would laugh off the question and shift the focus. I did not want teachers to feel awkward or parents to be upset with something

1. Prior to this, I was only out with a couple of close friends from high school. They knew I was questioning my gender, but I had not put a label on it yet. My official coming out expanded that circle into my familial, professional, and school life.

I said. Towards the end of my time with the Centre, in 2018, I began telling people I use they/them pronouns with more confidence and the questions would stop.

While with the SRSC, I worked on the redescription of collections and file-level descriptions for the Shingwauk Residential School and the Spanish Residential School. While I worked with these records, I often wondered how many queer Indigenous identities were erased or punished. When I was redescribing records, I would use terms like "a group of boys sledding." When I began to examine gendering the subjects of the records, I shifted my language to "a group of students sledding." It seemed more appropriate since I did not know the gender of everyone in the photo. I did not want my assumptions to erase them or take away what little agency they had left. The SRSC did not organize their resource library with the traditional Library of Congress Classification System or the Dewey Decimal Classification System; those systems present issues for Indigenous materials. Instead, the resource library was organized by author and theme, which would be more accessible for the community that utilized the space.

My work in the archive required me to work closely with the library and its staff. The library staff were primarily older women and students who changed almost every semester. I was misgendered often, but I never spoke up. I was worried I would be seen as too sensitive, looking for attention, or creating unnecessary problems. Because I looked female and had a male-presenting partner, I figured that advocating for my pronouns was pointless. Some older faculty and older library staff asked me what the point was in coming out or changing my pronouns if nothing else about my life was changing. I sometimes wanted to explain that it really was changing, but I often felt defeated at that moment or that they would not understand anyway.

There were no trans-specific resources within the library space. I did not see the integration of LGBTQA2SI+ materials, even during pride month. There was no discussion about including pronouns of staff or ways to make the library more inclusive for trans, two-spirit, and gender diverse folks. Because there were so few discussions about inclusion and no representation in the space, I kept allowing others to perceive me as female. I would refer to myself as they or them in bios, and I hoped others would understand what I meant. I was not ready to open myself up to bullying or explaining why I was identifying as non-binary. I did not take up any official roles in my community or receive teachings on what it meant to be two-spirit, so I felt uncomfortable taking on that identity at the time. That understanding would come later.

Experiences at the Graduate Level

I did not pursue an MLIS for my Master's level education. I decided that Public History would provide the skills I needed to work in an archives environment or create materials for the public. The SRSC taught me that libraries, archives, and museums could be social change spaces for crucial public discourse. I chose the University of Western Ontario's Public History program. Western was a much larger school than Algoma University. I correctly assumed that there would be more services and community for trans and gender diverse folks on campus. The program had us write a short profile for their website about ourselves, and I used they/them pronouns throughout my profile. Many of my cohorts asked what pronouns I prefer, and I met other queer folks in the main History program.

I was not misgendered often in the Public History program. When I was, I found it easier to quickly say, "I actually use they/them pronouns." No one was upset by it because it was more common at a larger campus. When I began as a Teaching Assistant, the professor respected my pronoun choices when introducing me to the class, and students generally did the same. My favourite space on campus quickly became Western's Pride Library. I was doing research on queer activism and the intersections with Public History when I found the space. The Pride Library marked their codes with PRI, indicating they could only be found in the Pride Library. I ended up also taking out books on two-spirit identity and gender. The space itself was welcoming. The staff person working in the small room was kind and helped me find what I needed. The posters celebrated queerness and queer history, and there were educational materials for those looking for more information or community resources.

In my second semester, I ended my Teaching Assistant position and began working as a Research Assistant with the Museum of Ontario Archeology. My supervisor and co-worker shared a small section of the museum. I helped with sections of the website and began writing a research piece on Elsie McLeod Murray Jury, the wife of the museum's founder. Elsie had written much of her husband's work but did not receive the same credits. I appreciated my supervisor giving me work to explore my interests and allowing me to talk about collections storage from an Indigenous perspective. There was a library in the museum; however, it was purely archaeological. The staff at the museum generally respected pronouns, but to my knowledge there was no official policy to support trans or gender diverse staff. No one else identified as non-binary or used they/them pronouns but, luckily, my gender identity did not come up often. Sometimes I felt anxious about having to talk about my gender identity when it did come up. While my supervisor was great, the collections staff were not as well integrated with the administration and archaeological team at the museum, and I was afraid of implications for my professional career if I had to come out.

Experiences in my Master's program were fair as well. There were still things that could have made it better. I always felt like the queer community was separate from the graduate department and that queer spaces on campus were a hideaway or oasis where we could relax and be ourselves. It would be better if all aspects of campus life felt open to trans and other queer voices. For students working with off-campus heritage institutions and the public as Research Assistants, there should have been more resources for trans and gender diverse students. During my time at Western, I had not seen any two-spirit representation or events with two-spirit teachings. I took an internship for the summer that required another move to a new city. I was going by myself to Ottawa.

Working in Heritage Research Consulting

Historical services research firms are an emerging field for public historians with archival and library skills. Our ability to research, organize, and present information is invaluable to projects. I was lucky to have my six-month internship turn into a permanent job. I am fortunate that the firm I work for offers permanent employment with benefits. I often slip back into anxiety thinking about the precarious contract work I faced in the archives, libraries, and museums. I feel guilt for spending and am always looking for contingency plans when I realize I do not need them.

The company I work for prides itself on a great culture, and I have been so impressed with the changes I have seen in my two years there. I never feel tokenized or used for being Indigenous or non-binary. The staff is predominately white, with some Indigenous senior advisors. We work with diverse clients exploring Indigenous clients' heritage needs, special projects on queer history, and passion projects on marginalized stories that need to be told. My manager asked me to research different policies around gender for a client and then forwarded my recommendations to our HR department. Our Directors realized that there were gaps between our staff's lived experiences and identities and the communities they were working with. The company mandated professional development for cultural competency training and gender and sexual diversity training. Our instructor for gender and sexual diversity training was non-binary. It was so validating to hear them explain to my co-workers the awkwardness and frustration of being a gender-diverse person in the workplace. After this training, we added pronouns to our email signatures. I was the only one who chose they/them.

I had many colleagues apologize to me after I came out. I have many colleagues misgender me in conversation, then immediately apologize. I receive some well-meaning but invasive questions, and being the only person out at work can be isolating and exhausting. I still get misgendered in emails and meetings, but I know it is getting better. I still wish there was an easier way to talk about misgendering without making my colleagues feel like I am calling them out. I also wish there was a formal policy concerning LGBTQA2SI+ identities in the workplace.

During this time in heritage consulting, I began to visit and reconnect with my father's community in Kahnawake, which became a process of discovering that I had ancestors and other family members who identified as queer. For so long, I felt abnormal because my queerness did not fit with who I was supposed to be with my maternal family. While I was living in the community of Sault Ste. Marie, active members of the two-spirit community shared and advocated for queer Indigenous people. They showed me those two identities did not need to be separate. I learned a Kanien'kehá:ka term for two-spirits, *Onón:wat*, which translates to "I have the pattern of two spirits in my body." I am non-binary, and I can define that for myself. That means even if my body is not super thin, it is still a non-binary body. If my hair is not short, or I wear beaded earrings, that does not mean I am now feminine. Gender expression through a colonial lens is not how I need to define myself, because those things are not the same in Indigenous gender expression.

Conclusion

This reflection has been hard to write. I have had to deal with a lot of internalized homophobia, fatphobia, and fear. I am working towards a better relationship with my identity and discovering more about myself. It is complex to look at gender intersections with Indigeneity and mixed-ancestry. I have white privilege, which removes many barriers. At the same time, I work through the intergenerational trauma that comes with a previously incarcerated Indigenous parent, off-reserve disconnection, and a non-Indigenous side of the family that struggles to understand me. Being non-binary in spaces designed for professional-looking white women supervised by white men can be isolating for Indigenous people who do not want to conform to the colonial standards of gender expression.[2] I found myself wishing throughout my time in heritage, archives,

2. Professional-looking here meaning business casual coded with natural hair

and libraries that there were more policies shaped by Indigenous folks and members of the queer community. I am still discouraged by slow career mobility, and I often ask myself if I would be further ahead if I weren't out. But I am hopeful that there are more visible trans, non-binary, two-spirit, and gender diverse people working in these sectors and thriving in them. The experiences across these spaces have been so different, yet so similar. I hope these reflections can help shape future conversations in our field and further show others that they are not alone.

About the Author

Skylee-Storm Hogan-Stacey (they/them) is a public historian currently living and working on the unceded territory of the Algonquin Anishinaabek in Ottawa, Ontario. A descendant of the Mohawk Nation of Kahnawà:ke, Skylee-Storm has explored Indigenous-Crown legal histories, Residential Schools, Indigenous stories of resistance, and oral histories of Kahnawà:ke elders. They are interested in Kahnawà:ke history, community-based and Indigenous archival systems, ownership, and collections access. Skylee-Storm began their work with the Shingwauk Residential Schools Centre in 2014 and graduated with a Master of Arts in History from the University of Western Ontario's Public History Program in 2019. Skylee-Storm works with Know History Historical Services as an Associate in their Ottawa office.

colours, no visible tattoos, or piercings. Also dress that is coded to assigned gender expectations in the workplace or that falls into a western ideal of gender binary.

Appreciative and Cautious: Thoughts on Community, Libraries, and the Spaces Between

Sophie Ziegler (they/them)

Keywords: community archives, oral history, trans history, Louisiana Trans Oral History Project

Introduction

The Louisiana Trans Oral History Project (LaTOHP) is a trans-run, community-focused effort to collect and preserve the voices of Louisiana's transgender and gender non-conforming communities. Started in 2020, the project has, at the time of this writing, completed over thirty-five interviews with individuals across the state. We have interviewed farmers, doctors, professors, students, political organizers, religious leaders, musicians, and librarians, among others, and we seek diversity of geographic location, racial identity, and gender expression.

LaTOHP's goal is primarily to create a resource for trans communities in Louisiana; secondly, it is to share these resources more broadly for anyone who would benefit. It's true of myself, and I've heard the same from others, that our lives would be very different had we had more examples of trans and gender non-conforming (TGNC) people in our early lives. In fact, interviewees regularly talk about first hearing the terms that they come to adopt for themselves. One interviewee tells of their discovery this way:

> So, I was on the website Autostraddle, and I was making a profile on there, and under gender they had all these different options. And I was like, "Wait, there's other ones?" And I started looking into it, and I found the word genderqueer, and I was like, "Oh my God. This is me. There's a word for it." I marched into the school that Monday, walked up to my friends. I was like, "Y'all, I'm genderqueer. There's a word for me."[1]

After a quick review of the project as it exists at the time of writing, the remainder of this chapter will attempt to have something to say to two different, but likely overlapping, audiences. The first audience is other TGNC people who work in cultural heritage institutions and who might start a project similar to LaTOHP. To this audience, I offer some thoughts on taking advantage of the benefits your institution might offer, while simultaneously keeping some distance between your job and your community work. The second audience is composed of library workers who hope to make libraries more responsive and avoid some of the pitfalls mentioned to the first audience. To you I offer thoughts on how initiatives such as LaTOHP can generate ideas for making cultural heritage spaces more welcoming and inclusive to TGNC individuals.

A Note About Me:

Before going further, I find it's useful to say something about my own situation and circumstances. I am a white, trans femme/gender queer librarian in Louisiana. My work and my life benefit from a number of privileges not available to many people, especially to many trans people of color. Furthermore, my perspective is influenced by the relative security of my library job. I am twelve years into my career and only one year out as trans. The emotional and psychological toll of not being out for the first decade of my career will be long lasting—as will the benefits. Had I been out earlier in my career, I believe it is unlikely I would be as professionally secure.

---

1. Interview with Dre Tarleton, September 2020. Full interview: https://www.louisianatransoralhistory.org/interview-with/dre-tarleton.

Furthermore, it's important to specify that my thinking, both about librarianship and the overlap of librarianship with queer issues, would not be possible without the work of many writers. I list some here as a record of respect and appreciation: Dorothy Berry, Jay Colbert, Jarrett Drake, Emily Drabinski, Fobazi Ettarh, April Hathcock, Stephen Krueger, Sofia Leung, Tonia Sutherland, Bri Watson, Erin White, Baharak Yousefi.

The Louisiana Trans Oral History Project (As of the Time of this Writing)

The Louisiana Trans Oral History Project (LaTOHP) is a trans-run, community-focused effort to collect, promote, and preserve the voices of Louisiana's transgender and gender non-conforming communities.

In 2021, the project received a grant from the Louisiana Endowment for the Humanities, the state affiliate of the National Endowment for the Humanities, to fund interview transcriptions and a series of public events. We held three public, remote panels. The first, "Storytelling and the Preservation of Our Trans History: A Community Panel," featured Black and Brown trans women discussing the role of storytelling in their life and work. The second, "Tomorrow's History is Gonna Be So Queer: A Panel on Queer Oral Histories," featured oral history practitioners from projects around the country. The third panel, "History is Big Enough for Us All: Using Trans Oral Histories in the Classroom," gathered educators at different levels to talk about how to ensure LaTOHP oral histories can be useful in the classroom. Having funds available to distribute for the first time, LaTOHP distributed them to the community by hiring a Louisiana-based genderqueer transcriptionist, and by building the public panels to include a majority TGNC involvement.[2]

In June 2021, the project launched a podcast, Trans Louisiane, which features interview segments as well as music from Louisiana TGNC

2. Recordings of panels and other events are available here: https://www.louisianatransoralhistory.org/events.

musicians. The project centers the safety and comfort of the interviewee over expectations of a specific product, so we encourage everyone who takes part to closely scrutinize their interview transcripts. Anything can be removed, altered, or temporarily redacted. It is not uncommon to have final transcripts that vary from the audio in significant and important ways. For this reason, while we post approved interview transcripts to the website, we often do not share the full interview audio. The podcast is a way to share the audio in segments that are approved by the interviewee. The podcast is also a means to lift up other people in the community. Thanks to the generosity of our patrons, in addition to promotion, we're able to offer every participating musician a small stipend for the use of their song.[3] As the podcast continues to grow, we hope to find additional ways to promote and advance members of the community.

LaTOHP also aims to be responsive to the needs and challenges of the TGNC communities in Louisiana. In April and May of 2021, Louisiana state legislators introduced four anti-trans bills. LaTOHP shifted gears and postponed the launch of the podcast to gather recorded statements of support from cis allies. This was a small gesture, especially given the magnitude of anti-trans laws, but one that aligned with the expertise of the project and that, hopefully, offered some counterweight to the feelings of isolation many in the community felt. In June 2021, LaTOHP teamed up with Last Call, a multi-racial collective of queer oral historians, artists, activists, and archivists, for a new series of interviews. This series of interviews focuses on the resistance to the state legislative session, a resistance that defeated all four bills.[4] It is difficult,

3. LaTOHP maintains a Patreon account, and benefits greatly from the support of our patrons. https://www.patreon.com/LouisianaTransOralHistory.

4. Three of the bills were defeated in the legislature thanks in very large part to the organizing of local trans activists. The fourth, SB 156, was vetoed by the Governor of Louisiana, again thanks to the work of local trans advocates. A first-ever veto override session was held by the legislature, but was ultimately unable to pass any of the anti-trans legislation. On a personal note, I'll say that it was a joy to be at the state house with so many trans siblings when the bills died. For more on Last Call, see: http://www.lastcallnola.org/. The video of Cis Statements of Support is available here: https://youtu.be/mH4qvh1eRJI.

in the format of this chapter, to convey how painful the legislative session was for me and many others in Louisiana. What might be easier to convey are the long-term changes that we expect will come of it. The following quote from an interview with an activist is indicative of the feeling many of us have that a significant shift has occurred during our resistance to the bills:

> I've learned a lot. I'll start with that. There's a lot that I've learned throughout this session and I've been in different sessions before. This has changed me in the sense that I am not nearly as intimidated by the legislative session or these representatives or these senators. These are some of the most asinine, quite frankly, idiotic people I have had the displeasure of being in the same room with. That changed me. That changed me. If these people can be elected, then hell! I need to go get me a seat! I need to go find a way to get myself in that room. And I should never, ever, ever be afraid of saying my piece. Because they say their piece all the time, and it's nothing of nothing.[5]

Because LaTOHP aims to be relevant and responsive to the TGNC communities in Louisiana, we've also changed during this time by emphasizing the documentation of people associated with the struggle for trans rights.

Since the beginning, LaTOHP has benefited from my association with Louisiana State University Libraries (LSU Libraries), where I work. Before the first interview was scheduled, I was in contact with the T. Harry Williams Center for Oral History at LSU to learn about oral history practice, and to ensure the interviews would have a long-term home, should interviewees want to donate them. I have used my LSU Zoom account, and the freedom to do so is tied to my faculty status at my institution. Furthermore, my faculty status gives me the flexibility to schedule, conduct, and edit interviews. For these and related reasons, I believe LaTOHP would not exist if I did not currently work at LSU Libraries.

---

5. Interview with trans activist Elliot Wade, recorded July 21, 2021.

However, I guard the distinction between LaTOHP and LSU Libraries. They are very much separate institutions. As is the case in many states, a tension exists between Louisiana's large institutions and the communities around them. I have been told by multiple interviewees that they would not participate if LaTOHP were an LSU project. And indeed, I would likely not participate in LaTOHP if it were an LSU project, given the loss of decision-making, flexibility, and responsiveness, to say nothing of branding, aesthetic choices, and technical challenges that often accompany small projects within large universities.

For TGNC Library Workers Who Want to Do Community Work

Based on the above overview of LaTOHP, I'll share some thoughts in this section for other TGNC library workers who currently do community work or would like to start doing it in the future. By library worker, I include anyone who works in a library or any other cultural heritage institution, such as an archive, special collection, or museum. Similarly, I mean community work in a broad way to include any work that focuses on your community outside of work but that might take advantage of your position at your library. My perspective is grounded in my experience with LaTOHP, whose community is TGNC folks in Louisiana. I hope you'll find this applicable to your situation.

My first suggestion is to talk to your community about how they feel about the place where you work. It might be that your organization is universally beloved, in which case all is great. However, if there is any animosity, or even vague distrust, it's good to know about it. In my case, Louisiana State University is a predominantly white institution with a long history of exclusionary practices toward students, staff, and faculty of color. LSU Libraries, being part of that history, rightfully carries those stains as well. Aside from the specifics of any given institution, many communities are wary of collecting institutions that are extractive and add nothing to the communities from whom the material originates.

After you talk to members of your community, you'll have a better sense of how explicit to be about your project's detachment from your day job.

In addition to the needs of your community, there are other reasons you might want to keep a distance between your community work and your job. One is community involvement and responsiveness. In the case of LaTOHP, people regularly reach out requesting trans resources and information. We also hear from people who are in crisis and desperate for someone to talk to. No one associated with the project is trained in crisis care, but we can relate and we know resources, such as Trans Lifeline, to suggest.[6] Depending on the circumstances, we sometimes follow up with the individual. This is certainly outside the scope of the project, but not outside of the mission to be responsive and accountable to the community. In my experience, I would not trust any library I've worked at to be in a position to offer an understanding ear or appropriate resources to a TGNC person in crisis.

Maintaining a distance doesn't mean there aren't ways to enrich community work by virtue of your institutional affiliation. Many well-established library principles are quite helpful in community settings. From digital file organization to basics of digital preservation and donation workflows, there's much to take from librarianship.[7] Additionally, on a more granular level, your library might have technology that you can use for community work. There might be training available for topics or skills, such as grant writing or website design, that would benefit both your work in the library and your work in the community. By considering where our library work overlaps with our community work,

6. It's outside of the scope of this chapter, but it's worth pausing to draw attention to this resource. If you or anyone you know in the TGNC community is in need of emotional or financial support, please consider contacting Trans Lifeline: https://translifeline.org/. Your life and well-being matters, you are important, and you have a community that cares about you.

7. I had occasion to write about this at more length in relation to an earlier community project. See: S. Ziegler, "Let's Use What Works: The Radical Archives of Philadelphia and Traditional Archival Literature," in *Informed Agitation: Library and Information Skills in Social Justice Movements and Beyond* (Sacramento, CA: Library Juice Press, 2014), 105–17.

we can see how the latter can benefit from the former, even when we keep them separate.

For Library Workers Who Want to Learn from Community Work

Having discussed some reasons that libraries might not be the best place for community work to take place, in this section I'll explore some ideas for how we, as library workers, could change our workplaces to make them better suited for such work. Please know that I'm presenting these thoughts with respect and appreciation for the work that all library workers do. I know this work. I do not intend to make recommendations that, in my experience, are not realistic. Rather, I want to tie my experience in libraries to my experience in community projects, and say something useful.

Let's start with how we pay people. This is an area many of us have no control over, though, to varying degrees, some of us do. Furthermore, regardless of where we fall on this spectrum, we can certainly advocate for change as Diversity, Equity, and Inclusion conversations arise. For the LaTOHP panels, we paid people using the payment app Venmo. It was very important that we did not require any paperwork from them. This is important for our TGNC community because tax forms will deadname many people. When we're paying people for their time and expertise, we do so out of respect for their lived experiences and personal interpretations of the world around them, and we should be looking to avoid ways of inadvertently causing harm. Additionally, because we know that the TGNC community is more likely than the general population to struggle to keep jobs and homes,[8] the faster we can pay people the better. For those of us in libraries, let's keep this in

8. I rely on the US Transgender Survey for this insight. Sandy E. James et al., "The Report of the 2015 U.S. Transgender Survey" (Washington, D.C.: National Center for Transgender Equality, 2016), https://www.ustranssurvey.org/reports. Note especially chapters 9 and 13.

mind when our institution wants to invite people to speak to us about Diversity, Equity, and Inclusion.

In cases where our libraries directly benefit from staff members being active in community work, we can be mindful of that struggle. In some cases, the community work directly benefits the library, as in the case of LaTOHP when oral histories were donated to the Special Collections.[9] Sometimes the benefit is less direct. For example, community work can cultivate staff who are sensitive to community needs and who bring that with them when they represent the library to patrons. There are many ways to communicate that this work is important and valued. In institutions with tenure requirements, we can advocate that this work is recognized for tenure and promotion. Less formally, management can communicate that community work can be done during the work day.

Additionally, we can be mindful when things are happening in the communities within which our colleagues work. For example, the 2021 Louisiana legislative session was a tough time, as four anti-trans bills were introduced and a significant amount of time, energy, and attention was required to combat them. As colleagues, we could let our co-workers know we understand that this is a distraction and a drain on an individual's energy and attention. As supervisors, we could let folks know that we give them space to take care of themselves, even if that means some deadlines will need extensions. It can be simple, and it could mean a lot.[10]

If we want our spaces to be a place for community participation, it's also important to think about access to them. Especially in the cases where our spaces are restricted, such as our special collections reading rooms, what steps could we take to make them more approachable for our communities? Do we require state identification for people to use

9. Though not affiliated with LSU, LaTOHP assists interested interviewees in donating their interviews to the T. Harry Williams Oral History Center at LSU for long-term preservation and access. The holdings of the Center eventually make their way to LSU Libraries Special Collections.

10. We focus on the TGNC community, but of course everything here is relevant to everyone and it's unfortunately easy to think of examples for the AAPI and Black communities, among others.

our space and collections? What level of wiggle room do we have for this? If we absolutely need patrons to show IDs, how can we train our front-facing staff to respectfully handle situations in which the names on identification cards do not match what staff might expect based on the physical appearance of the patron? In many places, names are difficult and expensive to change. We know that many of us in the TGNC communities can look very different in person than in our ID photos. We also know that not everyone wants to change their name or update gender markers on identification. When we acknowledge that the world is large and beautiful and diverse, we have to change some of our practices that were built for a world of static identity.

These changes can be easy. We can have training to prepare our front-facing staff for these scenarios, and a clear line of authority for whom to contact if questions arise. Especially in the case of those of us using student labor at front desks, let's ensure that they know whom to contact if they're unsure how to proceed.

A similar situation exists for registration requirements. Do our systems allow for easy name changes or use of non-legal names? If we're asking for gender information, do we really need it? What gender options are patrons presented with? Many of us in the library field do have some say over our forms and the training of our front-facing staff. I hope we'll consider opportunities that make our spaces more approachable.[11]

Lastly, I hope that we, as library workers, can all think about how to build a system of community engagement that will outlive us. Passionate people come and go, and leadership changes. What steps can we take to ensure that any progress we make doesn't simply get forgotten or reversed as soon as we retire or take other jobs? What policies can we create, what onboarding procedures can we adopt that pass values of inclusivity and connection to future generations of library workers? Again, to a significant extent, this is something we have some control

---

11. For additional reflections on creating respectful spaces for TGNC communities on forms and online, see Erin White, "Trans-Inclusive Design," A List Apart, May 9, 2019, https://alistapart.com/article/trans-inclusive-design/.

over in our libraries. We can help set a tone of acceptance and an expectation that new hires carry on the legacy of community engagement.

Conclusion

My experience in LaTOHP and other community projects, combined with my time as a library worker, allow me to see both the pitfalls and promise of combining and separating institutional work from community work. I am appreciative and cautious: appreciative of the resources and experience my role as a librarian affords, and cautious that too strong a link with my institution could undermine my community work. I hope that the thoughts and observations in this chapter assists library workers interested in starting community work, as well as all library workers hoping to make their institution a site of community engagement.

Bibliography

James, Sandy E., Jody L. Herman, Susan Rankin, Mara Keisling, Lisa Mottet, and Ma'ayan Anafi. "The Report of the 2015 U.S. Transgender Survey." Washington, D.C.: National Center for Transgender Equality, 2016. https://www.ustranssurvey.org/reports.

"Last Call: New Orleans Dyke Bar History Project." Last Call: New Orleans Dyke Bar History Project. Accessed October 4, 2021. http://www.lastcallnola.org/.

Louisiana Trans Oral History Project. "Interview with Dre Tarleton." Accessed October 4, 2021. https://www.louisianatransoral-history.org/interview-with/dre-tarleton.

Louisiana Trans Oral History Project. Messages of Support from Our Cis Allies. Accessed October 4, 2021. https://www.youtube.com/watch?v=mH4qvh1eRJI.

White, Erin. "Trans-Inclusive Design." A List Apart, May 9, 2019. https://alistapart.com/article/trans-inclusive-design/.

Ziegler, S. "Let's Use What Works: The Radical Archives of Philadelphia and Traditional Archival Literature." In *Informed Agitation: Library and Information Skills in Social Justice Movements and Beyond*, 105–17. Sacramento, CA: Library Juice Press, 2014.

About the Author

Sophie Ziegler (they/them) is a librarian with over ten years of experience in cultural heritage institutions; they are currently the Head of Digital Programs and Services at LSU Libraries in Baton Rouge. In 2020, they founded the Louisiana Trans Oral History Project to collect, preserve, and promote the transgender and gender non-conforming communities in Louisiana.

Section 6:

Professional Reflections

Visions of Liberation: Notes by a Trans Puerto Rican Librarian on LIS Oppression

Khalila Chaar-Pérez

Keywords: transgender BIPOC, social justice, LIS education, vocational awe, counternarratives

> "May you discover the enlivening power of darkness within yourself. May it nourish your rage. May your rage inform your actions, and your actions transform you as you struggle to transform your world."
> — Susan Stryker, "My Words to Victor Frankenstein above the Village of Chamounix: Performing Transgender Rage"[1]

> "In the future imperfect, which is to say, in that commingling of temporalities wherein the past is brought forth to the future to give rise to the present, Black (Trans) Lives Matter provides a conceptual framework to understand the ongoing struggle in the present by way of a future (aspiration) in which black lives *will have mattered* to everyone."
> —C. Riley Snorton, *Black on Both Sides: A Racial History of Trans Identity*[2]

When a friend shared with me the call for papers for this anthology, I felt elated. Finally, I told myself excitedly, there will be a book *about* and *by* trans voices in Library and Information Studies (LIS)![3] The lack of

1. Susan Stryker, "My Words to Victor Frankenstein above the Village of Chamounix: Performing Transgender Rage," in *The Transgender Studies Reader*, ed. Susan Stryker and Stephen Whittle (Routledge, 2006), 254.

2. C. Riley Snorton, *Black on Both Sides: A Racial History of Trans Identity* (Minneapolis, MN: University of Minnesota Press, 2017), 197-198.

3. I use trans here as an all-encompassing term for all possible identities and experiences outside the (cis)gender binary, from genderqueer and non-binary to trans women and men. I do acknowledge the term's limitations, especially its potential of erasing the many "gendered" forms of being

engagement with the needs and experiences of trans people is a deep-seated problem in LIS. This oppressive silence can be detected in many areas of the field today, from the limited amount of research about our communities to the frequent flattening of our identities beneath the LGBTQIA+ umbrella. For instance, this silence was evident in the 2021 conference of the Association of College & Research Libraries (ACRL). On one hand, I was heartened by how many of the presenters did the urgent work of confronting systemic racism through the lens of critical race theory. On the other hand, only one out of more than 300 presentations focused on the topic of trans inclusion; the four presentations that did examine LGBTQIA+ issues did so without touching on trans matters in a substantive manner. I was struck by the lack of discussion about trans people, especially since we were already witnessing the onslaught of anti-trans laws. As a non-binary trans woman, I couldn't help but feel disillusioned about this silence.

Throughout my experience as a full-time LIS student, I experienced a similar reticence. On the surface, I cannot say it was a directly oppressive environment. At the time, I had recently come out as trans and was a bundle of nerves. Like many other trans folks, I obsessed about how I would be perceived, how I would be read, how people would react to me, and how I would react to people's reactions, in a never-ending chain of dysphoric obsessions. I was relieved when I learned that my cohort and professors were seemingly accepting, at least in the courses I signed up for. There were some problems, serious problems that perhaps I should have confronted more actively and with more forcefulness, *in community* with my fellow non-cisgender students (aside from me, two of my peers identified publicly as such) as well as those instructors and students who were actively committed to social justice. Still, I should recognize that I did not have the drive to critique or protest much as the COVID-19 pandemic emerged during the halfway point of the program. Unlike the millions of folks who lost their jobs at this time, I was privileged to

that cannot be captured by the identity-based framework of Anglo-American trans studies.

have a part-time gig that was already remote. What little energy I had was focused on work, self-care, and trudging ahead amid a deepening crisis at the heart of a nation born out of racial capitalism. In admitting these limitations (my personal limitations and those that are imposed by my context), not only do I recognize my activist guilt but also seek to cultivate, as adrienne maree brown tells us in *Pleasure Activism*, a space for joy in the struggle for liberation.[4] This essay represents part of this process of reflective storytelling and hopes, not only to articulate a trans critique of LIS, but also to form ideas that help imagine, as the Zapatistas would say, "a world where many worlds fit."[5] There is an evident need for critical storytelling and self-ethnographies of the LIS graduate experience; such counter-narratives can provide a site that not only subverts the status quo but also imagines "many worlds" built on liberation and joy. This text aims to be part of this conversation.

Vocational Awe in the LIS Program

Months before classes started, I already had to face the problem of institutionalized oppression: the program's application form provided only two gender options, male and female. When I applied, things were clearing up for me in terms of my gender identity; after a few months of identifying as gender queer, I embraced myself fully as a transfeminine person and began my transitioning journey. As tends to happen when I encounter the gender binary in documents like this one, my body swelled up with frustration and dysphoria. But I breathed in and out and brushed aside those sensations and promptly filled out the form, not giving much thought to the experience until the fall semester began.

In my first meeting with the program's advisor, they made an effort to apologize about the application's lack of gender inclusion and promised

4. adrienne m. brown, *Pleasure Activism: The Politics of Feeling Good* (Chico, California: AK Press, 2019).

5. Subcomandante Marcos, "'No!' To the War in the Balkans," in *Our Word Is Our Weapon: Selected Writings*, ed. Juana Ponce de León (New York: Seven Stories Press, 2002), 197.

that it would be corrected in the future. As I corroborated the next year, the program's application did become more inclusive and now includes "non-binary" and "prefer not to disclose" options as well as an "another" field where the applicant can write in their gender. But this is not enough. The application form should be revised so that applicants can choose more than one option, such as when folks identify as both non-binary and woman. Individuals should have the freedom to fully identify as they desire when answering gender questions—in any context. At the same time, such an easily corrected issue is symptomatic of a more profound reality, a reality of less visible but harmful acts against trans people that was reproduced through the lack of any public recognition of the problem by the department. The issue of gender options could have (and should have) been seen as a useful starting point for discussing and addressing the broader patterns of exclusion of trans communities in and through LIS. LIS workers deal with gender-exclusionary attitudes, policies, and practices in the workplace all the time, and LIS programs should tackle these topics directly. Moreover, LIS faculty and staff have a responsibility to hold themselves accountable for their role in these marginalizing practices and the structures of oppression that generate them. Truth be told, the program's general aim is not to address the structures of oppression.[6] But in some classes I even failed to encounter the diversity practices that have become increasingly normalized in higher education, such as pronoun go-rounds.

In addition, two students were misgendered publicly on various occasions by both their cohorts and faculty members. As it happened with the application, nothing was said or done about these hurtful acts (at least not publicly). Having experienced the injury of being misgendered numerous times myself, I felt for my fellow students and was also concerned that it could happen to me (luckily this was not the case).

---

6. I should acknowledge that I had the luck of taking classes with two supportive professors who did recognize some of the systemic problems discussed here and addressed them in class. At the same time, their power in the program and the school that houses it wais limited by their status as non-tenure-track faculty.

However, aside from proposing a pronoun go-round in a class and reminding a student to use the correct pronouns for a peer, I did not do much to confront this pattern of affronts. Looking back, I sometimes tell myself that I could have been more critical and that I could have initiated some form of dissent or at least discussion among my cohort. But one must admit that it is hard to muster the necessary energy to protest and organize in the context of an intensive one-year program, where many if not all students have a side-job, especially when you are overworked and dealing with the pandemic.

The structures of contemporary graduate programs make transformative interventions difficult: in having to juggle numerous responsibilities, the only logical goal in the order of things is to plug away until you reach the finish line, if you have the luck and privilege to do so. Even then you must worry about finding a job that not only pays a living wage but also offers a welcoming environment. As is usually the case in higher education, gritty individualism represents the ideal path towards success, while building a critical sense of community and structural transformation is perceived as nonessential or even as creating professional barriers. Challenging structures of oppression is seen as a presumptuous act that interferes with the status quo, a culture where faculty rule over a paternalistic form of expertise that is passed on to students, who are then supposed to pass it on to users, patrons, and perhaps their own students, reproducing a hierarchy of power. It could be said that the seeds of vocational awe partly reside in LIS programs; these are spaces that require students (and non-tenure-track faculty) to sacrifice themselves for the greater good of an idealized profession. As Fobazi Ettarh indicates in "Vocational Awe and Librarianship," this type of awe cancels the possibility of critiquing the structures that shape LIS work, which reinforces the status quo.[7] In turn, this perpetuates the erasure of minoritized groups as well as discussions around how LIS participates in the marginalization of these groups, including trans peoples.

---

7. Fobazi Ettarh, "Vocational Awe and Librarianship: The Lies We Tell Ourselves," *In the Library with the Lead Pipe*, January 10, 2018, https://www.inthelibrarywiththeleadpipe.org/2018/vocational-awe/.

Towards a Trans-BIPOC Critique

Throughout the program, I witnessed this pattern of erasure and marginalization in courses where the discussion of trans issues should have been obligatory. As in the majority of LIS curricula, the content of these courses focused at various levels on how LIS workers engage with user communities (e.g., adult services in public libraries and reference). Sometimes these erasures were subtle. For instance, the subject of LGBTQIA+ users would be brought forward but without any in-depth analysis of LGBTQIA+ communities, their complicated history with libraries, and the differences within these communities. This problem was more evident in a required course that was supposed to deal with the relationship between communities and information professionals. At first, I was excited about the prospect of taking this course, imagining that it would give us the opportunity to scrutinize at least some of the problematic aspects of the treatment of marginalized groups in LIS. But the course ignored LGBTQIA+ issues altogether, except for a module about the conservative attempts to ban Drag Queen Story Hour in public libraries. The censorship of Drag Queen Story Hour certainly deserves critical attention as an example of social discrimination and intellectual freedom in libraries. But the fact that the plights of all LGBTQIA+ people were reduced to this example felt, to say the least, tokenizing. The relative absence of such conversations in the courses I took is characteristic of the generalized bias towards the status quo in LIS. Even as trans elements may be included in a course, they are reduced to being mere stand-ins for diversity that don't speak to the discomforting truths of structural oppression.

In the last semester of the program, the issue of white supremacy came to the forefront with the police murder of George Floyd and the eruption of anti-racist protests across the nation. Like thousands of other university administrators, the (white) dean of the school did the minimum that was required by his role: he denounced the killings of Floyd and other Black folks (but not the police); he condemned systemic racism (but not the school's unbearable whiteness and its own racialized history); and he asked for feedback on how to help the school become a more diverse, inclusive, and equitable place (without convening the school's community to discuss these problems). Meanwhile, the LIS program did not provide an official response, perhaps because the dean's words were perceived as sufficient. In our class on communities and the information professional, the professor also chose to remain silent, which spoke volumes about his position regarding communities of color. This string of silences reaffirmed yet again the LIS program's investment in the status quo, which represents the same status quo that Black folks were fighting against in the streets alongside their supporters.

My representation of these silences may sound too harsh to those who see them as unintentional. But intent is irrelevant when measuring the impact of one's words and actions. If there is a lesson to be learned, it is the need to hold both our institutions and ourselves accountable, which entails expanding our awareness of our own roles in the social hierarchy. This applies to those who, like me, may not be white but enjoy certain racialized or class privileges (full disclosure: I am a light-skinned Puerto Rican with upper-middle-class roots). Although I think of myself as a well-informed anti-racist, I have also had to do some deep soul-searching about my position in the scheme of things, from recognizing my shortcomings and privileges, to understanding how these parts of me have sometimes limited my ability to express solidarity with Black folks and other marginalized peoples. I have learned that I still have a lot to learn, through the process of active and compassionate listening with the knowledge that it is impossible to fully understand those who are not like me. If we wish to dismantle the structures behind trans injustice, we need to reflect on how our own words, actions, and silences might help sustain other structures of oppression, even though we may think our intentions are good. What is at stake in this intersectional approach is the building of a coalitional movement in LIS through which minoritized groups can support and empower each other while centering those who are most vulnerable.

After completing the program, I could not help but feel daunted by the difficulties of challenging the status quo in LIS. But I also looked back warmly to the many valuable exchanges that I had with my fellow students and esteemed mentors about the need to build equity in librarianship. Although those conversations did not seem to transcend the privacy of virtual meetings or the classroom, they still represented flashes of a social justice praxis that reverberates in the gaps and crevices of LIS, thanks to figures like Safiya Umoja Noble and organizations such as We Here.[8] Combining the traditions of critical race theory, feminism, and anticapitalism, this praxis represents a socially responsible thought and practice that addresses the inequities in the profession while also imagining worlds of liberation, including trans liberation. At the same time, the praxis of social justice teaches us that structural inequities are part of a broader intersectional process where the oppression of different social identities overlaps and often converges. From this lens, the struggle for trans liberation is necessarily *intersectional*: being trans and gender-nonconforming intersects with other forms of oppression, especially race. This means considering not only the fact that Black trans women transfemme folks bear the brunt of exclusion, but also how non-Black trans people might also be complicit with white supremacy.

A World Where Many Worlds Fit

How does this praxis of social justice translate to the LIS world then? I could propose a list of best practices, but the reality is that there is

8. I should highlight Noble's collaborations with Sarah T. Roberts, Miriam E. Sweeney, and Nicole Cooke, which articulate a forceful critique of LIS programs: Sarah T. Roberts, et al., "Empowered to Name, Inspired to Act: Social Responsibility and Diversity as Calls to Action in the LIS Context," *Library Trends* 64, no. 3 (2016): 512–32; Nicole A. Cooke, et al., "Social Justice as Topic and Tool: An Attempt to Transform an LIS Curriculum and Culture," *The Library Quarterly* 86, no. 1 (December 21, 2015): 107–24. We Here is a community space for supporting and empowering BIPOC in the field of LIS. The antiracist approach of We Here founders and members can be seen in key publications such as Jennifer Brown, et al., "We Here: Speaking Our Truth," *Library Trends* 67, no. 1 (2018): 163–81, and Sofia Y. Leung and Jorge R. López-McKnight, eds., *Knowledge Justice: Disrupting Library and Information Studies through Critical Race Theory* (Cambridge, MA: MIT Press, 2021).

already a variety of such lists from the perspective of trans people as well as BIPOC. As Z Nicolazzo argues in the conclusion to *Trans* in College*, it behooves us to move beyond the discourse of best practices.[9] Like the outpouring of Diversity, Equity, and Inclusion (DEI) policy statements in response to the George Floyd protests, best practices can easily leave structural oppression unaddressed by approaching inequity as if it were just a problem of individual behavior. Although these are important steps, trans liberation is not simply about respecting other people's pronouns or having more diverse programming. It is about cultivating a culture where, as Nicolazzo suggests, everyone is "involved in interrogating, exposing, and resisting the insidious ways gender regulates all our lives."[10] In comprehending how gender mediates our way of being and knowing, we can examine how LIS and library work are particularly gendered and how they might reinforce normative ideas of gender. The onus then is not on trans folks but on everyone to challenge the status quo and consider how they enable (or subvert) the gender conventions that fuel the fires of misogyny and transphobia. And since gender is embodied and constructed differently in different contexts, this also means looking at cisnormativity as it intersects with other structures of oppression, with racial capitalism at its center. In this way, trans liberation connects with other struggles and can attend to the broader, intersectional praxis of social justice.

Even as the fulfillment of this vision in LIS seems far away, imagining other worlds—worlds without patriarchy, white supremacy, and capitalism—is part of the process of liberation. If I were to imagine an LIS utopia, it would integrate an intersectional and transdisciplinary approach to all its curricula by fostering a critical community of practice where students, especially those who are most vulnerable, have a real voice and influence in the scheme of things. Such a community would address the oppressive structures that have shaped LIS while articulating

9. Z. Nicolazzo, *Trans* in College: Transgender Students' Strategies for Navigating Campus Life and the Institutional Politics of Inclusion*, First edition. (Sterling, VA: Stylus Publishing, 2017).

10. Nicolazzo, *Trans* in College*, 139.

a praxis of social justice, which teaches us that those structures affect us all. At the same time, this community would cultivate a pedagogy of care that, on one hand, understands learning as a joyful, open-ended journey and, on the other, rejects the hyper-productive, instrumentalist ethos of late capitalism. This would also necessitate full economic support, particularly for those who need it to join this community, a community where hierarchies should not be in place. There is much to be done to even begin imagining such a vision collectively. But as I write these words, dismay is displaced by a sense of radical hope that, inspired by this book and many other companions of liberation, looks to a future where actual equity is achievable. As Audre Lorde reminds us in "Learning from the 60s," "Revolution is not a one-time event. It is becoming always vigilant for the smallest opportunity to make a genuine change..."[11]

Bibliography

brown, adrienne maree. *Pleasure Activism: The Politics of Feeling Good.* Chico, CA: AK Press, 2019.

Brown, Jennifer, Jennifer A. Ferretti, Sofia Leung, and Marisa Méndez-Brady. "We Here: Speaking Our Truth." *Library Trends* 67, no. 1 (2018): 163–181. https://doi.org/10.1353/lib.2018.0031.

Cooke, Nicole A., Miriam E. Sweeney, and Safiya Umoja Noble. "Social Justice as Topic and Tool: An Attempt to Transform an LIS Curriculum and Culture." *Library Quarterly* 86, no. 1 (2015): 107–24. https://doi.org/10.1086/684147.

Ettarh, Fobazi. "Vocational Awe and Librarianship: The Lies We Tell Ourselves." *In the Library with the Lead Pipe*, (January 2018). https://www.inthelibrarywiththeleadpipe.org/2018/vocational-awe/.

---

11 . Audre Lorde, "Learning from the 60s," in *Sister Outsider: Essays and Speeches* (Berkeley, CA: Crossing Press, 1984).

Leung, Sofia Y., and Jorge R. López-McKnight, eds. *Knowledge Justice: Disrupting Library and Information Studies through Critical Race Theory*. Cambridge, MA: MIT Press, 2021.

Lorde, Audre. "Learning from the 60s." In *Sister Outsider: Essays and Speeches*. Berkeley, CA: Crossing Press, 1984.

Marcos, Subcomandante. "'No!' To the War in the Balkans." In *Our Word Is Our Weapon: Selected Writings*, ed. Juana Ponce de León. New York: Seven Stories Press, 2002.

Nicolazzo, Z. *Trans* in College: Transgender Students' Strategies for Navigating Campus Life and the Institutional Politics of Inclusion*. First ed. Sterling, VA: Stylus Publishing., 2017.

Roberts, Sarah T., and Safiya Umoja Noble. "Empowered to Name, Inspired to Act: Social Responsibility and Diversity as Calls to Action in the LIS Context." *Library Trends* 64, no. 3 (2016): 512–532. https://doi.org/10.1353/lib.2016.0008.

Snorton, C. Riley. *Black on Both Sides: A Racial History of Trans Identity*. Minneapolis, MN: University of Minnesota Press, 2017. https://doi.org/10.5749/j.ctt1pwt7dz.

Stryker, Susan. "My Words to Victor Frankenstein above the Village of Chamounix: Performing Transgender Rage." In *The Transgender Studies Reader*, eds. Susan Stryker and Stephen Whittle, 244–256. New York: Routledge, 2006.

About the Author

Khalila Chaar-Pérez (she/they) works as outreach and needs assessment archivist at the People's Media Record, the digital archive of the Movement Alliance Project. Her writings have appeared in *Small Axe*, *Global South*, *Uncle Tom's Cabins: The Transnational History of America's Host Mutable Book*, and the *U.S. Intellectual History* blog. She is interested in exploring civic data literacy, digital scholarship, and information literacy through a critical framework that challenges the historical marginalization of BIPOC, queer, trans, and disabled people.

Asking the Bigger Questions: The Problem with LGBT+ Allyship in Libraries

Jordan Dias Correia

Keywords: serving transgender patrons, transphobia, transgender support in libraries, library social media

The Library and Information Science (LIS) field often touts itself as a pillar of democracy, information access, and inclusion. It's based on the foundation that information and materials should be provided to patrons regardless of content, origin, etc. and that the spaces offered by the libraries are open to all, regardless of how they identify and how they will be using the space. There are some limitations, such as policies and community needs, but libraries are supposed to be safe havens and a resource for patrons. Based on my time working towards my master's degree in LIS and partnering with libraries, I've realized that libraries do not adequately support trans people. This is because library workers often fail to address bigger questions when concerns of inclusion and diversity occur.

Every few months, it is revealed that J.K. Rowling is transphobic; more specifically, as many scholars have observed, she is a trans exclusionary radical feminist (TERF). In the summer of 2020, she doubled down on her views and posted on her blog what some have called her "transphobic manifesto."[1] She lists concerns about the "transgender

1. Kalhan Rosenblatt, "J.K. Rowling Doubles down in What Some Critics Call a 'Transphobic Manifesto'," NBC News (NBCUniversal News Group, June 11, 2020), https://www.nbcnews.com/

phenomenon," concerns that many activist groups and advocates have debunked.[2] Her essay and views have had real-world impact on legislation in both the United Kingdom and United States. For example, a senator in the United States cited the J.K. Rowling essay to argue against expanding anti-discrimination protections for LBGT+ people.[3] As a result of this reassertion of misinformation (and perhaps disinformation) and the consequences it's generated, there have been numerous debates, arguments, and discussions about how transgender people are treated and portrayed within the publishing world and within novels.

There have been discussions within various online communities associated with the LIS field about what to do in light of this new revelation. I'm active in library groups on Facebook and Twitter where I've been able to observe some of the conversations that have emerged. The most joyful thing about reading these comments was the concern librarians showed for their trans patrons. They truly want to make their space safe, open, and accessible to underrepresented patrons and are trying their best to achieve this goal.

The least joyful, and sometimes downright offensive, part was the repetitive questions that were posed. Many librarians questioned whether they should continue carrying her books or holding the same Harry Potter-themed programs. Some argued that they shouldn't in light of this news or, at the very least, tone it down. Others stated that they have had high turnout for those programs or good circulation statistics for the books, so it would be impractical to weed them out. Reader's advisory was also debated, but with less frequency. Librarians mostly wanted alternative books that included similar themes to Harry Potter, but that were more diverse and affirming of others. Another question

---

feature/nbc-out/j-k-rowling-doubles-down-what-some-critics-call-transphobic-n1229351.

2 . Rosenblatt; Claire Lampen, "J.K. Rowling Triples down on Transphobia," The Cut (The Cut, July 5, 2020), https://www.thecut.com/2020/07/j-k-rowling-writes-essay-defending-her-transphobic-remarks.html.

3. Lily Wakefield, "Republican Senator Quotes JK Rowling's Essay on Trans People to Shut down a Vote on LGBT+ Rights," PinkNews, June 19, 2020, https://www.pinknews.co.uk/2020/06/19/jk-rowlings-lgbt-rights-trans-essay-republican-senator-james-lankford-equality-act-supreme-court-discrimination/.

that was constantly being brought up was whether those who had them should cover up their Harry Potter tattoos. Many felt that, while it had meant a lot to them at the time, it now felt uncomfortable to wear artwork inspired by someone who holds transphobic views. The tattoo conversation went into so much depth that people were discussing the intricacies of getting a cover up versus removing a tattoo, suggesting what to look for in a tattoo artist if they wanted a cover up, and some designs that would make for a good one.

I won't deny that these conversations are important. Views and stereotypes expressed by an author, whether consciously or unconsciously, can influence how a person thinks or feels about a group of people and can impact how people within that group feel about their identity. Small adjustments, such as restructuring reader's advisory or hosting programs based on more diverse literature, *do* help in my opinion. They can introduce new materials and views and can help marginalized patrons see themselves in media.

But there were two main problems with these conversations. The first was that librarians always seemed to center themselves when posing these questions. Even when asking about library services, it sometimes felt as if it was about the library looking bad rather than wanting to support trans people. This leads to the second major issue, one that librarians and professionals in other fields tend to have when discussing major changes: the conversations ran in circles and always went back to the same basic questions. Not once did I see a library worker stop to think about their current trans patrons, how they felt about these issues, and what changes they felt would be adequate. "Do trans people even go to your library?" was a question I repeatedly thought of when reading these comments. Making changes now is amazing, but what exactly were libraries doing before this happened to make trans people feel welcome in their spaces? These actions are only worth half their value if the intended audience isn't there to see it. So many times, it seems that libraries decide to be reactionary rather than proactive when it comes to reaffirming underrepresented groups, in order to save face and uphold their reputation as a progressive institution.

While it is understandably difficult for cis people to understand a trans person's journey, at times it feels as though a surface-level understanding is barely there. During an event, I introduced myself to a librarian. I had only just started hormones so my voice was still high and I was often misgendered as a woman, but my nametag stated my pronouns. When the librarian saw my pronouns, he seemed hesitant to continue speaking with me and soon walked away. In the best-case scenario, he just didn't want to chat with someone new. In the worst-case scenario, he was transphobic and refused to speak with a trans person. I spoke with a different librarian about the incident a few minutes later and she immediately asked if she should write her pronouns in support. I was completely bewildered. Pronouns were not the problem in the interaction; the problem was that the previous librarian read me as a certain gender, and when my pronouns didn't line up with his expectations, he clocked me as trans and refused to speak with me. I was not performing masculinity in a certain way, nor was I being transgender in the "correct" way (e.g., having gone through the physical changes associated with hormone replacement therapy). Putting pronouns in a nametag, while important and inclusive, will most likely not stop that librarian from associating each gender with certain acts and characteristics.

Missing these larger issues and questions leads to direct consequences. Competency courses about the trans community are often grouped with the rest of the LGBT+ community, despite trans people having specific needs that differ from those of the cis members of the community. Information that is about trans people only speaks about pronouns, respecting identity, and not making assumptions. Again, while this is important, it also leaves the burden of education on trans people to explain why certain situations and questions are not appropriate. Cis people also begin to think that these are the main issues facing the trans community, and they almost never deepen their perspective, activism, or critical thought about important topics and issues.

I think libraries and library workers do want to make their spaces welcoming for trans and other underserved patrons. But the hyperfocus on introductory bias trainings and the same circling questions makes it nearly impossible for real changes to be made. Libraries need to reach out to their trans communities to understand how to best serve their needs. They need to broaden their understanding of the trans experience, think more critically about how certain situations impact trans lives, and explore what exactly the real issues are behind their problems. They certainly need to make both minor and major improvements to their services, programs, and how they interact with patrons if they want to be a more welcoming space.

Bibliography

Lampen, Claire. "J.K. Rowling Triples down on Transphobia." The Cut. The Cut, July 5, 2020. https://www.thecut.com/2020/07/j-k-rowling-writes-essay-defending-her-transphobic-remarks.html.

Rosenblatt, Kalhan. "J.K. Rowling Doubles down in What Some Critics Call a 'Transphobic Manifesto'." NBC News. NBCUniversal News Group, June 11, 2020. https://www.nbcnews.com/feature/nbc-out/j-k-rowling-doubles-down-what-some-critics-call-transphobic-n1229351.

Wakefield, Lily. "Republican Senator Quotes JK Rowling's Essay on Trans People to Shut down a Vote on LGBT+ Rights." PinkNews, June 19, 2020. https://www.pinknews.co.uk/2020/06/19/jk-rowlings-lgbt-rights-trans-essay-republican-senator-james-lankford-equality-act-supreme-court-discrimination/.

About the Author

Jordan Dias Correia (he/him) is a PhD student at the Rutgers School of Communication and Information. His research focuses on transgender health within the library and information science field. He received his MLIS from Syracuse University.

Remixing LIS Leadership: Considering Gender-Variant BIPOC—*Are we there yet?*

kynita stringer-stanback & Lorin Jackson

Keywords: Audre Lorde, BIPOC, DEI, disability

The Warrior Poet

When we think of defying gender roles, Black identity, and libraries, one of the first luminaries who come to mind is Audre Lorde. In addition to being lauded as a writer, poet, activist, and librarian, Lorde also was Black, disabled, and a member of the LGBTQ+ community:

> When she returned from Mexico, she enrolled in Hunter College and graduated in 1959. While there she worked as a librarian and spent many leisure hours in Greenwich Village as a member of the gay community. Lorde earned her Master's degree in library science at Columbia University and at the same time worked as a librarian at the Mount Vernon Public Library...She became the head librarian at Town School Library in New York City and held that position until 1968...She [was also] briefly a librarian at Lehman College and City College, and a professor of English at John Jay College and Hunter College.[1]

While Lorde was able to ascend to leadership roles in library administration we wonder, as Black gender non-conforming librarians ourselves, what sacrifices she had to make to attain that leadership? What was the

1. Herb Boyd, "Audre Lorde, Activist, Librarian, Lesbian and Warrior Poet," New York Amsterdam News, December 22, 2016, https://amsterdamnews.com/news/2016/12/22/audre-lorde-activist-librarian-lesbian-and-warrior/.

cost to her well-being, in order to be a part of the oppressive structures built into and around the infrastructure of the library? Is it possible that her immune system was compromised by the work of having to balance her creative brilliance at a time when there were even fewer Black librarians, let alone disabled queer ones? We suspect that it was likely a struggle for her to work in libraries and that attaining leadership demanded much from her, which likely made it difficult for her to manage her health in sustaining ways.

> "I have been a woman for a long time…Beware my smile/I am treacherous with old magic/and the noon's new fury/with all of your wide futures promised/I am woman and not white."[2]

We know that there are several consequences in the library workplace for being Black, a woman, and disabled. There are additional struggles to be had by those who are members of these categories and who are also queer. For non-cisgender people in the library, there are even more significant challenges.

Making Space

Understanding the implications for the oft-touted neutrality of libraries requires an in-depth analysis of the concept of whiteness. In a 2005 article, "Trippin' Over the Color Line: The Invisibility of Race in Library and Information Studies," T. Honma provides context for the ways that whiteness functions as an enabler for the continued subjugation and oppression in the library field: "As these scholars indicate, 'whiteness' works as an invisible and elusive structure of privilege, one that allows for constant reinvention and rearticulation to protect the interests of a white racial ruling class."[3] Not fitting neatly into the status quo of

---

2. Boyd, "Audre Lorde, Activist, Librarian, Lesbian and Warrior Poet."

3. Todd Honma, "Trippin' Over the Color Line: The Invisibility of Race in Library and Information Studies," *InterActions: UCLA Journal of Education and Information Studies* 1 no. 2, pg. 6, (2005): http://dx.doi.org/10.5070/D412000540.

libraries, which are dominated by the employment and leadership of white cisgender women, constitutes a threat to the majority. The perceived threat is to the maintenance of white women's dominance, in numbers and presence, on library staff. If more are hired from other backgrounds, will white, cisgender women become outnumbered and struggle to keep the power systems that are currently in place?

Not representing the predominant cultural identities present in libraries breaks down the bodies, minds, and spirits of those who are not part of the majority. The price of the ticket we pay in order to be present or have the opportunity to work within these library environments is our health.

Many pieces of us are lost in the process of working in libraries. Our initial passion and wonderment at libraries often becomes subsumed by the trauma we experienced. Many BIPOC LGBTQ+ librarians decide to leave the profession due to the common mistreatment experienced. Recruitment and retention of librarians with marginalized backgrounds have been a recurrent issue for decades. These circumstances may be reasons why Lorde sought refuge in the process of creating her own poetry. We believe that her poetry was a balm for the wounds she likely suffered from just existing in the world, let alone her existence and leadership within the world of libraries.

"This shame is going to kill us."—Tarana Burke[4]

A recent podcast episode of "Unlocking Us," by social change leaders Brené Brown and Tarana Burke, included a conversation about their newly-released essay anthology, *You are Your Best Thing: Vulnerability, Shame Resilience, and the Black Experience* (2021). In this conversation, they discuss the notion of "shame resilience." Being shame resilient requires us to name the trauma we experience in order to confront it with the hope of remedying the wound. Burke describes the reality that "coerced

4. Brené Brown, Tarana Burke, and Jason Reynolds, "Brené with Tarana Burke and Jason Reynolds on 'You Are Your Best Thing,'" April 28, 2021, in *Unlocking Us*, podcast, 43:24, https://open.spotify.com/episode/06QDH5SNTwSHmFYN434X2S.

vulnerability"[5] is often required by Black people, whereas those with privilege are allowed to maintain their comfort, withhold vulnerability, and still be successful. Black peoples' lived experience often requires their continual subjugation to be successful, including enduring subjugation in the workplace. This is a direct attack and a denial of our humanity, as Menakem explains:

> ...The cultural operating system of white-body supremacy influences or determines many of the decisions we make, the options we select, the choices open to us, and *how* we make those decisions and choices. The operating system affects us all, regardless of the hue of our skin.[6]

When someone different is given the space to try and step into the leadership realm of the library, the possibilities awaken for a new day, replete with new choices. Opportunities grow to actively challenge the former established patterns that sought to keep libraries exclusionary and closed off from BIPOC and LGBTQ+ people. If we really want to be changemakers, we have to make space for change. We have to allow for differences to be perceived and acknowledge what the introduction of new people into roles that previously did not exist means for all of us. We also have to become okay with getting uncomfortable, as our learning is often predicated upon our ability to step outside of our comfort zone and into the future of libraries. If we require that some of us be vulnerable, we demonstrate equity when we ask that everyone be vulnerable.

While we can identify trends within the lived experiences of Black, disabled, LGBTQ+ people, we also want to acknowledge that part of moving into the future of libraries requires an acknowledgment of the diversity within these lived experiences. A frequent characteristic of discriminatory or oppressive behavior is that they minimize the experiences of different groups into a monolith. This is another form of

---

5. This is a term Lorin and kynita coined. This is not directly said, but is strongly implied by Tarana Burke.

6. Resmaa Menakem, *My Grandmother's Hands*, (Las Vegas, NV: Central Recovery Press, 2017), xix.

oppression that threatens the integrity and possibility of the library being more inclusive of marginalized people within it. We have similarities, but our lived experiences are grounded in our own individual truths. Acknowledging this is an allowance of a "both/and" framework that is more accepting and welcoming than not. We understand the simplicity and ease that comes from stereotyping a group different from your own, but acknowledging the complexity of what it is to be a person, regardless of your background, is a foundational value of truly engaging in diversity, equity and inclusivity (DEI) principles.

Post-Pandemic (Almost)

As we hopefully approach the end of the pandemic, we are facing a new world that is simultaneously more isolated and more open. Stakeholders with power are driving the priorities of institutions. Within library and information science (LIS) leadership, though, our users are pushing us to consider broader and more inclusive communities within libraries.

Public policy dictates social welfare priorities. Such priorities include whether the government invests in corporate welfare and weapons of mass destruction development or programs that increase access to food, healthcare, housing, transportation, and job placement and training. These policies are formed and shaped at universities and colleges across the nation. For example, currently our nation is debating Critical Race Theory. It all started with Christopher Rufo who works at the Heritage Foundation, a conservative think tank based in Washington, DC. Critical Race Theory has become the focus of a media onslaught. On June 24, 2021, the Washington Post reported that in 2020, Critical Race Theory had only been mentioned 132 times on Fox News. By June 24, 2021, it had been mentioned on Fox News close to 2,000 times.[7] This assault on Critical Race Theory by Fox News and the conservative media has

7. Jeremy Barr, "Critical Race Theory is the hottest topic on Fox News. And it's only getting hotter," The Washington Post, June 24, 2021, https://www.washingtonpost.com/media/2021/06/24/critical-race-theory-fox-news/.

led twenty-seven states to pass legislation against it.[8] This is how academics employed by think tanks make public policy changes in real time.

The voices of BIPOC and LGBTQ+ professionals within LIS have not been centered or amplified in the overall discourse about the field. If we articulate our own experiences, we can be discredited, marginalized, and threatened. Sometimes, members of these groups are directly undermined, coerced, harassed, and bullied more often than their white colleagues. Lalitha Nataraj, et al., explain this phenomenon in their article "Nice White Meetings: Unpacking Absurd Library Bureaucracy through a Critical Race Theory Lens" (2020):

> BIPOC, especially Black library workers, may struggle to "assert subjectivity" in collaborative settings because they are entangled in the formidable tasks of both decoding the absurd and naming these practices as absurd to white colleagues and administrators who have a vested interest in maintaining the dominant culture and its common practices. BIPOC risk being cast aside, picked on, terminated, and even chastised publicly and on a wide scale when directly challenging administration or the dominant culture. They are meant to look down or away.[9]

Some of us are fortunate to have the protection of a union in the workplace, but many of us do not. We are not just talking about race, gender, gender identity, gender expression, disability, age, nationality, or creed. We want to confront and include an intersectional perspective, which represents a conglomeration of several overlapping identities, because our focus is on when those identities converge into one body. A person may not be considered human or deserving of equitable treatment and consideration because of the intersecting parts of their

8. "Where Critical Race Theory Is Under Attack," Education Week, June 11, 2020, http://www.edweek.org/leadership/map-where-critical-race-theory-is-under-attack/2021/06.

9. Lalitha Nataraj, Holly Hampton, Talitha R. Matlin, and Yvonne Nalani Meulemans, "'Nice White Meetings': Unpacking Absurd Library Bureaucracy through a Critical Race Theory Lens," *Canadian Journal of Academic Librarianship* 6: (2020): 10-11. https://doi.org/10.33137/cjal-rcbu/v6.34340.

identities. In "Low Morale in Ethnic and Racial Minority Academic Librarians: An Experiential Study" (2021), co-authored by Kaetrena Davis-Kendrick and Ione T. Damasco, we learn that these phenomena impact morale and likely contribute to the low retention rate for BIPOC & LGBTQ+ LIS professionals:

> Minority academic librarians' low morale is not divorced from historic and contemporary events of racism and segregation in the United States and LIS. Respondents considered the ongoing outcomes of institutional racism as they moved through their experience. While historiographies and popular media chronicling LIS civil rights' missteps are increasing, the profession continues to struggle with consistently framing, promoting, and supporting the library profession and library spaces as welcoming to and safe for marginalized racial, cultural, and ethnic groups.[10]

We work in an extremely homogeneous industry as library and information science professionals. When we walk through the doors, we are usually one of one. How many BIPOC LGBTQ+ colleagues work in your library? We ask because the approach that BIPOC and LGBTQ+ perspectives can bring to LIS leadership is urgently needed. We must look at how we have been mentored and trained throughout our careers. What patterns, if any, emerge in our collective experiences? A lot of conferences might have talks about DEI issues around recruitment, but what about retention? How are our organizations demonstrating their commitment to DEI? Have goals and/or standards been set? What does accountability look like and who is being held accountable?

If we look at the stories of April Hathcock (at ALA Midwinter Conference, 2019) and Nikole Hannah Jones (UNC Chapel Hill, 2021), we see that Black intellectuals are often subjected to inhumane treatment

10. Kaetrena Davis-Kendrick and Ione T. Damasco, "Low Morale in Ethnic and Racial Minority Academic Librarians: An Experiential Study," *Library Trends* 68 no. 2, (2019): 193, doi: 10.1353/lib.2019.0036.

for speaking our truth.[11] Black women represent less than 3% of tenured faculty across the nation.[12]

Leadership Remix

It is imperative that administrators, department heads, and team leads understand how to create inclusive spaces within the LIS profession for the protected classes in our nation. People within these leadership positions should receive iterative training on how to better supervise and lead people from diverse backgrounds who may have distinct needs in order to be successful in the workplace.

> For those of us
> who were imprinted with fear
> like a faint line in the center of our foreheads
> learning to be afraid with our mother's milk
> for by this weapon
> this illusion of safety to be found
> the heavy-footed hoped to silence us
> For all of us
> this instant and this triumph
> We were never meant to survive.[13]

---

11. April Hathcock, "ALAMW: What Happened, and What Should Happen Next," *At the Intersection* (blog), January 30, 2019, https://aprilhathcock.wordpress.com/2019/01/30/alamw-what-happened-and-what-should-happen-next/; Nikole Hannah Jones, "Nikole Hannah-Jones Issues Statement on Decision to Decline Tenure Offer at University of North Carolina-Chapel Hill and Accepts Knight Chair Appointment at Howard University," Legal Defense Fund, July 6, 2021, https://www.naacpldf.org/press-release/nikole-hannah-jones-issues-statement-on-decision-to-decline-tenure-offer-at-university-of-north-carolina-chapel-hill-and-to-accept-knight-chair-appointment-at-howard-university/.

12. African American Policy Forum (@AAPolicyForum), "5. Only 2% of full-time professors at degree-granting postsecondary institutions across the country are Black women," Twitter, March 1, 2021, https://twitter.com/aapolicyforum/status/1366515218751385606.

13. Audre Lorde, *The Black Unicorn: Poems* (New York: W.W. Norton & Company, 1995), 31.

In order for our library and information science profession to continue to stay relevant, actionable, measurable steps must be taken toward implementing holistic DEI initiatives. We must put our money where our mouths are. We must have leadership that is willing to engage in brave, difficult conversations that interrogate the hiring practices of their organizations, as well as how to retain talented people from underrepresented backgrounds. We must investigate our Human Resources data and determine why people are coming to our organizations. What are the identities of the people applying to our organizations? Who is leaving? Why are they leaving?

> "If women in the academy truly want a dialogue about racism, it will require recognizing the needs and the living contexts of other women."[14]

The context we bring to research, programming and service helps us build inclusive models that impact our communities in ways that have yet to be imagined. We know why BIPOC & LGBTQ+ people should be in leadership, and all the skills we bring to our profession. Now is the time for those with the platforms to speak about our presence, what we bring, and how we all benefit. The LIS profession needs BIPOC & LGBTQ+ leaders. Making space for us to be in leadership positions in library and information science must become a priority if we truly want the field to be more inclusive and to meet the needs of our dynamic, culturally rich communities.

Bibliography

African American Policy Forum (@AAPolicyForum). "5. Only 2% of full-time professors at degree-granting postsecondary institutions across the country are Black women." Twitter, March 1, 2021. https://twitter.com/aapolicyforum/status/1366515218751385606.

---

14. Audre Lorde, "The Uses of Anger," *Women's Studies Quarterly* 9, no. 3 (1981): 8, http://www.jstor.org/stable/40003905.

Barr, Jeremy. "Critical Race Theory is the hottest topic on Fox News. And it's only getting hotter." *The Washington Post.* June 24, 2021. https://www.washingtonpost.com/media/2021/06/24/critical-race-theory-fox-news/.

Boyd, Herb. "Audre Lorde, Activist, Librarian, Lesbian and Warrior Poet." New York Amsterdam News. December 22, 2016. https://amsterdamnews.com/news/2016/12/22/audre-lorde-activist-librarian-lesbian-and-warrior/.

Brown, Brené, Tarana Burke, and Jason Reynolds. "Brené with Tarana Burke and Jason Reynolds on 'You Are Your Best Thing.'" *Unlocking Us.* April 28, 2021. Podcast, 43:24. https://open.spotify.com/episode/06QDH5SNTwSHmFYN434X2S.

Davis-Kendrick, Kaetrena, and Ione T. Damasco, "Low Morale in Ethnic and Racial Minority Academic Librarians: An Experiential Study. *Library Trends* 68 no. 2, (2019): 174-212. doi: 10.1353/lib.2019.0036.

Hathcock, April. "ALAMW: What Happened, and What Should Happen Next." *At the Intersection* (blog). January 30, 2019. https://aprilhathcock.wordpress.com/2019/01/30/alamw-what-happened-and-what-should-happen-next/.

Honma, Todd. "Trippin' Over the Color Line: The Invisibility of Race in Library and Information Studies." *InterActions: UCLA Journal of Education and Information Studies* 1 no. 2 (2005): http://dx.doi.org/10.5070/D412000540.

Jones, Nikole Hannah. "Nikole Hannah-Jones Issues Statement on Decision to Decline Tenure Offer at University of North Carolina-Chapel Hill and Accepts Knight Chair Appointment at Howard University." Legal Defense Fund. July 6, 2021, https://www.naacpldf.org/press-release/nikole-hannah-jones-issues-statement-on-decision-to-decline-tenure-offer-at-university-of-north-carolina-chapel-hill-and-to-accept-knight-chair-appointment-at-howard-university/.

Lorde, Audre. *The Black Unicorn: Poems.* New York: W.W. Norton & Company, 1995.

Lorde, Audre. "The Uses of Anger." *Women's Studies Quarterly* 9, no. 3 (1981): 7-10, http://www.jstor.org/stable/40003905.

Menakem, Resmaa. *My Grandmother's Hands*. Las Vegas, NV: Central Recovery Press, 2017.

Nataraj, Lalitha, Holly Hampton, Talitha R. Matlin, and Yvonne Nalani Meulemans. "'Nice White Meetings': Unpacking Absurd Library Bureaucracy through a Critical Race Theory Lens." *Canadian Journal of Academic Librarianship* 6 (2020): 1-15. https://doi.org/10.33137/cjal-rcbu/v6.34340.

"Where Critical Race Theory Is Under Attack." Education Week. June 11, 2020. http://www.edweek.org/leadership/map-where-critical-race-theory-is-under-attack/2021/06.

About the Authors

kynita stringer-stanback is an Information Activist.

Lorin K. Jackson (she/they) is the Executive Director of Region 2 Regional Medical Libraries at the Medical University of South Carolina. Their research interests include critical librarianship, social justice in librarianship, prison librarianship, community archives, and zines. Find out more about Lorin and their work at lorinj.dev.

LIS-Gendering: A Dialogue on Gender Diverse Labour in Libraries & Archives

Brian M. Watson (they/them), G Trupp (they/them), Magnus Berg (they/he), M'issa Fleming (they/them)

Keywords: equity, workplace environment, microaggressions, trans competency, precarious labor

Introduction[1]

While there is considerable scholarship on trans and gender diverse patrons, programming, and description, there is very little on the lived experiences of trans and gender diverse librarians, archivists, and information workers—particularly those operating as the sole trans and gender diverse person in their workplace.[2] Further, much of the scholar-

1. B.M. Watson wrote this introduction.

2. B. M. Jennings, "Serving Trans* Patrons in Public Law Libraries: Best Practices for Providing Superior Service to Transgender and Gendernonconforming Patrons," *AALL Spectrum* 21, no. 6 (2017): 33–35; Spencer D.C., Julie Leuzinger, and Jennifer Rowe, "Providing Inclusive Services to Transgender Customers," *Texas Library Journal* 93, no. 3 (2017): 82–83; Jami Kathleen Taylor, "Targeting the Information Needs of Transgender Individuals," *Current Studies in Librarianship* 26, no. 1/2 (2002): 85–109; Laura Wilson, "An Archive for All: How the Transgender Archives Work to Create Community Connections," *American Libraries Magazine* (blog), January 2, 2018, https://americanlibrariesmagazine.org/2018/01/02/uvic-transgender-archives-for-all/; Holling Smith-Borne, "Creating a Welcoming and Inclusive Environment for Transgender and Gender Fluid Music Library Users," *Music Reference Services Quarterly* 22, no. 1–2 (April 3, 2019): 18–29, https://doi.org/10.1080/10588167.2018.1536691; Jamie Campbell Naidoo, "A Rainbow of Creativity: Exploring Drag Queen Storytimes and Gender Creative Programming in Public Libraries," *Children and Libraries* 16, no. 4 (December 12, 2018):

ship on trans and gender diverse people in LIS is written by cis authors, often with little acknowledgement that trans people can, and do, work in LIS. This chapter aims to build community amongst ourselves, as the authors, and to broaden the conversation on our lived experiences and labour as trans and gender diverse librarians, archivists, and information workers. Prior to authoring this chapter, we had never met each other, and as a result of the call for proposals came together based on our shared experiences of being either the only or one of very few trans and gender diverse people in our workplaces.

As research on health problems of minoritized populations demonstrates, this is more than a philosophical problem: when already-marginalized individuals face feedback from others that is incompatible with their self-identity, it can cause an increase in the chances of individuals facing negative psychological effects including depression, anxiety, suicidal thoughts, or resulting physiological problems.[3] One way that

---

12, https://doi.org/10.5860/cal.16.4.12; Brandon Lyttan and Bikika Laloo, "Equitable Access to Information in Libraries: A Predicament for Transgender People," *Journal of Access Services* 17, no. 1 (January 2, 2020): 46–64, https://doi.org/10.1080/15367967.2019.1671850; Aira Huttunen, Noora Hirvonen, and Lotta Kähkönen, "Uncomfortable in My Own Skin – Emerging, Early-Stage Identity-Related Information Needs of Transgender People," *Journal of Documentation* 76, no. 3 (February 14, 2020): 709–29,https://doi.org/10.1108/JD-09-2019-0193; Jeanie Austin, "Chapter 7 Lines of Sight and Knowledge: Possibilities and Actualities of Transgender and Gender Non-Conforming Youth in the Library," in *Advances in Librarianship*, ed. Bharat Mehra, vol. 45 (Emerald Publishing Limited, 2019), 167–96, https://doi.org/10.1108/S0065-283020190000045012; Aubri A. Drake and Arlene Bielefield, "Equitable Access: Information Seeking Behavior, Information Needs, and Necessary Library Accommodations for Transgender Patrons," *Library & Information Science Research* 39, no. 3 (July 2017): 160–68, https://doi.org/10.1016/j.lisr.2017.06.002; Fiona M. Jardine, "Inclusive Information for Trans* Persons," *Public Library Quarterly* 32, no. 3 (July 2013): 240–62, https://doi.org/10.1080/01616846.2013.818856; K.R. Roberto, "Inflexible Bodies Metadata for Transgender Identities," *Journal of Information Ethics* 20, no. 2 (2011): 56–64, https://doi.org/10/bw6v92; Matt Johnson, "Transgender Subject Access: History and Current Practice," *Cataloging & Classification Quarterly* 48, no. 8 (2010): 661–83, https://doi.org/10/bxcvpx; Melissa Adler, "Transcending Library Catalogs: A Comparative Study of Controlled Terms in Library of Congress Subject Headings and User-Generated Tags in LibraryThing for Transgender Books," *Journal of Web Librarianship* 3, no. 4 (November 23, 2009): 309–31, https://doi.org/10/fvxmwg.

3. Ilan H. Meyer, "Prejudice, Social Stress, and Mental Health in Lesbian, Gay, and Bisexual Populations: Conceptual Issues and Research Evidence," *Psychological Bulletin* 129, no. 5 (September 2003): 674–97, https://doi.org/10/

individuals may ameliorate minority stress is through the finding or building of communities or resources from or about people similar to them as a bulwark against the larger society.[4]

At this point we would like to break from the pluralized voice to introduce ourselves:

G: I'm G (they/them), a white, queer, trans, able-bodied, nonbinary person working at a school library on the unceded traditional territory of the Kumeyaay Nation.
M'issa: I'm M'issa (they/them), a white, queer, able-bodied genderqueer raised primarily middle-class in the mid-Atlantic and working as a public librarian for teens in Bulbancha/New Orleans, unceded Chitimacha territory.
Magnus: I'm Magnus (they/he) and I'm an archivist turned special librarian in a broadcasting corporation. I'm also a queer transmasculine person, a person with invisible disabilities, and a white settler on S'ólh Téméxw, the unceded, shared territory of the Stó:lō Nation.
Bri: I'm Brian (bri) M. Watson (they/m) – I'm a white queer crip & nonbinary settler living in Tsleil-Waututh. I'm a PhD student at the University of British Columbia's iSchool focusing on equitable cataloging in Galleries, Libraries, Archives, Museums, and Special Collections (GLAMS). I also serve as the Archivist-Historian of APA's Consensual Non-Monogamy Committee and on the Editorial Board of the Homosaurus.

Bri: In absence of pre-existing literature and context, we as the authors of this chapter drew upon the methods of grounded theory—a qualitative research method that seeks to "ground" theory and academic

ctz7wp; Ilan H. Meyer and Mary E. Northridge, eds., *The Health of Sexual Minorities: Public Health Perspectives on Lesbian, Gay, Bisexual and Transgender Population* (New York, NY: Springer, 2007); Stephen T. Russell and Jessica N. Fish, "Mental Health in Lesbian, Gay, Bisexual, and Transgender (LGBT) Youth," *Annual Review of Clinical Psychology* 12, no. 1 (March 28, 2016): 465–87, https://doi.org/10/gfj4mw; Mike C. Parent et al., "Stress and Substance Use among Sexual and Gender Minority Individuals across the Lifespan," *Neurobiology of Stress* 10 (February 2019): 100146, https://doi.org/10/gf8zsq; Erin Baucom, "An Exploration into Archival Descriptions of LGBTQ Materials," *The American Archivist* 81, no. 1 (March 2018): 65–83, https://doi.org/10/gft4cf.

4. Meyer, 674–97.; Meyer and Northridge, eds.; Russell and Fish, 465–87; Parent et al., 100146; Baucom, 65–83.

discussion in the lived experience of participants.[5] To accomplish this, we set up biweekly discussions and reflections with each other over videoconferencing platforms. These conversations became a space and place for the sharing of stories, microaggression frustration, venting, and comfort. We discussed our experiences separately and in relation to each other, shared hopes for the future, and built community with each other in the process.

Collectively, we represent perspectives from academic libraries, school libraries, public libraries, and special libraries, from two generations of queer folks, but we are limited by being white settlers on stolen land, and we are all privileged by our ability to pursue advanced degrees. We conclude with a question regarding changes for LIS spaces that would welcome and uplift trans and gender diverse librarians, archivists, and information workers.

Dialogue

How do co-workers/staff-members respond to your pronouns?

M'issa: I've been wearing a large-ish button announcing "My pronouns are they/them" on my nametag for about 4 years. Many of my coworkers still struggle to use "they," a lingering inability that I'm sure wearing skirts and dresses to work contributes significantly to. Some are opposed to the grammar of "they" and get impatient when I remind them of my or someone else's pronouns. One joked during a diversity training introduction that his pronouns were "comrade," which was met with approving laughter. I spoke with the trainers afterwards and said that, while I had enough history with "comrade" to speak to him

5. Uwe Flick, *Doing Grounded Theory* (1 Oliver's Yard, 55 City Road London EC1Y 1SP: SAGE Publications Ltd, 2018), https://doi.org/10.4135/9781529716658; Antony Bryant and Kathy Charmaz, *The SAGE Handbook of Grounded Theory* (1 Oliver's Yard, 55 City Road, London England EC1Y 1SP United Kingdom: SAGE Publications Ltd, 2007), https://doi.org/10.4135/9781848607941.

directly, ideally they'd be prepared to address this kind of passive taunting in future introductions.

Luckily, my most direct, departmental co-workers adjusted without much trouble; several of our regular teens had asked for us to use "they" and folks had put in earnest practice. My then-boss allowed my pronouns in my email signature and followed up with HR and our Equity Taskforce to the extent that, eventually (three years later), they made a clear system-wide indication that everyone was welcome to do so. She is cisgender and opted to include her pronouns in her signature around the same time as I included mine, making it clear this was normal/acceptable. An educational article she posted on the managers' forum allowed other branches' managers a chance to consider this use of "they" as well.[6]

I don't have a lot of hope that we'll be able to staff-train resistance away, nor do I believe this should be given priority over the more immediate and pressing concern of addressing racial inequity and injustice in our system. I am attempting small-scale education for the sake of my own and other trans and gender diverse coworkers' comfort and safety, while advocating in whatever ways are available for our library to examine what we can do to dismantle systemic oppression in every form.

Magnus: Early in my career, and shortly after I first came out, this was a huge problem for me. I was misgendered constantly and each time it felt like a knife slicing through me. I initially only used they/them pronouns but eventually broke down and started using he/they because I couldn't handle the alternative any longer. This situation doesn't seem to improve no matter where you work. When I was volunteering at an LGBT archive, I had multiple people make ignorant remarks about how my pronouns were grammatically incorrect or asking why I "decided" to be trans. One of the most frustrating situations I've encountered is the defensiveness of colleagues when confronted about repeatedly

6. Alison Green, "How to Get Better at Using a Coworker's Nonbinary Pronouns," Ask a Manager, October 27, 2019, https://www.askamanager.org/2019/10/how-to-get-better-at-using-a-coworkers-nonbinary-pronouns.html.

misgendering me. I get misgendered far less often now that I pass more regularly, but similar to M'issa, I have noticed a reluctance among some members of the profession to change their pronoun use.

G: I feel that pain for sure, I'm definitely misgendered pretty much all of the time. I exclusively use they/them though, so I do recognize that because of the binary imposed by our white supremacist and colonial systems, this is likely going to happen a lot. I definitely feel myself restricting and changing my presentation to be more masculine at work, because I am usually read as a woman. I can also feel the discomfort coworkers have if I correct them on my pronouns, if they have to refer to me in the third person, or if they have to use an honorific to refer to me. This usually manifests in misgendering, an awkward moment of them realizing that they don't know how to refer to me but don't want to ask, or them just not addressing me at all.

How do patrons and library partners respond to unfamiliar pronouns?

G: I feel like I get a wide range of responses to my pronouns. I have a little pin on my work badge that says they/them, and when I do class visits, I use the title Mx. and explicitly give my pronouns, and explain what they mean. For almost all of the students, it is their first time meeting someone who uses they/them pronouns and a gender-neutral honorific. So, I usually have to answer a lot of questions. On the whole, once they get an explanation, they're pretty accepting. But many students and teachers still read me as a woman, which really contributes to a lot of daily dysphoria and anxiety around my gender presentation. I feel like I have to sacrifice fashion that I like in order to seem more androgynous and "believable" as a nonbinary person—which is incredibly messed up.

M'issa: I second G's emotion! I work with teenagers who, maybe even more so than adults, are looking to drag for cues on someone's gender (whilst figuring out their own). This means that it can feel a little weird to be wearing a dress with a fancy hairdo and trying to explain what being GNC (Gender Non-Conforming) means. Sometimes teens remember and remind each other that I use "they". I try to be as chill as possible when teens scoff; I want them to be able to use the library with as much ease and sense of belonging as is possible and, as the adult in the situation, I have more room to choose my reaction before I respond. The trick here is that I'm also modeling behavior for how any trans and gender diverse teens in the space might handle the situation, so I still want to indicate that it's acceptable to request the pronouns I prefer and ask people to respect them.

Magnus: I no longer work in a public-facing role but when I did, I had several situations at the reference desk where patrons made uncomfortable comments about my perceived age and how I looked too young to do my job, sometimes even going so far as to ask to deal with another staff member because they perceived me to be younger than the university students I was serving. This is a pretty common microaggression faced by trans masculine people, but one that's not talked about very often in my experience. I even had a colleague publish a social media post identifying me as a student despite the fact that I was a full-time staff member and had already completed my master's.

What has been your experience with conversations around gender in the field/workplace? How has being trans/gender diverse impacted that?

Magnus: This is obviously a huge problem when we talk about gender writ large within Western (neo-colonial) society, but these conversations look different in LIS because of the feminization of the profession as well as its demographic makeup. Since most librarians/archivists are white cis heterosexual women—in addition to being settlers, able-bodied, and neuro-typical—the frame of reference for most of my colleagues has been undoubtedly a white cis feminist one. Often when we talk about gender, both within the library/archive and the institution more broadly, we are talking about cis women specifically, and usually cis white women. Cis white women in the field are quick to complain about the feminization/sexualization of the field, the preponderance of cis men in leadership positions, parental leave, or imbalanced home responsibilities without considering how these issues impact, or do not impact, gender diverse and/or queer people. Issues that are specific to trans and gender diverse people are almost never discussed, considered, or advocated for during conversations about gender.

G: Exactly! In school libraries this is doubly true because the makeup of both education and librarianship are very similar when it comes to race, gender, sexuality, and ability. Whenever I am able to bring up trans and gender diverse-specific issues with regards to gender, I almost always get some variant of "I never even thought about that!"

How have you responded when facing harassment and microaggressions from coworkers and supervisors?

G: I have been privileged to have been in LIS spaces that are not overtly transphobic, but in my workspaces, I continue to experience lots of different microaggressions. I have had the legitimacy of my name and identity continuously called into question and have had co-workers be antagonistic about pronouns. I usually end up correcting in the moment and later venting to my friends or to colleagues that I'm close with. I recently joined the Trans and Gender Diverse LIS Network, which has definitely been helpful for my mental health.

Magnus: Similar to G, I have had co-workers not be respectful of my pronouns or question their legitimacy. I have also been in work situations where I faced repeated, targeted harassment from a co-worker based on my gender identity and sexual orientation, as well as on the race of my partner. In my personal experience, I have found the dismissiveness of colleagues about transness to be the most common microaggression and have been repeatedly silenced by cis colleagues who were more interested in having a token trans person on their committee than they were in considering the experiences of trans and gender diverse people and our legitimate grievances.

How has the emotional weight of being the only trans and gender diverse LIS worker impacted your work or life?

Magnus: While I have sometimes been around other trans and gender diverse people when volunteering in LGBT+ community archives, I have otherwise always been the sole out trans person in my workplace(s). I find the emotional weight that comes with that to be the most difficult aspect of working in this field. Especially as a precariously employed person, I often feel that I have to couch what I say and how I present myself. It is also worth considering not only the emotional weight of being the only trans and gender diverse worker but how that impacts wider policies and our ability to function within the system. Because I am precariously employed and have had to move cities/provinces/states/countries multiple times, I have had to put my transition on hold multiple times and have sometimes not been able to get on a waitlist because I wouldn't be in a particular area long enough. This presents an additional burden that, ultimately, negatively impacts my mental health and self-perception.

G: Magnus, I'm sorry. These systems are so incredibly fucked up. I totally feel all of what you said here. I was lucky when I was first entering the field to have met trans folks in LIS online and in person, but since then I've been the only out trans person at my workplace. In addition to being queer and trans, I'm also just in a very different place in terms of age, politics, and lifestyle (haha) than my colleagues, which can make it difficult to relate to coworkers.

Resilience is a common topic in LIS right now. How do you stay resilient? Alternatively, how do you problematize resiliency as a conceptual framework?

Magnus: I personally have a huge problem with resiliency as a management fad and am skeptical of any management/business fad that intersects with LIS. "Resiliency" is implicitly ableist, which is not usually acknowledged by those that champion it. What do we mean when someone is *not* resilient? That they suffered burnout? Or a mental health crisis? Why are we putting the onus on workers rather than management or the work environment? As marginalized people, we have already demonstrated resilience through our own survival, but what does that say about those of us that did *not* survive for any number of legitimate reasons? To champion resiliency in the field is to write off the labour issues that are currently vexing LIS and to place the responsibility on LIS workers to accept precarious, abusive, and/or toxic work environments with a smile.

G, Bri, and M'issa: [resounding agreement]

How does being trans and gender diverse influence the kinds of work we do in the library?

M'issa: It motivates me to press for more inclusive library policies, better staff training, and shifts towards equity on every level. I want teens of all varieties to see themselves in the collection and behind the desk, which requires this kind of pressing! I get to do a lot of relationship-building with teens, and conversations about gender are relatively frequent. These conversations and my own experiences informed a presentation on making public libraries welcoming to trans and gender diverse teens, which I gave at Young Adult Library Services Association Symposium.[7] I offered some basic suggestions like having trans and gender diverse folks represented in book displays during any month of the year (not just Pride month) and having these books represent folks with a variety of backgrounds and abilities whenever possible. This effort is only possible because the youth collection development librarian actively builds and maintains collections that prioritize Own Voices materials with an appropriately diverse representation of Black, Indigenous, people of color (BIPOC).

Also, having been an awkward and sometimes secretive queer teen, I'm extra-aware that they won't always ask for the information they need. I actively seek out resources that connect patrons to topics they are less likely to verbally request and make them available throughout the space.

---

7. Fleming, M'issa. 2017, "Supporting Trans* Teens in the Public Library." PowerPoint Presentation, Young Adult Services Symposium, Pittsburgh, PA, November 4, 2017, https://www.ala.org/yalsa/sites/ala.org.yalsa/files/content/events/supporting%20trans%20teens.pdf.

This necessity is not limited to local trans and gender diverse support agencies, help lines, and support groups—other examples include needle exchanges, where to find free showers, suicide hotlines, and domestic abuse support agencies. For as long as trans and gender non-conforming folks experience any level of stigma, reduced access to social services, and a higher need for support structures due to a variety of factors related to stigma, libraries will need to make information readily and visibly available.

G: Echoing all of what you said, because these are very much a part of my librarianship as well! I've definitely worked to push the library and my larger work environment to be a more inclusive space at multiple levels. In school cataloging systems we can be flexible with our cataloging, so I've been creating local subject headings that are much more accurate and affirming than the Library of Congress Subject Headings for trans-related subjects as well as for a variety of other subject headings that are harmful. Also, I get to have a lot of conversations about gender with younger kids that are really impactful. I haven't been on any of the committees you've mentioned, but I co-facilitated my previous school's LGBTQ group, and I also write about trans inclusion as a Writing Team member for a library organization that I'm in.

Magnus: Echoing M'issa and G, the outsider perspective has given me a lot of empathy when it comes to approaching records for my own community, as well as communities I'm not a part of. There are plenty of concepts, systems, or even core tenets to LIS that actively disservice marginalized people, and because I can see those cracks, I try my best to negotiate around, or change, policies and practices when I'm able to. In practice, this means actively redescribing records, not transcribing titles verbatim that use offensive terminology, creating custom thesauri, or modifying my approach to archival appraisal to take into account local record creation and collection practices, or a lack thereof. As trans and gender diverse people, we are forced to find ways of being and living that don't fit within dominant society, and that definitely has an impact on how willing I am to try something new rather than forcing a practice/policy/standard onto a situation that doesn't bear it out.

We often have to work with systems that invoke or enforce gender conformity, cis supremacy, and colonial ideas of gender. How do you work within, or in opposition to, these systems? How does being trans and/or gender diverse impact the kind of work you do?

Bri: There has been a lot of discussion about how diversity work is so often pushed onto those who are already minoritized or who can speak to the experiences of the minorities. For example, Black faculty or librarians being asked to serve on an anti-racist taskforce or initiative, or queer people being asked to serve on yet another gender and/or sexuality diversity committee. These conversations are absolutely valid—pushing identity work onto people on top of their other duties (especially librarians, who tend to be overworked anyways) should be acknowledged as oppressive at best, or actively harmful at worst. These sorts of requests should come with additional pay or other sorts of rewards.

But one of the things that I have not heard or read much discussion about are the *positive* reasons and rewards—excluding the obvious identity-based ones—why a minoritized person would choose to get involved in this work. Here I am thinking specifically of my work on The Homosaurus International LGBTQ+ linked data vocabulary (homosaurus.org) and the Name Change Policy Working Group (NCPWG).

Conversations around intersectionality from the beginning have been about the ways in which multiple marginalized identities further limit and marginalize the folks with them.[8] I think intersections can also be *generating* in that they allow those individuals a unique perspective, understanding, and interpretation of systems—especially systems that divide and classify people into specific groups.

8. Kimberlé Crenshaw, "Demarginalizing the Intersection of Race and Sex: A Black Feminist Critique of Antidiscrimination Doctrine, Feminist Theory and Antiracist Politics," *University of Chicago Legal Forum 1989*, no. 1 (1989): Article 8, https://doi.org/10.4324/9780429499142-5; Kimberlé Crenshaw, "Mapping the Margins: Intersectionality, Identity Politics, and Violence against Women of Color," *Stanford Law Review* 43, no. 6 (1991): 1241–99, https://doi.org/10.2307/1229039.

One reaction to this is to become highly critical, to point at the system as an oppressive force, and to reject it. This is an absolutely fair and important reaction, and I don't want to subtract or malign that reaction or the important work that is a result of it—especially because it's something I do myself! But I'm interested in talking about working within and without systems to make them better; something which is ultimately an act of optimism.

Being nonbinary, polyamorous, queer, and disabled places me in a lot of weird intersections to begin with, so much of my activism work (with the Homosaurus and the NCPWG) is because of these intersections.

Magnus: Bri's perspective here is a really important one and I wanted to respond to it as someone who has fallen into the camp of rejecting the Equity, Diversity, and Inclusion (EDI) industrial complex because of a combination of burnout and negative experiences on diversity and inclusion working groups/committees/task forces that have been less interested in substantive change than they have been on superficial Band-Aids on a broken system.[9] However, as Bri has pointed out, this kind of work is still extremely meaningful and rewarding, and doesn't always take place within a capital C committee. I'm a big believer in making local adaptations to standards to serve local contexts, and much of the work and research I do, particularly from a descriptive standpoint, is heavily influenced by radical empathy. Because I was doing this work as part of my research or regular job, and because I was doing this outside of an explicit EDI committee, I hadn't necessarily considered this to be EDI work. I think this boils down to a flaw, both in my own approach and the general approach, that EDI work reveals in the field: that it is a concerted effort left to a small group of people rather than something that is embedded in our everyday practice. Despite embedding identity work in my practice, I had internalized this viewpoint, which is ultimately a toxic one. Bri's view of working within or without, or

9. Kimberly Springer, "The Design of the Everyday Diversity Industrial Complex," *The Activist History Review*, accessed May 31, 2021, https://activisthistory.com/2018/02/26/the-design-of-the-everyday-diversity-industrial-complex.

against, systems as an act of optimism is a far more constructive way of approaching the potential futures of the field.

What kinds of barriers have you encountered as a trans and gender diverse LIS worker?

Magnus: Precarious labour is endemic to our field and has an adverse impact, not only on trans and gender diverse people, but on all marginalized folks in the field, particularly those of us whose material conditions were suboptimal to begin with. Precarious work has been my biggest barrier in this field and has had a significant impact on my financial, emotional, medical, and familial well-being. To date, I haven't had a single employer cover my moving costs, and at times I have lived out of a couple suitcases to cut down on the cost of relocation. The incessant relocation required to stay employed has made it impossible to save money long-term and has delayed my transition by several years due to constantly switching healthcare systems and providers. Even if I was able to get on a waitlist for surgery, the precarious nature of my employment status has meant that I don't have medical leave and can't afford to take unpaid leave for the amount of time I would need to take off in order to recover. Some of the more rural and/or smaller urban centers to which my partner and I have relocated for my work have had no, or extremely limited, trans competent healthcare options and limited resources/community available for people like us. At this point I have stopped making new friends, because I know I'm going to have to pick up and start over again in a short period of time. Considering that the medical system bars trans and gender diverse people from transitioning if they don't have an adequate support system, this could potentially lock people out of receiving life-saving care. These are major barriers for anyone entering the field and I have been extremely fortunate and privileged to stay in the field despite them.

G: As I mentioned earlier, I have encountered barriers surrounding name and pronouns being respected at work from both coworkers and at an HR level. Putting policies in place that make it easy to receive and enact name changes for emails, directories, and other workplace communication is crucial to changing this, as the lack of these policies in my workplaces has been a source of harm for me. Additionally, if someone has not had the ability to change their legal name, making sure that there is a separation between the internal documents that absolutely require a legal name (such as an employee's personal timesheet for payroll) and the documents shared with other employees, such as shared staffing schedules and directories.

What kinds of changes do you think are necessary for the future?

G: Our libraries and archives should have materials, resources, and programming that show a variety of different trans and gender diverse perspectives and experiences. This representation needs to explicitly include resources by, about, and for trans and gender diverse people who are BIPOC, disabled, neurodivergent, low income, sex workers, those who occupy the intersections of these identities, and more. We need collection development policies that explicitly address curating a collection that has varied representation, and that take into account the historical contexts that have led to marginalization and absence from collections, as well as routine collection assessments.

Bri: Yes, absolutely—collection development is so vital, as these stories, representations, and histories serve as sites of resistance, discovery, and power. I would extend this point a bit further and say that the use of appropriate cataloging, classification, and description becomes even more important in contexts like this. After all, institutions can spend (and after 2020, are spending) a lot of money in the name of Equity and Diversity to acquire the work of the marginalized and minoritized. But if these works are not represented in the catalogs of GLAMS, using accurate, relevant, and timely terminology, they remain undiscoverable and, therefore, cannot serve as sites of power, affirmation, or resistance. Until cultural heritage institutions use my identity terms (crip, queer, demisexual, polyam), they cannot represent me—and the same holds true for others. Much of my work—academic and personal—is oriented towards creating space for redescription, reappropriation, and renaming. In order to achieve these goals, I believe that GLAMS need to invite and encourage more diverse input and turn over "the power to name" to those who are named.[10]

One "imagined future" I have is that the changing of civic identity names would be just as easy as updating a metadata record.[11] Currently, changing one's legal name and gender marker is expensive, onerous, and in some cases not possible without the approval of a judge. Having processes in place to support trans and gender diverse people through this process, whether they are able or willing to do it legally or not, is necessary. Further, as our scholarship increasingly moves to the purely digital, there is no excuse but to allow trans and gender diverse people to change their name post-publication. We are heartened by publishers like the Public Library of Science (PLOS) who republish works with updated names for trans and non-binary authors and call on all publishers and journals to adopt the guiding principles and best practices set by Tanenbaum, et al.[12]

M'issa: I'd appreciate expanded and consistent staff education that includes security and custodial staff and does not rely on trans and gender diverse staff-members. Safety and comfort for trans and gender diverse staff and patrons alike relies heavily on all library workers having a basic understanding and comfort with trans and gender

---

10. Olson, Hope A. *The Power to Name: Locating the Limits of Subject Representation in Libraries*. Dordrecht, The Netherlands; Boston: Kluwer Academic Publishers, 2002.

11. Campt, Tina M. "Quiet Soundings: The Grammar of Black Futurity." In *Listening to Images*. Duke University Press, 2017. Anderson, Reynaldo, and Clinton R. Fluker. *The Black Speculative Arts Movement: Black Futurity, Art+Design*. Rowman & Littlefield, 2019.

12. "Implementing Name Changes for Published Transgender Authors," The Official PLOS Blog, PLOS, October 12, 2020, https://theplosblog.plos.org/2020/10/implementing-name-changes-for-published-transgender-authors/. Note that the policy refers only to trans and non-binary authors and does not mention other gender diverse people; Theresa Jean Tanenbaum, Irving Rettig, H Michael Schwartz, Bri M. Watson, Teddy G Goetz, Katta Speil, and Mike Hill, "A Vision for a More Trans Inclusive Publishing World: Guest Article," Committee on Publication Ethics, January 13, 2021, https://publicationethics.org/news/vision-more-trans-inclusive-publishing-world.

diverse identities. Since this isn't something everyone comes in with, it behooves the library to offer some education, especially as it relates to library policy. A circulation worker without context for trans issues may not understand why it's important to use the "Preferred Name" field in the Integrated Library System (ILS) instead of just the "Name on ID" field, any more than a circulation specialist would naturally understand why it's important to choose an ILS with these two distinct fields. Without context for trans issues, a security guard or custodian could easily mistake policing a trans or gender diverse patron's presence in the bathroom for doing their job to maintain library safety. All staff need this basic information but, if it is available, it is often reserved for the public-facing staff and not the security guards or custodians—a distinction that is problematic and potentially harmful to all parties involved. If the library does not provide education on gender diversity alongside other kinds of anti-oppression training, it leaves the onus of education on the individual trans and gender diverse staff and patrons. Some will be comfortable doing situational, person-by-person education, but certainly not everyone, so it is unwise and unfair to rely on trans and gender diverse patrons and staff to create a safe and welcoming library environment for themselves.

Magnus: Being precariously employed impacts our ability to receive medical care, our ability to transition (when desired), our ability to have community with one another, our level of comfort and safety in the workplace, our ability to care for our loved ones, and most importantly, our ability to feed, clothe, and house ourselves. Job precarity impacts many library workers, but has a disproportionate impact on people with disabilities; BIPOC; queer; neurodivergent; working class; and low-income people, in addition to trans and gender diverse workers.[13]

13. Christine M. Moeller, "Disability, Identity, and Professionalism: Precarity in Librarianship," *Library Trends* 67, no. 3 (2019): 455-70.; Ean Henninger, Adena Brons, Chloe Riley, and Crystal Yin, "Perceptions and Experiences of Precarious Employment in Canadian Libraries: An Exploratory Study," *Partnership: The Canadian Journal of Library and Information Practice and Research* 14, no. 2 (2019): 1-22.; Kaetrena Davis Kendrick, "The Public Librarian Low-Morale Experience: A Qualitative Study," *Partnership: The Canadian Journal of Library and Information Practice and Research* 15, no. 2 (2020): 1-32.; Nicole S.

As contended by Galvan, the current LIS labour landscape is inherently reliant on both "access to time and wealth" and performative whiteness.[14] As LIS becomes increasingly mired in credentialism, the implicit and explicit opportunity costs of years of precarious work, on top of one (or more) graduate degrees, prices out a large contingent of trans and gender diverse workers that face intersecting marginalization. The outright eradication of precarious labour is necessary to address the severe underrepresentation of BIPOC trans and gender diverse people, transfeminine people, and trans people with disabilities in the field.

Conclusion

The intent of this dialogue was to reflect on our experiences as trans and non-binary workers in information organizations and the ways that the field has failed to accommodate or account for our existence or material conditions. These issues are not unique to people of marginalized genders; as contended by Leung & López-McKnight, libraries are more interested in neoliberal progress narratives and cosmetic diversity initiatives and statements than substantive change towards dismantling White Supremacy.[15] White Supremacy, transphobia, cis-normativity, ableism, and colonialism are inextricably linked, and the dismantling of these interlocking oppressive systems is necessary to reach a state of trans and gender diverse liberation and empowerment within LIS.[16] Building community around our realities and discussing hopes for the future

Bernhardt, "Racialized Precarious Employment and the Inadequacies of the Canadian Welfare State," *Journal of Workplace Rights* 5, no. 2 (2015): 1-13.

14. Angela Galvan, "Soliciting Performance, Hiding Bias: Whiteness and Librarianship," *In the Library with the Lead Pipe* (2015), accessed August 29, 2021, https://www.inthelibrarywiththeleadpipe.org/2015/soliciting-performance-hiding-bias-whiteness-and-librarianship/.

15. Sophia Y. Leung and Jorge R. Lopez-McKnight, "Dreaming Revolutionary Futures: Critical Race's Centrality to Ending White Supremacy," *Communications in Information Literacy* 14, no. 1 (2020): 12-26, https://doi.org/10.15760/comminfolit.2020.14.1.2.

16. Brooklyn Leo, "The Colonial/Modern [Cis]Gender System and Trans World Traveling," *Hypatia* 35 (2020): 455, https://doi.org/10.1017/hyp.2020.27.

only represents a first step toward improving the inclusion and material conditions of people of marginalized genders working in information organizations and represents a call to action to our cis colleagues.

Bibliography

Adler, Melissa. "Transcending Library Catalogs: A Comparative Study of Controlled Terms in Library of Congress Subject Headings and User-Generated Tags in LibraryThing for Transgender Books." *Journal of Web Librarianship* 3, no. 4 (2009): 309–31. https://doi.org/10/fvxmwg.

Anderson, Reynaldo, and Clinton R. Fluker. *The Black Speculative Arts Movement: Black Futurity, Art+Design*. Lanham, Maryland: Rowman & Littlefield, 2019.

Austin, Jeanie. "Lines of Sight and Knowledge: Possibilities and Actualities of Transgender and Gender Non-Conforming Youth in the Library." In *LGBTQ+ Librarianship in the 21st Century: Emerging Directions of Advocacy and Community Engagement in Diverse Information Environments*, edited by Bharat Mehra, 45:167–96. United Kingdom: Emerald Publishing Limited, 2019. https://doi.org/10.1108/S0065-283020190000045012.

Baucom, Erin. "An Exploration into Archival Descriptions of LGBTQ Materials." *The American Archivist* 81, no. 1 (March 2018): 65–83. https://doi.org/10/gft4cf.

Bernhardt, Nicole S. "Racialized Precarious Employment and the Inadequacies of the Canadian Welfare State." *Journal of Workplace Rights* 5, no. 2 (2015): 1–13.

Bryant, Antony and Kathy Charmaz. *The SAGE Handbook of Grounded Theory*. London: SAGE Publications, 2007. https://doi.org/10.4135/9781848607941.

Campbell Naidoo, Jamie. "A Rainbow of Creativity: Exploring Drag Queen Storytimes and Gender Creative Programming in Public Libraries." *Children and Libraries* 16, no. 4 (December

12, 2018): 12–22. https://doi.org/10.5860/cal.16.4.12.

Campt, Tina M. "Quiet Soundings: The Grammar of Black Futurity." In *Listening to Images*. Durham, NC: Duke University Press, 2017.

Crenshaw, Kimberlé. "Demarginalizing the Intersection of Race and Sex: A Black Feminist Critique of Antidiscrimination Doctrine, Feminist Theory and Antiracist Politics." *University of Chicago Legal Forum* 1989, no. 1 (1989): 139-67. https://doi.org/10.4324/9780429499142-5.

Crenshaw, Kimberlé. "Mapping the Margins: Intersectionality, Identity Politics, and Violence against Women of Color." *Stanford Law Review* 43, no. 6 (1991): 1241–99. https://doi.org/10.2307/1229039.

D.C., Spencer, Julie Leuzinger, and Jennifer Rowe. "Providing Inclusive Services to Transgender Customers." *Texas Library Journal* 93, no. 3 (2017): 82–3.

Drake, Aubri A. and Arlene Bielefield. "Equitable Access: Information Seeking Behavior, Information Needs, and Necessary Library Accommodations for Transgender Patrons." *Library & Information Science Research* 39, no. 3 (July 2017): 160–8. https://doi.org/10.1016/j.lisr.2017.06.002.

Fleming, M'issa. "Supporting Trans* Teens in the Public Library." Presentation at the Young Adult Services Symposium, Pittsburgh, PA, November 4, 2017. https://www.ala.org/yalsa/sites/ala.org.yalsa/files/content/events/supporting%20trans%20teens.pdf.

Flick, Uwe. *Doing Grounded Theory*. London: SAGE Publications, 2018. https://doi.org/10.4135/9781529716658

Galvan, Angela. "Soliciting Performance, Hiding Bias: Whiteness and Librarianship." *In the Library with the Lead Pipe* (2015). Accessed August 29, 2021. https://www.inthelibrarywiththeleadpipe.org/2015/soliciting-performance-hiding-bias-whiteness-and-librarianship/.

Green, Alison. "How to Get Better at Using a Coworker's Nonbinary Pronouns." Ask a Manager. October 27, 2019. https://www.askamanager.org/2019/10/how-to-get-better-at-using-a-coworkers-nonbinary-pronouns.html.

Henninger, Ean, Adena Brons, Chloe Riley, and Crystal Yin. "Perceptions and Experiences of Precarious Employment in Canadian Libraries: An Exploratory Study." *Partnership: The Canadian Journal of Library and Information Practice and Research* 14, no. 2 (2019): 1-22.

Huttunen, Aira, Noora Hirvonen, and Lotta Kähkönen. "Uncomfortable in My Own Skin – Emerging, Early-Stage Identity-Related Information Needs of Transgender People." *Journal of Documentation* 76, no. 3 (2020): 709–29. https://doi.org/10.1108/JD-09-2019-0193.

"Implementing Name Changes for Published Transgender Authors." The Official PLOS Blog. PLOS, October 12, 2020. https://theplosblog.plos.org/2020/10/implementing-name-changes-for-published-transgender-authors/.

Jardine, Fiona M. "Inclusive Information for Trans* Persons." *Public Library Quarterly* 32, no. 3 (July 2013): 240–62. https://doi.org/10.1080/01616846.2013.818856.

Jennings, B. M. "Serving Trans* Patrons in Public Law Libraries: Best Practices for Providing Superior Service to Transgender and Gendernonconforming Patrons." *AALL Spectrum* 21, no. 6 (2017): 33–5.

Johnson, Matt. "Transgender Subject Access: History and Current Practice." *Cataloging & Classification Quarterly* 48, no. 8 (2010): 661–83. https://doi.org/10/bxcvpx.

Kendrick, Kaetrena Davis. "The Public Librarian Low-Morale Experience: A Qualitative Study." *Partnership: The Canadian Journal of Library and Information Practice and Research* 15, no. 2 (2020): 1-32.

Leo, Brooklyn. "The Colonial/Modern [Cis]Gender System and Trans World Traveling." *Hypatia* 35 (2020): 454-74. https://doi.org/10.1017/hyp.2020.27.

Leung, Sophia Y. and Jorge R. Lopez-McKnight. "Dreaming Revolutionary Futures: Critical Race's Centrality to Ending White Supremacy." *Communications in Information Literacy* 14, no. 1 (2020): 12–26. https://doi.org/10.15760/comminfolit.2020.14.1.2.

Lyttan, Brandon and Bikika Laloo. "Equitable Access to Information in Libraries: A Predicament for Transgender People." *Journal of Access Services* 17, no. 1 (2020): 46–64, https://doi.org/10.1080/15367967.2019.1671850.

Meyer, Ilan H. "Prejudice, Social Stress, and Mental Health in Lesbian, Gay, and Bisexual Populations: Conceptual Issues and Research Evidence." *Psychological Bulletin* 129, no. 5 (September 2003): 674–97. https://doi.org/10/ctz7wp.

Meyer, Ilan H. and Mary E. Northridge, eds. *The Health of Sexual Minorities: Public Health Perspectives on Lesbian, Gay, Bisexual and Transgender Population.* New York: Springer, 2007.

Moeller, Christine M. "Disability, Identity, and Professionalism: Precarity in Librarianship." *Library Trends* 67, no. 3 (2019): 455-70.

Olson, Hope A. *The Power to Name: Locating the Limits of Subject Representation in Libraries.* Dordrecht, The Netherlands; Boston: Kluwer Academic Publishers, 2002.

Parent, Mike C., Andrew S. Arriaga, Teresa Gobble, and Lexie Wille. "Stress and Substance Use among Sexual and Gender Minority Individuals across the Lifespan." *Neurobiology of Stress* 10 (February 2019): 100146. https://doi.org/10/gf8zsq.

Roberto, K.R. "Inflexible Bodies Metadata for Transgender Identities." *Journal of Information Ethics* 20, no. 2 (2011): 56–64. https://doi.org/10/bw6v92.

Russell, Stephen T. and Jessica N. Fish. "Mental Health in Lesbian, Gay, Bisexual, and Transgender (LGBT) Youth." *Annual Review of Clinical Psychology* 12, no. 1 (2016): 465–87. https://doi.org/10/gfj4mw.

Smith-Borne, Holling. "Creating a Welcoming and Inclusive Environment for Transgender and Gender Fluid Music Library Users." *Music Reference Services Quarterly* 22, no. 1–2 (2019): 18–29. https://doi.org/10.1080/10588167.2018.1536691.

Springer, Kimberly. "The Design of the Everyday Diversity Industrial Complex." *The Activist History Review*. Accessed May 31, 2021. https://activisthistory.com/2018/02/26/the-design-of-the-everyday-diversity-industrial-complex.

Tanenbaum, Theresa Jean, Irving Rettig, H Michael Schwartz, Bri M. Watson, Teddy G Goetz, Katta Speil, and Mike Hill. "A Vision for a More Trans Inclusive Publishing World: Guest Article." Committee on Publication Ethics. January 13, 2021. https://publicationethics.org/news/vision-more-trans-inclusive-publishing-world.

Taylor, Jami Kathleen. "Targeting the Information Needs of Transgender Individuals." *Current Studies in Librarianship* 26, no. 1/2 (2002): 85–109.

Wilson, Lara. "An Archive for All: How the Transgender Archives Work to Create Community Connections." *American Libraries Magazine*. January 2, 2018. https://americanlibrariesmagazine.org/2018/01/02/uvic-transgender-archives-for-all/.

Bursting Into the Building

Freyja T. Catton (he/they)

Keywords: job searching, disability, nonbinary, accessibility, surveys

Are you non-compliant?
Do you fit in your box?
Are you too fat, too thin, too loud, too religious, too secular, too prudish, too sexual, too queer, too black, too brown, too whatever-it-is-they'll-judge-you-for-today?
You just may belong on…
Bitch Planet[1]

This chapter is a personal reflection on my experiences as a new graduate of an online Master of Library and Information Studies (MLIS) program in Canada. While my other descriptors distinctly shape my experience of the world, the two identities I want to highlight in this chapter are the ones that are the most significant to me in social spaces and workspaces: that of a nonbinary trans and disabled person.

As I write this, I am in an extremely transitional space as I navigate both my gender transition and a career shift by post-degree job hunting during a pandemic. I started job hunting while in my last semester of school in Fall 2020, convocated in Spring 2021, and as of this writing in Fall 2021, I am still looking. Postings seem to have increased during

1. Kelly Sue Deconnick and Valentine de Landro. *Bitch Planet* (Portland, OR: Image Comics, 2017), back cover.

the summer, but competition continues to be tough, and I have so many barriers to shove past.

Never mind breaking the glass ceiling, how do us trans and gender diverse people get into the building?

Job Hunting

Between the pandemic, the oversaturated field of LIS, and physical limitations, I gotta say, it's not pretty out there. Over the past twelve months, I have submitted 130 applications for information management-related positions all across Canada. From this set of applications, I have had four interviews, all in the past four months. Two were for library positions (assistant and manager), one was for a programming position in a theatre company, and one was for general administration/office support. At this point in the job search, I would normally turn to retail, just to tide me over, but with the ongoing pandemic and my heavy reliance on lipreading, this is not an option. Instead, I am trying to stick it out as well as exploring the freelance consulting route.

During my job hunt, I have focused on openings in cultural institutions and administration in relation to my new MLIS, rather than my past direct experience in the print industry and customer service. I need to include a custom cover letter for every application to make my eclectic resume make sense for a career shift, which means I am unable to standardize and modify my cover letters for a more efficient application process. Every application requires between half an hour and two hours of attention, between writing a custom one-page cover letter, gathering references, revising my resume or CV, and filling out the various forms required. Some postings require creating yet another account and password to apply to a particular position. Some jobs simply require an email to human resources or to the library board, at which point I have to decide whether to include my pronouns in my email signature along with the notification that I am hard of hearing and prefer email correspondence. Is it too much to put "he/him or they/them" in my signature, or my cover letter? Do I come across as "too much" to even get my resume looked at?

Getting into the building is *really hard.* The LIS field is notorious for being difficult for new professionals to break into, let alone during a pandemic when there were lots of layoffs for more experienced professionals. Based on my observations of Library Twitter over the past year, it seems like unless MLIS graduates have previous library experience (as the vast majority of my MLIS classmates did), they can expect to job hunt for between six months to three years before finding a permanent library job. It also seems like, once they get into the field, it gets easier to find more LIS work (though still more precarious than we might like). We will have to see how the pandemic affects this pattern, but I would assume that multiple layoffs and restructuring in 2020 will have some lasting impact on job precarity.

I also learned from an online LIS job seeker panel that a lot of library workers get their start in the field by moving to places—often rural—where there is less competition for jobs. From a trans and/or disability standpoint, the logistics and finances involved in this method of getting a foot in the door is so much more complicated than simply driving to another city every day. For one thing, I have already moved cities once to try and improve my chances of getting a library job. Moving again will be expensive and my partner will need to find another job, too, or we would have to live apart and pay for two places and/or two cars. If I stay where I am now and work out of town, I will have to buy a second car and overcome my severe driving anxiety. What about people who are even less able to drive than I am? What if they have physical disabilities preventing them? LIS candidates being able to drive is not a guarantee. Additionally, access to healthcare is a concern when relocating or moving to small towns. Getting trans-friendly healthcare or specialists is difficult in large cities, let alone in small cities. I also think about how many of my classmates already have families and would have to relocate or move away from their family to get their first library job. Presuming that new librarians can move to smaller towns before getting work in their own town is a huge barrier for new librarians trying to get their foot in the door. Why does the LIS field assume that its professionals are all mobile?

Self-Identification

As a nonbinary person newly out as trans, I want to figure out my gender identity and pronouns well before starting my new job; my hope is that this will make it easier both for paperwork and for others to accept my pronouns, and I want to avoid transitioning at work if possible. From what I've experienced in personal interactions and on Library Twitter, many LIS environments and other non-profit organizations seem more accepting of trans and gender-nonconforming identities than most industries. This gives me a lot of hope that one day I can show up as myself, punk hair and nonbinary pronouns and all, so long as I can persist in the job hunt.

Some application processes in Canada involve filling out an employment equity survey in which applicants can declare themselves a minority. These surveys are intended to track progress towards hiring and retaining diverse staff. The general practice is to keep the diversity survey responses separate from the application so that they won't influence the hiring process. In Canada, applicants can typically select from the following: *Visible minority, Minority gender identity, Minority sexual orientation, Disability, Woman, Aboriginal person,* or *Not self-identified.* Shockingly, I even found one survey that had a drop-down menu where the applicant could select only a single minority we identified with, if any. This format was completely counterproductive—the effect was to erase people with multiple marginalized identities. The choices were accurate in terminology but instead of multiple checkboxes, we could only select one. In this case, I answered the question with the area I would need the most direct support in: *Disability.* I then emailed the institution's human resources department to let them know that their form needed to be revised to allow applicants to provide multiple answers or a write-in box. They answered back very quickly, thanking me for the feedback, and saying they would look into incorporating my suggested changes. It made me realize that employers rarely take that survey themselves or, if they do, may not realize the issues with it unless they are personally impacted—so feedback is needed. I have also found one survey which allowed for multiple selections, including both transgender and nonbinary identities. This one nearly made me cry when I saw it, because it really should be that easy.

In any case, very few of these survey questions provide accurate representation of nonbinary or transgender identities. I try to make a note of which institutions do include nonbinary options in their survey, as those are the workplaces at which I am most likely to be accepted. In Canada, most of the surveys simply ask if you identify as a woman, which is a protected class due to the gender pay gap. Some ask if you are transgender or minority gender identity, which is better. But for me, when I'm not offered the choice of nonbinary in those surveys, what do I do? There is no accurate way for me to answer, so my identity goes uncounted.

Learning about Leadership and Disability

One of the most intimidating tenets of LIS studies for me was leadership and management. I had to challenge my ideas of what leadership is to find my place within it. Having an introverted personality, a shorter stature, a hearing disability that interferes with my ability to use telephones, and no management experience made me deeply question my ability to be a leader. For me, experience would have to come after theory.

During my Leadership and Management course, as we learned about different leadership styles and theories to support our styles, our language shifted from observing other leaders to observing ourselves as leaders. We came to see how neither leaders nor librarians need to know how to do everything perfectly—instead, we can act as conduits. We can engage in conversations and pay attention to others' experiences, reach out for support in our weak areas, and use transparency to ensure that everyone knows what is going on and has the opportunity to pitch in.[2] When I think about management, I think about the supervisors I've had who were able to implement my needs into everyday routines with no questions asked. When I struggled to answer phones at work in a noisy print room, they were willing to take phone calls for me, even if I had to interrupt their lunch break.

I learned that I have other skills useful for leadership that can counteract those things that I felt held me back—I'm observant and compassionate, I'm interested in other people's experiences, I have a problem-solving mindset, I'm good at planning and organizing complex projects, I can gather resources before making a decision, I know how to navigate bureaucracy, I'm persistent, and I know how to pace myself and others to prevent burnout. I realized that being nonbinary trans and hard of hearing means I *do* have a right to take up space—as a representative of both leaders with gender diverse identities, and leaders with disabilities. Knowing what my own physical limits are means that I would work well in a collaborative leadership style. I am a very active listener, I ask a lot of questions, and I have a direct personality, so I am especially well equipped to navigate interpersonal communications and make decisions. I also need someone to help ensure that I accurately understand details, especially when phones are involved. This collaborative approach also would give me a chance to lift someone else up along with me because, while I can do a lot more than I initially thought, I still cannot do it alone.

For me, language exchange is central to my approach to advocacy because, when you have the words to describe your experiences, you are better able to advocate for yourself in the way you need to. I continually learn and re-evaluate ways to describe and convey my experiences,

---

2. Baharak Yousefi, "On the Disparity Between What We Say and What We Do in Libraries," in *Feminists Among Us: Resistance and Advocacy in Library Leadership,* ed. Shirley Lew and Baharak Yousefi, (Sacramento, CA: Library Juice Press), pp. 92-105; Jamie Green, Barbara Chivers, and Glen Mynott, "In the Librarian's Chair: An Analysis of Factors Which Influence the Motivation of Library Staff and Contribute to the Effective Delivery of Services," *Library Review*, V. 49, Issue 8, 2000, pp. 380-386.

and I listen to how people with different minority identities describe their experiences. I try to amplify their words so that when they need a break, I can step up, and when I need a break, someone else can fill in for me. Burnout is an issue in activism and advocacy both, and activism looks different for those with different abilities.[3] For me, activism involves discussions with others and learning words that can describe my experiences and that I can use to advocate for myself—skills that my LIS training has prepared me well for. This work is ongoing, and it is more important to put the continual effort into it than it is to be afraid of messing up.

The most surprising thing I noticed during my studies was the complete lack of literature about leaders with disabilities. Instead, support for disabilities was limited to supporting library users with disabilities, or the occasional staff member with disabilities. Resources involved legislation such as the Canadian Employment Equity Act, which recommends identifying and eliminating employment barriers and providing "reasonable accommodations," and some training on what support common disabilities require. None of it, however, discussed ways to support *leaders* with disabilities.[4] From talking to friends and observing discussions on Library Twitter, many of us with disabilities have impressive lists of work related to leadership, but not a lot of direct paid experiences in leadership and management that would allow us to move up within our careers. A study in 2011 showed that persons with disabilities are less likely to be employed but may also differ from non-disabled individuals

3. "Self-Care and Prevention of Burn Out Among Activists—Tools For Everyday Life," *International HIV/AIDS Alliance* and *Eurasian Harm Reduction Association*, 2018, https://frontlineaids.org/wp-content/uploads/old_site/self_care_workbook_(webready)_original.pdf?1532089391.

4. The definition of "reasonable accommodation" is regularly contended as it operates on a case-by-case basis that tends to rely on the employer's definition of what is too expensive. This duty to accommodate also applies to other grounds like family status, and employers must document the process of consideration and acting on the employee's request for accommodation. More information on Canada's Duty to Accommodate can be found at https://www.canada.ca/en/government/publicservice/wellness-inclusion-diversity-public-service/diversity-inclusion-public-service/working-government-canada-duty-accommodate-right-non-discrimination/duty-accommodate-general-process-managers.html.

in our employment profiles; for example, women with disabilities were less likely to be employed in management and professional occupations and more likely to be employed in personal service and customer information service occupations, although these statistics tended to reflect lower levels of education.[5] Taken together, these observations point to a need to give people with disabilities access to not just jobs, but jobs with leadership opportunities. Accessibility needs to be a bigger conversation within diversity, equity, and inclusion, but that is still developing.

Finding My Place

Shifting careers is not easy. It requires being able to frame our past experiences as useful to our new careers. I spend a lot of time trying to figure out what it is that I want to do in my future job. I have been attending virtual LIS conferences to help me network and to help me solidify what I think my place in LIS is. Many of the conversations from conferences that have caught my attention have focused on accessibility in practices and in staff support.

When I get hired as a leader someday, I want my library to be empowering for patrons and staff alike. I want to be able to advocate for better healthcare for my staff, because trans and disabled needs are expensive and usually not well covered by employers or by our healthcare systems.[6] Accessibility improvements to LIS environments also include more accessible spaces, and so I want to push for improvements to architectural and interior design challenges for users and staff who use the space—from historical buildings that are inaccessible to wheelchair users; to bathrooms that have heavy doors or are not on every floor; to

5. Martin Turcotte, "Persons with Disabilities and Employment," *Statistics Canada*, modified Nov. 27, 2015, para. 31 and 36. https://www150.statcan.gc.ca/n1/pub/75-006-x/2014001/article/14115-eng.htm.

6. As the Canadian healthcare system exists now, I must purchase my own hearing aids, which are approximately $2400 for the pair every five or so years, plus yearly molds at $90-200 for the pair. My healthcare over the years has yet to cover more than $500 per year, nor does this amount cover the molds, so the hearing aid coverage is abysmal. From other friends, I know that power wheelchairs have similar budgetary challenges.

spaces that are difficult to navigate for someone with a temporary disability like a broken arm or leg, who needs to rest frequently; to not being able to mingle in natural congregation areas. From the library perspective, conducting user and staff surveys prior to the request for proposal process would be good practice. I know how much I have learned from my previous experiences and from those of my friends and classmates, and I aspire to use those experiences to help me understand my staff and be willing to find and provide alternatives to problems, such as modifications to the workspace, equipment, job duties, break rooms, etc. I realize that as one person, I probably won't be able to make those changes, but at least I can help voice the need for them.

Regardless of identity or ability, what diversity, inclusion, and equity work have in common is requiring one to slow down and listen to individuals. This is true in disability advocacy, as well as in queer advocacy. Our experiences are all unique and require different support strategies. We need policies and procedures that are broad enough to encompass our common and collective needs, as well as staff training and compassion to address our individual needs. The most important thing I have learned from my MLIS is that we are not "too much." There's a building out there waiting for me; I just have to find it.

References

Deconnick, Kelly Sue and Valentine de Landro. *Bitch Planet.* Portland, OR: Image Comics, 2017.

Government of Canada. *Duty to Accommodate: A General Process for Managers.* Modified Nov. 4, 2011. https://www.canada.ca/en/government/publicservice/wellness-inclusion-diversity-public-service/diversity-inclusion-public-service/working-government-canada-duty-accommodate-right-non-discrimination/duty-accommodate-general-process-managers.html.

Green, Jamie, Barbara Chivers, and Glen Mynott. "In The Librarian's Chair: An Analysis of Factors Which Influence the Motivation of Library Staff and Contribute to the Effective

Delivery of Services." *Library Review*, 49, no. 8, (2000), pp. 380-386.

"Self-Care And Prevention of Burn Out Among Activists—Tools for Everyday Life," *International HIV/AIDS Alliance* and *Eurasian Harm Reduction Association*, 2018. https://frontlineaids.org/wp-content/uploads/old_site/self_care_workbook_(webready)_original.pdf?1532089391.

Turcotte, Martin. "Persons with Disabilities and Employment." *Statistics Canada*, modified Nov. 27, 2015. https://www150.statcan.gc.ca/n1/pub/75-006-x/2014001/article/14115-eng.htm.

Yousefi, Baharak. "On the Disparity Between What We Say and What We Do in Libraries." *Feminists Among Us: Resistance and Advocacy in Library Leadership*. Sacramento, CA: Library Juice Press, pp. 92-105.

About the Author

Freyja T. Catton, MLIS, BFA (he/they) is a hard of hearing nonbinary trans writer, artist, and researcher. He is an immigrant residing on traditional territories of the Blackfoot Confederacy (Siksika, Kainai, Piikani), Nehiyaw (Cree), Denesuliné (Dene), Nakota Sioux (Stoney), Anishinaabe (Saulteaux) and the Métis Nation (Region 4) lands. Catton grew up as a descendant of settlers on Ojibwe and Dakota Oyate lands. Catton is passionate about language, access to information, and communication. He provides independent writing and research services for the arts and culture sectors as Wordeater Consulting, and his art practice focuses on the connections between language and art. More of their work is available at their website, www.thewordeater.com.

all i am is grieving

kas (they/ᐃᔦ)

Keywords: transphobia in LIS, the paradox of tolerance, institutional trans-antagonism

When I first proposed this chapter, I wanted to use this space to reflect on my experiences studying and working in LIS during my transition, as well as after graduation. I wanted to do this for myself, first and foremost, to process my experiences, but also to offer help or hope to other trans folks who might be in similar situations. But I feel dishonest trying to give help and hope when I haven't found them myself. I want to believe that we can find transgender liberation and joy, and that libraries and LIS workers could be a part of the change that leads to that future. But it feels like every time I get my hopes up, I am disappointed. I cannot separate myself from my sorrow and my rage.

It has been over a decade since I started working in libraries and several years since I first began to transition. Although libraries have been an important space and resource for me as a trans person, I am frustrated by the hypocrisy that permeates the field's supposedly egalitarian ideals. This hypocrisy is evident in LIS treatment of transgender people. I have seen librarians and LIS administrators repeatedly refuse to act in support of trans people and instead enact policies that are antagonistic to us because they give space to transphobic people. LIS institutions claim to champion intellectual freedom and freedom of expression on the one hand, and equity, diversity, and inclusion on the other, but when they offer those freedoms and inclusion to bigots, they alienate marginalized people and undermine our place in LIS by showing that the "safe space" image of libraries is often a façade.

I have heard so many trans people pour out their life stories, their pain and struggles, in order to plead with library administrators to stop allowing transphobic vitriol to be platformed in libraries.[1] But too many cisgender LIS leaders and managers want to be seen as allies without being accountable to the trans people they claim to welcome into libraries. Instead of acting in solidarity, those LIS administrators say that they need to be neutral. But such statements are complicit, because they suggest that it is possible to question trans people's existence and our right to live as ourselves, without also promoting discrimination, harassment, and violence towards us—there can be no tolerance of intolerance, no neutral stance on discrimination, no objective view of oppression. Yet time and time again, trans people are met with minds closed and hearts hardened by this rhetoric of neutrality. LIS leaders appeal to objectivity and free speech to avoid addressing critiques and fulfilling their own responsibilities. I have no reason to believe that sharing my stories will elicit a different response. The self-serving indifference and the denial of critical thinking that I have already been met with is as exhausting as outright hatred.

I feel like the only advice I can truthfully offer to other trans folks in LIS is this:

Whether they're CEOs, deans, department chairs, board members, managers, or supervisors, and whether it's public libraries, archives, academic libraries, LIS schools, or any other LIS organization, don't trust the people in charge to care about you more than they care about their positions and reputations. They never have and they never will, as long as this field upholds the categories and worldviews of the colonial, white supremacist, cishetero-patriarchal death machine.

So, take care of yourselves and each other.
ᑭᓵᑭᐦᐃᑎᓈᐚᐤ
ᐋᐦᑲᒣᔨᒧᑖᑦ

1. Examples include the contestation of transphobic events held at the Vancouver Public Library and the Toronto Public Libraries in 2019, and at the Seattle Public Library in 2020."

About the Author

kas is a trans non-binary ᐅᑎᐯᔨᒥᓱᐤ (Métis person), also of mixed European settler ancestry. They worked in libraries for eight years and completed their MLIS in 2018. They are an amateur quilter and ᓀᐦᐃᔭᐍᐏᐣ (Plains Cree) language learner.

Towards an Illegitimate Present

Caleb Simone (they/he)

Keywords: trans imaginaries, normativity, legitimacy, futurity

Land Acknowledgment

I wish to acknowledge that I have written these words on Pawtucket, Nipmuc, and Massa-adchu-es-et land. There is neither liberation nor revolution outside of decolonization. All liberatory efforts must be done in solidarity with those whose lands you have settled on.

An Illegitimate Present

Library and Information Science (LIS) is a field dependent on classification and organization. Trans and queer bodies and modes of being are inherently resistant to such strict processes. They do not easily fit into cisnormative conceptions of gender and so elude the social, political, and medical schemas used to organize contemporary U.S. society. In his seminal work, *No Future: Queer Theory and the Death Drive*, Lee Edelman posits that queerness *is* tension; its purpose is to be non-definitional, yet imagining queerness against normativities automatically defines it as non-normative.[1] If queerness is best utilized as an oppositional chameleon or constant alternative, then it is not only possible but logical

1. Lee Edelman, *No Future: Queer Theory and the Death Drive* (Durham: Duke University Press, 2004).

for queerness to be in abstract opposition to LIS. So, what does that mean for trans folks in the field?

There is considerable literature on the relationship between queerness and librarianship. Discourse surrounding oppressive language within the catalog is extensive and growing.[2] Emily Drabinski has done much work to incorporate geo-spatial analyses of queerness in libraries.[3] However, there is a dearth of literature problematizing the relationship between trans bodies and academic LIS spaces. This is troubling, not least because much of LIS pedagogy hinges on legitimacy and futurity, two primary foci of contemporary queer theorists.

In this chapter I suggest that we, LIS students and professionals, move away from legitimacy and futurity to instead embrace an illegitimate present. An illegitimate present welcomes non-definitionality. It has room for trans imaginaries beyond one week of allotted readings in a syllabus. And it understands that which is "allowed" as one of many frameworks in the LIS multiverse. Before we can flesh out an illegitimate present, it is important to first understand how LIS's current emphasis on legitimacy and futurity is incompatible with transness. Using that understanding, I will illuminate why the shift towards an illegitimate present is crucial not only for trans people in LIS, but for the entire field and those we serve.

Legitimacy is the pipeline between recognition and authorization. It is the idea that true validation hinges on whether a ruling authority, often the State or a State-sanctioned body, has incorporated an entity

2. Sara A. Howard and Steven A. Knowlton, "Browsing through Bias: The Library of Congress Classification and Subject Headings for African American Studies and LGBTQIA Studies," *Library Trends* 67, no. 1 (Summer 2018): 74–88; Samuel J. Edge, "A Subject 'Queer'-y: A Literature Review on Subject Access to LGBTIQ Materials," *Serials Librarian* 75, no. 1–4 (2018): 81–90; Susan Brown and John Simpson, "The Curious Identity of Michael Field and Its Implications for Humanities Research with the Semantic Web," *2013 IEEE International Conference on Big Data*, December 23, 2013, 77–85, https://doi.org/10.1109/BigData.2013.6691674.

3. Emily Drabinski, "Queering Library Space: Notes Toward a New Geography of the Library" (presentation, Thinking Critically: Alternative Perspectives and Methods in Information Studies, University of Wisconsin-Milwaukee, Milwaukee, WI, May 15-17, 2008.

into their systems of organization. Legitimation relies on futurity, or the adherence to a trajectory of State-recognizable identity. This trajectory is grounded in the future as much as it is in the present and the past. It is about the linear path from point A to point B and the progress narrative attached to it. Futurity assumes and privileges a final and logical form.

Legitimacy and futurity are rooted in normativity, another concept present in my experience as a trans person in LIS. I take critical geographer Natalie Oswin's cue to think about normativity and queerness in terms of space rather than subject.[4] Normativity is something we perform; this performance is easier in some spaces and harder in others. My transness does not preclude me from engaging in gendered normativities. Imagining as much reduces all queer subjects to a hierarchy of radical identity in which certain populations are considered inherently more queer than others. A queer approach to space is critical of all normativities, regardless of who is deploying them. Legitimacy and futurity are two functions of normativity.

Below, I share a personal experience that has been pivotal in my ongoing academic and political radicalization. It was a conversation that served three broad functions. The first was a harsh and staying reminder that my transness informs aspects of my ideological and material realities that are *not* inherently shared by LGB communities. In other words, our relationships to normativity often differ. The second was my realization that LIS pedagogies and systems are built upon legitimacy and futurity. The third was recognizing that a crucial aspect of my identity was at odds with my chosen field of study.

The Conversation

The journey to this chapter began with a conflict during my first semester of graduate school. A conversation with a classmate about whether to include the sexual assault allegations against Donald Trump in his

4. Natalie Oswin, "Critical Geographies and the Uses of Sexuality: Deconstructing Queer Space," *Progress in Human Geography* 32, no. 1 (2008): 91.

authority record turned into an exchange about objectivity and legality. I criticized the notion of objectivity via its near synonymy with complicity in maintaining structures of oppression. The example I used was that allowing white supremacist groups to utilize libraries as meeting spaces renders libraries complicit in white supremacy.

My perspective did not land well with my classmate, a licensed attorney. His rebuttals were intelligent, well-formed, and hyper-rational. They were rooted in the conception of legality as paramount. Untouchable. *True.* I was warned that my thinking was in opposition to Constitutional law and that attempts to activate those thoughts would beget serious repercussions. It is true that prohibiting entire groups from libraries due to their "beliefs" could invite catastrophic legal and social consequences. This concern is an ongoing site of debate for librarians and their communities. What is not true is that US legal legitimacy is the universal moral framework for all realities. There are rich histories of movements and communities which act in accordance with their own systems of ethics and accountability, such as contemporary community responses like GenerationFIVE and Collective Action for Safe Spaces, to traditional Indigenous Peacemaking and governance practices.[5] I say this as a white person, recognizing my privilege of navigating the world legally unquestioned because of my whiteness. I also say this as a trans person, legally questioned at almost every turn because of my transness. Like many other trans folks, I have dedicated time and resources to legal legitimacies that neither validate nor invalidate my existence. Nor do legal legitimacies disrupt the nonconsensual cooptation of my body as a political site of debate.

5. Generation Five, "Toward Transformtive Justice: A Liberatory Approach to Child Sexual Abuse and Other Forms of Intimate and Community Violence; A Call to Action for the Left and the Sexual and Domestic Violence Sectors" (Generation Five, June 2007), http://www.generationfive.org/wp-content/uploads/2013/07/G5_Toward_Transformative_Justice-Document.pdf; "Collective Action for Safe Spaces," Collective Action for Safe Spaces, 2021, https://www.collectiveactiondc.org/; Native American Rights Fund, "Indigenous Peacemaking Initiative," Indigenous Peacemaking Initiative, n.d. https://peacemaking.narf.org/; The University of Arizona Native Nations Institute, "Peacemaking," Indigenous Governance Database, 2021, https://nnigovernance.arizona.edu/keywords/peacemaking.

These legitimacies are a Band-Aid. My license, with the name "Caleb Simone" and the signifier "M," offers a sense of security for surface-level interactions. That sense of security, however, prevents neither individual nor systemic transphobia. Indeed, displaying my name-change documents when required often feels like unveiling a duplicitous simulacrum to a jury of cis commentators. Prospective landlords have gone silent on me, medical professionals demand clarification about "who I was" when I was born, secretaries continually glance between me and my documents, checking. Maybe worst of all, the floor automatically opens to any and all questioning and commentary. "You totally look like a guy!" "So your parents were okay with you changing your name?" "Wait, were you born a boy or a girl?" The purported dedication of the American Library Association (ALA) to safety and equity feels the same: it looks good on paper, but the lack of systemic change continues to enable harmful interactions during which those experiencing harm must pander to those enacting it.[6]

There was no pandering on either side of the exchange with my classmate. I remember shaking, equally enraged at his tone and in disbelief that I had uncovered such a gulf between our realities. It shook me. Not least because this peer is a gay man. Our conversation was an instant and stark reminder of the vast nuances between the identities represented in our ever-growing acronym. It was a harsh demonstration of the ideological power of cisness and how divergent trans and queer realities can be beyond sexuality. In that academic space I was uncomfortably reminded of the reproduction not of heteronormativity, but of cisnormativity.

6. American Library Association, "ODLOS Glossary of Terms," About ALA, September 7, 2017, https://www.ala.org/aboutala/odlos-glossary-terms; American Library Association, "Hateful Conduct in Libraries: Supporting Library Workers and Patrons," Advocacy, Legislation & Issues, December 7, 2018, https://www.ala.org/advocacy/hatefulconduct; Stephanie Hlywak, "ALA Takes Responsibility for Past Racism, Pledges a More Equitable Association," News and Press Center, June 26, 2020, https://www.ala.org/news/press-releases/2020/06/ala-takes-responsibility-past-racism-pledges-more-equitable-association.

In the United States, non-normative sexualities have crept much closer to the normalized edge than have non-normative expressions and embodiments of gender. This spatial separation problematizes the notion of a cohesive LGBTQIA+ community. While all liberations are connected, there are distinct material realities between the letters in that initialism. Those distinct realities inspire unique liberatory imaginaries that affect how broad LGBTQIA+ communities interact within the spaces between them.

Cis camaraderie, with those of us whose transness engenders a spatial separation from cisnormativity, requires the active questioning of all normative realities, including that of legality. "Legal" does not automatically mean "safe" for us; it does not automatically mean "acceptable." Legality is not always the optimal route, and legal rulings in our "favor" do not always feel like wins. Unfortunately, a cisnormative relationship to legality takes precedence in LIS classrooms. This was made clear to me through the confidence with which my classmate utilized our shared academic space to criticize my response based on its relationship to legality rather than acknowledging its relationship to trans realities and imaginaries. I am not advocating for the pedagogical dominance of trans realities, but for upsetting the assumption that legality is the only legitimate framework.

This conversation was my first taste of LIS's attachment to legitimacy. My classmate's perspectives were bolstered by official ALA statements and stances that are reflected in much of our core course materials.[7] After the conversation, I began to see how legitimacy shapes other aspects of LIS.

Legitimacy

Though acronyms and initialisms are commonplace in scientific fields, the influx of condensed frameworks and LIS working groups perturbs me. There is: IFLA-LRM, FRAD, FRSAD, FRSAR, FRBR, FRBRoo,

7. American Library Association, "Hateful Conduct in Libraries."; American Library Association, "ODLOS Glossary of Terms."

LRMoo, FRANAR, CIDOC, RDA, RDF, RIF, SPARQL, OWL, DCMI, SKOS, and my personal favorite, WEMI (pronounced "wee-me"). Though the acronym deluge has become a running joke within the field, there are nefarious undertones to the sprawling acronymized universe. In essence, acronyms and initialisms exist to save time and space. However, function does not always mimic intention. When used in abundance, acronyms and initialisms also serve to alienate, gatekeep, and obscure knowledge.[8] They set a knowledge-based standard for entry and interest, barring novices while fostering "a sense of cohesiveness" to those already in the know.[9] In some scientific settings, "the creation of new acronyms...is a recognized form of branding," which simultaneously produces "pockets of hyperspecialization" and legitimizes the entrance barriers around them.[10]

LIS is facing a crisis of legitimacy, unable to divorce itself from Enlightenment era empirical ideals that gave rise to a number of epistemological crises within the social sciences throughout the past century-and-a-half. I am thinking particularly of the empirical influence of Leopold von Ranke on history and the European branding of archival *work* as archival *science*.[11] Both fields have since wrestled with

8. Andrew H. Hales, Kipling D. Williams, and Joel Rector, "Alienating the Audience: How Abbreviations Hamper Scientific Communication," *APS Observer* 30, no. 2 (January 31, 2017), https://www.psychologicalscience.org/observer/alienating-the-audience-how-abbreviations-hamper-scientific-communication; Hannah Seo, "Why Scientific Papers Are Growing Increasingly Inscrutable," *Popular Science*, August 25, 2020, https://www.popsci.com/story/science/science-journals-acronyms-communication/; Jonathan M. Jeschke, et al., "Knowledge in the Dark: Scientific Challenges and Ways Forward," *FACETS* 4, no. 1 (June 1, 2019): 423–41, https://doi.org/10.1139/facets-2019-0007.

9. Hales, Williams, and Rector, "Alienating the Audience."

10. Adrian Barnett and Zoe Doubleday, "Meta Research: The Growth of Acronyms in the Scientific Literature," ed. Peter Rodgers, *ELife* 9 (July 23, 2020), https://doi.org/10.7554/eLife.60080; Seo, "Why scientific papers are growing increasingly inscrutable."

11. Anne J. Gilliland, "Archival and Recordkeeping Traditions in the Multiverse and Their Importance for Researching Situations and Situating Research," in *Research in the Archival Multiverse* (Clayton, Victoria, Australia: Monash University Publishing, 2016), 31–73.

postmodernism and have been moving away from objectivity and neutrality in their own respective ways.

Though librarianship seems to be moving in the same direction, the field at large still suffers from scientific insecurity. Other scientific fields have fortified their academic positions through the widespread use of acronyms.[12] This practice provides an air of legitimacy. The semantic reduction of a concept into a palatable form suggests an inherent complexity which requires simplification if it is to be both explainable and understood. Through that process, the concept in question becomes a scientific and, therefore, legitimate subject. Complication and simplification are not unique to LIS.

Marie Draz speaks to how the complexities of transness are similarly legitimized in cisnormative narratives via reduction, primarily through the "born this way" model of acceptability.[13] Through the "born this way" narrative, it is easy to imagine that gender has a scientific permanence which ties it to fate. This dangerous form of trans-inclusive biological determinism presents transness as a binary of error and correction. Once our gender is "corrected," it is legitimate, and we are placed on the fast track to the normative edge where we are expected to identify with one of two genders. In theory, transness becomes palatable when it is defendable in relation to cisnormativity, and vice versa. However, the reality is far more complex. As shown by the ever-increasing violence against trans people, specifically Black and Latinx trans women, the gender binary is one of several power structures that contribute to anti-trans violence.[14] What, then, is the utility of the "born this way" cisnormative legitimization?

---

12. Barnett and Doubleday, "Meta Research: The Growth of Acronyms in the Scientific Literature"; Anton Pottegård et al., "SearCh for HumourIstic and Extravagant AcroNyms and Thoroughly Inappropriate Names for Important Clinical Trials (SCIENTIFIC): Qualitative and Quantitative Systematic Study," *BMJ* 349 (December 16, 2014), https://doi.org/10.1136/bmj.g7092.

13. Maria Draz, "From Duration to Self-Identification? The Temporal Politics of the California Gender Recognition Act," *Transgender Studies Quarterly* 6, no. 4 (November 2019): 593–607.

14. Human Rights Campaign, "Fatal Violence Against the Transgender and

While LIS is legitimized through the reduction of a manufactured complexity, and transness is legitimized through a manufactured reduction of its complex non-normative potentials, both processes are indicative of the normative need for defendable legitimacies. For LIS, the defendable legitimacies are the acronyms. For transness, it's the "born this way" binary narrative. Neither of those legitimacies serve the needs of the populations who interact with them. However, what makes them defendable is their teleological nature, meaning there is an expected deliverable that both justifies and defines the process.

Hil Malatino utilizes Lauren Berlant's concept of cruel optimism to explore "teleological narratives of transition," in which "that which you profoundly desire is also that which inhibits your flourishing."[15] I am still unlearning the desire of a gendered deliverable. After six years of steady testosterone injections and five years of a surgically flattened chest, I am beyond the point that a prior version of myself would have considered "transitioned." Should I be feeling complete? Am I now allowed to feel attractive or happy? Was my goal to move through a heteronormative world like a cis man or to actualize my own world? Why were those two questions once synonymous and when did they separate? Is it supposed to be a compliment when someone says, "Wow! I couldn't even tell!"? Couldn't tell what? That I had been keeping some sort of secret? How much joy do we surrender while we are "waiting" to reach some gendered finality? Do my full beard and thinning hair render me a legitimate trans subject?

The LIS deliverable is a traceable and legitimized complex roadmap of classification. Every acronym represents a piece of LIS that serves our primary goals of findability and accessibility. However, the increasing

---

Gender Non-Conforming Community in 2021," HRC, https://www.hrc.org/resources/fatal-violence-against-the-transgender-and-gender-non-conforming-community-in-2021; Ivan Natividad, "Why Is Anti-Trans Violence on the Rise in America?," Berkeley News, June 25, 2021, https://news.berkeley.edu/2021/06/25/why-is-anti-trans-violence-on-the-rise-in-america/.

15. Hil Malatino, "Future Fatigue: Trans Intimacies and Trans Presents (or How to Survive the Interregnum)," *Transgender Studies Quarterly* 6, no. 4 (November 2019): 635–36.

web of frameworks, the interoperability of which is confusing at best, has only complicated my understanding of records and data. It seems that new versions of frameworks are frequently generated to achieve some level of granularity or to acknowledge the specific categorizational needs of particular knowledge sets. These ends deserve cogitation. And yet the slate is never wiped clean for them. We continue to build on top of ourselves with acronyms that erect barriers around knowledge. This is the complexity that feels manufactured. These systems complicate themselves. The continuous resolutions to these ceaseless complications ensure a narrative of progress. Here, legitimacy ties into futurity.

Futurity

Bear with me as I provide a brief but chaotic snapshot of LIS's world of acronyms. The International Federation of Library Associations and Institutions Library Reference Model (IFLA LRM) is the consolidation of the Functional Requirements for Bibliographic Records (FRBR), the Functional Requirements for Authority Data (FRAD), and the Functional Requirements for Subject Authority Data (FRSAD), three distinct bibliographic conceptual frameworks created by separate IFLA groups.[16] Despite their distinct purposes, there is overlap. Because of their distinct purposes, there are inconsistencies between them. IFLA LRM aims to resolve the inconsistencies. So does FBRB-object oriented (FRBRoo), a different consolidated framework developed at the same time as IFLA LRM but as an extension of the International Committee for Documentation's Conceptual Reference Model (CIDOC CRM). But FRBRoo and IFLA LRM have distinct purposes, meaning they also have overlap and inconsistencies. So there is a working group to manifest LRM-object oriented (LRMoo), an updated version of FRBRoo that is consistent with IFLA LRM.[17] Are you following? This is one example of the overlap-

16. Pat Riva, "IFLA Library Reference Model a Conceptual Model for Bibliographic Information," n.d., 101; Chris Oliver, "IFLA Library Reference Model," n.d., 36.

17. International Federation of Library Associations and Institutions,

inconsistency-consolidation process that contributes to a broader and more tangled acronymized web of frameworks and standards.

This is our cruel optimism. The profession is dedicated to cycles of overcomplicated reinvention that monopolize current and future work. To what end and for whom? The cycle is driven by a desire to eradicate ambiguity and clarify relationships. Within a narrow LIS lens, that desire makes sense; the neat categorization that aids findability and accessibility is only achievable through consistency. But if we think of consistency as a state that is incompatible with nuance, the desire to achieve it begins to resemble the reduction of transness through the "born this way" framework of legitimacy.

My transness *is* nuance; it is an embrace of the ambiguous and a desire for fluid relationships to myself and the surrounding world. It is consistent only in that I am committed to those values. Learning about a profession that strives for comprehensive models is challenging. Interacting with knowledge that feels inaccessible due to its desire for legitimization is challenging. Engaging with frameworks that assess legitimacy based on their ability to convey clear and unambiguous relationships is challenging. Who is findable in these frameworks? Or rather, what reality is findable? In "The Curious Identity of Michael Field and its Implications for Humanities Research with the Semantic Web," Susan Brown and John Simpson explore the ontological complications of describing the late-nineteenth and early-twentieth century writer, Michael Field.[18]

Michael Field was a pseudonym assumed by partners Katherine Harris Bradley and Edith Emma Cooper, each of whom had respectively assumed previous pseudonyms. Bradley and Cooper were also aunt and niece through marriage. Mapping Field onto existing schemas resulted in a complete relational mess. Brown and Simpson note how existing "ontologies apply properties related to personhood in commonsensical

"IFLA," accessed September 17, 2021, https://www.ifla.org/working-group-on-frbr-cidoc-crm-harmonization/.

18. Brown and Simpson, "The Curious Identity of Michael Field."

and normalizing fashions that are inadequate for capturing the complexities of Field."[19] "Field" here can be replaced with any mode of being that is not aligned with cisnormativity.

The Michael Field case study is representative of how cisnormative realities are privileged in LIS systems. Ironically, the unsuccessful attempts to capture nuance secure a legitimate future for the field. Not for the obvious "if at first you don't succeed" rationale, but for the nature of the continued attempts. The preoccupation with updates means we will continue to build on top of frameworks that emphasize consistency and clarity as a means to comprehension. I have argued that those values are incompatible with ambiguity, nuance, and transness, meaning new iterations will be unable to meaningfully describe nonnormative relationships. This inability guarantees the need for future updates and consolidations, which signify moments of linear progression. As long as the framework is moving *closer* to something that really *works*, the cycle is justified.

Echoed here is the cisnormative idea of a body still "in transition." The anticipation of a final, better, *complete* form hinders the creation of flexible and nuanced potentials. Viewing this anticipated completeness through my transness, it is hard not to interpret each update as an attempt to push the ambiguous uncapturables, like Field, closer to the normative, and therefore categorizable, edge.

So, what exists outside of a normative and therefore legitimate progression? Individual semantic web projects are great examples. There are a growing number of resources that utilize linked open data in creative and inspiring ways: Linked Open Jazz, Connected Papers, DBPedia, etc.[20] Despite their brilliance, they have typically been presented to me as examples of what *could* be rather than as autonomous feats. The legitimacy attributed to future totalities is debilitating to present imaginaries.

---

19. Brown and Simpson, "The Curious Identity of Michael Field," 81.

20. "Linked Jazz | Revealing the Relationships of the Jazz. Community," n.d., https://linkedjazz.org/; "Connected Papers | Find and Explore Academic Papers," n.d., https://www.connectedpapers.com/; "Global and Unified Access to Knowledge Graphs," DBpedia Association, accessed November 28, 2021, https://www.dbpedia.org/.

In the classroom, the semantic web is often presented as a reality that has either yet to happen or probably will not. But isn't it happening? Why are these programs undeserving of their own universes and potentials? How do we begin to sever our frameworks, projects, and goals from future totalities, to release them from cisnormative expectations?

Emily Drabinski gives us some clues in "Queering the Catalog: Queer Theory and the Politics of Correction." She urges the field to divest from notions of "finally corrected" language, another concept that brings to mind a body still "in transition."[21] Language, like gender, has no absolute future. This is not a proposal to settle for the best option, but rather to emancipate ourselves and our ontologies from the idea that trans realities can and/or should be reduced to a choice term, phrase, or gender.

Language also has no absolute present. Take, for example, the January 2020 Library of Congress (LoC) Summary of Decisions regarding requested revisions to Library of Congress Subject Headings (LCSH). One proposed revision was to add *Gay newspapers* as a Genre/Form Heading. The proposal was rejected via the logic that *Community newspapers* "cover the important issues that affect a cohesive and well-defined geographic, ethnic or cultural community," and that "Gay people constitute a defined cultural community, so *Community newspapers* can be assigned."[22] When I think of community, I consider Cindy Patton's definition of communities as political rather than social entities, meaning community is formed not through social sameness but through the sharing of knowledge, experience, and solidarity.[23] Now I think of my aforementioned classmate who identifies as gay. I also sometimes use the word "gay" to describe my social, political, and sexual selves. However, my peer and I are clearly not in political solidarity, which leads me to conclude that our communities are different. Even if the LoC had

21. Emily Drabinski, "Queering the Catalog: Queer Theory and the Politics of Correction," *Library Quarterly: Information, Community, Policy* 83, no. 2 (2013): 95.

22. Library of Congress, "Summary of Decisions, Editorial Meeting Number 2001," Cataloging and Acquisitions, January 20, 2020, https://www.loc.gov/aba/pcc/saco/cpsoed/psd-200120.html.

23. Cindy Patton, *Inventing AIDS* (New York: Routledge, 1990): 8.

approved the incorporation of *Gay newspapers*, it would be no closer to capturing the nuance of identity than the broad stroke of *Community newspapers*, because the system requires totalities.

So what, then? Maybe I'm being unreasonably picky, simultaneously criticizing broad ontological efforts and the dangers of reduction. Maybe I'm forgetting that queerness asks us for constant revision. Or maybe I'm not the problem. As a trans student in LIS, it is exhausting to engage with systems and frameworks that were not built to capture the nuance of trans identity but continue to try to do so. As a field, LIS needs to rethink its foundations in legitimacy and futurity. And not just for trans folks, but for everyone.

An Illegitimate Present

I began this chapter with a proposition: that as a field we move away from legitimacy and futurity, and towards an illegitimate present. I have outlined how LIS is inherently tied to legitimacy and futurity, why those frameworks are incompatible with transness, and the interpersonal and systemic challenges produced by that incompatibility. My original question was: what does that mean for trans folks in the field? It means the tension is considerable. Now, my question is: what is the relationship between tension and an illegitimate present?

Initially, I wondered whether entering LIS was a mistake. For a moment, I assigned the same totalities to LIS that legitimacy and futurity assign to me. I believed that the tension was an indication that my transness did not belong, that because LIS is so bound up in legitimacy and futurity, it is *supposed* to be that way. But it's not. Neither transness nor LIS are *supposed* to be anything. And yet they are at odds with each other.

In keeping with Edelman's supposition that queerness *is* tension, I now wonder what we can uncover if we use tension as a lens to look at LIS. Through tension, we can question why legitimacy and futurity factor so heavily into our systems and frameworks to then imagine ways to dismantle their influence. We can question why LIS as it stands privileges totalities over fluid imaginaries, consequently isolating its trans students and professionals. This is the illegitimate present; it is not a set of standards or rules for a new framework, it is occupying tension to uncover and dismantle the myths of all that is *supposed* to be. We are all already everything we are supposed to be.

Bibliography

2021 ALA Annual Virtual Conference. "ALA CD 19.5-19.7 Intellectual Freedom Committee Action Items." American Library Association, June 29, 2021. https://www.ala.org/aboutala/sites/ala.org.aboutala/files/content/ALA%20CD19.5-19.7%20Intellectual%20Freedom%20Committee_action%20items.pdf.

2021 ALA Virtual Midwinter Meeting. "ALA CD 43 Resolution to Condemn White Supremacy and Fascism as Antithetical to Library Work." American Library Association, Winter 2021. https://www.ala.org/aboutala/sites/ala.org.aboutala/files/content/ALA%20CD%2043%20Resolution%20to%20Condemn%20White%20Supremacy%20and%20Fascism%20as%20Antithetical%20to%20Library%20Work%20Final_0.pdf?utm_source=newsletter&utm_medium=email&utm_content=ALA%20Resolution&utm_campaign=February%20News%20%26%20Updates.

American Library Association. "Hateful Conduct in Libraries: Supporting Library Workers and Patrons." Text. Advocacy, Legislation & Issues, December 7, 2018. https://www.ala.org/advocacy/hatefulconduct.

American Library Association. "ODLOS Glossary of Terms." About ALA, September 7, 2017. https://www.ala.org/aboutala/odlos-glossary-terms.

Barnett, Adrian, and Zoe Doubleday. "The Growth of Acronyms in the Scientific Literature." Edited by Peter Rodgers. *ELife* 9 (July 23, 2020). https://doi.org/10.7554/eLife.60080.

Brown, Susan, and John Simpson. "The Curious Identity of Michael Field and Its Implications for Humanities Research with the Semantic Web." *2013 IEEE International Conference on Big*

Data, December 23, 2013, 77–85. https://doi.org/10.1109/BigData.2013.6691674.

Collective Action for Safe Spaces. "Collective Action for Safe Spaces," 2021. https://www.collectiveactiondc.org/.

"Connected Papers | Find and Explore Academic Papers," n.d. https://www.connectedpapers.com/.

DBpedia Association. "Global and Unified Access to Knowledge Graphs." https://www.dbpedia.org/.

Drabinski, Emily. "Queering Library Space: Notes Toward a New Geography of the Library." Presentation at Thinking Critically: Alternative Perspectives and Methods in Information Studies, University of Wisconsin-Milwaukee, May 15-17, 2008.

Drabinski, Emily. "Queering the Catalog: Queer Theory and the Politics of Correction." *Library Quarterly: Information, Community, Policy* 83, no. 2 (2013): 94–111.

Draz, Maria. "From Duration to Self-Identification? The Temporal Politics of the California Gender Recognition Act." *Transgender Studies Quarterly* 6, no. 4 (November 2019): 593–607.

Edelman, Lee. *No Future: Queer Theory and the Death Drive.* Durham: Duke University Press, 2004.

Edge, Samuel J. "A Subject 'Queer'-y: A Literature Review on Subject Access to LGBTIQ Materials." *The Serials Librarian* 75, no. 1–4 (2018): 81–90.

Generation Five. "Toward Transformative Justice: A Liberatory Approach to Child Sexual Abuse and Other Forms of Intimate and Community Violence; A Call to Action for the Left and the Sexual and Domestic Violence Sectors." Generation Five, June 2007. http://www.generationfive.org/wp-content/uploads/2013/07/G5_Toward_Transformative_Justice-Document.pdf.

Gilliland, Anne J. "Archival and Recordkeeping Traditions in the Multiverse and Their Importance for Researching Situations and Situating Research." In *Research in the Archival Multiverse*, 31–73. Clayton, Victoria, Australia: Monash University Publishing, 2016.

Hales, Andrew H., Kipling D. Williams, and Joel Rector. "Alienating the Audience: How Abbreviations Hamper Scientific Communication." *APS Observer* 30, no. 2 (January 31, 2017). https://www.psychologicalscience.org/observer/alienating-the-audience-how-abbreviations-hamper-scientific-communication.

Hlywak, Stephanie. "ALA Takes Responsibility for Past Racism, Pledges a More Equitable Association." News and Press Center, June 26, 2020. https://www.ala.org/news/press-releases/2020/06/ala-takes-responsibility-past-racism-pledges-more-equitable-association.

Howard, Sara A., and Steven A. Knowlton. "Browsing through Bias: The Library of Congress Classification and Subject Headings for African American Studies and LGBTQIA Studies." *Library Trends* 67, no. 1 (Summer 2018): 74–88.

Human Rights Campaign. "Fatal Violence Against the Transgender and Gender Non-Conforming Community in 2021." HRC, n.d. https://www.hrc.org/resources/fatal-violence-against-the-transgender-and-gender-non-conforming-community-in-2021.

IFLA Functional Requirements for Bibliographic Records (FRBR) Review Group, Pat Riva, Patrick Le Boeuf, and Maja Žumer. "IFLA Library Reference Model A Conceptual Model for Bibliographic Information." *IFLA*, n.d. https://repository.ifla.org/handle/123456789/40.

International Federation of Library Associations and Institutions. "IFLA." Accessed September 17, 2021. https://www.ifla.org/working-group-on-frbr-cidoc-crm-harmonization/.

Jeschke, Jonathan M., Sophie Lokatis, Isabelle Bartram, and Klement Tockner. "Knowledge in the Dark: Scientific Challenges and Ways Forward." *FACETS* 4, no. 1 (June 1, 2019): 423–41. https://doi.org/10.1139/facets-2019-0007.

"Linked Jazz | Revealing the Relationships of the Jazz. Community," n.d. https://linkedjazz.org/.

Malatino, Hil. "Future Fatigue: Trans Intimacies and Trans Presents (or How to Survive the Interregnum)." *Transgender Studies Quarterly* 6, no. 4 (November 2019): 635–58.

Native American Rights Fund. "Indigenous Peacemaking Initiative." Indigenous Peacemaking Initiative, n.d. https://peacemaking.narf.org/.

Natividad, Ivan. "Why Is Anti-Trans Violence on the Rise in America?" Berkeley News, June 25, 2021. https://news.berkeley.edu/2021/06/25/why-is-anti-trans-violence-on-the-rise-in-america/.

Oswin, Natalie. "Critical Geographies and the Uses of Sexuality: Deconstructing Queer Space." *Progress in Human Geography* 32, no. 1 (2008): 89–103.

Patton, Cindy. *Inventing AIDS*. New York: Routledge, 1990.

Pottegård, Anton, Maija Bruun Haastrup, Tore Bjerregaard Stage, Morten Rix Hansen, Kasper Søltoft Larsen, Peter Martin Meegaard, Line Haugaard Vrdlovec Meegaard, et al. "SearCh for HumourIstic and Extravagant AcroNyms and Thoroughly Inappropriate Names for Important Clinical Trials (SCIENTIFIC): Qualitative and Quantitative Systematic Study." *BMJ* 349 (December 16, 2014). https://doi.org/10.1136/bmj.g7092.

Seo, Hannah. "Why Scientific Papers Are Growing Increasingly Inscrutable." *Popular Science* (blog), August 25, 2020. https://www.popsci.com/story/science/science-journals-acronyms-communication/.

Library of Congress. "Summary of Decisions, Editorial Meeting Number 2001." Cataloging and Acquisitions, January 20, 2020. https://www.loc.gov/aba/pcc/saco/cpsoed/psd-200120.html.

The University of Arizona Native Nations Institute. "Peacemaking." Indigenous Governance Database, 2021. https://nnigovernance.arizona.edu/keywords/peacemaking.

About the Author

Caleb Simone (he/they) is a white queer and trans graduate student at Simmons University, where he is currently enrolled in a dual-degree archives management program. He expects to graduate in the Spring of 2023 with a MA in History and an MLS. His academic interests include archival activism, community responses to the AIDS crisis, and Queer geographies.

Section 7:

Leaving Libraries

Burnout and the Binary

Evan Held

Keywords: burnout, leaving the library profession, changing careers, nonbinary, workplace protections

Southern summers are always merciless, and August 2020 was no exception. It was hotter than hell, tensions were high, and the pandemic was raging. The city was facing a budget crisis, and though the library had just opened for curbside pickup in June, the board was already pushing for more. In my four years at this public library, we had spent more time in a hiring freeze than out of one, but the specter of layoffs had never loomed this close before. My spouse and I spent a great deal of mental energy worrying and planning for what we would do if I lost my job. So it was something of a shock when, on a normal day at work, I suddenly got a text message from my spouse: "I just got fired." Numb and panicked, I immediately left. As I drove home, I began to slowly realize the truth: my spouse had just been fired for being non-binary.

My spouse, Felix (not their real name), worked for a Christian university as a digital reference librarian, primarily for adult learners. By August 2020, they had worked there for three years, staying in the closet and presenting as a cisgender woman. This university had an unofficial "live and let live" policy for employees with same-sex partners, so when we met and ultimately married, I agreed to also present as a cisgender woman to Felix's coworkers. I find explaining the intricacies of my identity as a non-binary person rather exhausting, particularly in the South, where everyone is either ma'am or sir, so I was happy to take the easy way out. For these first few years, there were no problems.

The trouble began in the first few weeks of 2020, when a new employee who joined Felix's small office discovered their gender identity and forcibly outed Felix to their boss and the Human Resources department. While her intentions were not malicious, her actions had consequences. Within a few weeks, Felix was written up for the first time in their career. The reason? A minor typo on a monthly report. Three months later, they received another identical write up. And then in August, they were fired for "poor performance." Looking back, I feel foolish for not seeing this coming, but I suppose 2020 taught us all a thing or two about hindsight.

In comparison, my library experience has been mixed as far as my gender identity is concerned. Our diversity training focuses on generational diversity rather than any category that might invite controversy, including queer issues. And my health insurance doesn't cover any trans-related expenses. But I am allowed to have my pronouns in my email signature and on my nametag, and some of my coworkers even use them correctly. Library administration largely pays lip service to equity, diversity, and inclusion concerns, but some of my cisgender colleagues are authentic in their advocacy and support. At the end of the day, I have never feared that I would lose my library job because of my gender identity—something that many transgender and gender diverse people, including my spouse, cannot say.

Despite all of this, in the fall and winter I began to think very seriously about changing careers. I struggled with my decision to leave libraries, because I know firsthand how fortunate I am to have this relative safety. And yet, here I am volunteering to leave a job where I'm protected by civil service, a union, and a nondiscrimination clause, where my boss uses my pronouns and advocates on my behalf to library administration, and where I can present myself however I decide. And I'm leaving it for a job in information security, an industry rife with cisgender, heterosexual, conservative white men. I feel a little bit like I've lost my mind.

What brought me to this point? As I said, with regards to my gender identity, my library experience has been mixed but, overall, I've been fortunate. Unfortunately, in many other areas it has not been nearly as innocuous. I think we all know the story: low pay, awful hours, job creep, and on and on and on. Burnout is a real problem in our field and I'm not ashamed to say that it's what happened to me. The work that I am required to do does not match the money that I make. Patrons in my community need an immigration lawyer, a social worker, a career coach, an accountant, and more. I am a librarian. I am tired.

My reserves of patience and empathy are spent. I feel brittle and jaded and I hate it, because I used to care. I used to believe in this work. I wanted to be a librarian and serve my community. I had ideas and wanted to use them to make the library better, safer, and queerer. But with every budget cycle, I got a little angrier. And with every hiring freeze, I felt more despair. Again and again, our administration brushed off our concerns, told us to tighten our belts, and traded away our work-life balance in the name of a balanced budget. I had to stop caring, or it would have eaten me alive.

But even though I knew I didn't want to work in libraries anymore, I almost stayed. According to the National Center for Transgender Equality, more than twenty-five percent of transgender people have been fired for their gender identity and more than seventy-five percent have experienced discrimination in the workplace.[1] As high as those numbers are, they are even higher for transgender people of color, so I would be remiss if I did not acknowledge that my white privilege affords me a level of safety. Still, it's not surprising that I truly believed that this library job was the best that I could hope for. I know that is not and should not be true, but that fear was hard to shake.

Ultimately, I've decided that fear is not a reason to stay. Token gestures of inclusion with no real effort behind them are meaningless; that shouldn't be a high bar to clear. When broken down to its bare bones, my library isn't that great. I don't want to spend my life tolerating less than I deserve because I'm afraid that other jobs might not offer even

1. "Employment," National Center for Transgender Equality, accessed April 12, 2021, https://transequality.org/issues/employment.

the meager protections that I have at the library. I believe that things can be better. It might take a long time to get there, but I'm not going to play it safe in the meantime.

The truth is, I can't do more with less anymore, because I simply have nothing left to give. So I'm quitting and by the time this book is published I will be in a new career that I have no emotional investment in at all. My goal is to make enough money to provide for my family, secure our future, and still have enough energy left over after work to do the things I like. My job will be just a job, not a vocation, and I can't imagine anything more perfect (at least not in our current late-stage capitalist hellscape).

My other goal is to use my position as a private citizen to advocate for library workers. Right or wrong (hint: it's wrong), the library board and administration are more likely to listen to a patron than a staff member. And as a patron, I will be unencumbered by the restrictions placed on staff. I will be able to advocate for my former colleagues and speak freely about the library's many shortcomings.

Until then, I'm speaking up as a library employee to help lay the groundwork for a better future. While I believe that I will be a better advocate for my library as a private citizen, there's still work to be done in my role as a public employee. The decision to leave has given me the clarity to push past my fear and start advocating for the type of working conditions my colleagues and I deserve. Even if my efforts don't bear fruit until after I'm gone, I believe that it's still a worthwhile investment.

My hope is that library workers everywhere start to demand better treatment. Our work has value, and so do we. Just because a branch *can* be run on a skeleton crew does not mean that it *should* be. Just because something is possible does not mean that it is right or sustainable. The library's investment in us should match the energy that we pour into our jobs. Otherwise, how can we avoid burnout? Whether we work in public, academic, school, or special libraries and whether we have multiple master's degrees or none, our employers have a responsibility to us and we have a responsibility to each other.

May we all stop tolerating less than we deserve.

Bibliography

"Employment." National Center for Transgender Equality. Accessed April 12, 2021. https://transequality.org/issues/employment.

About the Author

Evan is a public librarian who lives in the southeastern US with their spouse and what some people might call "too many cats."

Pushed Out: Why I Left Libraries and Stayed Gone

Loren R. Klein

Keywords: paraprofessional, coming out at work, public libraries, leaving the library profession

Given how it turned out, it's hard to talk about why I started working in public libraries. During my career I was a dedicated public servant and vocal champion of libraries and their importance. I was halfway through a Master of Library and Information Science (MLIS) program, had a robust professional network, and was an American Library Association (ALA) Emerging Leader when I came out as Transgender to my coworkers. Within a year, I had been forced out of my job and decided to leave the profession. While non-discrimination laws should have protected me, coming out without a local LGBTQ+ activist community to fight for my rights was all it took to undo years of dedicated work.

To help contextualize and describe my experience, I have to acknowledge my debt to Safehouse Progressive Alliance for Nonviolence and their concept of "pushout."[1] This concept was developed to describe the experiences of Black women in professional spaces. It is characterized by a progression of tokenization, microaggressions, gaslighting, and targeted attacks that are designed to force the woman out of an organization when she asks for accountability and change around interpersonal

1 . Kira Page, "The 'Problem' Woman of Colour in Nonprofit Organizations," COCo (December 12, 2019), https://coco-net.org/problem-woman-colour-nonprofit-organizations/.

and systemic oppression. While my individual experience is indelibly shaped by my whiteness, pushout is an illuminating tool in the context of my Queer and trans-ness and the way both were used against me in an all-too-common pattern.

I was working as a full-time paraprofessional in a small public library in the Northeast United States. A pattern of hostility and harassment began when I came out as transgender and asked co-workers to use my true name and pronouns. It started with microaggressions: staff responded to my coming-out email by asking how much time I would need off for surgery. This quickly turned into open aggression and gaslighting. I was regularly misgendered by coworkers and given written reprimands when I tried to remind them of the correct pronouns. State law requires that an employee's pronouns be respected immediately but a year after coming out, I was still being told that staff needed "more time to get used to it." I was also shouted at in front of staff and patrons by my supervisor. The verbal and emotional abuse by this supervisor continued on social media even after I left my position.

My experience illustrates many pushout tactics. Microaggressions (such as being asked about surgery) were held up as proof of workplace acceptance. Constant dehumanizing treatment (misgendering and hostility) were used to justify creating a paper trail (written reprimands for "insubordination") designed to eliminate me. All of this was in service of maintaining the institutional *status quo*.

During and after this experience, I reflected on and wrote publicly about the idea that state and national professional organizations could have intervened to save my career. For example, free mediation services or legal advice from ALA might have prompted my employer to follow the law. Instead, I wrote emails to national and state organizations that went unanswered. I didn't need diversity and inclusion statements or Transgender authors speaking at conferences where I couldn't even safely use the bathroom. What I needed was allies with institutional power who would fight for me.

Under the current system, the financial and logistical burden fell on me to fight my own abuse in court as it was happening. Of course, this abuse coincided with being forced out of my low-wage job, leaving me few resources with which to hire a lawyer. Because I was in a small workplace of less than fifteen workers, neither the Equal Employment Opportunity Commission nor any other non-discrimination agencies could get involved. Small employers, like many libraries, know of this loophole and exploit it to push out workers who challenge the power and control of management.

I may have been able to find another job in libraries after these experiences, but I was offered a position in a different field where I am treated with respect and earn a living wage. As a result, I withdrew from my MLIS program and have no plans to go back.

Now that I've been out of libraries for almost five years, I can see that there were other reasons for my permanent departure. Many of them were economic. Like so many library workers, my full-time job doing highly skilled work paid about $25,000 per year.[2] Without an MLIS degree, there was no hope of career advancement. As someone living with chronic illness, the exceptionally good health insurance benefits I received served more as a tool of coercion than a perk of the job.

The most persuasive reason for staying gone, however, was human. I was growing increasingly disgusted by the disconnect between the profession's stated values and the routine use of violence and discrimination to control patrons.[3] I was personally tasked with denying undocumented people access to free ESL classes and denying patrons access to library services based on unwritten, constantly shifting policies. After I allowed a Black woman experiencing homelessness to use the phone, staff called the police on her and banned her from the building. Routinely acting as an agent of white supremacy was dehumanizing. Resisting this violence

2. If you work in the US, I encourage you to look at the data and see if your "professional" wages qualify you as working poor: https://www.unitedforalice.org/national-overview.

3. For more insight on this topic, see Fobazi Ettarh on "vocational awe": Fobazi Ettarh, "Vocational awe and librarianship: The lies we tell ourselves," *In the Library with the Lead Pipe* (2018), https://www.inthelibrarywiththeleadpipe.org/2018/vocational-awe/.

felt hopeless because my colleagues, both locally and regionally, enthusiastically supported these tactics and outcomes.

I still love books and still work in public service to meet people's information needs. However, my trust in libraries as an institution was crushed by the violence I experienced and was expected to perpetuate. Nevertheless, it wasn't until I was on the receiving end of this discrimination and violence that I realized I had given up too much of myself for an institution that would not, and *could not,* love me back.

Bibliography

Ettarh, Fobazi. "Vocational awe and librarianship: The lies we tell ourselves." *In the Library with the Lead Pipe* (2018). https://www.inthelibrarywiththeleadpipe.org/2018/vocational-awe/.

Page, Kira. "The 'Problem' Woman of Colour in Nonprofit Organizations." COCo (December 12, 2019), https://coco-net.org/problem-woman-colour-nonprofit-organizations/.

About the Author

Loren is a white, Queer, gender non-conforming Transman living near the Hudson River. He spent more than five years working in public libraries before leaving to work on healthcare and community wellness. Reach out on Instagram @it_ain_t_me.

Acknowledgements

Thank you to Library Juice Press and the Series on Gender and Sexuality in Information Studies for providing a place for this project. Special thanks to series editor Emily Drabinski for guiding us through the book proposal process, supporting our learning curve as first-time editors, and trusting our judgment when we announced that this book had over fifty chapters in it.

Kalani is endlessly grateful to their friends for keeping them generously supplied with vegan baked goods throughout this project, and to their parents, William Adolpho and Beth Scrozzo, for their words of encouragement.

Continuing the theme of queer-friendly pastries, Stephen greatly appreciates Lucky's Coffee Garage in Lebanon, NH, and all its employees. It is possible that his part in the book would have happened without this institution, but the quality would very likely have suffered.

Krista is thankful for Shabby Motley, a queer-friendly Sault Ste. Marie, Ontario yarn store and cafe. The endless supply of local coffee, embroidery floss, and baked goods helped make this book possible.

Most of all, thank you to our authors. These experiences can be very difficult to write about for any number of reasons; we appreciate so much that you were willing to do so.

Index

CPSIA information can be obtained
at www.ICGtesting.com
Printed in the USA
JSHW010027130723
44420JS00001B/4